Hudson Taylor in Early Years

HUDSON TAYLOR IN EARLY YEARS

THE GROWTH OF A SOUL

HUDSON TAYLOR IN EARLY YEARS.

From a portrait by his aunt, Mrs. Richard Hardey, painted in 1852, just before he left Hull for London.

Frontispiece.

Hudson Taylor
IN EARLY YEARS

THE GROWTH OF A SOUL

WITH ILLUSTRATIONS
PORTRAITS, MAPS, Etc.

By
DR. AND
MRS. HOWARD TAYLOR
WITH INTRODUCTION BY
MR. D. E. HOSTE
GENERAL DIRECTOR, CHINA INLAND MISSION

NEW YORK:
HODDER & STOUGHTON; GEORGE H. DORAN CO.
CHINA INLAND MISSION,
PHILADELPHIA.
MCMXII

TO SHOW FORTH

THY LOVING-KINDNESS

IN THE MORNING,

AND THY FAITHFULNESS

EVERY NIGHT.

PREFACE

THIS book makes no claim to being anything but a true and grateful record of the Lord's dealings with our dear father in his early years. It is not fiction, though the form in which it has come to us is unusual, perhaps, for a biography. It is the faithful story of the growth of a soul in the knowledge and love of God. Drawn mainly from Mr. Taylor's own letters and recollections, which are freely quoted, it has been pondered and prayed over until it seems to have lived again in our hearts.

Many a time as it has grown to completion, in spite of hindrances from without and within that only the power of God has overcome, we have felt profoundly that the place whereon we stood was holy ground. Most gratefully do we thank all who have waited so patiently for this book, and to whose help in prayer we know it is largely due that it appears at length. May they find in its pages some fragrance of the life they loved, because it brought them nearer to God, and strengthened them in seeking to live for His glory and the good of many.

Praying that the cleansing of the precious blood of Christ may be upon all that is not of Him, we commit it now to His blessing whose touch alone can turn the water into wine.

MALVERN,
September 22, 1911.

vii
b

OUR INDEBTEDNESS

VERY thankfully we wish to acknowledge all the help that has come to us in compiling this record from sources other than Mr. Taylor's own writings and recollections. That his early letters have been preserved at all in an unbroken succession is due to the care of his mother, who filled twelve manuscript volumes with copies in whole or in part of his correspondence from the time his sister first went to school.

And then to that dear sister herself, now the widow of Mr. B. Broomhall, grateful acknowledgments are due. The writers trust that they may have her forgiveness for giving her name the prominent position in this record that it necessarily occupies, without her knowledge or consent. They can only plead that truth would have it so, well knowing that the best and sweetest her life has had to give have ever been held at the disposal of the Master.

And there are others, too numerous to mention individually, who have helped in various ways to make this book what it is. For letters, photographs, and personal reminiscences the writers tender heartfelt thanks.

They desire also to record their gratitude to God, that through the help of personal friends in England and in America they have been enabled to complete the manuscript of this volume without expense of any kind to the China Inland Mission. In this respect the narrative is in keeping with one important aspect of that life itself, for it was to

Mr. Hudson Taylor a matter for constant thankfulness that he was enabled from first to last to refrain from drawing financial aid from the Mission he founded, and so long sustained by faith and prayer. He was, on the contrary, a considerable donor to its funds, carrying out, through all his connection with it, the spirit of the last words quoted from him in these pages. That that spirit may be their own increasingly, in common with all who belong to and sustain the Mission, is the earnest prayer of the writers,

HOWARD AND GERALDINE TAYLOR.

CONTENTS

xi

PART III

PREPARATION FOR CHINA, IN LONDON AND ON THE VOYAGE

1852–1854. AET 20–21.

PART IV

SHANGHAI AND EARLY ITINERATIONS

1854–1855. AET. 22–23

PART V

SEVEN MONTHS WITH WILLIAM BURNS

1855–1856. AET. 23–24.

PART VI

NING-PO AND SETTLED WORK

1856–1860. AET. 24–28.

ILLUSTRATIONS

MAPS

ERRATA

Page ix, line 26, for "that" read "the."

,, 38, line 3, for "would" read "could."

,, 193, line 14, for "illuminating" read "illuminated."

,, 214, line 4, for "villages" read "villagers."

,, 221, line 8, for "really" read "nearly."

,, 228, line 17, for "ways" read "way."

,, 277, line 1, for "province" read "providence."

,, 281, line 2, for "talk" read "walk."

,, 300, line 12, for "Grave" read "Gravel."

,, 346, line 26, omit "his God."

,, 450, line 36, for "fifty" read "more than forty."

,, 461, line 1, for "the" read "their."

,, 501, line 6, for "gratified" read "justified."

INTRODUCTION

I FEEL it a great privilege to respond to the invitation to write a brief introduction to this, the first volume of the life of the Founder of the China Inland Mission. In doing so, I venture, first, to draw attention to the latter part of its title : " The Growth of a Soul." It will be found that this volume brings before the reader an account of the influences which, in various ways and in different degrees, contributed to the formation of the personal character of Mr. Hudson Taylor. At first sight it might appear to some that to devote not less than half of the biography of one who did a great public work, to a description of his preparation for that work, evidences some lack of the sense of due proportion. The authors were fully alive to this aspect of the subject; but as they studied and pondered over the materials at their disposal, it was impressed upon them, with growing force, that the experience and the career of Mr. Taylor furnished a notable illustration of the truth that when God raises up a man for special service He first works in that man the principles which later on are, through his labours and influence, to be the means of widespread blessing to the Church and to the world.

Hence, this book has been written not so much as a literary production, likely to be read with an interest such as is excited by the biography of a man of distinction in any walk of life, but with the earnest hope that it may be of practical service, in illustrating and emphasising the fact that, for the purposes of Christian work, personal character, formed on truly Christian lines, is the most important factor ; further, that the formation of such a character largely depends upon the choices made by the individual concerned in the opening years of life. The important part which the influences of heredity and early environment had in moulding the personality of Mr. Taylor is ably brought out in this work. The narrative makes it quite clear, however, that these influences in themselves would have been inadequate without a moral response on his part to the claims of truth and duty as they presented themselves to him in his youth.

Led by Divine grace, when still a boy, to see in a Crucified Redeemer the Divinely provided answer to the problem of his guilt as a sinner, it was not long before he was further led, in a very simple and direct way, to accept the teaching of that Redeemer as his supreme rule of life. It may seem a truism to say that the conduct of the Christian is to be governed by the precepts of Christ; and yet how many there have been, and, it is to be feared, still are, who, having, in the first flush of new-born faith and love, taken the New Testament as the one and only standard of discipleship, have either broken down under the tests and difficulties of such a course, or have gradually yielded to the deadening influences of conventional standards taught and practised around them   Through the grace of God it was not so with Mr. Hudson Taylor. Having accepted the Holy Scriptures as his rule of life, it was not long before he was led into circumstances that, in various ways, severely tested his fidelity to them; and it becomes apparent in the biography, that the manner in which he held on his way in spite of great difficulties and the spirit in which he accepted not a little severe discipline were, under God, the main factors in producing a strength and a quality of character, without which the work to which he was called could never have been accomplished.

A good deal is written in the present day as to the need of living our lives and doing our work in a scientific manner. It is to be feared that much weakness and failure in Christian life and service may be traced to a lack of the scientific spirit in our treatment of the Holy Scriptures. We hear much, for instance, of the need of a fuller enduement of spiritual power for the Church and her representatives in the mission-field, if the responsibilities involved by present opportunities are to be adequately met. Is it sufficiently realised, however, in practice, that such enduement, the outstanding instance of which is recorded in the opening chapters of the Acts of the Apostles, was bestowed upon people who, during the preceding three years, whatever their faults and limitations, had counted the cost and had, without any reservation, responded, in intention at all events, to the conditions of discipleship laid down by their Lord : so much so that He was able at the close of that time to say to them, " Ye are they who have continued with me in my temptations, and I appoint unto you a Kingdom." Just as the ministry of John the Baptist was antecedent and preparatory to that of our Lord, so the period of personal discipleship—involving as it did an unreserved placing of life and all it included at the disposal of the Divine Master—was essential and led up to Pentecost : nor is there any other path at the present time. Outward circumstances alter with each succeeding age, bringing with them a corresponding modification in the external application of the principles and practice of our Lord ; similarly, their application in the life of each individual will also have a character of its own. But the fact remains eternally true that the path of discipleship is the only road to spiritual power.

I venture to dwell upon this point as illustrated in the life of Mr. Taylor, because experience shows that nothing is easier than, in the words of the Prophet Isaiah, for the " wine to become mixed with water " ; that is to say, for the essential teachings as to conduct given us by Christ, and subsequently by His Apostles in the Epistles, to be toned down and adulterated by the admixture of ideas and maxims, not only foreign to, but repugnant to the spirit of Christianity.

The great truth which is complementary to the foregoing, that it is only in union with Christ by the Holy Ghost that the Christian has the power to carry into practice the precepts of His Lord, also receives powerful illustration in this biography. A single-hearted, unreserved intention to follow the Lord, whilst essential, is by itself as fruitless as the efforts of Sisyphus. But it is also true that the inworking of Divine grace will never be known in its victorious fulness where there is not such an intention.

It is perhaps the highest tribute to the character of Mr. Hudson Taylor that it is the recollection of what he was, almost more than what he accomplished, which is most treasured by those who were privileged to know and work with him. He possessed qualities both of heart and mind not often found highly developed in the same individual. Whilst it is no exaggeration to say he was literally consumed with a self-sacrificing zeal for the spread of the Gospel, yet he was never hard or unsympathetic towards those who, through various causes, were unable to toil and to suffer as he did : on the contrary, his tenderness and sympathy endeared him to his brethren, and ever cheered those who were disheartened in the fight, or laid aside by illness. His gracious, unassuming manner, his habitual kindness and gentle courtesy, his tact and patience under opposition and ill-treatment, combined to bestow a peculiar charm to his personality.

Though gifted with more than ordinary powers both of thought and action, his true humility, as well as his practical wisdom, were evidenced by his readiness to confer with his brethren, and by the deference with which he weighed the wishes and judgment even of those many years younger than himself. Never perhaps was there a man who, as he went on in life, was more free from the disastrous mistake of despising " the least of his brethren." There can be no doubt that to his habit of carefully weighing the views of younger men was due the receptivity and elasticity which his mind retained to the end of his service.

The fact that Dr. and Mrs. Howard Taylor are the authors of this book would seem in itself to render a reference to its workmanship superfluous. It seems well, however, to mention that they have bestowed upon it far more than ordinary care and labour, such as a work of this kind would naturally call for, as the sense has deepened in their minds, and in those of others, that there were features in this biography which, if truthfully and adequately presented, were eminently calculated, with the Divine blessing, to convey lessons of deep and permanent import both to the Christian community at large and also to individuals.

Hence, not only have exceptional pains, involving often much laborious research, been taken to secure the strictest fidelity to truth in every detail of the record, but also no labour has been spared to present in their right proportion and their true light the guiding principles of this remarkable life. It is the sober truth to say that every page, and even every sentence, has been the subject of many earnest prayers for the Divine blessing, and it may be added that the one desire of the authors has been that they may be the means of conveying a message of God which shall touch hearts and alter lives.

D. E. HOSTE.

CHINA INLAND MISSION, LONDON,
October 19, 1911.

PART I

ANTECEDENTS, HOME AND EARLY YEARS

1776–1849. AET. 1–17

Lord, Thou hast been our dwelling-place in all generations.
Before the mountains were brought forth,
Or ever Thou hadst formed the earth and the world,
Even from everlasting to everlasting, Thou art God. . . .

O satisfy us early with Thy mercy ;
That we may rejoice and be glad all our days. . . .

Let Thy work appear unto Thy servants,
And Thy glory unto their children.
And let the beauty of the Lord our God be upon us :
And establish Thou the work of our hands upon us ,
Yea, the work of our hands establish Thou it.

Psalm xc.

CHAPTER I

AS FOR ME AND MY HOUSE

1776–1786

It was James Taylor's wedding-day, a wintry morning long ago in the north country. The sun had not yet risen over Brierley Common, and in the snowy valley Royston still lay in shadow. But on Staincross Ridge the young stone-mason was up betimes, making ready for his bride. Was there not water to carry from the well and wood to prepare for the fire, as well as wheat to thresh and take to the mill to provide for her first baking ?

Full of life and good spirits, " a noted singer and extremely fond of dancing," [1] Taylor had hardly given a serious thought to the step he was about to take. He had fallen in love with bright little Betty, one of the Johnsons of Royston, in the fine old church of which he was a bell-ringer and member of the choir. There he had heard the Banns of Marriage published, with much satisfaction, on three successive Sundays after the New Year. And now the auspicious day had come, Thursday the 1st of February, and all was ready for the festivities. There would be music and dancing, feasting and merry-making, and he and Betty would be gayest of the gay. But beyond this they anticipated little save the cosy fireside in the home that was to be.

Now, however, as the young man went out into the frosty

---

[1] Quoted from an address by Mr. Edward Taylor of Barnsley, Yorkshire, reported in *The Barnsley Chronicle*, January 1880 See also note 1, page 6.

3

air to carry his sheaves to the barn,[1] a new line of thought
began to present itself. Was it the familiar cottage next
door to his own that suggested it, the home of Joseph and
Elizabeth Shaw, well known throughout the country-side ?
Was it the music of some hymn Dame Betty was singing as
she plied her morning tasks ?

Not long ago, as he could well remember, there had been
more sighing than singing in this good woman's lot. Crippled
by an acute attack of rheumatism, she had been confined to
bed month after month in weariness and pain. But since
that memorable day when all alone in the house she had
" trusted the Lord," as they put it, for immediate healing,
great indeed had been the change. How astonished her
husband must have been when he came back a little later
and found her not only up but sweeping the kitchen, as
well and happy as could be.[2] It had made much stir in the
neighbourhood, and Taylor, like every one else, was at a loss
to account for what had happened—every one, that is, except
the Methodists, who seemed to think it simple and natural
enough. But what credulity could surprise one in people
of such extreme religious notions !

Those notions seemed to haunt him this morning, however,
strange as it might seem. For what had he to do with
religion ! he, the leader rather in all that was opposed to
the " revival " that had invaded the neighbourhood of late.
Surely it was enough that Farmer Cooper and the Shaws
had turned Methodist, bringing from Wakefield preachers
of the new-fangled doctrines, who terrified people with
their earnestness about " the wrath to come." Had not
John Wesley himself appeared, one Mapplewell " Feast
Monday," boldly addressing the crowds in the Market
Place while the Midsummer Fair was going on ?[3] It was

---

[1] It was the custom in that part of England to leave the sheaves in
stacks instead of at once threshing out the wheat. As the flour was needed
for use, two or three sheaves would be threshed at a time and the grain
taken to the mill for grinding.

[2] See the *Account of an Extraordinary Deliverance*, by Rev. J. Pawson
in the *Arminian Magazine* for 1796, pp. 409-411. This experience was
related to him at Staincross by Dame Betty herself, in the year 1775, and
confirmed by many witnesses.

[3] This, we learn from Wesley's Journal, was on July 27, 1761. That it
was Mapplewell " Feast Monday " is given on the authority of *The Barnsley*

a courageous thing to do in that Yorkshire town, where "bating the Methodists" had become a favourite pastime with those of the rougher sort. But the white-haired preacher had so discoursed, that day, that all else had been forgotten, and he was allowed to pass unmolested to the Shaws' cottage on the Ridge, there to rest till the cool of the day.[1] Perhaps it was from his lips young Taylor had caught the words that returned to him now so persistently, as he worked away in the barn :

"As for me and my house . . me and my house . . . we will serve the Lord."

Yes, he knew what it meant to serve the Lord. His neighbours lived that sort of life. But he was no narrow-minded Methodist ! Besides, it was his wedding-day. He was threshing wheat for Betty's home-coming. It was no time to be thinking of religion.

" As for me and my house."

Yes, he was about to establish a new household that day. It was a serious step, a great responsibility. How careless had been his attitude hitherto, how unthinking ! But now the words would not leave him :

" We will serve the Lord."

Hour after hour went by. The sun rose high over the hills, lighting the white-roofed village where the bride was waiting. Taylor was due there long before noon, and had yet to don wedding apparel. But all, all was forgotten in this first, great realisation of eternal things. Alone upon his knees among the straw the young stone-mason was face to face with God. " As for me " had taken on new meaning.

Chronicle for Saturday, September 30, 1905, in an editorial entitled " History of Barnsley and the Surrounding District." To the late editor, Mr Alex Patterson, we are indebted for much information

[1] Mapplewell, as it was called in those days, is now the busy mining town of Staincross, near Barnsley, and the Shaws' cottage still stands on the Ridge which divides it from the neighbouring parish of Royston. Substantially built of stone, it hardly shows the wear and tear of two centuries, and is the best preserved of the few remaining dwellings that form the oldest part of the town How interesting it was to find oneself in the pleasant kitchen in which Wesley was once entertained, talking by the fireside with a member of the very family that had shown him hospitality. For the cottage still belongs to the Shaws, who have occupied it from the first ; and their next-door neighbours have been Taylors for many generations.

The fact of personal responsibility to a living though unseen Being—Love infinite and eternal, or Justice as a consuming fire—had become real and momentous as never before. It was the hour of the Spirit's striving with this soul, the solemn hour when to yield is salvation. And there alone with God James Taylor yielded. The love of Christ conquered and possessed him, and soon the new life from above found expression in the new determination:

" Yes, we will serve the Lord." [1]

.　　.　　.　　.　　.　　.　　.

Thus the critical moments of life come with little warning, silently as the sunrise often, shedding Divine illumination upon things unseen. All unexpectedly, one day, we see as we have never seen before. Duty becomes plain in the light of eternity. Then we have reached a turning-point indeed, and everything depends upon the response of the soul to the claims and promises of God. Had young Taylor decided otherwise that winter morning how different the sequel must have been ! It was the little beginning, the tiny spring from which was to flow blessing not for himself only and his house from generation to generation, but for an ever-widening circle in England, China, and throughout the Church of God. Such a moment may come for us to-day, fraught with far-reaching issues. What is our response to be?

" Speak, Lord, for Thy servant heareth."

.　　.　　.　　.　　.　　.

Were the church bells ringing over the valley when

[1] The definiteness of the stone-mason's conversion on the morning of his wedding-day, and under the circumstances narrated, is ascertained from the careful researches of Mr. Edward Taylor, embodied in several Lectures.

Mr. Edward Taylor's name is one of the most respected in Barnsley. He was for many years a Local Preacher and leader in the Methodist "Reform Movement" Omnivorous in his reading and of strongly antiquarian tastes, he made it his business to search out all available information regarding early Methodism and its supporters in the district, and left a considerable library now in the possession of his widow, his son Mr. William Taylor, and his son-in-law Mr. John Knee, to whom belong most of his Lectures and other MSS. To each of these members of Mr. Taylor's family we are indebted for valuable help. Though not related to James Taylor the stone-mason, Mr. Edward Taylor was specially interested in his history as the pioneer and practically the founder of the Methodist Movement in Barnsley, and to his records we owe many of the facts related in this chapter concerning the marriage and after experiences of the great-grandparent of Mr. Hudson Taylor.

Photograph by F. Howard Taylor.

A VIEW OF THE TOWER OF ROYSTON PARISH CHURCH.

Showing the clock beside the oriel window.

To face page 7.

James Taylor returned to consciousness of earthly things ? It was almost noon. The wedding-guests must be in consternation as to what had become of him. Never surely had the two miles to Royston seemed so endless as when, fearing he could not be in time, he ran down the long hill from Staincross Ridge, a new man in a new world.

Where the cross-roads met in the heart of the village he came in sight of the church at length. Glancing apprehensively at the clock by the oriel window,[1] what was his surprise to find that it had come to a standstill, as if in sympathy with his dilemma. Possibly it might not yet be too late !

Somewhere the bridal party was waiting. It was no moment for explanations. To church they went as speedily as possible. The Vicar asked no questions, unaware perhaps of the ruse whereby his bell-ringers had saved the day for their favourite. The service duly proceeded, the Register was signed in the vestry, and James Taylor and Betty Johnson were man and wife.

Very interesting it was more than a hundred years later to hunt up the old calf-bound volume and come upon the entry made that day—February 1, 1776. Much of the writing was faded on the discoloured page, but one signature stood out with startling clearness, vividly recalling the handwriting of another who long after was to bear the bridegroom's name. There was the same familiar shape of each carefully formed letter, the same firm, characteristic style, as though the quill had been guided by the very hand that so often wrote in recent years :

> " Affectionately yours in Christ,
> JAMES HUDSON TAYLOR."

And not the signature only is noteworthy in connection with this old-time story ; the later experiences of the stone-mason and his wife reveal traits of character that also appear,

[1] This beautiful window high up beside the clock is one of the distinctive features of Royston Church. There is said to be only one other like it in England. Built by the monks of Bretton not far from their monastery, the church is provided with a chamber in the tower, designed apparently for meditation and prayer. Sunny and silent, lighted by the oriel window, it was probably a favourite resort of the monks through many generations.

by the blessing of God, in the great-grandson whose life we trace. There is the same singleness of purpose, strength of principle, love for the Lord Jesus Christ and faithfulness in His service : a rich inheritance, bringing with it the blessing promised " to the third and fourth generation."

To begin with, there was no compromise about the James Taylor of long ago. Up to the hour of his wedding he had been as far from religious impressions as the most thoughtless of his companions. Now as they left the church he did not hesitate to confess all that had taken place. Simply and earnestly with his young wife on his arm he explained that he had enlisted in the service of a new Master. This meant among other things no dancing at his wedding or unseemly jollification. Hearing which the bride exclaimed in dismay :

" Surely I have not married one of those Methodists ! "

But that was just what she had done, little as either of them expected it. For the warm love and living faith of the Staincross Society soon drew James Taylor into its membership. From the Shaws, Coopers, and others he learned more of what it really means to serve the Lord. His voice and fiddle, formerly much in request for revels throughout the country-side, were now used only for his Master, and before long he was gladly telling what great things had been done for his soul.

And meanwhile what about Betty ? Well, she was far from happy. Her heart told her James was right, but she was most unwilling to share with him the reproach of Christ. So she grumbled and scolded, and managed to make things generally uncomfortable. From the first day of their life together James had commenced " family prayers," but Betty refused to join him and busied herself ostentatiously about other things. At last one evening she was more trying than usual, and more unreasonable in her reproaches. James bore it as long as he could, and then before she knew what was happening Betty found herself lifted in his strong arms and carried to the room upstairs. There he knelt down and keeping her still beside him poured out all his sorrow and concern in prayer. She had not realised before how much he cared. His earnestness solemnised and impressed her, and though she would not show it she began to be troubled by a sense of sin. All next day her distress deepened. How willingly, then, would she have been as her husband was! In the evening the Bible was brought out as usual and Betty was glad enough to listen. The prayer that followed seemed just what she was needing, and that night while James was still on his knees she entered into peace with God.[1]

Thus at the outset of their married life these two were united in the best of ways, and as the years went on they became increasingly happy and helpers of one another's faith.

. . . .

It was a wonderful movement of the Spirit of God into which James Taylor and his wife were thus introduced in a remote corner of Yorkshire. All over Great Britain and Ireland similar conversions were taking place. Breaking in upon the darkness of the eighteenth century, a glorious Revival swept the land, saving it from threatened destruction. In the Established Church, dead though it was for the most part, mighty men of God were raised up—Whitfield, the Wesleys, Grimshaw, Rowlands, Berridge, and many another, with whom wrought a multitude of unlettered evangelists, proclaiming in humble spheres the saving grace of God.

How terrible was the state of things before this work began it is hard for us now to realise. In town and country alike, people were abandoned to vice and irreligion well-nigh incredible in our day, " for the most part," as the Churchman Southey records, " in a state of heathen or worse than heathen ignorance." The immorality of the wealthy classes and the indifference of the clergy were no less menacing than " the rudeness of the peasantry, the brutality of the

[1] The details of Betty Taylor's conversion are gathered from an address by Mr. Edward Taylor, already quoted, and from the written *Recollections* of the Rev. Samuel Taylor, late of St Leonards, the last surviving grandson of James and Betty Taylor, and uncle of the subject of this Memoir. With his death in 1904 there passed away a man of God indeed, whose memory will long be fragrant.

town populace, the prevalence of drunkenness, the growth
of impiety, and the general deadness to religion." [1]

Men who in the face of such conditions, with the pulpits
of the land closed against them, fearlessly took their stand
for God and righteousness, " stormed the strongholds of
Satan, plucked thousands like brands from the burning,
and altered the character of the age," needed an enduement
of the Holy Spirit no less mighty than that of the first
evangelists who " turned the world upside down." Like
them too they had to be prepared to " die daily," that they
might fill up that which was lacking of " the afflictions of
Christ." For only through lives laid down could such
regenerating work be done. And not the leaders only, men
whose names are honoured now the wide world over :—the
strength of the Revival lay in the great host of men and
women, unknown to fame, who everywhere rejoiced to share
their apostolic labours, sufferings, and success.

Amongst these came to be numbered James and Betty
Taylor, in a peculiarly dark and needy corner of the dark
and needy England of those days. And who shall say
that the courage, steadfastness and dependence upon
God developed by the conditions they had to face do
not lie at the foundation of much that is recorded in this
book ?

A serious accident some years after his marriage obliged
James Taylor to face the fact that he must give up his work
as a stone-mason and find other means of supporting his
family. It was a gloomy outlook, for there were fewer ways
of earning a livelihood in those days than at present, and
country occupations to which he was accustomed were all

---

[1] " In this we cannot be mistaken," said an archbishop of the time, " that
an open and professed disregard of religion is become, through a variety
of unhappy causes, the distinguishing character of the age. Such are the
dissoluteness and contempt of principle in the higher part of the world,
and the profligacy, intemperance, and fearlessness of committing crimes
in the lower part, as must, if the torrent of impiety stop not, become
absolutely fatal." See Archbishop Secker's *Eight Charges*.

Bishop Butler went further when he wrote in the preface to his *Analogy* :
" It has come to be taken for granted that Christianity is no longer a subject
of inquiry, but that it is now at length discovered to be fictitious. And
accordingly it is treated as if, in the present age, this were an agreed point
among all persons of discernment, and nothing remained but to set it up as
a principal subject for mirth and ridicule."

beyond his strength. The only course open to him was to leave the little home on Staincross Ridge and seek in some manufacturing centre the lighter employment factory or workshop might afford.

Barnsley was the nearest place of the kind, a notoriously wicked, mining town, just across the valley of the Dearne. "Drunkenness, licentiousness, and gambling, the three great sins of the nation," were there especially rife, and " scarcely any people," William Bramwell tells us, " raged against the Methodists or persecuted them with such ferocity as the people of Barnsley." The churches were deserted and the ale-houses overflowing, with what results may be judged from notices such as the following which were only too common :

 "*Drunk—a penny : dead-drunk—two-pence : clean straw for nothing*" 1

It must have been hard for James and Betty Taylor to bring their children into the atmosphere of a place like this, but when employment was offered him in the linen-warehouse of Joseph Beckett, a local magistrate, at a wage of thirteen shillings and sixpence weekly they could no longer hesitate. At the top of Old Mill Lane on the outskirts of the town stood a four-roomed cottage from which might be seen the wooded hills of their childhood. It was a busy corner, for the cross-roads met at their door, and the London coach coming up from the Market Place paused there to adjust its brakes before turning down the steep lane on its way to Wakefield and Leeds. Travellers were constantly passing on the Sheffield highway, and so frequent were the inquiries as to various destinations that the occupant of the mansion opposite went to considerable expense to settle the questions once and for all. The obelisk he erected is useful still, with its modern lamps and full directions, and when the sun is setting its shadow falls upon the site once occupied by James Taylor's modest dwelling.[1]

Here then the new arrivals settled, finding it a great

---

[1] The Taylors' cottage has recently been demolished, with several others, to make room for a row of shops and houses at the top of Old Mill Lane

change from their old surroundings. Living was more
expensive than in the country, and though the father was
earning what was then good wages it was far from easy to
make both ends meet. Besides rent and taxes, there were two
sons and three little daughters to provide for, and all they
had to live on was the small sum of twelve shillings a week.
But what of the remainder of the father's earnings, the
extra one and sixpence he received weekly ?   Was it reserved
for special comforts, tobacco, tea, or snuff ?   Was it set
aside for winter clothing, or against " a rainy day " ?   No,
it was given, sacrificed rather, for love of One dearer to
them than their children, more considered than themselves.
Poor as they were in this world's goods, they had learned
the secret of being " rich toward God "

In Betty's kitchen stood a corner-cupboard containing
a special cup into which, as James brought home his earnings,
one shilling and sixpence always found their way.   This
was consecrated money, never to be touched save for " the
support of God's cause and the relief of the poor." [1]   Thus
they always had something ready for the Master's use ; and
the remainder of their little income proved sufficient and
unfailing, because the blessing of God rested on it.   It was
the old story of the widow's meal and oil, for the Lord will
be no man's debtor.   Oh, that cup in the corner-cupboard,
that faithful giving of a ninth of everything (a tenth could
not suffice them) to the Lord, how much it explains of
blessing in the lives of their children's children !

The loss of Christian fellowship was the change they felt
most keenly during those early days in Barnsley.   The
beautiful church of St. Mary's a few steps from their door
offered no substitute for the meetings in Betty Shaw's
cottage, and of helpful, spiritual ministry there seems to
have been none.   True, the Friends had a Meeting House
a mile or two from the town, and the Independents were
building on Crow-well Hill the first Nonconformist place of
worship.   But there was little to choose between church
and chapel in those days.   Deadness and indifference
paralysed both alike, so that as Bishop Ryle puts it they

[1] From Rev. Samuel Taylor's *Recollections*

" seemed at last agreed on one point, . . . to let the devil alone and do nothing for hearts or souls." [1]

This state of things became a heavy burden on the new arrivals, and they longed unspeakably for some voice to tell the glad tidings that had set them free. But preachers rarely came from more favoured localities, and when they did it was a sorry welcome they found in Barnsley. Year in and year out James Taylor and his family were distressed to see " the Sabbath profaned and all kinds of brutal, ferocious, and licentious games practised." [2] It was little they could do to stem the torrent of iniquity, but it was better than nothing, and they could not hold their peace.

And so it came to pass that Betty's kitchen was swept and garnished, and a few neighbours gathered in for informal meetings. The singing no doubt was an attraction, and both James and his wife were among " the people that do know their God " and so can be a help to others. Some evidently received blessing, for in time a Class was formed which met regularly in the little cottage.[8] Eventually a Methodist Society was fully organised, and James Taylor appointed as the first Class Leader and Local Preacher in Barnsley.

Long before this, however, he had been privileged to " make full proof " of his ministry in truly apostolic ways. Down on the Old Bridge and in the Market Place he had been in danger of his life once and again while preaching in the open air. Pelted with stones and refuse, struck down and dragged through the mire, he had been rescued at the last moment—only to preach again.

Returning from a meeting on one occasion he was accosted by a couple of men who appeared to be friendly. Engaged in conversation with one of them he did not notice the movements of the other, who suddenly rubbed into his eyes a mixture of pounded glass and mud calculated to blind him

---

[1] See *The Christian Leaders of the Eighteenth Century*, by Bishop Ryle
[2] See *Life of Henry Longden*, by the Rev. William Bramwell.
[8] " The first Methodist Class Meeting in Barnsley was composed of seven members, i.e. James and Betty Taylor, Jonathan Pashley, John Denton, weaver, Timothy Peckett, mason, Thomas Blackburn, farmer, and his wife " (*Early Methodism in Barnsley and District*, by Mr. John Knee).

for life. Sightless and in desperate pain Taylor was wholly at their mercy, and there is no knowing what might have happened had not Joseph Beckett coming down Church Street at the time hastened to his assistance. Seeing the magistrate the ruffians made off, but not before Mr. Beckett had recognised one of them, a professed infidel and no friend to the Methodists in Barnsley. Poor Taylor was taken home in great suffering, and it was fully three months before he could return to work again. His employer urged him to take out a summons, having himself witnessed the occurrence. But James would not hear of it.

" No," he said, " the Lord is well able to deal with them. I would rather leave it in His hands."

This did not satisfy the magistrate, however, who decided to carry the prosecution through on his own account. In the witness-box the culprit denied the charge, calling upon God to strike him blind if he had had anything to do with the outrage. Shortly after, all Barnsley knew that he had lost his sight. For the rest of his life he had to be led by a dog through the familiar streets, and ultimately sunk into extreme poverty. His accomplice also was obliged to confess that nothing ever prospered with him from the time of their cruel attack upon James Taylor.

Such experiences in common with others of a less serious character afforded abundant opportunity for putting into practice the teachings of the Sermon on the Mount, opportunities not lost upon James Taylor and his fellow-Methodists.

It was an eloquent sermon he preached in Eastgate, for example, when an angry woman ran after him, frying-pan in hand. She had seen the good man go by wearing a light-coloured overcoat, and thought it an excellent opportunity of provoking him into a quarrel. Coming up behind, she vigorously rubbed the greasy, sooty utensil all over the back of his tidy garment, using her tongue meanwhile to the amusement of onlookers. But it was her turn to be discomfited when Taylor turned round with a smile, suggesting that if it afforded her satisfaction she might grease the front as well. Covered with confusion the woman retired, but the incident was not easily forgotten.

It is said that on his deathbed the infidel above-mentioned sent for the man he had injured, hoping to find comfort in his prayers. But eager as he was to help his former enemy, James Taylor could not pray. He tried and tried again, but his cry seemed to return from an unanswering heaven. The solemn words then came to mind : " He that being often reproved hardeneth his neck, shall suddenly be cut off, and that without remedy." To see an unrepentant soul pass into eternity was far more terrible to him than all the persecutions he had endured.

For none of these things moved him. He found that it was a safe thing and a blessed to trust in the living God. The little home at the top of Old Mill Lane was increasingly happy and a centre of blessing to others. Dame Betty in spite of her household cares found time to be useful as a Class Leader among the women. Their children grew up a joy and comfort to them, and in all that makes for true prosperity they were enriched of God. Attempts to do them harm were so manifestly overruled that they helped rather than hindered their influence. And one is not surprised to learn that as time went on they with others of " these early Methodists, by their meekness, uprightness, and consistent conduct, lived down opposition and took their place among the most respected inhabitants of the town." [1]

A like change was becoming apparent all over England. The close of the century that overwhelmed the land of Voltaire with the unspeakable horrors of the French Revolution witnessed, in the home of Whitfield and the Great Revival, a peaceful transformation of national life and character.[2] Long surviving his own generation, Wesley at eighty years of age could look out upon a revived and purified Church leading a people's progress toward righteousness, liberty and enlightenment, and welcome the dawning of the day of Modern Missions that was to extend these blessings to a waiting world. His evangelistic journeys were now " religious ovations," and he himself, " the best-

[1] *Recollections* of the Rev Samuel Taylor.
[2] " Whitfield and Wesley transformed England by giving to conversion once more its proper value."—Rev. R. F. Horton, D.D.

known man in England," was honoured and beloved for his work's sake where so long he had been hated and despised.[1]

This was the period of his long-expected visit to Barnsley, the first and only recorded occasion of his preaching there. Great must have been the joy of James Taylor and his friends as they prepared to welcome this father in the faith. In numbers the little Society had not made much progress, for those had been difficult years, but in knowledge of God and influence with those around them great headway had been won. They were able to look forward to the coming of the great evangelist without anxiety as to the reception that awaited him, and could even arrange with the landlord of the Old White Bear to make use of his spacious yard near the Market Place for an open-air meeting.

Wesley came to them from Epworth, the home of his childhood, having recently celebrated his eighty-third birthday. How unusual was the vigour he enjoyed both of mind and body may be judged from the following entry in his Journal, penned two days before he reached Barnsley :

Wednesday, June 28, 1786 : I am a wonder to myself. It is now twelve years since I have felt any such sensation as weariness. I am never tired, such is the goodness of God, either with writing, preaching, or travelling.

Thursday night was spent at Doncaster, and from thence he drove over the Hickleton Hills and through the lovely valley of the Dearne. Somewhere on the road no doubt

---

[1] Well might John Wesley be called " the best-known man in England." His labours had been prodigious for well-nigh fifty years. Travelling on horseback or by chaise from four to five thousand miles annually, he had established in Great Britain alone more than a hundred circuits, in which three hundred ministers and over a thousand local preachers were making known the truth as it is in Jesus. Acting on his own memorable words, " simplify religion and every part of learning," he had enlisted the press in the work of popular reformation. " Cheaper, shorter, plainer books " was his motto. Amid all other labours he found time to keep up a constant supply of pamphlets, tracts and sermons, carried by his preachers to the remotest parts of the country, besides providing them with a library of over two hundred volumes on a great variety of subjects, written or edited by himself, five works on music and forty-nine collections of hymns.

He preached in all 42,400 sermons after his return from Georgia in 1738, an average up to the time of his death in 1791 of more than *fifteen every week for fifty-three consecutive years*. His last words were, " The best of all is God is with us." See *History of Methodism*, by Abel Stevens, LL.D., vol. ii. pp. 320, 494, 508, etc.

the Barnsley friends would meet him, but it is hardly likely that James and Betty Taylor were among their number. For them the morning hours would be busy, as theirs was to be the honour of entertaining the distinguished guest.

Picture then the preparations in the little cottage that was to shelter John Wesley that night beneath its roof. Thousands of homes he had visited, in which his chamber may have been finer and the table spread before him more ample in its provision, but it is doubtful whether he ever met with warmer welcome or more genuine love for himself and for his Master.

"Methodism had no truer friends than this worthy couple," writes a well-known citizen of Barnsley.[1] "Their devotion increased with their difficulties. Persecution did but sharpen the edge of their attachment to Wesley and his cause. Their home seems to have been the chief resort of preachers who came from Wakefield and other places. What more fitting than that they should entertain the great evangelist himself, and so receive a distinction not soon to be forgotten."

That June day of a hundred and twenty years ago has left its mark on Barnsley. The arrival and progress of Mr. Wesley through the crowded streets, the scene in the yard of the Old White Bear with its stone stairway from which his discourse was delivered, the excitement and eager attention of the multitude, the appearance of the venerable speaker, his earnestness and power in setting forth eternal things— these and many other recollections are treasured on the library shelves of that Yorkshire town and in the warm hearts of its people.

But our present concern is chiefly with the close of the day when, the great meeting over, the preacher was escorted to the home of his humble friends. It had been a notable address, lengthened and increasingly earnest as the response of the audience was evident ; and now the simple meal was welcome and fellowship with the inner circle around Dame Betty's hearth. Interested in all that concerned them

---

[1] The late William Woodcock, Esq., one of the chief authorities upon the history of Methodism in the Barnsley district. This gentleman left a valuable library and collection of manuscripts, now in the care of his daughter Miss L. Woodcock, who generously spared no pains in making them available for the purposes of this book.

Wesley would soon make his sympathy felt, winning the hearts of the children and the confidence of the older people. He may even have heard the story of James Taylor's conversion on his wedding-day, and the consternation of the bride on learning that she had actually " married one of those Methodists ! "

And then as twilight deepened one can well imagine the earnestness with which he would seek to strengthen and encourage those he might never meet on life's pilgrimage again.

" Remember," we can almost hear him say, " remember, you have nothing to do to compare in importance with saving souls. Therefore spend and be spent in this work. Observe, it is not your business to preach so many times a week, or to take care of this or that Society, but simply to save as many souls as you can, to bring as many sinners as you possibly can to repentance, and with all your power to build them up in that holiness without which no man can see the Lord.

" Only through unwearied labour and perseverance can we really be ' free from the blood of all men.' Go into every house and teach every one therein, young and old, if they belong to us, to be Christians inwardly and outwardly. Make every particular plain to their understanding, fix it in their memory, write it on their hearts. In order to do this there must be line upon line, precept upon precept. I remember to have heard my father say to my mother, ' How could you have the patience to tell that child the same thing twenty times over ? ' ' Why,' she answered, ' if I had told him but nineteen times, I should have lost all my labour.' What patience indeed, what love, what knowledge, is requisite for this !

" Oh, why are we not more holy ! " he would exclaim with loving insistence. " Why do we not live in eternity, walk with God all the day long ? Why are we not all-devoted to God, breathing the whole spirit of missionaries ?

" Alas, we are too much enthusiasts, looking for the end without faithfully using the means. Do we rise at four or even five in the morning to be alone with God ? Do we fast once a week, once a month ? Do we even know the obligation or benefit of it ? Do we recommend the five o'clock hour for private prayer, at the close of the day ? Do we observe it ? Do we not find that ' any time ' is no time ?

" Oh let us stir up the gift of God that is in us. Let us no more sleep as do others. Let us take heed to the ministry that we have received in the Lord, that we fulfil it. ' Whatsoever thy hand findeth to do, do it with thy might.' " [1]

---

[1] Quoted from the excellent *Rules* drawn up by John Wesley for the guidance of his young preachers ; and from the bright, practical *Con-*

In some such helpful intercourse the hours would fly, until candles had to be lighted and the guest who was to depart on the morrow escorted to his chamber under the cottage eaves. Was it that night, beneath James Taylor's roof, he penned the entry in his Journal that seems so pertinent to the story of this book ?

Friday, June 30, 1786 : I turned aside to Barnsley, formerly famous for all manner of wickedness. They were then ready to tear any Methodist preacher in pieces. Now not a dog wagged its tongue. I preached near the Market Place to a very large congregation, and I believe the truth sank into many hearts. They seemed to drink in every word. Surely God will have a people in this place.

---

versations with his fellow-workers that have come down to us   The full title of this interesting work is ·   *Minutes of several Conversations between the Rev. John Wesley, A M., and the Preachers in connection with him, from the year 1744;* published in Leeds in 1803.

CHAPTER II

UNTO CHILDREN'S CHILDREN

1786–1824

" For myself and for the work I have been permitted to do for God I owe an unspeakable debt of gratitude to my beloved and honoured parents who have entered into rest, but the influence of whose lives will never pass away."

Thus wrote many years later the child who came to gladden James Taylor's home in Barnsley in 1832. This was not of course the first James Taylor, who had long since passed to his reward, nor was it even the son who had grown up to take his place. Two generations had come in between the visit of John Wesley to Barnsley and the birth of the child whose experiences we are to trace, in whose life the character-building of those early days was to bear rich fruit.

That at fifty years of age, amid all the responsibilities of a great mission in China, he should look back with " unspeakable gratitude " upon the training of his childhood, shows that there must have been right influences at work in that quiet home. What were they ? Wherein did these parents lay their son under such indebtedness ? What had they received themselves that was to prove of so much value to others ? These are important questions, the answers to which reveal the faithfulness of a covenant-keeping God, whose blessing is promised " unto children's children."

James Taylor the stone-mason, with whom our story opened, had the joy of seeing the beginning of this blessing before he passed away. The little Society he had been the means of founding seems to have grown rapidly after Wesley's visit. Dame Betty's kitchen was no longer able to accommodate the services, and step after step they were led into building for themselves a modest Chapel on Pinfold Hill, near the busiest part of the town.[1] Among the first to be received into fellowship in the newly completed building was young John Taylor, the stone-mason's eldest son. This double joy must have been the crowning experience in his father's life, which only a few months later drew to its unexpected close. Nothing is known about his passing away, save that it took place in 1795, and even his resting-place cannot now be traced. His was a lowly life, and he waits the resurrection in an unrecorded grave ; but in the family he founded and the cause he loved there remain to this day better memorials of his faithful service than any the recognition of man can raise.

Well it was for Dame Betty and the younger children that John was able in some measure to take his father's place. He was now seventeen and in regular employment, having learned the trade of a reed-maker, at which he ultimately achieved success. Linen-weaving was then as it still is one of the principal industries of Barnsley, and many were the hand-looms needing the slender reeds between which the shuttles flew. John Taylor worked hard and conscientiously, and by degrees became " of great consequence to the staple trade of the town." [2] He was able

---

[1] In the Public Library of Barnsley may be seen to-day a record of no little interest in this connection. It was penned by one Hugh Burland, who filled several large calf-bound volumes with the ancient " Annals " of the town, among which we come upon the following in his handwriting :

" 1791—The Wesleyans of Barnsley determined to build themselves a Chapel. Since the visit of John Wesley they had held Divine Service in a room in Eastgate. In about three years they accomplished their object ; for their Chapel, which was erected on Pinfold Hill, was opened for public worship in 1794. The whole was accomplished, including the cost of site, for the sum of £473 : 18 : 3½."

But old Hugh Burland does not tell of all the love and self-denial, the faith and prayer that went into that building ; the hours of unpaid labour James and his friends devoted ; the care they lavished upon every detail, and the joy that came to them when at length the whole was completed and dedicated to the service of God.

[2] The following quaint epitome of the life of John Taylor appeared in the *Leeds Intelligencer* for October 11, 1834 :

" October 6, Died, Mr John Taylor, Linen-reed Maker, Barnsley, aged

from the first to take his share in the support of the family,
and ere long began to look forward to a home of his own
on a very simple scale.

For hardly had he grown to manhood before he came
to know and love Mary the daughter of William Shepherd
of Bradford, who happily returned his affection. The
parents seem to have been of Scotch extraction, and one
cannot but be interested in them because of this union
which was to bring into the Taylor family qualities of inestimable value. All researches hitherto have failed in
discovering much about William Shepherd, save that he
was Governor of a gaol, probably in Yorkshire, " the best-
tempered man in the world " and a consistent Christian.
Tradition adds that he was one of Wesley's earliest preachers
and occupied a position of influence among the Methodists.
Be that as it may, he certainly handed on to his daughter
unusual strength of mind and body as well as principles of
sincere and simple godliness.

It was not in Bradford, apparently, that the Shepherds
were living at the time of the engagement. That would
have been a far cry for busy people—twenty miles' coach-
ride from Barnsley. In the Register still preserved in the
beautiful Church at Darfield, the bride is entered as " Mary
Shepherd of this Parish," and Darfield is within easy reach
of Old Mill Lane. There it was at any rate that the young
folks did their courting, when Mary was a tall, stately lassie
with a warm heart under a quiet exterior, and John with
all his practical qualities was a music-loving, merry lad of
only twenty-one.

But young as they were, he was able to provide for the
girl he loved. On Pinfold Hill near the Chapel a little
home was waiting, and Mary was fitted to make it all a
home should be. And so in All Saints' Church overlooking
the valley where the Dove runs into the Dearne they were
married one May morning in 1799, and thence through

56 : an excellent man and most highly respected. Mr. Taylor has been
an inhabitant of Barnsley a great number of years, and in his business
has been of great consequence to the staple trade of the town He was a
member of the Methodist Connexion, and evinced a remarkable fondness
for sacred music. His voice was a powerful counter, and was considered
by men of science to possess great harmony."

blossoming hedgerows wended their way together to the neighbouring town.

It still stands, that quaint old cottage, with its sunny kitchen and hospitably open door : the last house in a quiet court that ere long was to resound with children's merry laughter.[1] Across the street, also, may still be seen the outside stairway leading to John Taylor's workshop. It was a steep climb for little feet, but doubtless they helped to wear the stones so smooth with many a journey to call father when he stayed away too long. For the cottage overflowed with boys and girls and the factory with business, till the reed-maker must often have been conscious of the blessing of his father's God.[2]

In the Chapel, too, an overflowing blessing had been given. There John and Mary were both Class Leaders among the younger people, and his voice and musical ability were greatly valued. " Instead of the fathers shall be the children " was a promise so abundantly fulfilled that the premises, amply sufficient in James Taylor's day, were all too small for the succeeding generation. John Whitworth the young architect increased the difficulty when he started an excellent innovation known as the " Sunday School." Following the example of Mr. Raikes of Gloucester, he set about gathering in the untaught children of the streets. Few could be found to encourage, and even he had no idea of the magnitude of the work he was undertaking. But when on the day of opening no fewer than six hundred children crowded in, all eager to be taught, it was evident not only that the school was needed but that it must have larger premises.

And soon even opposers were surprised into approval. The changed demeanour of the children impressed the town

[1] The old home of John and Mary Taylor is now known as " Sten Court, five house," and is occupied by an elderly couple, Mr and Mrs. William Irving, who well remember its former owners

[2] Seven of John Taylor's children lived to grow up : Elizabeth became Mrs. Cope ; John took up his father's business and left a large family , Mary became Mrs. Norman , James was the father of Hudson Taylor ; William was a stockbroker in Manchester ; Sarah died unmarried ; and Samuel was for many years useful and beloved as a Wesleyan Minister. He had a great admiration for his mother, and used to say that he owed everything to her, his father dying while he was still a child.

so much that the landlord of a well-known tavern went in search of Mr. Whitworth and handed him a guinea with the request that he would never overlook the White Hart Inn when calling for subscriptions. Others helping in the same way it was soon possible to erect a suitable building near the Chapel, which gave the name of School Street to the hitherto quiet lane on which the Taylors lived.

Not long after, it became necessary to enlarge the Chapel also, which was so much altered and improved that James Taylor would hardly have recognised it had he come back again. The reopening just after Christmas, 1810, was a great occasion, when curly-headed little James, the grandson who bore his name, was not yet four years old. Young as he was, however, the rejoicings of that day, the decorations, singing and crowded meetings, made an impression that never passed away, and long years after he loved to recall the joy with which the Chapel his grandfather had helped to build was rededicated to the service of God.

From the first, the Divine hand was upon this little lad in the reed-maker's home, preparing him for usefulness. Educationally, he and his brothers had advantages unknown to the older generation, for their parents were able to keep them at school and let them choose their own line of life within reasonable limits. One took up the father's business, another became a stockbroker and a third a minister. James wished to be a doctor, and would have studied medicine had circumstances permitted. This being beyond his reach he went in for chemistry as the next best thing, and was indentured to a friend in a neighbouring town.

Seven years' apprenticeship away from home made a man of him before he was twenty-one, and the even tenor of a country business gave opportunities for study. He was quick and painstaking, an omnivorous reader and methodical in all his habits. Next to the Bible, theology was his favourite study. Sermons he read extensively, as well as good biographies. In order to make the most of his reading, he developed a system of shorthand on his own account, which he improved and made much use of in later years.

He had some aptitude for music as well as mathematics, and was devoted to the study of birds, plants, and nature generally. Though not tall in figure he was strong and active, and with a bright smile and pleasant manner was decidedly prepossessing.

At least so thought his mother, when occasional holidays brought him home. And from the course of events it would appear that she was not alone in this opinion. " Home " was no longer the cottage near the Chapel to which Mary Shepherd had come as bride. Prospered in business, John Taylor had built a plain but substantial stone house at the corner of Pitt and York Streets. The situation was good and the property large enough for the erection of work-shops and other premises. Thither the family had moved some years previously, and a brighter spot it would have been hard to find when all the young folk gathered home.

Though the Manse near by need not have feared comparison. This was another roomy, pleasant home, on the opposite side of Pitt Street, occupied about this time by a family with the same number of girls and boys. Naturally there was a good deal of intercourse between the households. The eldest daughter of the Manse had a voice so sweet that John Taylor called her " the nightingale." The minister himself and Mrs. Hudson were among the reed-maker's warmest friends, and many were the Sunday evenings when they walked home together from Chapel and joined forces at the corner house for an informal service of song.

It was in 1824 that the minister's family was transferred to the Barnsley Circuit. To the parents it must have seemed like coming home, for their native place, the little town of Holmfirth, lay only a few miles westward on the edge of the great grouse moors. There both Benjamin Hudson and his wife had been born and bred, and from that Yorkshire valley, running back into the Peak country and many a mile of mountain, dale and moor, had come the artistic temperament and courageous spirit of their children, enriched by a heritage of godliness.

Mr. Hudson, though not a gifted speaker, was a faithful and devoted minister of the Gospel. He was an artist, with a decided talent for portrait-painting, inherited by three at least of his children. But his most prominent characteristic, and one that gave him difficulty at times, was an irrepressible fund of humour. Happily this also was passed on in measure to his descendants. Reproved in the Methodist " Conference " on one occasion for not sufficiently restraining this tendency, he apologised in a reply so witty that the whole assembly was overcome with laughter. But in Barnsley he was on his native heath. Yorkshire folk could appreciate his dry, droll speeches and pointed exhortations. There and in many other places he exercised a helpful ministry, and was valued not for his own sake merely, but also on account of his family.

As for Mrs. Hudson, one look at her face was enough to inspire confidence and esteem. The accompanying portrait painted by her daughter Hannah gives some idea of what she was in later years, though it reveals but little of the strength and sweetness of spirit that made the minister's wife a blessing to many. Three boys and four girls completed the family, Amelia the eldest being only fifteen when they first came to Barnsley.

Young as she was, however, this daughter was a comfort to her parents in no ordinary degree. In addition to careful home-training, she had had the benefit of several years in the Friends' School at Darlington. Sincerity, thoroughness, and love of industry had become as natural to her as the thoughtfulness for others that made her everywhere beloved; and all she was and did told of a heart wholly given to the Lord.

Had it been financially possible Amelia would have continued her studies at Darlington. But younger sisters needed education, and with cheerful courage she took it for granted that she must make way for them and obtain remunerative employment. It was the only way to lighten home-burdens. And if her parents never knew how much she felt the sacrifice, Amelia on her part could little realise the mingled feelings of regret and thankfulness with which they saw her set to work before she was sixteen to earn her living. The right thing is not always the easiest; but God

THE REV. BENJAMIN HUDSON AND MRS. HUDSON.

Painted by their daughter, Mrs. Richard Hardey, some years after they had left Barnsley.

To face page 26.

has His schools for training, and a life left in His hands will never fail of its highest development here and hereafter.

So Amelia went to Castle Donnington as governess to three little children in the family of a gentleman-farmer. Her pupils were devoted to her and her surroundings congenial. But though happy in her work and gifted for it, she could not but long at times for home, and the holidays that enabled her to visit Barnsley seemed few and far between.

Thus it was that although a special favourite with John Taylor and his family she was rarely able to join the Sunday evening gatherings at the corner house. Like James in his apprenticeship, she was early feeling the discipline of life. Perhaps this very fact helped to draw them together. He was her senior by about a year, and prepared through what he had seen of the world to appreciate her brave, beautiful character. For as was purposed by the Heart that planned, those welcome holidays sometimes brought the young governess to the Manse just when James Taylor was also able to visit Barnsley. Short indeed would seem the ten miles' walk when he was homeward bound. And more than usual eagerness winged his feet when he came to know for himself the sweet singer of whom he had heard so much. To his delight he found Amelia to be lovely in disposition as well as in appearance, and that she thought and felt as he did about the deeper things of life.

The result was inevitable. A warm affection sprang up between these two, so suited to each other, and before the minister left Barnsley, an engagement had been hallowed by the love and prayers of both families that from that day united the names—Hudson Taylor.

CHAPTER III

1824–1832

IT was long, however, ere the young people were to see much of one another. James had his way to make in the calling he had chosen, and Amelia's holidays came no oftener than before, though more eagerly desired. But at sixteen and seventeen a long engagement is inevitable, and brings with it so much of hope and happiness that it is comparatively easy to bear.

When the young apprentice returned to Rotherham, it was with stronger incentives than ever to do well. There was new zest in business and study, and the blessing of the Lord so filled his heart that it could not but overflow to others. His employer perceiving his reliability, decided to put him in charge of a branch-establishment in the neighbouring town of Conisborough. Here James Taylor found, as others before him, that " prayer and pains with faith in Jesus Christ will do anything." The business prospered, and better still he prospered in it, according to the suggestive promise of the first Psalm.[1]

With comparatively little leisure in the years that followed he had a growing love for study, especially of a kind that would throw light upon the word of God. The Bible was his chief delight, and he longed to share the wealth he found in it with others. At no great distance from Conisborough were many neglected villages to which he made his way Sunday by Sunday, telling in out-of-the-way places the

[1] *In whatsoever he doeth, he shall prosper* (Psalm i. 3, R.V. margin).

28

wonderful love of God. He could not but speak, for his own heart was brimming over, and not a few among his hearers were awakened and blessed. Seeing which, the authorities of the Church to which he belonged recognised that the lad was called to this much-needed ministry, and at nineteen years of age his name was added to the list of Barnsley local preachers, of whom his grandfather had been the first.

Meanwhile his fiancée was still at Castle Donnington gaining health and experience for days to come. Constant reading kept her mind bright, and regular correspondence cultivated a habit of rapid, easy writing, of more value than she could suppose at the time. Her letters were full of interest and did much to encourage the one who received them as he took up on his own account the responsibilities of life.

His apprenticeship over James Taylor had returned to Barnsley, and with money advanced by his father rented one of the best shops in town. It was a step of faith, for 21 Cheapside was a serious undertaking for so young a man. But the premises were in a good situation, right on the busy Market Place, and large enough to afford a permanent home. One of his sisters took charge as housekeeper for the time, leaving him free to devote his energies to business six days a week and to his preaching appointments on Sunday. At least as much work and prayer were given to the shop as to his sermons, with the result that he succeeded in both and became known as a reliable man of affairs as well as a helpful, popular preacher throughout the Circuit. At length after years of uphill work the way seemed clear before him. He was able to repay his father's loan, and with a home and sufficient income of his own, felt he might claim his bride.

It was in the quaint old town of Barton-on-Humber that the Hudsons were living when the long engagement drew to a close. Seven years' friendship had done much to develop the boy and girl into earnest manhood and womanhood and to prepare them for the union to which they now looked forward. James had learned to pray his way through

difficulties and was full of confidence in God, and Amelia
at twenty-three more than fufilled the promise of her girl-
hood. Her father, whose ministry had taken him to Chester-
field and elsewhere since Barnsley days, was still in the North
country, in charge of the Barton Circuit, and had it all been
planned on purpose, nothing could have been more delightful
under the circumstances than the Manse and its surroundings.
No little comfort this, amid the varying fortunes of an
itinerant preacher's life.

For a something indescribable of old-world loveliness pervaded the little town, seen at its best no doubt through
lovers' eyes that sweet spring-tide in 1831. From the
famous Ferry of the Doomsday Book to the fine old churches
on the Green, dating back to Norman and even Saxon times,
the cosy, straggling place breathed an air of comfort and
repose. About it lay an undulating country noted for its
corn, malt, bricks and tiles. The spacious Market Place and
numerous windmills bore witness to a measure of commercial
activity ; but the quaint, irregular streets and picturesque
houses, half hidden among trees and flowering creepers,
were more in keeping with the spirit of a bygone time.

In the very heart of the town, the preacher's house near
the Chapel seemed specially a bower of greenery and bloom.
" Maltby Cottage, Maltby Lane," was an address with
which James Taylor was familiar, but even he can hardly
have anticipated the charm of that sheltered home. Within
the high, old-fashioned wall lay a spacious garden with
its lawn and flowers, its fruit-trees all in blossom, and a
green field beyond, where quiet cattle fed. Looking out
upon this pleasant scene stood the square, red-brick house
covered with creepers, whose wide windows welcomed the
sunshine and almost made the lower rooms seem part of
the out-of-doors. A sweeter spot could hardly be imagined
for a homelike, happy wedding, nor a more charming bride
than the minister's daughter whom James Taylor had loved
so long.

Here then they were married on April 5, 1831, in the
beautiful church of St. Mary's just beyond the trees.

Busy and happy were the days that followed when

Photographs by   F. Howard Taylor.

1. THE PARISH CHURCH OF ST. MARY, BARTON-ON-HUMBER, IN WHICH
MR. AND MRS. JAMES TAYLOR WERE MARRIED.

2. THE HOME OF THE BRIDE, "MALTBY COTTAGE, MALTBY LANE."

To face page 80.

Amelia found herself again in Barnsley.   The John Taylors were still living in the house on Pitt Street, and both there and in the Chapel the welcome she received was warm and true.   And the more she became known among her husband's friends the more she was beloved for the sweet spirit that seemed to have no thought or consciousness of self.   Intelligent and attractive as she was, there was no desire to shine or make an impression on others.   Her voice alone would have brought her notice, but there was a shrinking from display of this or any other gift.   Yet she enjoyed society, loved to see others admired, and was so good a listener that men and women alike found her companionship delightful.

But it was the chemist's home on the Market Place that really saw her shine.   There the qualities that made her an ideal wife could not be hidden, and James Taylor must often have realised at his own fireside the truth of that word : " Whoso findeth a wife findeth a good thing, and obtaineth favour of the Lord."

In all his work and interests she bore a cheerful part, while caring for domestic matters with a thoroughness and perfection of detail that characterised all she did.   His " Class " of forty or fifty lads felt the influence of her sympathy and prayers only less than the girls who became her special care, and one of the joys of their early married life was an old-time revival in the Chapel that resulted in the conversion of many of these young people.[1]

In his preaching engagements throughout the Circuit she also proved an unexpected help.   Preparing his sermons was no longer the solitary task it had been.   Together they prayed and studied, and when James Taylor's heart was full and his pen could not keep pace with the thoughts he longed to utter, his wife would take rapid notes and write out for

[1] The revival commenced in Westgate Chapel, as it was then called, with the Watch Night Service on December 31, 1832, and one of the lads converted in James Taylor's class was his cousin John Bashforth, whose mother was a daughter of James and Betty Taylor, brought up in the little cottage on Old Mill Lane.   The Bashforths became one of the leading families in Barnsley   Young John Bashforth from this time onward lived a consistent Christian life, and was for many years Superintendent of the Sunday School.

him many a sermon delivered as he paced the little room
behind the shop. He was a gifted speaker, and gave much
care to the preparation of his discourses.[1] In this work
Amelia's pen proved invaluable through many a long year,
and the joy of seeing souls brought into blessing through
his ministry more than repaid the sacrifice of time and
strength.

And then the young wife had the happiness of finding
her expectations more than realised in the character her
husband sustained as a business man. He was an excellent
chemist and highly respected for his influence in the town.
So scrupulous was he in financial matters that he made it a
rule to pay every debt the very day it fell due.

" If I let it stand over a week," he would say, " I defraud
my creditor of interest, if only a fractional sum."

In dealing with his customers he was upright to a farthing
or a grain, and full of genuine sympathy. He never sued
for a bill, and did not think it desirable for Christians even
to press for the payment of an account. On the contrary,
he frequently returned in whole or part sums that his
customers could ill afford to spare. More than one neighbour
barely able to settle an account was cheered by his generosity

" It's all right, John," he would exclaim. " We'll send
that bill up to heaven and settle it there."

Genial and kindly to all he was specially so to the poor
and to strangers in sickness or trouble. A foreigner or
traveller far from home could always find a friend in the
busy chemist.

" Come again, come again," he would say if he thought
they needed help. " Bring the bottle back when the
medicine is done and I will gladly fill it."

Yet he was a keen man of affairs and made his business
successful. This was partly on account of skill in the
management of money-matters, and partly through careful

[1] " Possessing good natural abilities, which he carefully improved by
study, James Taylor was a most able and effective preacher. His manner
was at once pleasant and dignified. His sermons bore evidence of much
thought and study, and as literary compositions were considerably above
the average of lay discourses " (from the Obituary Notice in *The Barnsley
Chronicle*).

attention to detail. His fellow-townsmen recognising his financial ability appointed him Manager of their " Building Society," an office he continued to fill for two-and-twenty years. That he did not regard lightly the duties of such a position may be judged from the fact that he worked out lists of interest at various rates to four or five places of decimals, and compiled tables of logarithms to assist his calculations. Public funds were to him a sacred trust, demanding the greatest care and fidelity in their administration.[1]

But it was to God above all James Taylor sought to be faithful, and he was possessed by a profound conviction of His infinite faithfulness. He took the Bible very simply, believing it was of all books the most practical if put to the test of experience. In this too he met with fullest sympathy from the young wife who was herself so loyal to the Lord.

On a day they could never forget, in their first winter together, he sought her Bible in hand to talk over a passage that had impressed him. It was part of the thirteenth chapter of Exodus, with the corresponding verses in Numbers :

" Sanctify unto me all the firstborn . ."
" All the firstborn are mine . . ."
" Mine shall they be . . ."
" Set apart unto the Lord."

Long and earnest was the talk that followed in view of the happiness to which they were looking forward. Their

[1] " He was one of the founders and for many years Acting Manager of the Barnsley Permanent Building Society. . . . After his retirement from business, about 1864 or 1865, he was able to devote a considerable amount of time to the work of the Society, which had by this time attained important dimensions, and all its members will agree that from first to last he had its interests thoroughly at heart . . . On the eve of his leaving Barnsley he was presented by the directors, officers, and members of the Society with a solid silver tea-service and an illuminated address ' as a mark of their esteem for his personal character, and in recognition of his faithful services as Manager of the Society from 1853 to 1875.'

" During the long period of his residence in Barnsley, Mr Taylor enjoyed the confidence and esteem of all sections of his fellow-townsmen, and of him it could with truth be said as his active, well-knit figure was seen passing along our streets :

' An honest man, close-button'd to the chin,
Broadcloth without, and a warm heart within.' " *Ibid.*

D

hearts held back nothing from the Lord. With them it was not a question of how little could be given, but how much. Did the Lord claim the best gift of His own giving? Their child was more their own for being His. To such parents what could be more welcome than the invitation, nay command, to set apart their dearest thus to Him? And how precious the Divine assurance, " It is Mine," not for time only but for eternity.

Together they knelt in the silence to fulfil as literally as possible an obligation they could not relegate to Hebrew parents of old. It was no ceremony to be gone through merely but a definite transaction, the handing over of their best to God, recalling which the mother wrote long after :

" This act of consecration they solemnly performed upon their knees, asking for the rich influence of the Holy Spirit," that their firstborn might be " set apart " indeed from that hour.

And just as definitely the Lord responded, giving them faith to realise that He had accepted the gift ; that henceforth the life so dear to them was their own no longer, but must be held at the disposal of a higher claim, a deeper love than theirs.

Thus spring-time came again touching with tender loveliness those Yorkshire hills and valleys, and on May 21, 1832, this child of many prayers was born, and named after both parents, James Hudson Taylor.

CHAPTER IV

NURTURE AND ADMONITION

1832–1839. AET. 1–7.

HE was a sensitive, thoughtful little fellow from the first, though bright and winsome as any heart could wish. It almost seemed as though he brought more love than usual into the world, with his great capacity for loving and the frailty of health that drew forth all the tenderness of those about him. For he was delicate, unusually so, as his parents soon discovered. This was no little sorrow, and added difficulty to the task of bringing him up to be a brave and faithful follower of the Lord Jesus Christ. As time went on he was often so far from well that it seemed almost impossible to insist upon obedience and self-control. Yet the very difficulty only made it the more necessary. For nothing in after-life, his parents realised, could ever compensate for the injury of an undisciplined childhood. But they knew where to turn for strength and grace. Were they not workers together with God in moulding this little life for His holy service ? If they lacked wisdom for so high a task, as indeed they did, would He not give it liberally according to His promise ?

So the child grew under a watchful care that could not in present happiness forget its responsibility to coming years. And his parents grew with him. The young mother, lovely as she had always been, developed new depth of character in dealing with this son, and into the father's life came added sympathy and strength.

It was around his grandfather's figure, strange to say,

35

and the Chapel on Pinfold Hill that his earliest recollections centred. Taken almost from infancy to the House of God, he retained a distinct remembrance of the old-fashioned gallery as it then was, and his father's pew right opposite the pulpit. Immediately behind was the seat occupied by John and Mary Taylor, whose presence usually inspired a wholesome sense of awe. But Hudson only remembered the smile that lighted his grandfather's face. For when he had been specially good he was sure to be handed over the back of the pew, at the close of the long proceedings, to receive his grandfather's commendations and be carried home to sit on his knee by the fireside and at the well-filled table. This was a regular custom as long as the reed-maker lived and kept open house on Pitt Street. That dizzy transit from pew to pew and the clasp of his grandfather's arms bringing a consciousness of duty well done were the first memories of his childhood.

And with them came another, of the last time he saw that dear, familiar face. His grandfather was lying very quiet then, and the wondering child was told that he had gone to be with Jesus. There was no fear in the impression, only surprise that he should be so cold and still. It was his first sight of death, and never to be forgotten, although at the time he was only two and a half years old.

There were other childish memories also of an unusual kind. One was of learning the Hebrew alphabet as he sat on his father's knee, and another his first attempt at authorship a little later. By this time he was four, and could read and write a little, for he embarked courageously on this literary effort.

" Was it a fairy-tale or story of adventure ? " we inquired when he spoke of this recollection.

" No, it was a serious recital of a matter that was burdening my mind. It was about an old man of eighty, who had led a very improper life and had not truly repented. His chances were growing small. I only finished one chapter, laboriously inscribed in large print. It was not very long."

From which it will be seen that this child of quick susceptibilities entered more perhaps than was good for him

into the life of older people, until little playfellows grew up
to claim their share of attention. This happily was the
case before long, and by the time he was five years old a
younger brother and sister were quite companionable.
They were a merry trio, and kept each other busy all day
long. Teaching Amelia [1] to walk became a great interest
to the boys, as Hudson recalled long after, when writing
from China for her nineteenth birthday. Another performance into which they put their whole hearts was the Sunday
evening " meeting " in which one of the brothers was
audience and the other speaker. The father's chair was
pulpit in the little sitting-room behind the shop, and it was
doubtless his example and the stories told them of James
Taylor and the days of Wesley that fired their imagination
and made them want to be " brave preachers " too.

For at no time is there greater capacity for devotion or
more pure, uncalculating ambition in the service of God
than in early childhood, when the heart is full of love to
Christ. Little Hudson, for example, was deeply impressed
at four or five years of age by what he heard about the
darkness of heathen lands.

" When I am a man," he would often say, " I mean to be
a missionary and go to China."

It was only a childish impulse ? Yes, but he meant it
with all his heart, and meant it because he loved the Lord
and wanted to please and follow Him. In the same spirit
was the prayer of another little one of five years old :

" Lord Jesus, help us to be *good* brothers to You, and to
do some of Your hard work in Africa and in China." [2]

The first sorrow that overshadowed Hudson's life was
the death of his brother, called after their great-grandfather,
William Shepherd. This was a loss indeed, for they had
been inseparable companions, and there was no one to fill
the empty place. Theodore was still a baby, and he too was
taken before long to be with Jesus. Hudson from this time
onward was an only son ; but two little sisters were spared

----

[1] Afterwards Mrs. Benjamin Broomhall.
[2] " Whosoever shall do the will of God, the same is my brother, and
sister, and mother " (St. Mark iii. 35).

to grow up, the elder of whom was near enough in age to become his special friend. These early bereavements, following the loss of their grandfather, would not but make him feel the reality of unseen things and develop his thoughtful tendencies.

But though he took life seriously from the first, he was sunny and bright by nature and dearly loved boyish fun. He had eyes and a heart for everything, and retained to the end a capacity for enjoyment that was remarkable. Nature was his great delight, and he had the patience, sympathy, and power of observation needed for entering into her secrets. He would take any amount of trouble to cultivate a little fern or flower brought home from the woods, or to learn about the ways of birds, animals and insects. All living, growing things seemed to possess a charm for him that years only increased.

On one occasion in his early childhood a fair of unusual interest was held in the town. The open space behind St. Mary's Church was covered with stalls and shows of every kind, and the usual attractions of circus, music, and merry-go-round were not lacking. But this fair was specially fascinating to Hudson on account of an exhibition of stuffed birds and animals, in which their natural habitats were reproduced as far as possible. Nothing could exceed the expectation with which he set out for the Green, the proud possessor of a penny, that open-sesame of all delights.

Now it was a rule of the family that pennies could be had if they were earned, but not otherwise. The parents recognised the importance of teaching their children the value of money, and that honest work is necessary if it is to be obtained. Simple tasks suited to their capacity were devised, such as hemming dusters, cleaning windows, or helping in the shop. When they were too young to do anything but play, small coins might be earned by what was called "a game of still," which meant just sitting perfectly quiet for a measured time by the clock, five or ten minutes or longer as the mother might decide. And Mother had more in view than the children thought, having discovered how much good was accomplished by these resting-times for mind and body. Of course all this was much more troublesome than the ordinary methods of obtaining pocket-money, but it had the desired effect, and the pleasure of giving and receiving pennies genuinely earned was sufficient reward for parents and children alike. Thus the unfortunate habit of teasing for money was entirely obviated. " Work for it and you shall have it " proved a much more satisfactory basis.

Well, this particular fair came just when Hudson was rejoicing in the possession of his first whole penny, obtained at what had been to him no little cost. Of course, it seemed a fortune. The largest, most precious coin he had ever possessed, what would it not purchase of delight ?

Joyfully he climbed the hill to St. Mary's, ran along the lane to Church Fields, and sought among the bewildering variety of attractions for the birds and animals of his dreams. It was disconcerting to find a fence around the enclosure, and at the gate an imposing personage of doubtful disposition toward little boys. But producing his penny he summoned up courage to ask admission. To his surprise this was denied, the man gruffly intimating that the entrance fee was " tuppence."

In a moment the child's mind grasped the unreasonableness of the situation. No doubt the man would like to have two pennies. So would he himself. But that was out of the question. There was only one.

" I haven't got another penny," he explained timidly. " But I will give you this one, if you will let me in ; and wouldn't it be better for you to have one penny than none at all ? "

But the man in uniform was not able to see the point.

Nothing daunted, the curly-headed little fellow continued his attempt. Reasonableness and perseverance were among the strongest traits in his character, and surely even a grown-up person would see, in time, what a mistake it was to refuse one penny just because you could not have two at once. But alas, the gate-keeper was obdurate.

At length the failure of his arguments and the inaccessibility of the treasures beyond that closed door were too much for the sensitive child. Turning away with tears in his eyes, he ran home sobbing as if his heart would break.

Happily his mother found him and was able to understand. Taking him in her arms she said quietly :

" But the man was doing his duty, my son. He didn't mean to be unkind. Every one has to pay two pennies to see those lovely birds and animals. You have been so good and industrious lately that Mother will give you another penny as a reward. Run off again, now, and the man will be glad to let you in."

This unexpected turn of events put everything right, and sent such gladness thrilling through the little heart that seventy long years after it had not died away.

The mother's gentle discipline had much to do with the happiness of his childhood, and gave rise to more than one situation that was long remembered. Such, for instance, was the company dinner when in attending to her guests she overlooked the needs of her little son. The meal went on and still the child said nothing, knowing he must not ask for things at table. At length, however, an expedient suggested itself, and a little voice was heard requesting for salt. That at any rate was permissible.

" And what do you want the salt for ? " questioned his neighbour, seeing the empty plate.

" Oh," he replied, " I want to be ready. Mamma will give me something to eat by-and-by."

On another occasion he called attention to his needs by inquiring in a pause in the conversation :

" Mamma, do you think apple-pie is good for little boys ? "

It was not often he attempted to evade home-regulations, partly no doubt because he knew it would be useless, and partly for fear of giving his mother pain. In all her dealings with the children she was reasonable and consistent. She made few rules, and avoided unnecessary commands. But they well knew that what she said she meant, for she never gave instructions she was not prepared to see carried out. Sometimes Hudson was tempted, like other boys, to see how far he could go in taking his own way ; but one distressing experience taught him a lesson that was not soon forgotten.

He was intensely fond of reading, and was absorbed one winter in a delightful book. He was all eagerness to finish it, but daylight hours were short and full of other occupations, and bed-time could not be postponed. If only he might read at night! But Mother always came to tuck him up and take the light away. The story grew in interest, and at length a plan suggested itself. He knew, as every one did in that orderly household, just where the candle-ends were kept for use in kitchen or cellar. It would never be noticed if he took a few of these. Then he could light them, one by one, and lying cosily in bed make progress with his book. At first the thought was startling and not to be entertained for a moment. But it came again and again, until conscience was silenced and he decided to carry it out.

A visitor came to spend the evening with his parents just when this stage was reached, and perceiving his opportunity the child filled his largest pocket with the coveted candle-ends and went in earlier than usual to say good-night. In the drawing-room the older people were gathered round the fire. The visitor was fond of children, and taking the little fellow on his knee asked if he would like to hear a story. Dearly as Hudson loved stories, however, especially at bed-time, the warmth of the fire made him anxious to escape. He was painfully conscious that the pocket full of candle-ends was on the fire side, and eagerly explaining that it was time to go to bed, tried to slip off the too-friendly knee.

But his mother's voice detained him. It was early yet, and as a special treat he might stay a little longer to hear the story. But instead of being delighted, the poor child was restless and miserable. The candles must be melting. He knew they were! What if Mother should smell the tallow, or it should trickle down upon the carpet? At the first pause in the recital, he urged again, more earnestly than before, that it really was bed-time and he ought not to stay up any longer. The gentleman was disappointed and the parents greatly puzzled. But still the story went on.

Finally, after what seemed hours of suspense, he was released and hurried away to his room. His mother quickly followed, to find him weeping bitterly over a pocketful of melted tallow and a story of his own that he was only too glad to pour forth without extenuation. Needless to say her sorrow over it all impressed the lesson for which in after-life he could not be too thankful.

One chief advantage of his childhood was that he was so continually under his mother's care. This in itself was sufficient compensation for the limited means that made it necessary. The father's business prospered and brought in more than enough for present needs. But with the welfare of his family at heart, he felt it desirable to lay by for the future, as well as to purchase the premises in which they lived and other properties. This necessitated careful economy in everyday matters. Household expenditure was reduced as far as possible, luxuries were unknown, and active, practical habits were the order of the day. The children learned to be independent and were well drilled in thoughtfulness for others. But above all they grew up in close contact with their parents, as children never can in a house with many servants, or if they are sent to school. The mother was their companion from morning till night. She it was who worked with them, taught them, did everything for them, and was the sun and centre of their little system, radiating light and love without end.

This accounted largely for the influence she exerted over her little people. It was second nature to obey her, and she was always there to encourage or restrain. She was a woman of few words and unusual tact, with a quiet way of saying and doing things that was very effective. A mere suggestion from her lips went further than repeated injunctions from some people.

" My dear, it is nearly time for dinner," or " for tea."

This meant clean hands, fresh pinafores, tidy hair, and a race to see who would be first at table before Father appeared.

How she managed it no one could tell ; but with the entire care and education of the children, cooking to attend to, washing to be done at home, and all the housework, sewing and mending necessary, and the help of only one maid, she invariably kept her surroundings neat and attractive, down to the brightly burning fire and clean-swept hearth. The little parlour behind the shop, though constantly in use for meals and lessons, needlework and play, was a picture of comfort and good order ; and this not by virtue of the distracting process known as " setting-to-rights " so much as by a happy knack of never letting things go wrong or stray far out of place.

It was a cosy spot, this family sitting-room, and well in keeping with the simple life to which Hudson Taylor owed so much. Entering from the shop, a long, old-fashioned couch occupied the wall to the right, beyond which a china-cupboard filled the corner with shining rows of crockery and glass. Next came the fireplace at a right angle with the sofa, making that end of the room attractive on winter evenings. The other end was taken up with a window and door, leading to the little yard, across which was the ware-house where the father's stores were kept. This window, facing west, let in the sunshine when the children were busy in the afternoon with needlework and lessons. A spacious bookcase filled the wall between the fireplace and window, and opposite stood a chest of drawers used as a sideboard, between two doors, one leading upstairs and the other down to the kitchen premises. A square table in the middle of the room was protected from draughts by a folding screen in the corner farthest from the fire. And last, but not least in the estimation of the children, a little window over the sofa afforded interesting glimpses into the shop and Market Place beyond.

The chief feature in the room, undoubtedly, was the bookcase, and it had also much to do with the order that prevailed. Over the lower shelves hung a curtain, concealing a characteristic device of the mother's household manage-ment. Everything in use for meals or lessons, work or play, had its appointed place in sideboard or cupboard, while magazines, books, and papers found hospitality upon the ample shelves. But one shelf behind the crimson curtain was unappropriated. Clean and empty, it stood ready for emergencies. Was the room needed for unexpected visitors ?

The work in hand, whatever it might be, was laid away without embarrassment and just as easily brought out again. Were the older people busy with letters or accounts when the table was wanted for a meal ? A place was ready in which ink and papers would be accessible and out of danger. It was a convenient receptacle at tea-time for the mother's sewing or the children's toys. But whatever its uses in the day-time, it was always cleared and dusted before night. Simple as such a plan may seem, it was effective because of the orderly mind that carried it out, and went far toward solving the problem of how to turn one room to so many uses without litter or confusion.

Not that a litter was objected to at the right time and in the proper place ; but the little hands that made it were expected to put things straight, before turning to other work or play. The children came to feel that their amusements must never give other people trouble, and that it is wiser to do at once what has to be done, rather than leave it to another time. " A place for everything and everything in its place " was the working rule of the household ; and that extra, empty shelf behind the curtain was more effective than many exhortations. One thing only made a deeper impression in this connection, and that was the fact that Mother's belongings never needed tidying. Other people's possessions might be more or less topsy-turvy on occasion, as bright eyes had not failed to discover. But Mother's drawers and cupboards stood the test. They never needed setting to rights, because, strange as it might seem, they were never out of order.

Personal neatness she taught them in the same practical way, until it became second nature to feel that one must be clean and tidy, however simply dressed. A fresh apron was ready for their father's use in the shop every morning, and the mother's print gown and closely fitting cap were just as pretty for breakfast, six days in the week, as her black satin and white crêpe shawl reserved for Sunday. She was very pleasing in appearance, and the children were like her. The muslin cap tied under the chin, with its soft tulle edging and white ribbons, well became her calm, sweet face. She

From an Oil Painting by
Mrs. Hardey.

MRS. JAMES TAYLOR OF BARNSLEY, IN THE DAYS OF HUDSON TAYLOR'S
CHILDHOOD.

To face page 44.

had donned it on her wedding-day according to the custom of the times, when a dainty cap was always waiting the bride's return from church. Mother would hardly have seemed Mother without that modest headgear. But whether it were the Sunday cap, its gauze ribbons edged with satin, or the more durable muslin for daily use, it was equally fresh and becoming.

Slovenliness in dress under any circumstances she could not endure. Pretty washing frocks were prepared for the little girls, with black alpaca aprons piped at the edges, and they were trained to feel that it was just as important to be neat and attractive for household work before breakfast as for entertaining friends at tea. A work-basket was always ready on their dressing-table, and stitches were put in as soon as needed. Even if it meant getting up ten minutes earlier on a winter morning, clean tuckers must be sewn in to everyday dresses just as carefully as to best ones. And their brother too was made to realise that clean hands and shoes, nicely kept nails, and well-brushed garments were quite as necessary at home as in any company. It was a question of thoroughness and self-respect, and those were essentials their parents required in everything.

In the same way the servant, probably an inexperienced little maid when she came to them, was taught to leave the kitchen in order before she went upstairs to other duties. The mother herself undertook most of the cooking, and it was while dinner was preparing that the morning's lessons were done. But thanks to careful management, the kitchen was just as pleasant as the parlour. The stone floor was well scoured, and a white border made on all four sides to match the spotless hearth. The kitchen range was clean and bright, no matter what might be cooking, and Mother's rocking-chair made the whole room look cosy. Here at a table reserved for the purpose, the little girls worked at their lessons, while Hudson was similarly employed under his father's supervision upstairs. There was no shirking work or playing truant if their parents were called away. Lessons had to go on just the same, and did with wonderful regularity.

Then in the afternoon, their mother had the older children with her while she was busy with her needle. A great deal of sewing had to be done, but she was able to go on with it while they read aloud or wrote from dictation. Many were the hours thus spent over history, literature and travels. Hard names or unfamiliar words they might not hurry over. No, the dictionary had to be brought and each difficulty mastered as they came to it. A real lover of books herself, she early inspired them with a taste for reading, and to her accuracy and thoroughness may be traced the unusual power of attention to detail that characterised her son in later years. Industry and perseverance also the children could not but learn from her example. So busy was she that it was the rarest thing to see her take time to enjoy a book, but she often had one propped up before her while her needle flew, that she might catch a sentence now and then without interrupting her work.

And the father in his department was just as busy. Through the little window over the sofa, he might be seen hard at work in the shop, morning, noon and night. The children lived in touch with him almost as much as with their mother, and he felt himself no less responsible for their training.

Though stern and even quick-tempered at times, the influence James Taylor exerted in the life of his son can hardly be overestimated. He was decidedly a disciplinarian. But without some such element in his early training who can tell whether Hudson would ever have become the man he was, by the grace of God. Do we not suffer in these days from too great a tendency to slackness and easy-going? Even Christian parents seem content if they can keep their children moderately happy and good-tempered. But with James Taylor this was not the point. Life has to be lived. Work must be accomplished. People may be consecrated, gifted, devoted, and yet of very little use, because undisciplined. He was a man with a supreme sense of duty. The thing that ought to be done was the thing he put first, always. Ease, pleasure, self-improvement had to take whatever place they could. He was a man of faith, but faith that

MR. JAMES TAYLOR IN LATER LIFE.

"For myself and for the work I have been permitted to do for God, I owe an unspeakable debt of gratitude to my beloved and honoured parents, who have entered into rest, but the influence of whose lives will never pass away."—J. HUDSON TAYLOR.

To face page 46.

went hand in hand with works of the most practical kind. It was not enough for him that his children were happy and amused, well-cared-for and obedient even. They must be doing their duty, getting through their daily tasks, acquiring habits that alone could make them dependable men and women in days to come.

The importance of punctuality, for example, he impressed both by teaching and example. No one was allowed to be late for meals or any other engagement. The mother called the children herself, at seven every morning. No bells were rung, but when the clock struck eight every one had to be at table.

" If there are five people," he would say, " and they are kept waiting one minute, do you not see that five minutes are lost that can never be found again ? "

Dinner was at half-past twelve and tea at half-past four ; but if these meals were delayed five minutes it would mean nearly an hour wasted out of one little day. And what would that amount up to in a week, a month, a year ?

Dilatoriness in dressing or undressing, or in beginning when the time came to begin, he also reprehended as a serious waste of time. " Learn to dress quickly," he would say, " for you have to do it once, at least, every day of your life. And begin promptly whatever the work in hand. To loiter does not help, it only makes the task more difficult."

" See if you can do without " was another of his maxims. This of course applied, among other things, to the simple pleasures of the table. Porridge with bread and butter for breakfast, meat once a day, and bread and butter or toast for tea was the usual routine. But sugar and preserves were allowed in moderation, and extra-nice cakes or puddings occasionally found a place. As a rule the children shared whatever was provided, their parents delighting to give them pleasure no less than other fathers and mothers the wide world over. At the same time they fully realised the lifelong influence of little habits. At any cost to themselves and within wise limits to the children, they felt they must secure to them the power of self-control.

" By-and-by," the father would explain, " you will have

to say ' No ' to yourself when we are not there to help you ; and very difficult you will find it when you want a thing tremendously. So let us try to practise now, for the sooner you begin the stronger will be the habit."

It was a principle difficult of application, no doubt, when a favourite dish was in question. But though it was at least as hard for him as for them, he would encourage them to go the whole length on occasions, saying cheerfully :

" Who will see if they can do without to-day ? "

The children were not blamed if they could not respond as he desired, but were commended if they did, the mother generally arranging some little surprise at night—a few almonds and raisins, or an orange, with an extra-loving kiss.

Sweets or confectionery they never thought of buying for themselves. Pennies honestly earned were far too precious to be squandered thus. Each one had a little brown earthenware jar in the sitting-room cupboard, in which their savings were kept. Whenever eleven pennies could be produced, their father would add one, giving in exchange a bright new shilling. This was a transaction much looked forward to, and encouraged the children in thoughtfulness about the use of money. These may seem trivial details, scarcely worth recording, but it is just such little habits that in the long run strengthen character and make all the difference between weakness and power to do and be one's best.

The spiritual life of his children was equally the father's care. Family worship he conducted regularly, after both breakfast and tea. Every member of the household had to be present, and the passage read was explained in such practical fashion that even the children could not fail to see its application. He was very particular about giving them the whole Word of God, omitting nothing. The Old Testament as well as the New was taken in regular course, and at the close of every day's reading the date was carefully entered in the family Bible. On Sundays he gave even more time to this home-ministry, in spite of the services for which he was responsible, and that often involved a considerable journey on foot. While thoroughly approving of Sunday Schools for those who needed them, he did not consider his own children to be among the number, and would relinquish to no one the privilege of teaching them in the things of God.

He gave time also to earnest, detailed prayer on their behalf, and taught them to pray. From infancy, the little happenings of every day were made occasions for drawing near to God   Nothing was too trivial to interest Father and Mother, because the little folk were dear to them, and nothing was too small to bring to Him who loved them better still.   If there were something to thank their parents for, or obtain help in, they would not wait till the end of the day to do so.   And in the same way they learned to come " without ceasing," with thanksgiving and prayer, to the greater Father in heaven.   It was just as natural to Amelia at three years old to say reverently, " O Lord, take away my naughty temper and give me a new heart," as to ask pardon of the mother she had grieved ; and, baby as she was, she felt it no less important.

At one time the father made it a practice to take the older children to his room every day for prayer.   At the big four-post bed, all three would kneel beside him while with his arm about them he poured out his heart to God for each in turn in a way they never could forget.   It was not much he could give them of wealth or worldly advantage, but he could and did imbue them with a strong, simple faith like his own.   He taught them to reverence the Bible as the Word of God from cover to cover, trusting every promise to mean at least all it says.   " God cannot lie," he would exclaim with intense conviction, " He cannot mislead you, He cannot fail."   And instinctively the children began to trust in the same way.

As they were able to understand, he explained to them the necessity for maintaining the life of the soul by prayer and Bible study, as the life of the body is maintained by exercise and food.   To omit this was to neglect the one thing needful.   He spoke of it frequently as a matter of vital importance, and arranged for every one in the house to have at least half an hour daily, alone with God.   The result was that even the little ones began to discover the secret of a

E

happy day.   Before breakfast in the morning, and again
as evening was drawing in, they went up to their own rooms
for reading and prayer.   They needed it just as much as
older people, and in their childish way came to realise that
no one can be good and happy all day long without heart-
to-heart fellowship with the Lord.   But it was example
that impressed these things upon them more than precept.
" Let them see thee talking to thy God " was golden counsel
these parents did not fail to improve.

Thus the children grew in body, mind, and spirit as the
days went on.   Hudson was still too delicate to go to school,
but the education he received at home more than made up
for this loss.   Not only were his studies systematic and his
general intelligence developed, but the conversation of his
parents and their visitors awakened thought and purpose
to which the average schoolboy is a stranger, and his father's
daily life, as he grew old enough to share it, in no wise
weakened these impressions.

James Taylor was sociable and talked freely in congenial
company.   He was gifted with warm sympathies and sound
common sense ; so much so indeed that few men in Barnsley
were more sought after for advice in temporal as well as
spiritual things.   Over the counter and in the little room
behind the shop, many an hour was spent with those who
came to him in trouble.   On Market Days another class of
visitors would drop in—friends from the country, to many
of whom he was indebted for Sunday hospitality, and brother
local preachers sure of a welcome.   A cup of tea by the
fireside gave opportunity for many a " dish of chat,"
seasoned with kindly humour, in which the children could
not fail to be interested.

But Quarter Day was looked forward to with still more
lively expectation.   For then fellow-workers came in from
every part of the circuit, bringing the contributions of those
they represented toward the support of the ministry.   In
the Chapel on Pinfold Hill their business was transacted.
Arrangements for the following quarter were considered,
missionary meetings planned, and financial matters settled ;

after which, luncheon was served in the vestry by the Circuit stewards and their wives. Then came an opportunity for private hospitality, which James Taylor frequently improved by inviting one and all to tea at 21 Cheapside. This was a favourite rendezvous, and at five o'clock the drawing-room over the shop would be well filled with guests. Those were times when conversation was at its best ; good, homely Yorkshire talk, as racy as it was profitable. And how the children listened ! Half a century later the remembrance had not faded from their minds.

I used to love to hear them talk—those local preachers gathered round our table for high tea. Theology, sermons, politics, the Lord's work at home and abroad, all were discussed with so much earnestness and intelligence. It made a great impression upon us as children.[1]

It was on these occasions, chiefly, that the subject of Foreign Missions came up, and the little folk were delighted by many a story from far-off lands. China still held, as it always had, the first place in their father's sympathies, and he used often to lament the indifference of the Church to its appalling need. It specially troubled him that the denomination to which he belonged should be doing nothing for its evangelisation. Methodists, who in the days of Thomas Coke had been foremost in sending missionaries to the heathen, still gloried in Wesley's motto, " The world is my parish." A hundred years had passed since the birth of the great Revival, and in the summer of 1839 (when Hudson was seven years old) the " Centenary Jubilee " was celebrated on both sides of the Atlantic in a spirit worthy of the memories it recalled. Methodists everywhere exceeded themselves in liberality and zeal for the cause of God. Thank-offerings filled their treasuries, world-wide prayer resulted in a great increase of spiritual blessing, and notable advance was made in evangelistic labours both at home and abroad. But among the new Missions projected and the new workers sent out, none were destined for China. It seemed to be taken for granted that nothing could be done or even attempted there. Morrison, the lonely pioneer of Protestant

[1] To Mrs. B. Broomhall, the " little Amelia " of those days, we are indebted for many of the recollections incorporated in this chapter.

Missions in that land, had passed away five years previously, and no one had been able to take his place. Canton was still the only mission station, recently manned by a few American workers, including Dr. Peter Parker, who had just opened the first hospital on Chinese soil. But beyond the narrow limits of that one settlement lay the whole vast empire with its four hundred millions, amongst whom no one was living and preaching Christ.[1] These things pressed as a burden on the heart of Hudson Taylor's father.

" Why do we not send our missionaries there ! " he would exclaim. " That is the country to aim at, with its teeming population, its strong, intelligent, scholarly people."

He could not understand the apathy of the Church about this magnificent field, the Gibraltar of heathenism. And the listening children were confirmed in their conviction that this was indeed the greatest, the most neglected and most promising of missionary lands.

Later on their interest was increased by Peter Parley's *China*, a little book they read and reread until they knew it almost by heart. It had many illustrations, tiny pictures of the old-fashioned kind, and so impressed Amelia that she decided to cast in her lot with Hudson, who had long ago made up his mind to go to China as a missionary. The parents did not fail to notice these childish purposes, though with some sorrow of heart. It had been their chief desire that Hudson might be called to just such service, but on account of his continued delicacy the hope had been gradually abandoned. He, at any rate, would never be strong enough for such a life.

It was manifest, however, that the Holy Spirit was working in his heart, for nothing interested him so deeply as the things of God. He loved to go with his father to the country chapels in which he was preaching Sunday by Sunday. The quickening impulse of the great Centenary was being felt in that Yorkshire district, and James Taylor's

[1] Romanism in China was just recovering from its second period of decline, and foreign priests were to be found at a few points in the interior on the ground of ancient rights. The Order of Jesuits, suppressed by Pope Clement XIV. in 1773, had been re-established half a century later, and from that time (1822) the Roman Catholic Church entered upon a stronger, more aggressive policy in China.

ministry was in power and blessing. Even his little son entered into the spirit of the time. Love for Christ, the master-passion of his life, and the unquenchable longing to bring others to know and love Him too, evidently had their beginning as early as the Jubilee of 1839 ; for it was of those days his mother wrote .

When about seven years of age, Hudson frequently accompanied his father into the country, when he was going to preach. It was a time of religious revival, and an after-meeting was usually held at the conclusion of the service to pray for blessing upon the Word and for the conversion of sinners. On such occasions persons deeply convinced of sin and desiring to obtain peace with God were invited to come forward to be prayed with and pointed to " the Lamb of God that taketh away the sin of the world." In these meetings his devout and prayerful earnestness were often remarked ; and when, as was frequently the case, burdened souls found comfort by resting on Jesus and His atonement, and believers sang " Praise God, from whom all blessings flow," he would join as heartily as any, while his face glowed with delight.

But this spirit of joy in the Lord and concern for the welfare of others did not depend upon revival meetings. It was fostered by the influence of his parents and the daily atmosphere of home. Much of their conversation was about spiritual things, and of a kind that made salvation and living for God appear, as indeed they are, the most important matters under the sun. And the children could easily see that this was no mere talk, but that their parents were consistent in putting God first and in seeking to help others to do the same. The mother was for many years too delicate to carry on her weekly class or attempt much outside work. Her hands were more than full with household duties. But in her own circle her heart still burned with love for souls that could not rest till all within its reach were won. The children knew how she thought of and prayed for the servants that came under their roof and for the successive assistants in the shop. Did they not share her joy when these young people were brought, as sooner or later they always were, to a living faith in Christ ? Mother's closed door in the middle of the busy day had a world of meaning for the household. Those were the seasons of quiet waiting upon

God that renewed her strength, and enabled her to make so attractive to others her unseen Friend.   Happy the son whose every remembrance of his mother affords fresh inspiration to a life of Christlike love and service.

Happy too the children so trained in habits of obedience to their earthly parents that they learn almost instinctively to obey and honour God.   To James Taylor this was a matter of supreme importance.   He felt with a deep sense of responsibility that Christian parents are placed at the head of the family as the direct representatives of Him " from whom every fatherhood in heaven and on earth is named."   To permit disobedience would be not only unfaithfulness to God, but cruel injustice to the children, wholly misleading them as to the character of the Heavenly Father with whom through life they have to do.   His duty on the contrary was to train them to such prompt and loyal obedience to their earthly parents that they would be prepared to render like submission to the will of God.   He showed them that such obedience requires the exercise of the highest powers, faith, love, patience, self-control, and is a faculty not easily acquired.   Unless they learned the lesson in childhood, they would grow up with unyielded wills, too wayward and undisciplined to be of use in the service of God.   The sorrow and danger of such a position he showed them from many passages of Scripture, dwelling especially on Eli's failure in governing his sons, the sin and misery it entailed, and the dishonour brought upon the name of God.

So much did he dread the consequences of over-indulgence that he went, perhaps, too far in the opposite extreme.   But even when he seemed most severe and the children were tempted to rebel, their mother's voice quickly recalled them :

" My dear, he is your father.   Not a word !   Remember, ' Honour thy father.' "

But there were aching hearts, at times, over what seemed a reproof or punishment of needless asperity, as when Amelia was sent to bed one Sunday afternoon for leaving a morsel on her plate at dinner, unfinished.   But though it cost tears at the time, she came to feel that Father had erred on the safe side, if he had erred at all, and that he and Mother sacrificed themselves in this as in everything else for the good of those entrusted to their care.

For the children's pleasures too their parents thought and planned, and many were the red-letter days that dotted the calendar throughout those early years. Saturday afternoon was always much looked forward to, for then visits might be paid to their friends across the Green, to the Neatbys, or the Cope cousins whose beautiful garden offered endless attractions. Or better still, Hudson and Amelia would take their hoops in spring and summer, and run off alone to the Lunn Woods down the Cudworth Road. Perfectly happy in each other's company, they would wander for hours up and down those shady glades, chasing butterflies and gathering flowers to their hearts' content. They never thought of quarrelling. Hudson was his sister's protector rather, and considered himself responsible to take care of and keep her happy, though he could not always overcome a boyish tendency to tease.

" Now, my child, don't *be* teased, and he will soon leave off," the mother would say with a smile, well knowing that Hudson's teasing was never more than fun.

As a matter of fact there was nothing he would not have denied himself for the good of this dearly loved sister. While she was still little and afraid to be left in the dark, he would frequently sacrifice an hour with his book by the fireside to keep her company. When it was cold he would sit beside her on the pillow with his feet under the bedclothes, telling the most fearsome, fascinating stories, until she drifted happily into the land of dreams.

Their enjoyment of the country was greatly increased by the companionship of their father, who often went with them on Saturday afternoon for long, delightful walks. How they loved the butterflies, birds, and flowers about which he told them ! It was better to wander with him in such company than even to visit the wonderful fairs on the Green. Twice every year these great occasions came, with all the excitement of shows, menageries, and merry-go-rounds, to say nothing of stalls passing description. But though they enjoyed the bewildering scene, keeping close to their father's side as he led them through the crowds, it was a different and doubtful joy, not to be compared with the other. The green woods never palled, or left one jaded and dissatisfied.

And then at home one could pursue the subject still. Careful and orderly as she was, the mother fully entered into the feelings of her little naturalists, and afforded every facility for the wonderful collections that grew from these country walks. Their father encouraged them too, and subscribed for a magazine of Natural History that coming month by month did not a little to deepen intelligent interest.

One thing the parents specially inculcated was thoughtful consideration for living creatures. To wilfully hurt a fly would have been an offence severely punished; and from babyhood the children were made to realise that all cruelty to dumb, helpless creatures was a sin against God Himself.

"What you sow in this way," the father would assure them, "you will certainly reap. You will be made to suffer for all the suffering you inflict, as God is God and knows everything."

Even flowers they might not gather unless they really wanted to keep them, and over their collections of insects and butterflies the greatest care was exercised. Hudson, who was intensely interested in these beautiful creatures, fully shared the solicitude of his parents that they should not be made to suffer. Pill-boxes large and small were supplied him from the shop, in which air-holes were carefully pricked, so that he might bring home his treasures "comfortably," and then a little chloroform precluded the possibility of pain.

Other happy memories for children and parents alike centred round the festivities that once a year gathered the family circle at "Grandmamma's." On Christmas Day her sons and daughters dined with her in state, and on New Year's Day she resigned possession to the younger generation. Tall and stately as she was, Mary Shepherd of the long-ago days inspired only gratitude and affection among her numerous grandchildren. Troops of merry boys and girls played hide-and-seek all over the house, and revelled in the good things her hospitality provided. They were quite a clan by this time, though the invitation extended to first cousins only ; and certainly none among them had more capacity for enjoyment than the unspoiled little people from the chemist's home on the Market Place.

But to them the happiest days of all were not those high days and holidays. Through the mists of childhood the brightest associations lingered about one dear figure in the repose that always seemed to accompany a white crêpe shawl and satin gown. Sunday was the day on which Mother gave herself to them as she could not through the week, and if there was one thing she cared about, it was that that day should be to every member of the household the happiest and most helpful of the seven. In the morning the children went with her regularly to the House of God, and there was more leisure to enjoy companionship at home on Sunday. But in addition, Mother had ways and means for making that day different from all others and much to be desired. The nicest toys and picture-books belonged to Sunday, as well as the prettiest frocks and a cosy fire in the drawing-room because the piano was there. Mother's sweet voice made hymn-singing a delight. No talks were like her talks over the Bible, not to speak of *Pilgrim's Progress* and other books that only appeared that day. Then she always had a basket of fruit for her little people in the afternoon. And just to see her looking so sweet and restful as she shared their enjoyments was not the least part of the happiness of the day.

Yes, home was home indeed and the nearest place to heaven, because it held that mother in whose heart was shed abroad the very love of God.

CHAPTER V

THE FINISHED WORK OF CHRIST

1843–1849. AET. 11–17.

> Upon a life I did not live,
> Upon a death I did not die,
> Another's life, Another's death,
> I stake my whole eternity.

THUS childhood's years passed by, and all unconsciously Hudson Taylor was drawing near the crisis of his life.

Outwardly he was now a bright lad of seventeen, with few anxieties or cares, but inwardly he was passing through a period of trial. Events that had transpired since the close of the preceding chapter had brought him into contact with the world as it is beyond the shelter of a Christian home. Under the stress of new experiences he had begun to think for himself and live his life more or less independently of others, and a difficult business he found it, until he learned to trust a higher strength than his own.

His troubles seem to have begun when at eleven years of age he was first sent to school, though it was only a day-school, conducted by Mr. Laycock, a friend of the family. After John Taylor's death and the removal of the reed-making business to larger premises, Mr. Laycock had rented the long, low factory near the corner of Pitt and York Streets and had turned it into class-rooms for the accommodation of fifty or sixty lads. The situation was good, and his able management attracted the best pupils in town. Here then, close to the home in which his grandmother still lived, Hudson began his brief career as a schoolboy.

It was brief for several reasons, one of which was the continued delicacy of health that made it impossible for him to be regular in attendance. Hardly a week passed without his having to miss one or more days on account of illness, and at other times it was difficult to avoid over-study. Still, association with boys of his own age was felt to be so desirable that every effort was made to continue it.

He intensely enjoyed study, and was so eager to work that the arithmetic master often handed over to him problems that he had hardly time for himself. "See that you bring them back in the morning," he would say with a smile. And Hudson, who knew why they were wanted, worked with a will, falling back upon his father's help if they proved too intricate. He was not sufficiently a lover of boyish sports to become a general favourite, but some enduring friendships were made, and the pursuits of the playground, though not for him specially attractive, had their valuable effect on character.

On the whole, however, his school-life seems to have been neither happy nor helpful. It was a great change from home, and he missed the spiritual atmosphere to which he had been accustomed. Needing more than ever the resource of prayer, he allowed the busy days to pass without taking time to be alone with God.

"His religious earnestness began to abate," his mother tells us, "and gradually declined, until he lost peace with God."

The joyous faith of childhood passed away, and he awoke to find the world a very different place without the sunshine of the Presence he had loved in earlier days. His mother's concern was deep and prayerful, but do what she would, nothing seemed to restore that lost God-consciousness.

For six years altogether he was in an unsettled state spiritually, trying hard to "make himself a Christian," but finding it of all efforts the most discouraging, and sure to end in failure if not despair. He was early proving the truth of the profound though simple warning: "Without Me ye can do nothing."

Yes, those are difficult years, from eleven to seventeen.

The young heart finds itself assailed by perplexing problems, attracted by undreamed-of possibilities, disturbed by unreasoning hopes and fears. They are often lonely years, for we outgrow the associations of childhood and do not quickly find our own real friends ; years in which God is more than ever needful to us, and yet the first force of temptation, the first glamour of the world, the first suggestion of doubt, reinforced it may be by love, or sin, or sorrow, obscure the shining of His face. Many a seemingly careless lad and schoolgirl carries an aching heart, a heart just hungry for the touch of sympathy older people often fail to give, because they do not understand. But often, too, that touch can come from God alone. Surely, did we see but deep enough, the spiritual needs and longings of childhood would drive us to our knees in earnest prayer. For only God can make us wise to speak the " word in season " to the soul whose very existence perhaps we hardly realise, because it dwells in the boy or girl to whose noise and merriment we are so accustomed. Pray, pray ! These young souls are awake, and moving rapidly for good or ill beyond our care.

Such a word in season came to Hudson Taylor in his first year at school, and was never forgotten. It was the summer of 1844, and he went with older people to a Camp Meeting in a park near Leeds. Among the speakers was Mr. Henry Reed of Launceston, Tasmania, who in the course of his address told the story of a man named Gardener whom he had known in the Colonies years before. His subject was the sin and peril of resisting the Holy Spirit, and upon the little lad from Barnsley it made an impression that never passed away.[1]

Gardener was one of six convicts under sentence of death, with whom Mr. Reed spent the last, terrible night before

[1] Long years after, when Mr. Henry Reed had become a warm friend and supporter of the China Inland Mission, Mr. Hudson Taylor, writing to him about other matters, recalled these facts.

" It must be about thirty years ago that I had the privilege of hearing you speak at a missionary meeting in a park near Leeds　I was then a boy, and unconverted　But one incident you narrated, showing the danger of quenching the strivings of the Spirit of God, riveted itself on my memory, and in after years has been often repeated by me to Chinese audiences. . . . I believe that in several instances in China it has been used of God to bring persons in a hesitating state of mind to the point of decision for Christ."

their execution. Condemned for murder, he had long denied the charges brought against him, but finally through his own confession the truth was brought to light. It then appeared that shortly before the crime was committed he had been conscious as never before of the pleading of the Holy Spirit, and of the nearness of God.

Walking up Cataract Hill, a beautiful spot near Launceston, he had even been startled by a voice behind him, earnestly saying :

" Gardener, give Me thy heart."

He turned to face the speaker, but no one was in sight. He was alone under the open sky, alone with an awakened conscience and the all-seeing God.

" My son, give Me thy heart."

His Maker must have spoken. No other voice could stir the soul like that. What should he do ? Yes, that was the question.

Long and troubled were his ponderings, for the call was unwelcome. He did not want, just then, to be a Christian. It would upset his plans, interfere with his prospects of success. No, he must make money first, come what might. Later on, at another time, a " more convenient season," he would reconsider the matter. God was merciful. There would be another chance. And so, deliberately resisting the Holy Spirit, he went on up the hill—went on to meet the tempter in his own strength.

That night alone in their shack he saw his partner begin to count a little store of savings as he sat over the fire. Seven one-pound notes lay in his hand. Gardener became interested. Then all at once an overwhelming desire to obtain that money took possession of him. Never before had he felt such a passion for gold. All restraints of conscience were swept away. His one, his only thought became:

" I must and will have it. But *how* ? "

Then followed the awful suggestion, " Dead men tell no tales."

Though it meant murder, this aroused neither fear nor compunction. A few hours before he had been powerfully drawn toward God and happiness and heaven. Now he seemed given up to evil   Three days and nights went by, while he waited his opportunity.   It came at last, and Gardener's hands were stained with the blood of one who had trusted him as a friend.

As Mr. Reed described that last, long night, when at their request he had been locked up with this man and five others about to be ushered into the presence of God, a profound impression was made on many a listener besides young Hudson Taylor.   Returning to Barnsley, and for long after, he was deeply troubled about spiritual things.   Amid all his waywardness he was conscious of that inward pleading, " My son, give Me thy heart."   But the change went no further while he remained at school.

This was two years in all, a period that transformed the open-hearted child into a boy of thirteen with some experience of the harder side of life.   His education had made progress, but on account of changes in the school that were not satisfactory it was decided he should leave.   His father needed assistance in the shop, and Hudson was delighted to be earning his own living, in part at any rate, while carrying on his studies at home.   Thus ended, just before Christmas 1845, his first and only experience of school-life.

The new arrangement worked well.   In his white apron behind the counter, the curly-headed boy with his bright face and pleasant ways soon became a favourite among the customers.   He was keenly interested in compounding and dispensing medicines and everything to do with doctor's work.   His father's library afforded all the books he required, and in the helpful companionships of home the troubles of his inner life began to pass away.

To this time he himself attributed [1] the first conscious surrender of his heart to God.   A leaflet published by the Religious Tract Society brought him blessing.   It was the story of a poor, half-witted fellow who was only able to grasp one great truth, but rested his soul upon it as he passed into the unseen.

" Yes, Joseph is the chief of sinners," he kept repeating. " But it is ' a faithful saying ' that Jesus Christ, the great

[1] In a letter given on page 102.

Photograph by

FRUDD'S BANK.

F. Howard Taylor.

God who made all things, ' came into the world to save sinners.' And *why not poor Joseph ?* "

The question brought its own answer.

While reading this little tract, the simplicity of faith was made clear to him as never before, and then and there he took the sinner's place and came back to God.

The days that followed were quiet and happy. He was busy with his lessons and work in the shop, and resumed the habits of prayer and Bible study in which he had been trained from childhood. But another testing-time awaited him, a further experience of the weakness of his own heart, out of which he was to be brought into a life of stedfast dependence upon the Lord for keeping as well as saving grace.

For though real and true as far as it went, this improvement in his spiritual condition was more or less evanescent. There were the ups and downs so characteristic of childhood, and from the point of view of later years he seems hardly to have considered it a true " conversion " at all. At any rate it did not stand the test when, a little later, he found himself plunged into an atmosphere of worldliness and unbelief.

This unlooked-for experience began in 1847, when at fifteen years of age he went as junior clerk into one of the best banks in Barnsley. An opening having occurred, his father was anxious that he should avail himself of it, feeling that whatever the future might bring he would always be thankful for a thorough business training. Out of many applicants Hudson was chosen, and after eighteen months at home entered with high hopes upon the duties of his new position.

The daily routine in which he was now engaged did undoubtedly prove of value in preparing him for responsibilities as yet unforeseen. He was well drilled in account-keeping and business correspondence, and in the absolute necessity for promptness and accuracy in financial matters. He also found his level in a little corner of the busy world, and learned to do his part as a man among men. But he was not ready, spiritually, to stand alone. Indeed he was not standing firm in Christ at all, and was easily carried away by the ungodliness of those around him.

For most of his new associates were thoroughly worldly. Sceptical views to which he was a stranger were freely discussed among them, and religion seldom spoken of without a sneer   To add to these dangers, the lad came under the influence of an older clerk who, though handsome and popular, was anything but a desirable friend. He took every occasion to laugh at what he called Hudson's " old-fashioned notions," and did all he could to make him as light-minded as himself.

" I well remember," Hudson wrote a few years later, " how I used to wish for money and a fine horse and house when I was in the Bank. Then my whole heart was set on this world's pleasures, and I longed to go hunting as some did who were about me. What a mercy that I had to leave that place ! "

It was weary work, with a heart set on this world's pleasures, to try to keep up the outward forms of Christian life. Yet he struggled to do so for a time. " Religious duties," however, could not satisfy, and were a poor substitute for the living Christ. He longed for gaiety and distraction ; ambitions that could not be realised made him miserable, and the sceptical views of his companions for a time carried him away. But the faithfulness of God did not fail.

In another letter he wrote of this period :

I began to set too great a value on the things of this world, and to neglect private prayer. Religious duties became irksome to me, and I fell from grace. But God in His infinite mercy caused my eyesight to fail, and I had to leave the Bank.

This was no doubt a bitter disappointment to the lad himself if not to his parents. Overtime-work by gas-light had brought on serious inflammation of the eyes. Nothing seemed to relieve them, and after nine months at book-keeping he was obliged to resign his position and return to the more varied duties of assistant in his father's shop.

But the unhappy state into which he had fallen continued long after he left the bank. His sight recovered and outwardly all went well, for the restraining grace of God kept him from open evil. But inwardly he was rebellious and full of unbelief. At times he knew himself to be in " a sinful and dangerous state " from which he struggled in vain to be free. At other times he tried to believe that his friends in the bank were right, and there really was no God and no hereafter.

There is something deeply touching about his own reference to these experiences, revealing as it does the exercise of soul through which an apparently careless lad may pass unknown to those around him :

> Often had I tried to make myself a Christian, and failing of course in such efforts, I began to think that for some reason or other I could not be saved, and that the best I could do was to take my fill of this world, as there was no hope for me beyond the grave. While in this state of mind I came in contact with persons holding sceptical and infidel views, and quickly accepted their teachings, only too thankful for some hope of escape from the doom which if my parents were right and the Bible true awaited the ungodly.

He had certainly travelled far in those difficult years from the love and faith of childhood. And there had yet to be sad revelations of his own heart ere he was to know that wonderful rest of faith into which he was privileged to lead so many others. Meanwhile the unrest deepened, and he began to prove how little the world has to give in exchange for the presence and blessing of God.

Needless to say, this state of things marred the happiness of home and overclouded his naturally sunny disposition. He was all wrong, and his parents could not but see it. The father tried to help him, but found it hard to be patient with the phase through which he was passing. The mother understood him better, and redoubled her tenderness and prayers. But it was his sister Amelia, now thirteen years of age, who was nearest to him and best able to win his confidence.

To her he could speak more freely than to grown-up people, and his indifference and unhappiness so affected her that she determined to pray about him three times every day until he was really converted. This she did for some weeks, going alone to plead with God for the salvation of her brother, and even making a note in her journal that

F

she would never cease to pray for him until he was brought into the light, and that she believed her petitions would be answered before long.

Thus wearied by failure, harassed by doubt, disappointed in all he had most wished to do and be, Hudson Taylor drew near the crisis of his life, held by the faith and prayers of a few loving hearts that did know their God.

" It may seem strange," he said in later years, " but I have often felt thankful for this time of scepticism. The inconsistencies of Christian people who while professing to believe the Bible were yet content to live just as they would if there were no such book, had been one of the strongest arguments of my sceptical companions ; and I frequently felt at that time, and said, that if I pretended to believe the Bible I would at any rate attempt to live by it, putting it fairly to the test, and if it failed to prove true and reliable, would throw it overboard altogether. These views I retained when the Lord was pleased to bring me to Himself. And I think I may say that since then I have put God's Word to the test. Certainly it has never failed me. I have never had reason to regret the confidence I have placed in its promises, or to deplore following the guidance I have found in its directions.

" And now let me tell you how God answered the prayers of my mother and of my beloved sister, now Mrs. Broomhall, for my conversion.

" On a day I can never forget, . . . my dear mother being absent from home, I had a holiday, and in the afternoon looked through my father's library to find some book with which to while away the un-occupied hours. Nothing attracting me, I turned over a basket of pamphlets and selected from amongst them a Gospel tract that looked interesting, saying to myself : ' There will be a story at the commence-ment and a sermon or moral at the close. I will take the former and leave the latter for those who like it.'

" I sat down to read the book in an utterly unconcerned state of mind, believing indeed at the time that if there were any salvation it was not for me, and with a distinct intention to put away the tract as soon as it should seem prosy. I may say that it was not uncommon in those days to call conversion ' becoming serious ' ; and judging by the faces of some of its professors it appeared to be a very serious matter indeed ! Would it not be well if the people of God had always tell-tale faces, evincing the blessings and gladness of salvation so clearly that unconverted people might have to call conversion ' be-coming joyful ' instead of ' becoming serious ' ?

" Little did I know at the time what was going on in the heart of my dear mother, seventy or eighty miles away. She rose from the dinner-table that afternoon with an intense yearning for the conversion of her boy; and feeling that, absent from home and having more leisure than she could otherwise secure, a special opportunity was afforded her of pleading with God on my behalf. She went to her room and turned the key in the door, resolved not to leave the spot until her prayers were answered. Hour after hour that dear mother pleaded, until at length she could pray no longer, but was constrained to praise God for that which His Spirit taught her had already been accomplished, the conversion of her only son.

" I in the meantime had been led in the way I have mentioned to take up this little tract, and while reading it was struck with the phrase : ' The finished work of Christ.'

" ' Why does the author use this expression ? ' I questioned. ' Why not say the atoning or propitiatory work of Christ ? '

" Immediately the words ' It is finished ' suggested themselves to my mind.

" ' What was finished ? '

" And I at once replied, ' A full and perfect atonement and satisfaction for sin. The debt was paid for our sins, and not for ours only, but also for the sins of the whole world.'

" Then came the further thought, ' If the whole work was finished and the whole debt paid, what is there left for me to do ? '

" And with this dawned the joyful conviction, as light was flashed into my soul by the Holy Spirit, that there was nothing in the world to be done but to fall down on one's knees and accepting this Saviour and His salvation praise Him for evermore.

Nothing either great or small,
Nothing, sinner, no :
Jesus died and did it all,
Long, long ago.

' *It is finished,*' yes, indeed,
Finished every jot.
Sinner, this is all you need,
Tell me, is it not ?

When He from His lofty throne
Stooped to do and die,
Everything was fully done—
Listen to His cry.

Weary, working, burdened one,
Wherefore toil you so ?
Cease your doing, all was done,
Long, long ago.

Cast your deadly doing down,
Down at Jesus' feet ;
Stand in Him, in Him alone,
Gloriously complete.

.   .   .   .   .   .

" Thus while my dear mother was praising God on her knees in her chamber, I was praising Him in the old warehouse to which I had gone alone to read at my leisure this little book.

" Several days elapsed ere I ventured to make my beloved sister the confidante of my joy, and then only after she had promised not to tell any one of my soul-secret. When Mother returned a fortnight later I was the first to meet her at the door and to tell her I had such glad news to give. I can almost feel that dear mother's arms round my neck as she pressed me to her heart and said :

" ' I know, my boy. I have been rejoicing for a fortnight in the glad tidings you have to tell.'

" ' Why,' I asked in surprise, ' has Amelia broken her promise ? She said she would tell no one.'

" My dear mother assured me that it was not from any human source she had learned the tidings, and went on to tell the incident mentioned above. You will agree with me that it would be strange indeed if I were not a believer in the power of prayer.

" Nor was this all. Some time after, I picked up a pocket-book exactly like my own, and thinking it was mine, opened it. The lines that caught my eye were an entry in the little diary belonging to my sister, to the effect that she would give herself daily to prayer until God should answer in the conversion of her brother. One month later the Lord was pleased to turn me from darkness to light.

" Brought up in such a circle and saved under such circumstances, it was perhaps natural that from the commencement of my Christian life I was led to feel that the promises were very real, and that prayer was in sober matter of fact transacting business with God, whether on one's own behalf or on the behalf of those for whom one sought His blessing."

CHAPTER VI

JUNE TO CHRISTMAS 1849. AET. 17

IT was the month of June 1849, when this definite apprehension of the atoning work of Christ changed the whole
of life for Hudson Taylor. Henceforward he rejoiced in
conscious acceptance with God, not on the ground of anything he could do or be, but simply because of what the Lord
Jesus is and has done. " Not I, but Christ," brought
freedom, joy and rest. It was the turning-point in his
experience, the commencement of a new order of things
that little as he realised it at the time meant for him—China.

And now became apparent the unspeakable value of
early training such as he had received, and years of steady
discipline in a Christian home. He was in a position to
make rapid progress. The Bible was no strange book to
him, but familiar territory, a land of promise waiting to be
possessed. Prayer was no unwonted effort, but the natural
outgoing of a heart long accustomed to turn to God. There
was much yet to learn, but mercifully there were few habits
or memories of evil to erase. The Holy Spirit had, comparatively, a free field in his heart. And at seventeen years
of age, all life was yet before him in which to spend and be
spent for the Lord he loved.

It is a little difficult at this point to determine the exact
order of the spiritual experiences that follow. They were
of such importance, however, in the light of after-events,
that nothing has been omitted, and it will readily be seen how
true to life the record is and how encouraging to other far
from perfect people.

Very manifest for one thing is the joy that overflowed those summer days, as Hudson Taylor realised himself to be indeed a child of God. He was happy. He found it a glad life, full of heart-rest and satisfaction. For "the Spirit Himself beareth witness with our spirit, that we are children of God." And the sweetness of this fellowship could never be forgotten. It embraced all who were dearest to him on earth. For he found that being right with God put things right with those around him. It restored the happiness of home, made him a better son and more useful assistant to his father, and deepened especially the love that bound him to the dear sister whose prayers for him had been unfailing. Well may we doubt the reality of any blessing that does not make us easier to get on with, sweeter and more loving, especially to those at home.

Another outcome of the change that had taken place was a longing every true child of God must know, the longing to give all in return for all that has been given. In the spirit of the Hebrew bondman this young heart cried : " I love, I love my Master, I will not go out free." He longed for some work to do for God, some service that might prove his gratitude, some suffering even that might bring him into deeper fellowship with the Lord he loved. A leisure afternoon gave opportunity for prayer, and with this desire filling his heart he went up to his room to be alone with God. And there in a special way the Lord met him.

" Well do I remember that occasion," he wrote long after, " how in the gladness of my heart I poured out my soul before God, and again and again confessing my grateful love to Him who had done everything for me—who had saved me when I had given up all hope and even desire for salvation—I besought Him to give me some work for Him, as an outlet for love and gratitude ; some self-denying service, no matter what it might be, however trying or however trivial ; something with which He would be pleased, and that I might do for Him who had done so much for me. Well do I remember, as in unreserved consecration I put myself, my life, my friends, my all upon the altar, the deep solemnity that came over my soul with the assurance that my offering was accepted. The presence of God became unutterably real and blessed, and I well remember . . . stretching myself on the ground, and lying there before Him with unspeakable awe and unspeakable joy. For what service I was accepted I knew not. But a deep consciousness that I was not my own took possession of me, which has never since been effaced."

It was an hour that left its mark on life ; an hour in which the soul began to apprehend " that for which also " it " was apprehended by Christ Jesus." The lad who closed his door that day to be alone with God was a very different being from the lad who rejoined the family-circle some hours later. A purpose and a power possessed him, unknown before. He had given himself to God. His offering had been accepted. And though he knew not for what special service the Lord had need of him, he knew that he was no longer his own, and must be ready for the call whenever it might come.

One result of this definite consecration was that he began to care about the welfare of others. Hitherto he had been concerned chiefly with his own growth in grace ; now he must be about his Master's business, which was the salvation of those around him. He was not deterred by the fact that he could do but little, nor did he excuse himself on the ground of unworthiness. If he could not preach or lead a class as yet, he could at any rate give away tracts and invite people to the House of God. Busy from morning till night in the shop, it was not easy to make time for this work. But he found that by denying himself one of his chief pleasures on Sunday, he could gain a few hours just when people would be most accessible. The enjoyment that had to be forgone was the Sunday evening service to which he had been accustomed from childhood. But much as he loved those helpful seasons, he could no longer be satisfied to feed his own soul continually and do nothing to carry the Bread of Life to the perishing around him. It was " a day of good tidings." He was rejoicing in wealth and blessedness untold. And like the lepers in the Syrian camp, he and his sister Amelia felt as they talked it over, " we do not well to hold our peace."

Instead of attending chapel therefore on Sunday evenings, they went out as soon as tea was over and made their way to the poorest parts of the town. In Wilson's Piece behind their own home and Kingston Place toward the race-course, they became familiar figures, passing from door to door with bright faces and kindly words. Tracts were handed to all who would receive them, and the message of salvation simply given as opportunity offered. Even the poorest lodging-houses were not passed over. And though it cost an effort to go down those dark, narrow passages into the crowded kitchens, they were more than rewarded by a sense of His approval whose they were and whom they sought to serve.

But joy in the Lord and in His service was not the only experience as summer passed away. There were also " times of painful deadness of soul and much conflict." The heart that had so gladly accepted the finished work of an all-sufficient Saviour, now knew what it was to be " wearied and disappointed in its struggles with sin." Somehow there seemed a gap between the power of the Lord Jesus to save " to the uttermost " and the needs of everyday life in shop and home. He found himself yielding to temptation, ease-loving, self-indulgent, and often disinclined for private prayer and study of the Word of God. Nothing can have been more real than his consecration; nothing plainer than the disappointment that followed when he discovered his inability to do and be what he would. It even seemed to make matters worse instead of better. For things that before would not have troubled him were now intolerable. He had given himself to God without reserve, longing to be always and only His. And yet he could not maintain that attitude. Coldness of heart crept in, forgetfulness, indifference. The good he longed to do he did not, and the evil he hated too often had the mastery. He did delight in the law of God after the inward man, but there was that other law bringing him into captivity to sin with all its deadening influences. And he had not yet learned to cry : " Thanks be to God. . . . The law of the Spirit of *life in Christ Jesus* hath made me free from the law of sin and death."

At such times two courses are open to the perplexed and troubled soul. One is to abandon the ideal, and gradually

sink down to a low-level Christian life in which there is
neither joy nor power. The other is just to go on with the
Lord, and because of His " exceeding great and precious
promises " to claim complete deliverance not from the
guilt only, but also from the mastery of sin ; just to go
on with the Lord, trusting His strength and faithfulness
to pardon, loose and cleanse, to sanctify us wholly, and
make our own every blessing promised in the eternal
covenant.

Nothing less than this could satisfy Hudson Taylor.
Conversion with him had been no easy-going assent of the
mind to an abstract creed. No, it was a change deep and
real. The cross of Christ had cut him off for ever from the
old life, and from rest in anything the world could give.
Nothing could satisfy him now but genuine holiness, unbroken fellowship with God who was his life, his all. Hence
times of spiritual lethargy and indifference were alarming.
Deadness of soul was painful beyond endurance. He could
not take backsliding easily. Thank God, even the beginnings
of backsliding were worse to him than death.

Moreover he recognised that he was saved to serve, and
that a work was waiting for which a life of inner victory and
power would be essential. He had had his unsatisfactory
experiences, and deeply knew how little a man has for others
who is not himself walking at liberty within. During his
sceptical days he had seen that the only logical position
for the Christian is to go all lengths with God. He had
then determined to throw off religion altogether, unless it
were possible to obtain in actual reality the promises held
out to simple faith. There could be no middle course for
him. If his life were to be of any use to God or man he
must have that " love out of a pure heart and a good conscience and faith unfeigned " which is sanctification indeed.
This was the only power to make even the most whole-
hearted consecration practical and enduring.

And this was a gift from above, like the fire that fell in
answer to Elijah's prayers ; the supernatural, Divine response to a heart that having laid all upon the altar would
not be denied the cleansing, sanctifying power.

It is not to be wondered at that in seeking this promised blessing the Barnsley lad should have times of conflict and defeat. In comparing his experience with that of other men of God one is surprised, rather, that he did not suffer more from the opposition and assault of the devil. For it was nothing less than full deliverance upon which he had set his heart : that was the point—real holiness, and daily victory over sin.

The conflict lasted all through the autumn, apparently, and outward circumstances were not wanting to increase his sense of failure and need. For September brought the first break in the family circle, when Amelia went from home to complete her education, and her place was taken by a lad of his own age who was not a Christian. At Barton-on-Humber their mother's sister, Mrs. Hodson, had an excellent school for girls and received a few resident pupils under her own roof. Her eldest son, John, was apprenticed to his uncle in Barnsley, and it was arranged that the cousins should exchange homes for the time being, without additional expense to either family. To the brother and sister who had never been parted before it was a painful separation, and Amelia was hardly more lonely during those first few weeks in Barton than Hudson was in the old home without her. The cousin who shared his room, though bright and attractive, was no help spiritually, so that with less privacy for prayer and Bible study Hudson had also less fellowship in the things of God. There was more provocation to exuberance of spirits in the presence of such a companion, and more tendency to friction in business hours, especially as the busy season drew on. With all his excellent qualities the father had a somewhat hasty spirit, and as Hudson grew to manhood it was a discipline that called for constant grace. All this combined to make things difficult, until early in December it would seem a crisis was reached.

Outwardly things were much as usual, but inwardly he was almost driven to despair. A terrible deadness of soul had begun to steal over him. Prayer was an effort and the Bible devoid of interest. Christmas was close at hand and business correspondingly pressing. There seemed no time for quiet waiting upon God, even had the desire been present. But it was not. And at times a terrible fear assailed him, that he was drifting he knew not whither and might "fall away from grace," missing the purpose of God for his life now, if not hereafter.

Just how and when he was recalled from this dangerous state does not appear, but there are indications of some providential happenings that could not but be helpful. His attention was arrested, for example, by an article in the November *Wesleyan Magazine*, setting forth in glowing terms the very experience he needed. It was entitled "The Beauty of Holiness," and quickened again the longing of his heart for victory over self and sin. Then, in the Pitt Street Chapel,[1] a mission was held that resulted in so real a revival of spiritual blessing that within a few days more than a hundred converts were gathered in. This was encouragement indeed, and Hudson as he sought to lead others into blessing found himself drawing nearer the One for whom his heart longed supremely and through all. And finally a definite promise from the Word of God came home to him with power :

I will sprinkle clean water upon you, and ye shall be clean : from all your filthiness, and from all your idols, will I cleanse you. A new heart also will I give you, and a new spirit will I put within you : and I will take away the stony heart out of your flesh, and I will give you a heart of flesh. And I will put my Spirit within you, and cause you to walk in my statutes, and ye shall keep my judgments, and do them.[2]

. . . .

Sunday morning came, December 2, 1849. He was not able to go out as usual, and was glad rather than otherwise of the cold that gave him time to be quiet and alone. The Lord was consciously with him, and yet things were far from right. He rejoiced as he remembered one after another entering a few days previously into the rest of faith, but mourned his own inability to possess to the full his possessions in Christ. His thoughts turned naturally to the beloved

---

[1] Three years before, in 1846, the congregation had migrated from the old Chapel on Pinfold Hill to larger premises. The new building on Pitt Street was very near the Methodist Manse in which the Hudsons had lived.

[2] Ezekiel xxxvi. 25-27

sister far away, and taking up his pen he poured out his
heart to her in the following simple, earnest letter.

BARNSLEY, *December 2, 1849.*

MY DEAR SISTER—" Grace to you and peace, from God our Father
and the Lord Jesus Christ " : " Who gave Himself for our sins, that He
might deliver us from this present evil world." . . . " The very God
of peace sanctify you wholly, and I pray God your whole spirit and
soul and body be preserved blameless unto the coming of our Lord
Jesus Christ. Faithful is He that calleth you, who also will do it."

Pray for me, dear Amelia. Thank God, I feel very happy in His
love, but I am so unworthy of all His blessings. I so often give way
to temptation. I am apt to be frothy and giddy, and I sometimes
yield to my teasing disposition. Pray for me, dear Amelia, pray for
me. I am seeking entire sanctification. Oh that the Lord would take
away my heart of stone and give me a heart of flesh ! Mr. Simmons
gave us our tickets last Sunday. The verse is : " Then will I sprinkle
clean water upon you, and ye shall be clean " (Ez. xxxvi. 25, etc.). Oh
that I could take hold of the blessed promises of God's Holy Word !
My heart longs for this perfect holiness. I have read a very interesting
paper on the beauty of holiness in the *Wesleyan Magazine* for
November. What a happy state it must be !

> Oh, for a heart to praise my God !
> A heart from sin set free ;
> A heart that always feels Thy blood,
> So freely shed for me.
>
> A heart in every thought renewed,
> And full of love divine ;
> Perfect, and right, and pure, and good,
> A copy, Lord, of Thine !
>
> Thy nature, gracious Lord, impart ;
> Come quickly from above ;
> Write Thy new name upon my heart,
> Thy new, best name of Love.

I never can sufficiently praise God for all His mercies to me. He
has striven with me times without number, and I have resisted Him.
And yet after all, He has pardoned all my sins. The earnest desire
of my heart is that He will sanctify me wholly and make me useful
in His cause.

When Mr. Greenbury was here, in only four nights the names of
more than one hundred persons were taken who had found peace. I
went to the prayer-meeting on Wednesday night after shutting up
shop. I sat in the free seats as there was no room elsewhere, and asked

several to go to the penitent form. One went. He told of it after-wards in the Class Susan attends, and said he had found peace. I was very thankful to hear it. It shows the necessity for doing all the good we can. I went again on Thursday night, after eight o'clock, and got a place on the pulpit stairs There was no standing room in either pews or aisle. I took down the names of those who found the Lord. On Friday John and I were both there. I got six names and addresses. Mr. Keeling told me to go inside the communion rail to talk to the inquirers better. Oh we had a gracious time of it !

Our cousin John is deeply impressed. He is not far from the Kingdom. I believe he would have gone to Class with me if I had been able to go to-day. I have been so poorly that I have not been out. But the Lord has been with me. God bless you, my dear sister. I cannot help wishing that instead of a slight cold I had some sickness that would take me to heaven. For though to me to live is Christ, still, to die is gain, eternal gain. I have a desire to depart and be with Christ, which is far, far better. . . .

We all unite in love to you.—Believe me, your very loving brother,

J. H. TAYLOR.

That night upon going to bed he was deeply troubled. His soul was athirst for God, and yet an intense realisation of failure and unworthiness almost overwhelmed him. "Draw nigh to God and He will draw nigh to you " is a promise always fulfilled to the sincere and humble spirit, but how often the vision granted calls forth the cry, "Woe is me | for I am undone ; because I am a man of unclean lips."

Nor was this all.

Absorbed in his own need the lad was longing for true holiness, the life that is " no longer I, but Christ " in every-thing. The Lord with wider needs in view was seeking him for this, but not for this only. In His great purposes the time had come when the Gospel could no longer be withheld from the " uttermost parts of the earth." China even must be opened, and its most distant provinces gladdened with tidings of a Saviour's love. There it lay in agelong darkness, its teeming millions—a quarter of the human race—living, dying without God. It was of China the Lord was thinking, may we not say it reverently, as well as of Hudson Taylor. But the lad was not ready yet to hear the call, " Whom shall I send, and who will go for us ? " The work of the convicting Spirit must go deeper ere he could be fully blessed and brought into harmony with the mind of God. Thus his sense of sin and need became more intense as he wrestled for the deliverance without which he could not, dared not go on.

What was it that kept him from the life for which he longed ? What was the secret of his frequent failure and backsliding in heart ? Was there something not fully surrendered, some disobedience or unfaithfulness to light ? Fervently he prayed that God would show him the hindrance whatever it might be, and enable him to put it away. He had come to an end of self, to a place where only God could deliver, where he *must* have His succour, His enlightenment, His aid. It was a life and death matter. Everything seemed at stake. Like one of old he was constrained to cry, " I will not let Thee go except Thou bless me."

And then, alone upon his knees, a great purpose arose within him. If only God would work on his behalf, would break the power of sin and save him, spirit, soul and body, for time and for eternity, he would renounce all earthly prospects and be utterly at His disposal. He would go anywhere, do anything, suffer whatever His cause might demand, and be wholly given to His will and service. This was the cry of his heart ; nothing held back—if only God would deliver him and keep him from falling.

.   .   .   .

Instinctively we pause and turn aside from a scene so sacred. The place is holy ground. Of what transpired further we know no more, save for a few lines written when occasion required it in the following year. For he rarely referred to this experience, though all life lived it out.

" Never shall I forget," he wrote, " the feeling that came over me then. Words can never describe it. I felt I was in the presence of God, entering into covenant with the Almighty. I felt as though I wished to withdraw my promise, but could not. Something seemed to say ' Your prayer is answered, your conditions are accepted.' And from that time the conviction never left me that I was called to China."

For distinctly, as if a voice had spoken it, the command was given : " Then go for Me to China." [1]

[1] This is stated in his mother's written recollections.

Silently as the sunrise over a summer sea dawned this
new day upon his waiting soul. China? Yes, *China*.
That was the meaning of his life—past, present, and to
come. Away beyond himself, outside the little world of
his own heart-experience, lay the great, waiting world,
those for whom no man cared, for whom Christ died. "*Then
go for Me to China.*" Your prayer is answered: your conditions are accepted. All you ask and more, far more, shall
be given. There shall be deeper knowledge of the Lord;
fellowship in His sufferings, His death, His resurrection;
a life of inner victory and power. "For to this end have I
appeared unto thee, to appoint thee a minister and a witness
both of the things wherein thou hast seen me, and of the
things wherein I will appear unto thee; delivering thee from
the people and from the Gentiles unto whom now I send thee,
to open their eyes, that they may turn from darkness to
light, and from the power of Satan unto God."

A little slip of paper tells the rest—all, that is, that can
be told; a brief postscript to his letter written that very
night, the outpouring of a heart so full that it must overflow.

Bless the Lord, O my soul, and all that is within me shout His
praise! Glory to God, my dear Amelia. Christ has said "Seek and
ye shall find," and praise His name, He has revealed Himself to me in
an overflowing manner. He has cleansed me from all sin, from all
my idols. He has given me a new heart. Glory, glory, glory to His
ever blessed Name! I cannot write for joy. I open my letter to
tell you.

Yes, it was done. From that day onward life was on
another plane. The Lord had met him, satisfied his soul,
and spoken again the sweet, compelling word "Follow Me."
Outwardly it was manifest that a great change had come
over him.

"From that hour," the mother wrote, "his mind was made up.
His pursuits and studies were all engaged in with reference to this
object, and whatever difficulties presented themselves his purpose
never wavered."

For inwardly there was a deep subjection to the will of

God, resting upon a profound and unalterable sense of what that will was for him.　And with this came new purity and power, a steady growth in grace, and fulness of blessing that carried him through all the testing and preparation of the next few years.

" Faithful is He that calleth you, who also will do it."

That was what made him and kept him, the real beginning of his walk with God as a man set apart.

PART II

PREPARATION FOR CHINA, IN BARNSLEY AND IN HULL

1850–1852. AET. 17–20.

G

Christ to the young man said : " Yet one thing more ;
  If thou wouldst perfect be,
Sell all thou hast, and give it to the poor,
  And come and follow Me ! "

Within this temple Christ again, unseen,
  Those sacred words hath said,
And His invisible hands to-day have been
  Laid on a young man's head.

And evermore beside him on his way,
  The unseen Christ shall move,
That he may lean upon His arm, and say,
  " Dost Thou, dear Lord, approve ? "

Beside him at the marriage-feast shall be,
  To make the scene more fair :
Beside him in the dark Gethsemane
  Of pain and midnight prayer.

O holy trust ! O endless sense of rest !
  Like the beloved John,
To lay his head upon his Saviour's breast,
  And thus to journey on !

HENRY W. LONGFELLOW.

CHAPTER VII

THE NEW STARTING-POINT

1850. Aet. 17.

THUS closed the old year and the old life, and with the dawn of 1850 came a new beginning of things for Hudson Taylor. He was seventeen and a half years of age, and employed as we have seen in his father's shop. Good prospects were opening before him as a chemist, and the powers he after-wards displayed in the development of a great mission would have made him successful in this or any other line of business. But now all was changed. A work of which he knew next to nothing claimed him ; a work that must absorb every energy of his being, and might require the sacrifice of life itself. How to set about it he had no idea ; how even to make preparation was difficult to discover. But the call of God had come, and there could be no looking back. Whatever might be involved, the future held but one thing for him—to do his Master's will in and for China.

But what problems faced him as he thought of it ! He, a mere lad, a chemist's assistant in a provincial town, what could he do for China ? Wrapped in the proud exclusiveness of centuries, there it lay, that mightiest empire of the East— vast in size and population, shrouded in mystery, fascinating, repellent ; appalling in its need, inaccessible in its seclusion. How could he hope to forward there the coming of the Kingdom of God ? *" Then go for Me to China."* That was definite and final. So he began at once to pray for guidance and to learn all he could as to his future field.

And here it is necessary to remind ourselves how very

83

little was known about missionary work and lands even so recently as the middle of last century. China especially was *terra incognita*. True, five ports had been opened along the coast to the residence of foreigners,[1] and the London Missionary Society, for nearly forty years the only British Mission at work in that land, had been reinforced by several newly organised efforts.[2] But they were all in their infancy ; and beyond the Treaty Ports practically nothing was being attempted. In the absence of definite knowledge about the interior, exaggerated rumours were afloat. The wealth and learning of the people and the wonders of their ancient civilisation, as reported by some travellers, were only exceeded by the cruelty and ignorance enlarged upon by others. But travellers of any kind who had penetrated beyond the coast were few and far between.

Of course, no one familiar with the far East was to be found in Barnsley. The circle in which Hudson Taylor had been brought up had no connections there, and even for books upon the subject he hardly knew where to turn. One friend might be able to help him, and that was Mr. Whitworth, the founder and superintendent of the Sunday School, who had recently become connected with the British and Foreign Bible Society. He would know something at any rate about the circulation of the Bible in China, and might possess a copy of the Chinese Scriptures in whole or part. So to Mr. Whitworth he went.

The visit was encouraging, for his old friend was able to give him a copy, in the Mandarin dialect, of the writings of St. Luke. This was a treasure indeed. And from him too he may have heard that Medhurst's standard work on

---

[1] The Treaty Ports of Canton, Amoy, Fuchow, Ningpo and Shanghai, opened by the Treaty of Nanking, which concluded the first opium war with England, in 1842.

[2] The order in which the British Societies commenced work in China, up to this point, is as follows :

1807. The London Missionary Society ; sending Robert Morrison to Canton.

After the Treaty of Nanking—

1843. The British and Foreign Bible Society.

1844 The Church Missionary Society.

1845. The Baptist Missionary Society.

1847. The English Presbyterian Mission, whose first representative was the Rev. William Burns ; see Part V., Chaps XXV.-XXIX.

China was to be found in Barnsley, in the library of the Congregational minister.

Moved by desires he could not put into words, the eager lad called upon the gentleman in question.   It is interesting to have his own account of the visit, accompanied as it is with a glimpse into his deeper feelings at the time and the earnestness with which he sought to prepare for the future before him.

" It seemed to me highly probable," he said long after,' " that the work to which I was thus called might cost my life.   China was not open then as it is now.   Few missionary societies had representatives there, and few books on the subject were accessible to me.   I learned, however, that a minister in my native town possessed a copy of Medhurst's *China*, and calling upon him ventured to ask a loan of the book.

" This he kindly granted, inquiring why I wished to read it.   I told him that God had called me to spend my life in missionary service in that land.

" ' And how do you propose to go there ? ' he inquired.

" I answered that I did not at all know; that it seemed to me probable that I should need to do as the Twelve and the Seventy had done in Judea, go without purse or scrip, relying on Him who had sent me to supply all my need.

" Kindly placing his hand on my shoulder, the minister replied, ' Ah, my boy, as you grow older you will become wiser than that.   Such an idea would do very well in the days when Christ Himself was on earth, but not now.'

" I have grown older since then, but not wiser.   I am more and more convinced that if we were to take the directions of our Master and the assurance He gave to His first disciples more fully as our guide, we should find them just as suited to our times as to those in which they were originally given.

"Medhurst's book on China emphasised the value of Medical Missions there, and this directed my attention to medical studies as a mode of preparation.

" My beloved parents neither disapproved nor encouraged my desire to engage in missionary work.   They advised me, with such convictions, to use all the means in my power to develop the resources of body, mind and soul, and to wait prayerfully upon God, quite willing, should He show me that I was mistaken, to follow His guidance, or to go forward if in due time He should open the way to missionary service. The importance of this advice I have since had occasion to prove.   I began to take more exercise in the open air to strengthen my general health. My feather bed was soon dispensed with, and as many other comforts as possible, in order to prepare for a rougher sort of life. I began also to do what Christian work was in my power, in the way of tract distribution, Sunday-school teaching, and visiting the poor and sick as opportunity afforded." [1]

His purpose went deep, and from the first he realised that a call to missionary work in China involved the beginning of true missionary-life at home. " A voyage across the ocean," he often said in later years, " does not make any man a soul-winner." So to humble, loving efforts for the good of those around him he gave himself with renewed diligence, and especially to the practice of his life-calling as " a fisher of men."

Another form of preparation entered upon with ardour was the study of Chinese, that formidable task requiring, as Milne put it, " bodies of iron, lungs of brass, heads of oak, hands of spring-steel, eyes of eagles, hearts of apostles, memories of angels and lives of Methuselah." [2] Courageous in his inexperience Hudson Taylor set to work, despite the fact that he had neither teacher nor books with the exception of that one little volume of the writings of St Luke. A grammar would have cost no less than four guineas, and a dictionary could hardly have been purchased for fifteen. Needless to say he had neither. But hard work and ingenuity accomplished wonders, as may be judged from the fact that within a few weeks he and the cousin who was with him in the shop had found out the meaning of over five hundred characters.

" The method we pursue is as follows," he wrote to his sister on February 14. " We find a short verse in the English version, and then look out a dozen or more (also in English) that have one word in common with it. We then turn up the first verse in Chinese, and search through all the others for some character in common that seems to stand for the English word. This we write down on a slip

---

[1] Quoted from his own brief but well-known Autobiography, *A Retrospect*, from which extracts have already been made.

[2] The Rev. William Milne, who joined Dr. Morrison in 1813. A man of remarkable linguistic gifts, he took a large share in Morrison's literary labours. His lamented death took place in 1822 ; but far and wide, wherever Chinese is spoken, Milne is at work to-day. His well-known dialogue *The Two Friends* is circulated still by tens of thousands, and is generally regarded as " the most popular tract in China."

of paper as its probable equivalent. Then we look all through the
Chinese Gospel for this same character in different connections. It
occurs as a rule pretty frequently. And if in every case we find the
same word in the English version, we copy the character in ink into
our dictionary, adding the meaning in pencil. Afterwards, if further
acquaintance shows it to be the true meaning, we ink that over also.
At first we made slow progress, but now we can work much faster, as
with few exceptions we know all the most common characters. In our
dictionary we have four hundred and fifty-three put down as certain,
and many others that are not fully proved. About two hundred more
we know as certain that we have not copied into the dictionary yet,
and many besides that are only probable.

"I have begun to get up at five in the morning," he continued,
"and so find it necessary to go to bed early at night. I must study if
I mean to go to China. I am fully decided to go, and am making every
preparation I can. I intend to rub up my Latin, to learn Greek and
the rudiments of Hebrew, and to get as much general information as
possible. I need all your prayers."

But in preparing for the future Hudson Taylor did not
neglect present opportunities. With his practical turn of
mind he saw that something might be done without delay,
even in Barnsley, to forward the cause to which his life was
given. Go himself he could not, perhaps for years to come ;
but he was none the less responsible here and now for the
salvation of perishing souls in China. He could pray and
lead others to pray, give and encourage others in giving.
And just at this juncture a new movement set on foot by
Dr. Gutzlaff of Hong-kong came to his knowledge that
seemed to afford the very channel needed.

For hitherto he had hardly known how to communicate
with China. Large as was the field, the Wesleyans had no
mission there. Work in the Treaty Ports was being carried
on by other societies ; but even then Hudson Taylor longed
after the unreached interior—that vast waiting world, still
destitute of the Gospel. If only some one were seeking
to carry the light farther afield ! But every way seemed
blocked. Missionaries were restricted to the coast-board
provinces, and the Chinese Christians were so few and far
between that even had they been fitted for it none could
be spared for this pioneering work.

What was the joy therefore with which Hudson Taylor

learned of this new movement, through papers lent him by
Mr. Whitworth, and that a society had been organised in
London to do the very work on which his heart was set.
Interdenominational in character "The Chinese Association," as it was called, aimed at employing native evangelists
to co-operate with any existing missions, but chiefly with
Dr. Gutzlaff of Hong-kong in an enterprise that bid fair to
solve the problem of how to send the Gospel to the unreached
interior. Quite a number were already working under his
supervision, and great was the success that seemed to attend
their efforts.

Burning with love to Christ and zeal for the advancement
of His cause Dr. Gutzlaff had returned from Hong-kong a
few months previously,[1] and had commenced in London as
a starting-point a missionary crusade of the most remarkable
kind. From Ireland to Hungary he passed, proclaiming in
all the leading capitals of Europe the duty of the Christian
Church toward the unevangelised millions of China. For
the first time the need and claims of that great land came
home to many a heart, with the result that multitudes were
on their knees praying as never before. It was prayer for
which Gutzlaff primarily appealed, prayer for the outpouring
of the Spirit of God upon China in its agelong darkness.
But true prayer, potent in itself, is sure to bring about
practical results, and in this case quite a number of organised
efforts grew up in London and on the Continent that resulted
in permanent blessing.

Gutzlaff's piety was deep and real, his schemes were
large and his optimism unbounded. He was a man of unusual gifts, and as Interpreter to the British Government
in Hong-kong occupied a position of influence. So great
was his enthusiasm for the spread of the Gospel that he had
risked his life repeatedly in daring attempts to reach the
interior, as well as in voyages along the entire coast.[2] With

---

[1] Dr Gutzlaff reached Europe early in 1850.

[2] Dr. Gutzlaff, wearing Chinese dress, made seven journeys during the
years 1831-35 along the Chinese coast, landing at places even as far north
as Tien-tsin, and risking his life again and again in earnest efforts to make
known the Gospel. Dr. Medhurst, at the request of the L.M S., made a
similar journey in 1835, seven years before the opening of the Treaty
Ports.

DR. CHARLES GUTZLAFF IN THE DRESS OF A FU-KIEN SAILOR.

The devoted missionary often referred to by Mr. Hudson Taylor as "the grandfather of the China Inland Mission."

To face page 89.

considerable experience as a sailor he even engaged himself
as mate on a Chinese junk, and at another time as cook, in
order to visit places to which no foreign vessels sailed and
obtain opportunities for making known the truth as it is
in Jesus.[1] Though not strictly speaking a missionary, he
lived for one thing only—the extension of the Kingdom of
God. To this he devoted his large salary, his remarkable
powers of mind and body and all his available time. He
wrote and published eighty works in no fewer than eight
different languages, including a translation into Chinese of
both the Old and New Testaments. He founded " The
Chinese Union," a native missionary society whose members
were to carry the Gospel far and wide to every part of the
eighteen provinces, and he awakened Europe one may almost
say with enthusiasm in support of this cause, everywhere
organising prayer-meetings and associations to carry on the
work. The new society in London was one of these, and
immediately claimed the sympathy of Hudson Taylor.

According to tabulated reports brought home by Dr.
Gutzlaff, the evangelists of " The Chinese Union " in-
augurated six years previously had met with amazing
encouragement. They now numbered a hundred and
thirty men, engaged in systematic preaching throughout
the interior and in the distribution of Christian literature.
They had circulated over ten thousand New Testaments,
besides many Bibles and countless books and tracts. They
wrote long and detailed letters from almost all the provinces
of China, telling of journeys even to the borders of Mongolia
and Tibet. And last but not least, they had baptized, "upon
examination and satisfactory confession of their faith,"
no fewer than 2871 converts. Such results, within so short
a time, could not but arouse the deepest interest.

All through the spring and summer these developments
were delighting the earnest lad in Barnsley. An excellent
magazine, quite above the average of religious papers, was
commenced in March of this year to supply the latest tidings
from Dr. Gutzlaff's workers, as well as missionary information from other parts of the world. Hudson Taylor took

[1] See Ball's *China*, published in 1854, pp. 59, 60.

it in from the first, and the careful study with which he followed it for years formed in itself a valuable education in missionary principles and practice. From its pages he learned of many on the Continent as well as in Great Britain who were engaged in active efforts for the evangelisation of China. The undertakings represented at Barmen and Cassel, the Pilgrim Missionary Institution of St. Chrischona, John Evangelist Gossner and his devoted workers, the Moravians of Herrnhut, and the Missionary Societies of Basel and Berlin all became familiar to him as the months went by. It informed him also of the varied labours of George Muller of Bristol, who during this and the previous year had expended more than £2500 on missionary work in Roman Catholic and heathen lands. This well-directed magazine, in short, was used of God to introduce Hudson Taylor into a new world of Christian enterprise, unsectarian in its character and international in its interests, preparing him while still in his teens for the far-reaching associations of coming years.[1]

By means of *The Gleaner* also he was enabled to follow the operations of the new society in London. Its character so impressed him that he ventured after a time upon the following letter, little realising to how much its modest overtures would lead.

21 CHEAPSIDE, BARNSLEY,
July 29, 1850.

To Mr. George Pearse, Secretary of the Chinese Association.

SIR—Some time ago, Mr. Whitworth, the respected Local Treasurer of the Bible Society, directed my attention to the Chinese Association, as advertised in *The Watchman*, and in *The Gleaner in the Missionary Field* I have seen several notices of its usefulness.

Feeling deeply interested in the spread of Christianity among the Chinese, and having determined as soon as Providence shall open my way to devote myself to that extensive and almost unbounded field of Christian enterprise, I wish during the interval to promote the work

---

[1] This interesting paper, *The Gleaner in the Missionary Field*, seems to have been edited by the Secretaries of the Chinese Association, or, as it was afterwards called, the Chinese Evangelisation Society. Although no names are given, it is easy to recognise Mr George Pearse of the London Stock Exchange as well as Mr. Richard Ball of Taunton in many of its articles. The latter was a man of literary gift as well as spiritual insight, and both were deeply taught in the Word of God.

as much as possible. I have therefore taken the liberty of addressing you as Secretary. I shall be much obliged if you will forward at your earliest convenience a few circulars or collecting cards, as well as any information, rules, etc., calculated to assist me in introducing the work to my friends.

Praying the great Head of the Church, without whose blessing nothing can prosper, greatly to forward your efforts,—I remain, Sir, yours respectfully,

JAMES H. TAYLOR.

But reports had begun to reach England by this time of the doubtful character of Dr. Gutzlaff's organisation, and the reply from Mr. Pearse was evidently discouraging. Further developments tended only to confirm the fear that, with all his brilliant gifts and rare devotion, Gutzlaff sadly lacked common sense and that "discernment of spirits" so necessary in dealing with an oriental people. In a word, he had been systematically swindled, as the German missionary acting as his *locum tenens* in Hong-kong discovered. Few of his so-called evangelists had travelled beyond Canton, and many of their glowing reports had been concocted in opium-dens a few minutes only from his own door. It was a painful and almost incredible exposure, and no one suffered more from grief and disappointment than the noble-minded leader, who did not long survive the failure of his work.[1]

And yet—had Gutzlaff failed? His plans miscarried grievously and his projects came to nothing. But prayer and faith cannot fail. More perhaps than any man in his day he had seen the commanding vision—China won for Christ—and had given himself, his all, to bring it to pass. "God buries His workmen, but carries on His work." Gutzlaff died in faith, entering, as was said of him, the presence of the Lord with the millions of China on his heart. And the aims he had never been able to realise, the ideals

---

[1] Dr. Gutzlaff passed away at Hong-kong on the 9th of August 1851, devotedly labouring among the Chinese until his brief but fatal illness came on. *The Gleaner* for January 1852 supplied the following details.

"Even in his last hours, all his thoughts were directed to the evangelisation of China. He spoke of it with great confidence, and in the delirium of fever frequently expressed bright hopes for the blessing and regeneration of his beloved Sinim   Truly of him it may be said that he departed this life and entered the presence of the Lord bearing the millions of China upon his heart."

that seemed to fail—of a native agency and widespread evangelistic work—fell as good seed into other hearts, to bear fruit at last in every part of China

Long years after, when the China Inland Mission had become a fact in all the inland provinces, its founder loved to refer to Dr. Gutzlaff as in a very real sense the father of the work. It was in any case a remarkable providence that brought this burning spirit with his prophetic vision across the orbit of Hudson Taylor's life just at this time. It could not but be that he was disappointed and in a measure discouraged by the turn events had taken. Among the friends and supporters of Gutzlaff's enterprise, whose interest had been aroused chiefly by his own enthusiasm, there was naturally a swing of the pendulum in the other direction when these disclosures came to light. A strong reaction set in, and for a time it seemed as though the whole movement would flicker out and leave no permanent results. But those whose hearts God had touched felt only the more responsible for the enlightenment of a people so obviously in need of the Gospel. It was a period of sifting that revealed the true character of many in the homelands as well as in China. But out of it all grew clearer knowledge, stronger faith, and a few undertakings of the right sort. Among these were the Moravian Mission to Tibet, with other German efforts, and in London the work with which Mr. Pearse was connected, the society that ultimately sent Hudson Taylor to Shanghai.

And lastly Hudson himself came out of it by the grace of God, more than ever determined to give his life to China. It was a test that might well have turned back one whose " call " depended chiefly on emotion. But, as the following letter shows, it only stirred the Barnsley lad to deeper earnestness and prayer, and served to teach him lessons of inestimable value.

21 CHEAPSIDE, BARNSLEY,
August 7, 1850.

To Mr. George Pearse.

DEAR SIR—I write to acknowledge your kindness in answering my note, to thank you for the Report and to avail myself of your permission to write again for further information.

I think, though the aspect of the Institution is at present in many respects discouraging, we may hope for better days. Notwithstanding that the character of the Chinese seems very unfavourable for the reception of the Gospel, we have the promise that all shall know Him, whom to know is life eternal. We know not what we might have been, had it not been for Christianity. Christ has died that all might turn, repent and live. We who do know the advantage, and experience the renovating influence of religion are bound to propagate the Gospel among all peoples. I think with you that under the supervision of European and American missionaries much good may be done by native agency.

" The harvest truly is great, but the labourers are few." We cannot be too much in earnest in the prosecution of this great work. The missionaries should be men of apostolic zeal, patience and endurance, willing to be all things to all men. May the Lord raise up suitable instruments, and fit me for this work.

On Dr. Gutzlaff's return to China, will the Institution be remodelled, or can further frauds be prevented in any way? Have you any collecting books or cards? If you will kindly forward me a few, or otherwise authorise me to collect, I will endeavour to gather a few pounds if possible. Apologising for troubling you,—I remain, dear Sir, yours respectfully,

J. HUDSON TAYLOR.

Thus amid all the discouragements of a peculiarly difficult time, we see his stedfast figure pressing on.

CHAPTER VIII

NO GOOD THING WILL HE WITHHOLD

1850–1851.   AET. 17½–19.

But disappointment in the work was not the only thing that came to test the reality of Hudson Taylor's call to China. Even before his eyes were opened, through the failure of Gutzlaff's plans, to the darker side of missionary experience he was overtaken by trial of a very different kind, that went with him through long months and years, bringing the strongest influences to bear against unquestioning obedience. It was a test of faith, a call to sacrifice, perhaps the hardest that can come in a young man's life.   And it began so soon —with that same Christmas of 1849.

For then it was, almost immediately after he had come to know the will of God for his future, that a counter-current set in, as powerful as it was unexpected.   He had just received a wonderful baptism of love and power, and was entering with unreserved consecration upon his life-service.   And at that very point the tempter met him, met him with suggestions so natural and attractive that it seemed hardly possible they could be contrary to the mind of God. And yet those suggestions had he followed them would have led far away from China and effectually hindered the Lord's first, best plan for his life.

It was as will be anticipated a question of " falling in love," seriously, tremendously, and for the first time.   But why not draw a veil over matters so intimate, especially if they were to end in disappointment ?   That certainly would be the easier course and one we would willingly pursue but for the constant recurrence of the same danger in other lives.   For many a young, intending missionary has made shipwreck upon the rocks that threatened Hudson Taylor now, and it may be that his experience will be used of God to safeguard some whose peril is known to Him alone.

It all began with the Christmas holidays and an ordinary friendship arising out of his sister's return from school. For Amelia did not come alone.   The young music-teacher to whom she had become much attached during the term accompanied her, and added not a little to the brightness of the family-circle that already included their cousin from Barton-on-Humber.

To Hudson and his sister this reunion was delightful after their first long parting, and many were the hours spent in fellowship and prayer such as only young hearts know. To no one else could he speak so freely of the things that mattered most, and there was much to talk over concerning his new-found joy in the Lord as well as his call to China. And when the little sister discovered that some one else was beginning to take a first place in his affections she rejoiced unselfishly.   Life would not be so lonely far away from home.

But Hudson saw difficulties ahead.   True it had not occurred to him that the one he loved might be quite un-suited for the life he hoped to live in China.   She was a Christian, a Methodist, and so bright and gifted that he could not imagine her to be lacking in missionary devotion. As a matter of fact Miss V. was decidedly attractive, and in addition to some musical training had a voice so sweet that it was a constant pleasure to those around her.   She was happy among her new friends, and interested especially in the son of the household.   But while sympathising to a certain extent with his feelings about China there was a something lacking, and she would gladly have held him back.

This of course he did not realise, or if he felt it intangibly from the first he was far from admitting even to himself that it might prove a serious obstacle.   No, the difficulties he felt, and felt increasingly as time passed on, arose from the uncertainties of his position and his lack of means, prospectively, to support a wife. Had there been any opening before him he might have had more hope. But how he was to go to China he had no idea, nor how he would be supported there. He knew of no society that sent out unordained men, unless perhaps the Chinese Association, and that soon came into such low water financially that it seemed doubtful whether it could continue to exist. The collapse of Dr. Gutzlaff's enterprise was seriously affecting missionary interest in China. On the whole it seemed more than likely that he would have to be a self-supporting missionary, or go in simple faith, trusting the Lord who sent him to provide. But that precluded any thought of marriage, at any rate for a long time to come. And meanwhile his lips were sealed. Some one else was sure to love her. Every one must who was near her and free to win her love. No one could care as he did! That was beyond question. And yet, with such prospects or lack of prospects before him he must be silent.

This was the ground, then, on which the conflict commenced : not so much a struggle between love and duty, though it came to that at last, as a long fight of faith with questionings and fears. *" No good thing will He withhold."* Would it prove really true ? Surely his heart's desire was a good thing : yet how was it to be accomplished ? Could he leave all in the hands of God and simply trust—nothing but uncertainty ahead ?

The year that followed was full of perplexity and pain, in the midst of which his spiritual life was deepening, as may be seen from frequent letters to his sister who had returned to school.

" Dear Amelia," he wrote in September, " remember me in all your prayers. Never did I feel a greater need of watchfulness and prayer than at present. Praised be God, I know that the blood of Jesus cleanses from all sin ; but I feel my own weakness, my own nothingness. Without His aid I cannot stand for one moment ; but I look to the Strong for strength ; and though he that trusteth in man shall be disappointed, blessed are all they that put their trust in the Lord. I realise this blessedness. I feel that I can trust Him with all my concerns. I can and do ' praise Him for all that is past, and trust Him for all that's to come.' He has promised to withhold ' no good thing '

from those that walk uprightly. I do love Him, and am determined
to devote myself, body, soul and spirit, to His work.

"I have a stronger desire than ever to go to China. That land is
ever in my thoughts. Think of it—three hundred and sixty million
souls, without God or hope in the world ! Think of more than twelve
millions of our fellow-creatures dying every year without any of the
consolations of the Gospel. . . . Barnsley including the Common has
only fifteen thousand inhabitants. Imagine what it would be if all
these were to die in twelve months ! Yet in China *hundreds* are dying,
year by year, for every man, woman and child in Barnsley. Poor,
neglected China ! Scarcely any one cares about it. And that immense
country, containing nearly a fourth of the human race, is left in
ignorance and darkness.

> Shall we whose souls are lighted
> With wisdom from on high ;
> Shall we to men benighted
> The lamp of Life deny ? . . .

"Pray for me, dear Amelia, that I may have more of the mind of
Christ ; that I may be guided in all things by His Spirit and made very
useful. Pray for the cause of God and expect an answer. Pray on
for China. . . .

"You say ' let us leave all in the hands of God.' You are right.
' The Lord God is a sun and shield : the Lord will give grace and glory :
no good thing will He withhold from them that walk uprightly.' But
remember His own word, ' I will yet for this be enquired of by the house
of Israel to do it for them.' Make it a matter of prayer, Love, and
then leave it in the hands of God our Father. I have prayed about
it, and I am sure I can trust God. He will do all things well. God
knows what is best, and we must learn to welcome His will, which is
' good, acceptable and perfect.' "

He was very busy at this time, rising early every morning
for study. Latin, Greek, theology and medicine occupied
every available moment even during business hours, and
Sunday brought opportunities of ministry to others. Sharing
a room with his cousin made it difficult to obtain much
privacy, but

"I go into the warehouse, stable, or anywhere," he wrote, " to be
alone with God. And some most precious seasons I have. . . . Do
your best to keep hold of Jesus. And if in an unguarded moment
you should fall, humble yourself before God   ' If we confess our sins,
He is faithful and just to forgive us our sins and to cleanse us from all
unrighteousness.' We cannot be perfect as angels who have never

H

sinned, nor as Adam before he fell. Sin always has had and always will have a power over us, if we look not to the Lord for strength. Yet, though we are vile in ourselves, we may be made ' pure in heart ' through the all-prevailing blood of Jesus. Washed in His blood we are even now ' whiter than snow.' But it must be constant washing. Grace we every moment need. Oh seek this grace, strive for it, and may God bless you with ' a pure heart ' for Christ's sake."

As the unstudied correspondence of a lad of only eighteen with a sister several years younger the above quotations have a special interest, and so also has the following letter bearing more directly upon the matter that was exercising his heart.

BARNSLEY, *Nov.* 11, 1850.

MY DEAR AMELIA—I have to write to you at sundry times and in divers places, here a little and there a little. . . .

In your last note you suggest that it might be a good plan to write to the Chinese Association and ask whether they could send me out as a married man. You must excuse my differing from you in opinion. I think that to do so would be to effectually prevent them. They would naturally conclude that I wanted to get married without means, and that I hoped they would insure me from the consequences of such conduct. It would not do to write to them at all at present.

I have not, as you know, the slightest idea how I shall go. But this I know, I shall go, either alone or married. . . . I know God has called me to the work, and He will provide the means. But as you see I cannot send the information you desire. It is not reasonable to suppose that Miss V. would be willing to go and starve in a foreign land. I am sure I love her too well to wish her to do so. . . . You well know I have nothing, and nothing (financially) to hope for. Consequently I can enter into no engagement under present circumstances. I cannot deny that these things make me very sad: But my Father knows what is best. " No good thing will He withhold." I must live by faith, hang on by faith, simple faith, and He will do all things well.

Think not I am cold or indifferent. But what *can* I do ? I know I love her. To go without her would make the world a blank. But I cannot bring her to want. Oh, pray for me ! It is enough to distract me. May God bless and enable me to trust Him fully.

> Through waves, and clouds, and storms,
>   He gently clears thy way :
> Wait thou His time, so shall this night
>   Soon end in joyous day.

I trust it will be so : God grant it may !

You say you are sure I might win her if I could see my way to provide for her. But you see I cannot. And if I could, how do you know that I might have her? Do let me know, for I am so anxious about it. You say I should ensure this best by being sent out. Very true. But who is to send me? The Wesleyans have no station in China. . . . The Established Church have one or two, but I am not a Churchman . . . and would not do for them. The Baptists and Independents have stations there, but I do not hold their views. . . . The Chinese Association is very low in funds. So God and God alone is my hope, and I need no other.

> Except the Lord conduct the plan,
> The best-concerted schemes are vain
> And never can succeed

With you I could wish, were it possible, that the matter should be decided at Christmas. But what reason have you for thinking it might if circumstances were favourable? Do you suppose she thinks or knows that I love her? Or does she, think you, care about me? Do answer these questions plainly.—Your affectionate brother,

J. H. TAYLOR.

A reply seems to have come from his sister that perplexed while it encouraged him.

" I wonder how often I have read and reread your letters," he wrote a fortnight later, " especially the last. As I do so, my mind is filled with conflicting hopes and fears. But I am determined to trust in God."

Thus winter passed slowly by, and with early spring came a first step toward China. It was now more than a year since the purpose of God had been made known to him, and he felt the time had come for more definite preparation for his life-work. Five years in his father's business had made him quite at home in dispensing medicines and even prescribing for ordinary ailments. He needed still to earn his own living, but felt that as assistant to a doctor in good practice he might at the same time make progress with his medical studies. It seemed but a small step in the direction desired, but it was all that was open to him, and the Lord would guide as to what was to follow.

" I am determined," he wrote to his sister, " to be more than ever His, and to redouble my diligence to make my calling and election sure. Continue to pray for E. Pray in faith and leave the results with God. . . . I am determined not to waste time any more in writing letters as I have done, but to endeavour in all things to be about my Master's work. May He help me. . . . It is my desire in all my ways to acknowledge Him : and He shall direct my path.

"Now that I have decided to leave home, I want you to ask that the Lord will guide me into a suitable situation, where I may get and do good and become fitted for China. . . "

Shortly after this he had occasion to write again to Mr. Pearse in London   The letter is worth quoting, as illustrating his careful attention to detail, and sense of stewardship in connection with money given for the Lord's work, even the smallest sums.

21 CHEAPSIDE, BARNSLEY,
March 31, 1851

Mr. George Pearse.

DEAR SIR—You will almost think I have forgotten the Chinese Union and have not its interests at heart, on account of my long silence. Such, however, is not the case, although from pressure of business I have not been able to devote to it the attention it deserves.   I have collected rather more than two pounds.   Please send me word as to how I shall remit this sum to you   If I send a post office order it will cost sixpence , but I can get it placed to your credit at Glynn & Co. or any other London banker's for two or three pence.   Meanwhile I will do all in my power to get a few more subscribers, as the interests of China lie very near my heart.   May I be fitted to engage in this great work. Please excuse haste, and—Believe me, yours in our Risen Lord,

J. H. TAYLOR.

Had Mr. Pearse replied that the money might be sent by post office order, as the difference of two or three pence was a small matter, it is doubtful whether he would have heard much more from Hudson Taylor. To him every penny was a trust to be used for his Master.   "A little thing is a little thing," he often quoted in later life, " but faithfulness in little things is a great thing." Mr. Pearse, however, appreciated his inquiry, and wrote mentioning a bank through which the money might be forwarded ; to which the Barnsley lad replied—

. . . I have paid through our Bankers £2 : 5 to your credit at Messrs. Jones, Lloyd & Co., Lothbury, according to your directions, and you will receive it on Monday. Please acknowledge the receipt of this sum, that I may be able to show the subscribers that it has been remitted. Have you a Report, or any other publication telling of the work done by your Society, and how the funds are applied ? . . . I enclose a list of the contributors. The amounts are small, but I have no doubt that when more is known about the Society and its operations I shall be able to collect more.

The field truly is great, and the means at present employed for its cultivation appear very inadequate. But . . . it is " not by might nor by power " but by the influence of the Holy Spirit alone that good can be accomplished, and God often makes the weak things of this world to confound the mighty. He and He only can raise up and qualify suitable labourers and own and bless those already on the field. . . .

I have devoted myself to missionary work in China in obedience I believe to His call, and am at present studying medicine and surgery that I may have more opportunities of usefulness and perhaps be able to support myself when there. This, however, I leave in His hands, believing that if I seek first the Kingdom of God and His righteousness all these things shall be " added " according to His promise.

Any suggestions you may be able to give me as to means for promoting the cause or fitting myself for more extensive usefulness would be thankfully received by—Yours in our Risen Lord,

J. H. Taylor.

Mr. Pearse was evidently interested. He seems to have consulted his Committee and to have written intimating that the Society might be willing to help in the expense of a medical education if they considered Mr. Taylor a suitable candidate for China. This letter with its inquiries as to his religious views, education, etc., called forth the following reply. Though long, it is given in full, as manifesting the spirit that actuated the young intending missionary, a spirit at once appreciative, dignified, independent and humble.

21 Cheapside, Barnsley,
April 25, 1851.

To George Pearse, Esq., Hackney.

Dear Sir—I have not been able hitherto, from press of business, to answer your kind favours of the 17th and 21st inst., and am sorry that, in haste, I neglected to enclose the list of contributors. Herewith you will receive it.

I feel obliged to you for mentioning the work on China, which I shall endeavour to procure ; and am grateful to your Committee for their kindness in promising access to a London hospital and lectures. I fear, however, that I shall not be able to avail myself of these privileges, as I have no means of supporting myself in London, and may not be able to obtain a situation there that would allow sufficient time to make use of them.

I have for some time past been looking out for employment in a Surgery, as I think that would afford better opportunities than I at present enjoy for acquiring medical and surgical knowledge. My present position is perhaps as favourable as most with regard to opportunities for self-improvement. It consists chiefly in prescribing and dispensing, and we have the privilege of reading during business hours if all the work is done. But the number of anatomical and similar works that I have access to is limited, and their price is very high, placing many altogether beyond my reach. So that apart from the benefit to be gained from practical surgery, the acquirement of the theory would be facilitated by the situation I am seeking.

As you are so kind as to interest yourself in my case, I may now perhaps state the reasons that make me think myself called to the work of evangelisation in China.

From my earliest childhood I have felt the strivings of the Holy Spirit, and when about fourteen years of age I gave my heart to God. About six months after that time I went into a bank as clerk, and remained about nine months, when I had to leave on account of my sight, which was injured through much writing by gas-light. The others in the bank were worldly men, and religion was seldom spoken of without a sneer. I began to place too great a value on the things of this world and to neglect private prayer Religious duties became irksome to me and I fell from grace. But God in His infinite mercy caused my eyes to fail, and I was obliged to leave.

I continued in a state of religious unconcern until June 1849, when God was pleased to strike home a conviction of my sinful and dangerous state while I was reading a tract accidentally left by a friend. I have not the slightest doubt but that this was in answer to the prayers of my parents, and of my sister, who had even made a memorandum a month or two previously to the effect that she would never cease praying for me until I was saved, and that she believed her prayers would be answered before long. I thank God that through His grace I was enabled to resolve never to rest until I found peace with Him through our Lord Jesus Christ. Shortly afterwards it pleased Him again to cause His face to shine upon me, and I was enabled by faith to realise the merit of His atonement.

About Christmas 1849, I am sorry to have to say, that notwithstanding all the love the Saviour had manifested to me, I began to slacken in my closet duties. A spiritual lethargy seemed to have crept over me. I did not enjoy communion with God as heretofore, and felt something was wrong, so wrong that I feared I might fall away from grace and be finally lost. Earnestly I cried to God to show me the hindrance and take it away, promising Him, if He would only save me completely, that I would do anything in His cause He might direct.

Never shall I forget the feeling that came over me then. Words can never describe it. I felt that I was in the very presence of God, entering into covenant with the Almighty. I felt as though I wished to withdraw my promise, but could not. Something seemed to say : " Your prayer is answered, your conditions are accepted." And from that time the conviction has never left me that I was called to China.

I obtained all the works I could on that interesting country, and read them as I was able. I see there an unbounded field of usefulness, and there by the grace of God I mean to go. I feel my own salvation depends on it. May I be made the humble instrument of much good.

Mr. Whitworth, the respected Local Treasurer of the Bible Society, lent me several numbers of *The Watchman* in which were papers on China. There I first saw a notice of your Society. Afterwards, seeing more about it in *The Gleaner*, I ventured to write to you in the hope of being able to do a little to forward the cause.

I obtained through Mr. Whitworth a copy of the writings of St. Luke in Chinese, and discovered the meaning of many characters by comparing passages with the aid of an English Concordance. I also procured a copy of Marshman's *Clavis Sinica*. Medhurst's Grammar was ordered but could not be procured. But I found I could not with advantage continue the study of the language without a Dictionary, which I was not able to afford. So I thought I should do more good by studying necessary subjects such as Anatomy, Physiology, Medicine and Surgery, which accordingly I have done.

I will now endeavour to answer your questions :

I. Some of the reasons that make me think, nay, make me *sure* (for I have no doubt on the matter) that I am truly converted to God are as follows :

The things I used formerly to delight in now give me no pleasure, while reading the Word, prayer and the means of grace, which were formerly distasteful to me, are now my delight.

> Once the world was all my treasure,
>   And the world my heart possessed :
> Now I taste sublimer pleasure
>   Since the Lord has made me blest.

I know I have passed from death unto life because I love the brethren. The Spirit of God bears direct witness with my spirit that I am His child. My mind is kept in perfect peace because I trust in Him. And I feel no doubt that should I be called hence, when this earthly tabernacle is dissolved I have a building of God, a house not made with hands, eternal in the heavens. I feel I am but a stranger here. Heaven is my home . . I know that in myself there is nothing that can merit Heaven. I am a poor, helpless, hell-deserving sinner. But in Him all fulness dwells. I am, praised be God, a sinner saved by grace

II. My age will be nineteen on the 21st of May 1851. Of course I am unmarried.

III. As to the general state of my health : I have never had any serious illness, but cannot be called robust. I have never been better than at present, and intend to take more care of my health than I have previously done, having often neglected exercise for weeks together in order to have more time for study.

IV. My occupation has been, since Christmas 1845, with the exception of nine months spent in the bank, that of assistant to my father, who is a chemist and druggist.

V. My education was carried on at home until I was eleven years of age. Then I went to school, and continued there until I was thirteen, when the master resigning without arranging for an efficient substitute, I left at the Christmas vacation and came into the shop. Besides the regular routine of study, I worked at Latin, Euclid and Algebra, in which I took great interest. Since then I have had access to a tolerably good library, and have acquired the rudiments of Greek as well as of Anatomy and Physiology.

VI. With regard to denominational views : at first I joined the Wesleyan Methodists, as my parents and friends were members of that body. But not being able to reconcile the late proceedings with the doctrines and precepts of Holy Scripture, I withdrew, and am at present united to the branch Society.

Apologising for thus intruding upon your time—I remain, dear Sir, yours in our beloved Redeemer,

JAMES HUDSON TAYLOR.

Meanwhile his prayers for guidance were being answered through an opening that occurred in Hull for an assistant to one of the busiest doctors there. An aunt on his mother's side was married to a brother of this Dr. Hardey, and it was probably her influence that secured the position for her nephew in Barnsley. In many ways it seemed the very thing he needed, and from his point of view was none the less desirable for being within easy reach of Barton, where Amelia and the young music-teacher were still in Mrs. Hodson's school. It was not London, nor did it enable him to avail himself of the aid Mr. Pearse and his Society had offered. But it was the way providentially opened after much prayer, and as such was thankfully accepted.

On one of the last days before leaving Barnsley, Hudson

spoke for the first time in public. This was at Royston, within sight of the fine old church in which James and Betty Taylor had been married. There on his wedding-day the stone-mason had first confessed his allegiance to a new Master, and there seventy-five years later came the great-grandson who bore his name to give his first public testimony to that Master's saving grace.

" On Tuesday I went to preach at Royston," he wrote to his sister the following day. " The room was crowded ; there would be from fifty to sixty present. I never was so blessed in my life. We had a prayer-meeting afterwards in which ten or twelve took part. One little girl of about thirteen came to the penitent-form and professed to find peace. She is young, but Jesus can keep her."

Thus the quiet years of life at home drew to a close, and early in May the separation came that meant so much for both Hudson and his mother. Full well they knew it was but the beginning of that longer parting toward which their faces were set. But they spoke much of the joy and privilege of suffering for Jesus' sake and trusted Him about the sorrow.

It was on his nineteenth birthday that after a brief visit to his grandparents in Hull the new apprentice took up his duties with Dr. Hardey. The day was naturally a busy one, and not till nearly midnight did he find time for the few lines to his sister that could not be omitted.

" From what I have seen of my situation," he wrote, " I think I shall like it exceedingly. Of course I felt very strange and awkward at first, but I have begun to be more at home now and to know better where to find things and what to do."

And then his thoughts carried him away from his new surroundings and across the Humber to the quiet, old-world township in which his dear ones lived. How near he was to them at last ! His heart beat quick with hope as he realised that almost any day he might see them.

" I am to have an hour to myself at dinner and another at tea-time," he continued eagerly. " I almost think I shall be able to run over to Barton sometimes in the evening, by a little arrangement and being willing to stay over-time when needed. . . .

"Go on praying for me and all the others. You cannot think how happy I feel in my Saviour's love. Oh, He has loved me, the chief of sinners! I love Him for it. He has hitherto granted all my prayers and He will grant me more before midsummer. 'The crooked shall be made straight.' You understand, Love. Farewell."

NO. 13 CHARLOTTE STREET, HULL, THE HOME OF DR. ROBERT HARDEY.

The surgery at the end of the garden (now half hidden by a conservatory) in which much of Mr. Taylor's work was done.

To face page 107.

CHAPTER IX

THAT I MAY WIN CHRIST

MAY–DECEMBER 1851. AET. 19.

DR. ROBERT HARDEY of 13 Charlotte Street was widely esteemed in the city of Hull as a reliable medical man and a consistent Christian. He was very busy, having in addition to a large, general practice the surgical oversight of a number of factories and a lectureship in the School of Medicine. Tall and vigorous in appearance he was unusually gentle and full of fun, and was beloved by little children and the poor who crowded his dispensary no less than by wealthy patients in their beautiful homes. His humour seems to have been irresistible, and in spite of themselves those under his care had to look on the bright side of things. Often indeed he made people laugh so much that they were cured of half their ailments without recourse to medicine at all. And better still, in troubles medicine could not touch, he knew how to bring help and healing to the soul.

His home of which Hudson Taylor was now an inmate was the city doctor's house of the old-fashioned type. The broad thoroughfare, like Harley Street in London, was a centre for the profession in those days and quite aristocratic. Number 13 stood on the sunny side and was specially attractive for the Virginia creeper that framed the windows in a wealth of green. To the right of the hall as one entered was the consulting-room, beyond which the dining-room overlooked a narrow strip of garden with the dispensary at its farther end. This garden, much traversed by the doctor and his assistant, consisted mainly of a lawn, on one side of which a pathway overarched with roses led to what had been the stables but was now an out-patient department, conveniently accessible from a back street.

Here then in what was called the Surgery Hudson Taylor found himself at home. Mrs. Hardey's supervision had not extended apparently to this branch of the establishment, but the new assistant was equal to the occasion and soon had everything in apple-pie order, after the fashion to which he had been accustomed at home. His knowledge of book-keeping also proved of value to Dr. Hardey, who had much work of that sort on hand and was glad to leave it to so competent a helper. Thus the doctor's relations with the Barnsley lad soon came to be of a cordial character. He was so bright and eager to learn, so willing and good-tempered, that to work with him was a pleasure, and before long the busy doctor found that it was a help to pray with him too. Many were the quiet times, after that, from which the older man came away refreshed and strengthened. Needless to say there was no familiarity or presuming on these relations. The young assistant respected himself and his employer far too much for that. He did his work faithfully, as in the sight of God, and Dr. Hardey showed his appreciation by giving him opportunities for study and by directing his reading as much as possible.

But there were drawbacks to the life at Charlotte Street, of which Hudson Taylor himself was largely unconscious. For one thing it was too comfortable, too easy-going in certain ways, and failed on that account to afford some elements needed in a missionary's training. Quite in another part of Hull amid very different surroundings was a little " prophet's chamber," bare in its furnishings and affording neither companionship nor luxury, where a stronger if a sterner life could be lived, apart with God. Moses at the backside of the wilderness, Joseph in Pharaoh's prison, Paul in the silence of the Arabian desert—lived that sort of life, and came out to do great things for men in the power of God. That was the life Hudson Taylor needed and to which he was being led. He did not choose it for himself, at any rate not at first or consciously. The Lord chose it

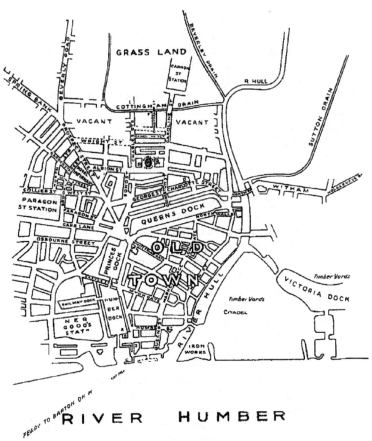

F. Howard Taylor, del

MAP OF HULL AS IT WAS IN 1851.

Showing (D) location of Dr Hardey's house on Charlotte Street; (H) of Mrs Richard Hardey's home on Kingston Square; and (F) of Mrs Finch's cottage, facing Cottingham Drain, also (B) the old Humber Dock and the crowded neighbourhood of the Royal Infirmary, where Mr. Taylor used to preach and distribute tracts on Sunday.

for him, and so ordered circumstances that he was brought to see and to embrace it, finding in self-denial and the daily cross a fellowship with his Master nothing else can yield.

So there came a day, providentially, when the young assistant could no longer be domiciled at Dr. Hardey's. His room was needed for a member of the family, and as the Surgery was not provided with sleeping accommodation he had to seek quarters elsewhere. But it was too much, perhaps, of a transition to that other, better life which awaited him, without some intermediate experience, and for the time being Hudson Taylor found himself welcomed by his aunt, Mrs. Richard Hardey, into her pleasant home.

This was in some ways more congenial than the first arrangement, and quite as convenient for his daily work. The Richard Hardeys lived on Kingston Square, opposite the Medical School at which Hudson was attending lectures and within two minutes of the Surgery. They were not wealthy people, indeed Mrs. Hardey's skilful brush supplied the larger part of their income. But they were generous and warm-hearted, and having no children of their own were glad to entertain a sister's son. Mrs. Hardey inherited the family gift for portrait-painting,[1] and her attractive personality in addition to her husband's genial spirit gathered about them a large circle of friends. All this Hudson enjoyed to the full, especially when his sister came over from Barton to spend a Sunday with them.

But though happy in outward circumstances he was anything but free from anxiety and unrest. Life was opening before him, and away from the scenes of childhood, dependent for the first time upon his own earnings, he was feeling the seriousness of his position as never before. He had taken as he thought a step toward China, and yet his hope of getting there, his ideal of a life devoted to its evangelisation seemed more and more remote as time went on. He had come to Hull eager to fit himself for medical work, but his busy days with Dr. Hardey left little time for study, while they showed him with increasing clearness how far he was from the end in view. Though he said little about

[1] See Frontispiece.

it, the call of God was as a fire burning within him. The thought of perishing souls in China was ever present. Day and night he pondered the problem of how to prepare for and enter upon his life-work. To his youth and inexperience no answer seemed forthcoming ; yet how hard it was to wait in patience, to wait for God alone. In the main he did, as before leaving Barnsley, rest in the Lord and count upon His working. Yet the quiet Surgery witnessed many an hour of anxious thought as well as many an hour of prayer, and all through that summer and autumn there was a good deal of unnecessary exercise of heart.

Perhaps also there was another reason for those months of trouble and unrest, just as another fire was consuming within him not a little spiritual strength. For he was out of harmony with God in the matter of his deepest affections, that inner citadel of being so often the last stronghold yielded to His control. Unconsciously it may be he was holding something back—something, the best thing in his manhood—not recognising that in that realm also " every thought" must be brought into subjection to " the obedience of Christ." He was giving far too much of himself to the one who had come as a bright, beautiful vision into his life a year and a half before. It was one thing, he discovered, to think of her in Barnsley out of reach, and quite another in Hull, where any day they might meet. His love was growing too strong for him, quickened by hopeful indications of its being returned on her part.

And yet he had begun to feel instinctively that her life was not fully yielded to God. Though there was no engagement between them they understood one another without words, and he could not but be conscious that her influence was all against a future she was unwilling to face.

" Must you go to China ? " she questioned at times, her tone clearly implying, " How much nicer it would be to stay and serve the Lord at home ! "

Fervently he prayed that she might come to feel as he did ; for nothing, not even the loss of her love, could alter his call from God. But how could he go forward at such a cost ? How face the anguish of losing her just when it seemed she might be won ?   Oh the struggle of those autumn days when he could no longer escape the fear that their paths must lie apart !   Older people may pass on, perhaps, with little perception of what such a situation means ; but young hearts understand, and there is one infinite Heart that is always young, always touched with the feeling of our griefs.   That Friend did not fail Hudson Taylor.

And so it came to pass that helpful experiences found their way into his life at this time.   He was strengthened by association with fellow believers who were able to lead him into a deeper knowledge of God ; he was encouraged in work for others, simple efforts to help the poor and suffering and to win the most degraded to a new life in Christ ; and the way opened, strange to say, for a visit to London, just when the first International Exhibition was attracting thousands to the far-famed Crystal Palace : all providential happenings, no doubt, in view of the trial through which he had yet to pass.

It was no small mercy, for example, that led him during this sojourn in Hull into fellowship with a company of Christians exceptionally fitted to meet his need.   Shortly before leaving home he had for conscientious reasons resigned his connection with the denomination in which he had been brought up.   During the progress of a widespread Reform Movement he and his parents had felt obliged to side with the minority, at no little sacrifice of personal interests.   This had led Hudson to the study of Church history and government, and opened his eyes to the limitations of all human systems, even the best.   He had followed his parents in joining " the Reformers," afterwards known as the Methodist Free Church, but personally had begun to feel himself something more than a Wesleyan, bound by more important ties to all who love the Lord Jesus Christ in sincerity and truth.   While still in Barnsley he had enjoyed the meetings of the so-called Plymouth Brethren, ministered to by Mr. William Neatby, and now in Hull was glad to renew associations that had already proved helpful.

The Hull Meeting at that time was a strong, united body, profiting greatly from the ministry of Mr. Jukes, a man of culture and spiritual illumination.[1] Their quiet gatherings on Sunday morning were specially suited to help young Hudson Taylor. He was hungry for the Word of God, and their preaching was for the most part a thoughtful exposition of its truths. He needed a fresh vision of eternal things, and the presence of Christ was often so real on these occasions that it was like heaven on earth to be among them. He was facing a difficult future, and they set before him an example of faith in temporal as well as spiritual things that surpassed his utmost thought. For this meeting was in close touch with George Müller of Bristol, whose work was even then assuming remarkable proportions. He had already hundreds of orphan children under his care, and was looking to the Lord for means to support a thousand. But this did not exhaust his sympathies. With a deep conviction that these are the days in which the Gospel must be preached " for a witness unto all nations," he sustained in whole or part many missionaries, and was engaged in circulating the Scriptures far and wide in Roman Catholic as well as heathen lands. All this extensive work, carried on by a penniless man through faith in God alone, with no appeals for help or guarantee of stated income, was a wonderful testimony to the power of " effectual, fervent prayer." As such it made a profound impression upon Hudson Taylor, and encouraged him more than anything else could have in the pathway he was about to enter.

And then his work helped him, not only the daily round of duties in the Surgery but the service he had undertaken in addition for the Lord. A little to the west of Dr. Hardey's stood the Royal Infirmary, the largest hospital in the city, about which lay a network of squalid streets culminating in the Irish quarter. Here drinking saloons and tramps' lodging-houses abounded, and the police hardly ventured to appear in less force than three or four at a time. Riots and drunken brawls were of frequent occurrence, and nothing was more common than for the priest to be called in to thrash his tipsy parishioners. Garden Street, one of the

[1] The Rev. Andrew Jukes, previously a clergyman of the Church of England, did not hold in those days, or at any rate did not teach, the views with which his name was afterwards connected.

I

larger thoroughfares through this district, and West and Middle Streets close to the Infirmary seemed specially the haunts of misery and vice.   It required courage, as Hudson Taylor found, to go among that bigoted population as a preacher of the Gospel, but a little knowledge of medicine with a great deal of love and prayer opened the way and gave access to many a heart.

" The people seemed pleased to see us," he wrote of one sultry evening in July, " and received the tracts willingly. We went to several lodging-houses.   In one, Kester read the story of the Prodigal Son and said a little about it, and in another I read the fifty-fifth chapter of Isaiah.   People kept dropping in until we had forty or fifty listeners. I spoke a little and so did Kester.   Last Sunday I went again and felt very happy."

" I think it is very difficult," he continued in a later letter, " to set our affections wholly on things above. I try to be a ' living epistle ' of the Lord's, but when I look within I wonder many a time He does not cast me off. I seek to subdue my will, to blend it with His, and say and feel in all things ' Thy will be done.' But even while I try, I can scarcely keep back the tears. For I seem to have an impression that I shall lose my Dear One, and God only knows the struggle it is to say, ' Nevertheless, not my will but Thine be done.'

" Do you think I should be justified in going to London shortly ? If it were only for pleasure, I could decide at once ; for much as I should like to go, my pleasures must not stand in the way of duty. But sometimes I think that Lobscheid might give me information worth going for.   I shall be glad to hear from you and have your advice."

That idea about going to London certainly came at the right time. The German missionary Lobscheid, to whom he referred, had recently returned from China and was one of the few people who could speak from experience of the practicability of missionary work away from the Treaty Ports. Possessing some medical knowledge he had been enabled to travel repeatedly in what was then considered " the interior," a populous district on the mainland, north of Hong-kong ; and now that he was for a short time in England Hudson Taylor was anxious to profit from his advice.

His parents approving the idea, and Dr. Hardey giving him a week's holiday, he decided to take advantage of a special train running up to the Exhibition, and (at his

AMELIA HUDSON TAYLOR, AFTERWARDS MRS. BENJAMIN BROOMHALL.

The sister next in age to Mr. Taylor and closely associated with his life-work.

To face page 115.

expense) it was arranged that his sister should accompany him. This seemed almost too good to be true, until they were actually speeding southward in the express bearing hundreds of excursionists to London. Never had they visited the great Metropolis before, and he was just as eager to meet Mr. Pearse and the missionary from China as she was to explore the wonders of the Crystal Palace. An artist uncle arranged accommodation for them in his Soho lodgings, and proved a delightful cicerone for his niece when Hudson was otherwise occupied.

That was a memorable time in London, from the moment they caught sight of its lights shining like stars in the distance to the journey home together when they lived it all over again.

Amelia remembered best, perhaps, the glittering Palace as it broke upon their sight from Piccadilly, the sun shining on its crystal dome amid the greenery of Hyde Park. It was her sixteenth birthday, and Hudson was free to spend it with her, which made their happiness complete. Together they went to the Exhibition and wandered among the ferns and flowers in which its fairy-like scenes were set. They lunched at a restaurant in proper style, investing in a pine-apple, a rare luxury in those days. Then they traversed the gay, crowded city to the Bank of England, where a rendezvous had been arranged with Mr. Pearse.

A busy member of the Stock Exchange as well as Secretary of the Chinese Evangelisation Society, Mr. Pearse had not much time for visitors in office hours. He was glad, however, to meet his correspondent from Barnsley, and as he talked with the bright earnest lad whose face bore unmistakable testimony to the spirit within, and the little sister as modest and lovely in appearance as she was in heart, interest soon deepened to a warmer feeling. Tottenham—yes, he must take them to Tottenham and the Brook Street meeting. There they would be sure to find a welcome and a real spirit of prayer on behalf of China. So to Tottenham they went with him the following Sunday.

And this to Hudson at any rate was the most delightful of all their experiences. For the Tottenham friends, once seen, could never be forgotten. He was familiar already with the names of John Eliot Howard and his brother Robert Howard of Bruce Grove, who since the visit of Dr. Gutzlaff to England had been on the Committee of the C.E.S. He knew from *The Gleaner* also of the activity of the ladies in their Auxiliary Society, and that they were considerable donors to the work. But how little could he have anticipated the charm and culture, the gracious spirit and generous hospitality of their homes!

If anywhere on earth ideal Christian families were to be found in surroundings as nearly perfect as wealth and refinement could make them, it was in the pleasant suburb of Tottenham in those days. Not that there was lavish expenditure on luxury, for they came of a Quaker stock with simple tastes and habits; but the beauty of the inward life imparted to it all a something money could not buy. About the parents, still young or in the prime of life, large families were growing up, trained in an atmosphere of Christian courtesy. All was cheerful, orderly, unostentatious. Home-like rooms, beautifully furnished, opened on lawns shaded by spreading cedars. Friends from far and near gathered around the ample board, where quiet talk flowed freely on the deepest interests of the Kingdom of God. And best of all, the love of Christ possessed and permeated everything.

The Brook Street meeting that gathered these families on Sunday was also exceptional in its ministry and spirit. Many well-known Brethren were among the speakers in those days, including the heads of the Howard family, men greatly beloved for their works' sake. What it must have been to Hudson Taylor to be welcomed in such a circle, words are poor to express. It was a new world to him then, full of help and inspiration, but a world of which he was to become a part. For the friendships begun that day endured throughout a lifetime, strengthening his hands in God until his work on earth was done.

"I love Tottenham," he wrote from China a few years later. "I love those I know there dearly. Of no other place can I say that my every recollection is sweet and profitable, marred by no painful thought or circumstance, save that I see it no more."

And the Tottenham friends on their part, what did they think of him ?   They saw a simple, Yorkshire lad quiet and unassuming.   Introduced by their friend Mr. Pearse as an intending missionary, he was observed more closely than he might otherwise have been, and the conclusions come to by some of the younger people are remembered to this day. He did not fit in exactly with their idea of a missionary, for he looked young and delicate and was evidently full of fun.   But they liked him none the less for that, and felt his earnestness and absorbing interest in China.   In a word, he won their confidence just as his little sister won their hearts.   These also were conclusions confirmed in the case of parents as well as children by lifelong fellowship in service for the Lord.

With the missionary they had come so far to see, their intercourse seems to have been less encouraging.   He too must have visited Bruce Grove that day, for one still living in the dear old home recalls a conversation that took place. Mr. Lobscheid, besides being bright and forceful, was full of information about his field.   He may have been superficial in matters of judgment, and at any rate formed no favourable impression of the north-country lad who asked so many questions.

" Why, you would never do for China," he exclaimed at length, drawing attention to his fair hair and grey-blue eyes. " They call *me* ' Red-haired Devil,' and would run from you in terror !   You could never get them to listen at all."

" And yet," replied Hudson Taylor quietly, " it is God who has called me, and He knows all about the colour of my hair and eyes."

It was during this visit to London, as Hudson long remembered, that he gained his first impression of the Society of Friends.   Passing Devonshire House in the City, he was struck by the calm and gracious bearing of both men and women as they passed out from " Yearly Meeting," in their old-time Quaker dress.   Could they be really denizens of this lower sphere ?   The ladies especially, in snowy kerchiefs, with silk or satin gowns, perfect in their simplicity, looked to him like " the Host of the Shining Ones " coming to

welcome the pilgrim of Bunyan's immortal dream.   Later
on he found that the Howards of Tottenham had been
brought up as Friends, and learned from their beautiful
lives the value of much that is distinctively " Friendly "
in thought and spirit.

Refreshed and encouraged by these experiences, Hudson
Taylor resumed his duties with Dr. Hardey at the end of
September, and shortly after this it was that the nest began
to be stirred up about him.   He was again settled in the
home of his relatives on Kingston Square, where every want
was anticipated and pleasant companionship afforded out
of working hours.   The neighbourhood was one of the nicest
in Hull, and as far as circumstances were concerned nothing
could have been more desirable.   But this was not all His
love had planned who was moulding this young life in view
of China.   Already, through discipline of heart, the lad was
learning lessons of patience and submission to the will of
God.   But something more was needed, something even of
outward trial to prepare him for the life-work that was to
be.   Away in an unfrequented suburb that little home was
waiting—a single room in which he could be alone as never
before, alone with God.   The steps by which he was led to it
were very simple, beginning, as he himself records, with a
conscientious difficulty about remaining where he was.

" Before leaving Barnsley," he wrote, recalling this experience,
" my attention was drawn to the subject of setting apart the first-
fruits of all one's increase and a certain proportion of one's possessions
for the service of the Lord.   It seemed to me desirable to study the
question Bible in hand before one went from home and was placed in
circumstances that might bias one's conclusions by the pressure of
definite wants and cares.   In this way I was led to the determination
to set apart not less than one-tenth of whatever moneys I might earn
or become possessed of, for the Lord.

" The salary I received as medical assistant in Hull would have
allowed me to do this without difficulty, but owing to changes in the
family of my kind friend and employer it was necessary for me to reside
out of doors.   Comfortable quarters were secured with a relative, and
in addition to the sum I had previously received, the exact amount
was allowed me that I had to pay for board and lodging.

" Now arose in my mind the reflection, ' Ought not this also to be

Photographs by   *F. Howard Taylor.*

KINGSTON SQUARE AND "DRAINSIDE."

1. The home of Mrs. Richard Hardey— first house on the right.
2. Mrs. Finch's cottage—last on the left. The room Mr. Taylor occupied is to the left of the front door.

To face page 119.

tithed ? ' It was surely a part of my income, and had it been a question of government income tax would certainly not have been excluded. But to take a tithe from the whole would have left me insufficient for other purposes, and for a time I was embarrassed to know what to do.

"After much thought and prayer, I was led to leave the comfortable home and pleasant circle in which I resided, and engage a little lodging in the suburbs, a sitting-room and bedroom in one, undertaking to board myself. I was thus enabled to tithe the whole of my income ; and while one felt the change a good deal, it was attended with no small blessing. More time was given in my solitude to the study of the Word of God, to visiting the poor and to evangelistic work on Sunday evenings than would otherwise have been the case. Brought into contact in this way with many who were in distress, I soon saw the privilege of still further economising, and found it possible to give away much more than I had at first intended."

It all reads so simply and naturally that one can hardly imagine any special sacrifice to have been involved. Let us hunt up this " sitting-room and bedroom in one," however, and find out what were in actual fact the surroundings for which he had given up his home on Kingston Square. The change could scarcely have been more complete.

" Drainside," as the neighbourhood was termed, could not under any circumstances have been considered inviting. It consisted of a double row of workmen's cottages facing each other across a narrow canal, connecting the country district of Cottingham with the docks and estuary of the Humber. The canal was nothing but a deep ditch into which Drainside people were in the habit of casting their rubbish, to be carried away in part whenever the tide rose high enough. It was separated from the town by desolate spaces of building-land, across which ran a few ill-lighted streets ending in makeshift wooden bridges. The cottages, like peas in a pod, were all the same size and shape down both sides of the long row. They followed the windings of the Drain for half a mile or more, each one having a door and two windows, one above the other. The door opened straight into the kitchen, and a steep stairway led to the room above. A very few were double cottages with a window to right and left of the door and two rooms overhead.

On the city side of the canal, one of these larger dwellings stood at a corner opposite The Founder's Arms, a countrified public-house whose lights were useful as a landmark on dark nights, shining across the mud and water of the Drain. The cottage, known as 30 Cottingham Terrace, was tenanted by the family of a seafaring man, whose visits home were few and far between. Mrs. Finch and her children occupied the kitchen and upper part of the house, and the downstairs room on the left as one entered was let at a rental of three shillings a week. It was too high a charge, seeing the whole house went for little more. But the lodger in whom we are interested did not grudge it, especially when he found how much it meant to the good woman whose remittances from her husband came none too regularly.

Mrs. Finch was a true Christian and delighted to have " the young Doctor " under her roof. She did her best no doubt to make the little chamber clean and comfortable, polishing the fireplace opposite the window and making up the bed in the corner farthest from the door. A plain deal table and a chair or two completed the appointments. The whole room was less than twelve feet square and did not need much furniture. It was on a level with the ground and opened familiarly out of the kitchen. From the window one looked across the narrowest strip of " garden " to the Drain beyond, whose mud banks afforded a playground for the children of the neighbourhood.

Whatever it may have been in summer, toward the close of November, when Hudson Taylor made it his home, Drainside must have seemed dreary enough, and the cottage far from attractive. To add to the discomforts of the situation, he was " boarding himself," which meant that he lived upon next to nothing, bought his meagre supplies as he returned from the Surgery, and rarely sat down, with or without a companion, to a proper meal. His walks were solitary across the waste, unlighted region on the outskirts of the town ; his evenings solitary beside the little fire in his otherwise cheerless room ; and his Sundays were spent alone, but for the morning meeting and long hours of work in his district or among the crowds that frequented the Humber Dock.

And more than this, he was at close quarters with poverty and suffering. Visiting in such neighbourhoods he had been accustomed to for a few hours at a time, but this was very different. It belonged to him now in a new way, and outwardly at any rate he belonged to it. He had cast in his lot with those who needed him, and needed all the help and comfort he could bring. This gave new purpose to his life and taught him some of its most precious lessons.

" Having now the twofold object in view," he wrote, " of accustoming myself to endure hardness, and of economising in order to be able more largely to assist those amongst whom I spent a good deal of time labouring in the Gospel, I soon found that I could live upon very much less than I had previously thought possible. Butter, milk and other luxuries I ceased to use, and found that by living mainly on oatmeal and rice, with occasional variations, a very small sum was sufficient for my needs. In this way I had more than two-thirds of my income available for other purposes, and my experience was that the less I spent on myself and the more I gave to others the fuller of happiness and blessing did my soul become."

For the Lord is no man's debtor ; and here in his solitude Hudson Taylor was learning something of what He can be to the soul that leaves all for Him. In these days of easygoing Christianity is it not well to remind ourselves that it really does cost—to be a man or woman God can use ? One cannot obtain a Christ-like character for nothing ; one cannot do a Christ-like work save at great price. And is there not a sense in which even Christ Himself is to be *won* ? It is easy to pray a little, help a little, love a little ; but the missionary apostle meant more than this when he said :

What things were gain to me, those I counted loss for Christ. Yea doubtless, and I count all things but loss for the excellency of the knowledge of Christ Jesus my Lord : for whom I have suffered the loss of all things, and do count them but refuse, *that I may win Christ*, and be found in Him : . . . That I may know Him, and the power of His resurrection, and the fellowship of His sufferings, being made conformable unto His death ; if by any means I might attain unto the out-resurrection from among the dead : . . . If I may apprehend that for which also I am apprehended of Christ Jesus.[1]

Much prayer, as we have seen, was going up for China,

[1] Phil iii. 7-12.

and countless hearts were stirred more or less deeply for
its evangelisation. But when disappointment came and
unexpected failure the great majority ceased to help or care.
Prayer meetings dwindled to nothing, would-be missionaries
turned aside to other callings, and contributions dropped
off to such an extent that more than one society in aid of
the work actually ceased to exist. But here and there in
His own training-schools were those the Lord could count
upon : little and weak perhaps, unknown and unimportant,
but willing to go all lengths in carrying out His purposes,
ready through His grace to meet the conditions and pay
the price.

Here in his quiet lodging at Drainside was such a man.
With all his youth and limitations, Hudson Taylor desired
supremely a Christ-like character and life. As test came
after test that might have been avoided he chose the pathway of self-emptying and the cross, not from any idea of
merit in so doing, but simply because he was led by the
Spirit of God. Thus he was in an attitude that did not
hinder blessing.

Behold, I have set before thee an open door, and no man can shut
it : for thou hast a little strength, and hast kept My word, and hast
not denied My name.
A great door and effectual . . . and there are many adversaries.[1]

Adversaries there certainly were to oppose Hudson
Taylor's progress at this time. He was entering upon one of
the most fruitful periods of his life, rich in blessing for himself and others. Is it any wonder that the tempter was at
hand ? He was alone, hungry for love and sympathy,
living a life of self-denial hard for a lad to bear. It was just
the opportunity for the devil, and he was permitted for a
while to do his worst, that even that might be overruled
for good.

For it was just at this juncture, when he had been a few
weeks at Drainside and was feeling his position keenly,
that the dreaded blow fell, and the one he loved most in all
the world seemed lost to him for ever. For two long years

----

[1] Rev. iii. 8; 1 Cor. xvi. 9.

he had hoped and waited. The very uncertainty of the future had made him long the more for her presence, her companionship through all changes. But now the dream was over; and how bitter the awakening! Seeing that nothing could dissuade her friend from his missionary purpose, the young music-teacher made it plain at last that she was not prepared to go to China. Her father would not hear of it, nor did she feel herself fitted for such a life. This could mean but one thing, though the heart that loved her best was well-nigh broken.

It was not only an overwhelming sorrow, it was a tremendous test of faith. The tempter, naturally, did everything in his power to call in question the love and faithfulness of God. Only break down his trust, make him give up the struggle now, and the usefulness of all his after-life would be marred.

Sunday morning came, December 14. It was cold and cheerless in the little room at Drainside. The lad was benumbed with sorrow, for instead of turning to the Lord for comfort he kept it to himself and nursed his grief. He did not want to pray. The trouble had come in between his soul and God. He could not, would not go as usual to the morning meeting. He was too full of bitter questionings and pain. Then came the cruel, insidious suggestion:

" Is it all worth while ? Why should you go to China ? Why toil and suffer all your life for an ideal of duty ? Give it up now, while you can yet win her. Earn a proper living like everybody else, and serve the Lord at home. For you can win her yet."

Love pleaded hard. It was a moment of wavering and peril. The enemy came in like a flood. But enough ! The Spirit of the Lord lifted up a standard against him.

"Alone in the Surgery," he wrote the following day,[1] " I had a melting season. I was thoroughly softened and humbled and had a wonderful manifestation of the love of God. ' A broken and a contrite heart ' He did not despise, but answered my cry for blessing in very deed and truth. May He keep me softened, and thoroughly impress on me the seal of His own nature. I see this to be my privilege. Oh

---

[1] A letter to his mother, dated December 15, 1851

may I be filled with His Spirit, and grow in grace until I reach ' the measure of the stature of the fulness of Christ.'

" I am happy · not without trial, anxiety or care ; but by the grace of God I no longer bear it all myself. ' The Lord gave, and the Lord hath taken away.' . . .

> We will praise Him for all that is past,
> And trust Him for all that's to come.

" Trusting God does not deprive one of feeling or deaden our natural sensibilities, but it enables us to compare our trials with our mercies and to say, ' Yet, notwithstanding, I will rejoice in the Lord, I will joy in the God of my salvation.' It enables us to see . . . the Refiner watching the fire, and be thankful.

" ' Our fathers trusted in Thee . . . and Thou didst deliver them.' In Thee, O God, put I my trust."

To his sister he opened his heart more freely. It is to be regretted that the earlier part of the letter has not been preserved. It is dated December 16, 1851, and begins *in medias res* :

For some days I was as wretched as heart could wish. It seemed as if I had no power in prayer nor relish for it ; and instead of throwing my care on Him I kept it all to myself until I could endure it no longer.

Well, on Sunday I felt no desire to go to the Meeting and was tempted very much. Satan seemed to come in as a flood and I was forced to cry: " Save, Lord ; I perish." Still Satan suggested, " You never used to be tried as you have been lately. You cannot be in the right path, or God would help and bless you more," and so on, until I felt inclined to give it all up.

But, thank God, the way of duty is the way of safety. I went to the Meeting after all, as miserable as could be ; but did not come away so. One hymn quite cut me to the heart. I was thankful that prayer followed, for I could not keep back my tears. But the load was lighter.

In the afternoon as I was sitting alone in the Surgery I began to reflect on the love of God ; His goodness and my return ; the number of blessings He has granted me ; and how small my trials are compared with those some are called to endure. He thoroughly softened and humbled me. His love melted my icy, frost-bound soul, and sincerely did I pray for pardon for my ungrateful conduct.

Yes, He has humbled me and shown me what I was, revealing Himself as a present, a very present help in time of trouble. And though He does not deprive me of feeling in my trial, He enables me to sing, " Yet I will rejoice in the Lord, I will joy in the God of my salvation'' Thus I do rejoice by His Grace, and will rejoice, and praise Him while He lends me breath .

> And when my voice is lost in death,
> Praise shall employ my nobler powers .
> My days of praise shall ne'er be past,
> While life, and thought, and being last,
>   Or immortality endures.

Now I am happy in my Saviour's love. I can thank Him for *all*, even the most painful experiences of the past, and trust Him without fear for all that is to come.

CHAPTER X

FROM FAITH TO FAITH

JANUARY–MARCH 1852. AET. 19.

" I NEVER made a sacrifice," said Hudson Taylor in later years, looking back over a life in which to an unusual extent this element predominated. But what he said was true. For as in the case in point, the first great sacrifice he was privileged to make for China, the compensations that followed were so real and lasting that he came to see that giving up is inevitably receiving when one is dealing heart to heart with God.

It was so, very manifestly, this winter. In the hour of trial, a step of faith had been taken and a victory won that made it possible for the Holy Spirit to lead him on. Not outwardly only but inwardly he had accepted the will of God, giving up what seemed his best and highest, the love that had become part of his very life, that he might be unhindered in serving and following Christ. The sacrifice was great, but the reward far greater.

" Unspeakable joy," he tells us, " all day long and every day was my happy experience. God, even my God, was a living, bright Reality, and all I had to do was joyful service."

A new tone is perceptible about his letters, which are less introspective from this time onward and more full of missionary purpose. China comes to the front again in all his thinking, and there is a quickened longing for likeness to Christ and unbroken fellowship with Him. Jesus

Himself was filling the empty place and drawing His servant on to deeper love and closer following.

"I feel my need of more holiness," he wrote to his sister early in the New Year, "and conformity to Him who has loved us and washed us in His blood. Love so amazing should indeed cause us to give our bodies and spirits to Him as living sacrifices. . . . Oh, I wish I were ready! I long to be engaged in the work. Pray for me, that I may be made more useful here and fitted for extended usefulness hereafter."

And again a few weeks later ·

I almost wish I had a hundred bodies. They should all be devoted to my Saviour in the missionary cause. But this is foolishness. I have almost more than I can do to manage one, it is so self-willed, earthly-minded, fleshly. Constantly I am grieving my dear Saviour who shed for me His precious blood, forgetting Him who never has relaxed His watchful care and protection over me from the earliest moment of my existence. I am astonished at the littleness of my gratitude and love to Him, and confounded by His long-suffering mercy. Pray for me that I may live more and more to His praise, be more devoted to Him, incessant in labours in His cause, fitted for China, ripened for glory.

But though he was happy and full of blessing, his mother at home was not a little troubled. She had a good idea by this time of his surroundings at Drainside, and read between the lines of his own cheery letters. It distressed her to think of what seemed unnecessary privations, especially when she learned from others that he was looking pale and thin.

"I am sorry you make yourself anxious about me," he wrote in January. "I think it is because I have begun to wear a larger coat that everybody says, 'How poorly and thin you look!' However, as you want to know everything, I have had a heavy cold . . . that lasted a week. But since then I have been as well as ever in my life. I eat like a horse, sleep like a top and have the spirits of a lark. I do not know that I have any anxiety save to be more holy and useful.

"I was in Garden Street on Sunday. We seemed welcome and were heard with great attention. When there, it would save me ten or fifteen minutes' walk if I came home by Drainside.[1] But I always go round at night, though ever so tired, because you wish it. So I am sure you need not be concerned about me. As to my health, I think

---

[1] Along the little canal, in the dark.

sometimes I have too much; for I have such a flow of spirits! and often have to restrain myself from idle conversation and jokes. ' In the multitude of words there wanteth not sin.'

" Praise God, I have much to be thankful for. ' The lines have fallen unto me in pleasant places.' Dr. Hardey talks to me more like a friend than an employer. Of course I know how to keep my place. And I can truly say I am thankful for the reading habits you implanted in me that make me more or less independent of companions."

But the one he sought to comfort was far from satisfied. He was well apparently for the moment, and happy in the Lord, but if this were the line he was taking up what would it mean for the future ? Yes, the future—that was the trouble. In the light of present privations she saw with painful clearness all that life in China might bring. And he was her only son.

Ah, that shrinking of mother-hearts ! God only who made us fully understands. " He that spared not His own Son, but delivered Him up for us all," how shall He not fathom the depth of even that anguish. Yes, He has borne it too. God Himself suffered most for a sinning, sorrowing world, and He does not forget. He knows all it costs to give up home and loved ones and go alone to earth's dark places to lay down life itself, it may be, in seeking souls for whom the Saviour died. And He knows too the sacrifice of those who cannot go, but send their dearest—life of their life, soul of their soul—and with bleeding, thankful hearts look up into His face saying, and saying truly, " I have nothing too precious for Jesus."

HE did not blame this mother that for a moment she seemed to waver. It is only " through the Eternal Spirit " such sacrifices can ever be unreservedly offered. And for the passing hesitation we may well be thankful, seeing it called forth the following, that might not otherwise have been written :

Do not let anything unsettle you, dear Mother. Missionary work is indeed the noblest mortals can engage in, and angels would be proud, if I may use such an expression, if they could be permitted to share so glorious an undertaking. We certainly cannot be insensible to the ties of nature, but should we not rejoice when we have anything we can give up for the Saviour ? You would be far more unsettled if I were to turn away from this work, and if the Lord were to withdraw His restraining grace and I fell into sin in consequence, would you not ? It is all of His mercy that I am preserved from many of the pitfalls that ensnare other young men.

As to my health, I think I never was so well and hearty in my life. The winds here are extremely searching, but as I always wrap up well I am pretty secure. . . . The cold weather gives me a good appetite, and it would be dear economy to stint myself. So I take as much plain, substantial food as I need, but waste nothing on luxuries. In going to my lodgings I have somehow got into one particular route, and always go the same way and cross at the same place. I have never passed the gate once, and at night the reflection of the lamps and windows opposite are always shining on the Drain.

I have found some brown biscuits which are really as cheap as bread, eighteen pence a stone, and much nicer. For breakfast I have biscuit and herring, which is cheaper than butter (three for a penny, and half a one is enough) with coffee. For dinner I have at present a prune-and-apple pie. Prunes are two or three pence a pound and apples tenpence a peck. I use no sugar but loaf, which I powder, and at fourpence halfpenny a pound I find it is cheaper than the coarser kind. Sometimes I have roast potatoes and tongue, which is as inexpensive as any other meat. For tea I have biscuit and apples. I take no supper, or occasionally a little biscuit and apple. Sometimes I have a rice pudding, a few peas boiled instead of potatoes, and now and then some fish. By being wide awake, I can get cheese at fourpence to sixpence a pound that is better than we often have at home for eightpence. Now I see rhubarb and lettuce in the market, so I shall soon have another change. I pickled a penny red cabbage with three halfpence worth of vinegar, which made me a large jar-full. So you see, at little expense I enjoy many comforts. To these add a home where every want is anticipated ,and " the peace of God which passeth all understanding," and if I were not happy and contented I should deserve to be miserable.

I am enlarging on these trifles, though they are not worth writing about, because I know they will interest you and perhaps help you to feel more settled about me. If not, please tell me and I will not do so any more. . . .

Continue to pray for me, dear Mother. Though comfortable as regards temporal matters, and happy and thankful, I feel I need your prayers. . . . Oh Mother, I cannot tell you, I cannot describe how I long to be a missionary ; to carry the Glad Tidings to poor, perishing sinners; to spend and be spent for Him who died for me. I feel as if for this I could give up everything, every idol, however dear.

Think, Mother, of twelve millions—a number so great that it is

K

impossible to realise it—yes, twelve million souls in China, every year, passing without God and without hope into eternity. Oh, what need for earnestness in the Church and in individual believers ! Do we not deserve, by our worldly-mindedness, our indolence, our apathy, our ingratitude and disobedience to the Divine command, " Go teach all nations," do we not deserve to experience little of the love of God and the peace of Christianity ?

Oh, it is a noble, an honourable calling ! I feel my utter unworthiness and unfitness for it. I want more of the Divine life, more of the Spirit of God to make me a faithful servant and witness. Oh for more grace, love, faith, zeal, holiness !

Please tell Father that I have been going to write to him several times this week to say, If he will only go to China and preach the Gospel, I will work like a slave, and live cheap, and send him twenty-five or thirty pounds a year myself until he gets established. Or if he prefers it I will give up my situation and come home and manage the business for him for five or six years. Tell him the voyage would probably lengthen his life. He has a gift for languages. The Rev. William Burns preached his first sermon in Chinese only six months after landing. Does he not think there are plenty of Christians in Barnsley ? But who cares for China ? They are dying, dying, dying, 250,000 every week, without the knowledge of God, of Christ, of salvation. Oh, let us look with compassion on this multitude ! God has been merciful to us : let us be like Him. The cry comes " Help us, Help us ! Will no man care for our souls ? " Can we refuse ?

> Shall we whose souls are lighted
> With wisdom from on high ;
> Shall we to men benighted
> The lamp of Life deny ?

I must conclude. Would you not give up *all* for Jesus who died for you ? Yes, Mother, I know you would. God be with you and comfort you.

Must I leave as soon as I can save money enough to go ? I feel as if I could not live, if something is not done for China.

What a glimpse is here afforded into his deeper life during that winter at Drainside ! " I cannot tell, I cannot describe how I long to be a missionary, to carry the Glad Tidings to poor, perishing sinners. . . . For this I could give up everything, every idol, however dear . . . *I feel as if I could not live if something is not done for China.*"

This was no mere emotion, no superficial interest that might give place to considerations of personal advantage.

It was not that he had taken up missionary work as a congenial branch of Christian activity, but that the need of the perishing in heathen lands, the need and longing of the heart of Christ—" them also *I must bring* "—had gripped him and held him fast. He believed that the heathen are perishing, and that without a knowledge of the one and only Saviour they must be eternally lost. He believed that it was in view of *this*, and because of His infinite love, that God had given " His only-begotten Son that whosoever believeth in Him should *not* perish, but have everlasting life." And these convictions pledged him to the only life possible in view of such stupendous facts—a life wholly given to making that great redemption known, especially to those who had never heard.

Yet much as he longed to go, and go at once, there were considerations that held him back.

" To me it was a very grave matter," he wrote of that winter, " to contemplate going out to China, far from all human aid, there to depend upon the living God alone for protection, supplies, and help of every kind. I felt that one's spiritual muscles required strengthening for such an undertaking. There was no doubt that if faith did not fail, God would not fail. But what if one's faith should prove insufficient ? I had not at that time learned that even ' if we believe not, yet He abideth faithful, He cannot deny Himself.' It was consequently a very serious question to my mind, not whether He was faithful, but whether I had strong enough faith to warrant my embarking in the enterprise set before me.

" ' When I get out to China,' I thought to myself, ' I shall have no claim on any one for anything. My only claim will be on God. How important to learn, before leaving England, to move man through God by prayer alone.' "

He knew that faith was the one power that could remove mountains, conquer every difficulty and accomplish the impossible. But had he the right kind of faith ? Could he stand alone in China ? Much as he longed to be a missionary, would such faith as he possessed be sufficient to carry him through all that must be faced ? What had it carried him through already, here at home ?

He thankfully realised that faith, the faith he longed for, was a " gift of God," and that it might " grow exceedingly." But for growth, exercise was needed, and exercise of faith was obviously impossible apart from trial. Then welcome trial, welcome anything that would increase and strengthen this precious gift, proving to his own heart at any rate that he had faith of the sort that would really stand and grow.

And here it should be remembered that in taking this attitude before the Lord, Hudson Taylor was wholly earnest and sincere. He was bringing " all the tithes into the storehouse," a most important consideration ; living a life that made it possible for him to exercise faith to which God could respond in blessing. In a word, there was no hindrance in himself to the answer to his prayers ; and experiences followed that have been made an encouragement to thousands the wide world over.

The story though well known will bear repeating here, illustrating as it does the only principle of growth in spiritual things—" From faith to faith " ; the law reiterated by our Lord Himself—" He that hath, to him shall be given."

" To learn before leaving England to move man through God by prayer alone," this and nothing less was the object Hudson Taylor had before him now, and it was not long before he came to see a simple, natural way of practising this lesson.

At Hull my kind employer, always busy, wished me to remind him whenever my salary became due. This I determined not to do directly, but to ask that God would bring the fact to his recollection, and thus encourage me by answering prayer.

At one time as the day drew near for the payment of a quarter's salary I was as usual much in prayer about it. The time arrived, but Dr. Hardey made no allusion to the matter. I continued praying. Days passed on and he did not remember, until at length on settling up my weekly accounts one Saturday night, I found myself possessed of only one remaining coin, a half-crown piece. Still, I had hitherto known no lack, and I continued praying.

That Sunday was a very happy one. As usual my heart was full and brimming over with blessing. After attending Divine Service in the morning, my afternoons and evenings were taken up with Gospel work in the various lodging-houses I was accustomed to visit in the lowest part of the town. At such times it almost seemed to me as if heaven were begun below, and that all that could be looked for was an enlargement of one's capacity for joy, not a truer filling than I possessed.

After concluding my last service about ten o'clock that night, a poor man asked me to go and pray with his wife, saying that she was dying. I readily agreed, and on the way to his house asked him why he had not sent for the priest, as his accent told me he was an Irishman. He had done so, he said, but the priest refused to come without a payment of eighteen pence which the man did not possess, as the family was starving. Immediately it occurred to my mind that all the money I had in the world was the solitary half-crown, and that it was in one coin; moreover, that while the basin of water-gruel I usually took for supper was awaiting me, and there was sufficient in the house for breakfast in the morning, I certainly had nothing for dinner on the coming day.

Somehow or other there was at once a stoppage in the flow of joy in my heart. But instead of reproving myself I began to reprove the poor man, telling him that it was very wrong to have allowed matters to get into such a state as he described, and that he ought to have applied to the relieving officer. His answer was that he had done so, and was told to come at eleven o'clock the next morning, but that he feared his wife might not live through the night.

" Ah," thought I, " if only I had two shillings and a sixpence instead of this half-crown, how gladly would I give these poor people a shilling ! " But to part with the half-crown was far from my thoughts. I little dreamed that the truth of the matter simply was that I could trust God *plus* one-and-sixpence, but was not prepared to trust Him only, without any money at all in my pocket.

My conductor led me into a court, down which I followed him with some degree of nervousness. I had found myself there before, and at my last visit had been roughly handled. My tracts had been torn to pieces and such a warning given me not to come again that I felt more than a little concerned. Still, it was the path of duty and I followed on. Up a miserable flight of stairs into a wretched room he led me; and oh, what a sight there presented itself ! Four or five children stood about, their sunken cheeks and temples all telling unmistakably the story of slow starvation, and lying on a wretched pallet was a poor, exhausted mother, with a tiny infant thirty-six hours old moaning rather than crying at her side, for it too seemed spent and failing.

" Ah ! " thought I, " if I had two shillings and a sixpence, instead of half-a-crown, how gladly should they have one-and-sixpence of it." But still a wretched unbelief prevented me from obeying the impulse to relieve their distress at the cost of all I possessed.

It will scarcely seem strange that I was unable to say much to comfort these poor people. I needed comfort myself I began to tell them, however, that they must not be cast down ; that though their circumstances were very distressing there was a kind and loving Father in heaven. But something within me cried, " You hypocrite ! telling these unconverted people about a kind and loving Father in heaven, and not prepared yourself to trust Him without a half-a-crown."

I was nearly choked. How gladly would I have compromised with conscience, if I had had a florin and a sixpence ! I would have given the florin thankfully and kept the rest. But I was not yet prepared to trust in God alone, without the sixpence.

To talk was impossible under these circumstances, yet strange to say I thought I should have no difficulty in praying. Prayer was a delightful occupation in those days. Time thus spent never seemed wearisome and I knew no lack of words. I seemed to think that all I should have to do would be to kneel down and pray, and that relief would come to them and to myself together.

" You asked me to come and pray with your wife," I said to the man, " let us pray." And I knelt down.

But no sooner had I opened my lips with " Our Father who art in heaven," than conscience said within, " Dare you mock God ? Dare you kneel down and call Him Father with that half-crown in your pocket ? "

Such a time of conflict then came upon me as I have never experienced before or since. How I got through that form of prayer I know not, and whether the words uttered were connected or disconnected I cannot tell. But I arose from my knees in great distress of mind.

The poor father turned to me and said, " You see what a terrible state we are in, sir. If you can help us, for God's sake do ! "

At that moment the word flashed into my mind, " Give to him that asketh of thee." And in the word of a King there is power.

I put my hand into my pocket and slowly drawing out the half-crown, gave it to the man, telling him that it might seem a small matter for me to relieve them, seeing that I was comparatively well off, but that in parting with that coin I was giving him my all ; what I had been trying to tell them was indeed true—GOD really was a FATHER and might be trusted. The joy all came back in full flood-tide to my heart. I could say anything and feel it then, and the hindrance to blessing was gone—gone, I trust, forever.

Not only was the poor woman's life saved ; but my life, as I fully realised, had been saved too. It might have been a wreck—would have been, probably, as a Christian life—had not grace at that time conquered, and the striving of God's Spirit been obeyed.

I well remember how that night, as I went home to my lodgings, my heart was as light as my pocket. The dark, deserted streets resounded with a hymn of praise that I could not restrain. When I took my basin of gruel before retiring, I would not have exchanged it for a prince's feast. I reminded the Lord as I knelt at my bedside of His own Word, " He that giveth to the poor lendeth to the Lord " ; I asked Him not to let my loan be a long one, or I should have no dinner next day. And with peace within and peace without, I spent a happy, restful night.

Next morning for breakfast my plate of porridge remained, and before it was finished the postman's knock was heard at the door. I was not in the habit of receiving letters on Monday, as my parents and most of my friends refrained from posting on Saturday, so that I was somewhat surprised when the landlady came in holding a letter or packet in her wet hand covered by her apron. I looked at the letter, but could not make out the handwriting. It was either a strange hand or a feigned one, and the postmark was blurred. Where it came from I could not tell. On opening the envelope I found nothing written within ; but inside a sheet of blank paper was folded a pair of kid gloves, from which, as I opened them in astonishment, half-a-sovereign fell to the ground.

"Praise the Lord," I exclaimed. "Four hundred per cent for twelve hours' investment—that is good interest ! How glad the merchants of Hull would be if they could lend their money at such a rate." Then and there I determined that a bank that could not break should have my savings or earnings, as the case might be—a determination I have not yet learned to regret.

I cannot tell you how often my mind has recurred to this incident, or all the help it has been to me in circumstances of difficulty in after-life. If we are faithful to God in little things, we shall gain experience and strength that will be helpful to us in the more serious trials of life.

But this was not the end of the story, nor was it the only answer to prayer that was to confirm his faith at this time. For the chief difficulty still remained. Dr. Hardey had not remembered ; and though prayer was unremitting, other matters appeared entirely to engross his attention. It would have been so easy to remind him. But what then of the lesson upon the acquirement of which Hudson Taylor felt his future usefulness depended—" to move man through God, by prayer alone " ?

" This remarkable and gracious deliverance," he continued, " was a great joy to me as well as a strong confirmation of faith. But of course ten shillings however economically used will not go very far, and it was none the less necessary to continue in prayer, asking that the larger supply which was still due might be remembered and paid.

All my petitions, however, appeared to remain unanswered, and before a fortnight elapsed I found myself pretty much in the same position that I had occupied on the Sunday night already made so memorable. Meanwhile I continued pleading with God more and more earnestly that He would Himself remind Dr. Hardey that my salary was due.

" Of course it was not the want of money that distressed me. That could have been had at any time for the asking. But the question uppermost in my mind was this : ' Can I go to China ? or will my want of faith and power with God prove so serious an obstacle as to preclude my entering upon this much-prized service ? '

" As the week drew to a close I felt exceedingly embarrassed. There was not only myself to consider. On Saturday night a payment would be due to my Christian landlady, which I knew she could not well dispense with. Ought I not, for her sake, to speak about the matter of the salary ? Yet to do so would be, to myself at any rate, the admission that I was not fitted to undertake a missionary enterprise. I gave nearly the whole of Thursday and Friday, all the time not occupied in my necessary employment, to earnest wrestling with God in prayer. But still on Saturday morning I was in the same position as before. And now my earnest cry was for guidance as to whether I should still continue to wait the Father's time. As far as I could judge I received the assurance that to wait His time was best, and that God in some way or other would interpose on my behalf. So I waited, my heart being now at rest and the burden gone.

" About five o'clock that Saturday afternoon, when Dr. Hardey had finished writing his prescriptions, his last circuit for the day being taken, he threw himself back in his arm-chair, as he was wont, and began to speak of the things of God. He was a truly Christian man, and many seasons of happy fellowship we had together. I was busily watching, at the time, a pan in which a decoction was boiling that required a good deal of attention. It was indeed fortunate for me that it was so, for without any obvious connection with what had been going on, all at once he said :

" ' By the by, Taylor, is not your salary due again ? '

" My emotion may be imagined. I had to swallow two or three times before I could answer. With my eye fixed on the pan and my back to the doctor, I told him as quietly as I could that it was overdue some little time. How thankful I felt at that moment ! God surely had heard my prayer and caused him in this time of my great need to remember the salary without any word or suggestion from me. He replied,

" ' Oh, I am so sorry you did not remind me ! You know how busy I am. I wish I had thought of it a little sooner, for only this afternoon

I sent all the money I had to the bank. Otherwise I would pay you at once.'

" It is impossible to describe the revulsion of feeling caused by this unexpected statement. I knew not what to do. Fortunately for me the pan boiled up and I had a good reason for rushing with it from the room. Glad indeed I was to get away and keep out of sight until after Dr. Hardey had returned to his house, and most thankful that he had not perceived my emotion.

" As soon as he was gone I had to seek my little sanctum and pour out my heart before the Lord for some time before calmness, and more than calmness, thankfulness and joy were restored. I felt that God had His own way, and was not going to fail me. I had sought to know His will early in the day, and as far as I could judge had received guidance to wait patiently. And now God was going to work for me in some other way.

" That evening was spent, as my Saturday evenings usually were, in reading the Word and preparing the subject on which I expected to speak in the various lodging-houses on the morrow. I waited perhaps a little longer than usual. At last about ten o'clock, there being no interruption of any kind, I put on my overcoat and was preparing to leave for home, rather thankful to know that by that time I should have to let myself in with the latchkey, as my landlady retired early. There was certainly no help for that night. But perhaps God would interpose for me by Monday, and I might be able to pay my landlady early in the week the money I would have given her before had it been possible.

" Just as I was about to turn down the gas, I heard the doctor's step in the garden that lay between the dwelling-house and Surgery. He was laughing to himself very heartily, as though greatly amused. Entering the Surgery he asked for the ledger, and told me that, strange to say, one of his richest patients had just come to pay his doctor's bill. Was it not an odd thing to do? It never struck me that it might have any bearing on my own case, or I might have felt embarrassed. But looking at it simply from the position of an uninterested spectator, I also was highly amused that a man rolling in wealth should come after ten o'clock at night to pay a bill which he could any day have met by a cheque with the greatest ease. It appeared that somehow or other he could not rest with this on his mind, and had been constrained to come at that unusual hour to discharge his liability.

" The account was duly receipted in the ledger, and Dr. Hardey was about to leave, when suddenly he turned and handing me some of the banknotes just received, said to my surprise and thankfulness :

" ' By the way, Taylor, you might as well take these notes. I have no change, but can give you the balance next week.'

" Again I was left, my feelings undiscovered, to go back to my little closet and praise the Lord with a joyful heart that after all *I might go to China.* To me this incident was not a trivial one ; and to recall it sometimes, in circumstances of great difficulty, in China or elsewhere, has proved no small comfort and strength."

CHAPTER XI

IF IT BE THOU, BID ME COME

MARCH–SEPTEMBER 1852.   AET. 19–20.

IT is perhaps hardly to be wondered at that in the light of these experiences the importance of something higher far than money, in relation to the service of God, began to impress Hudson Taylor.   His quiet life at Drainside was working a change in his attitude toward many things. There were memorable hours that winter in which he saw from the divine standpoint as never before, and a spirit shines out in his letters of the early spring that is clearly traceable to the trials into which he had been brought and the faith and prayer that overcame them.

"I feel I have not long to stay in this country now," he wrote to his sister on March 1.   "I do not know what turn Providence is about to take, but I think some change is coming, and I am forewarned that I may be prepared.   Pray for me that my faith fail not . . . I am so unworthy, so unfit for the Lord's service !   But that will only make the glory more entirely His.   Oh to be instrumental in bringing many to His fold !

"I feel the Lord is saying, ' If I open the door or bid thee go, *wilt thou go*, even if thou canst not see the way clearly ?   Wilt thou trust in Me ?   The very hairs of your head are all numbered.   Ye are of more value than many sparrows.'   I do not feel sure that He does not intend me to give up my situation and work my passage out to China : to go in faith, nothing doubting.   I am waiting patiently on Him for guidance.   In due time He will manifest His will, and then He, and He alone, can give me grace to fulfil it."

Only two weeks previously he had written to his mother. " Must I leave as soon as I can save money enough to go ? "

Now it was no longer a question of money. It was the far more important question of souls.

"Oh Amelia," he continued, "my heart is bound to you by ten thousand ties! But if my Saviour calls, shall I not obey? If He has left His throne in glory to come and bleed and die for us, shall we not leave all, *all*, and follow Him? If I stay here another two years and save fifty or sixty pounds to pay my expenses to China, I shall land there no better off than if I go at once and work my passage out. In two years there will die in that land at least twenty-four million people. . . . In six or eight months I should be able to talk a little Chinese. And if I could instruct in the truths of the Gospel one poor sinner, and the Spirit accompanied the word with power to his soul and he were saved—to all eternity he would be happy, praising the Redeemer. Then what would the hardships of a four or five months' voyage weigh in comparison? These 'light afflictions which are but for a moment' work out 'a far more exceeding and eternal weight of glory.'"

To his mother also he wrote a characteristic letter about this thought of working his passage out to China. His idea was, failing a berth as assistant to a ship's surgeon, to go as a sailor before the mast, and he had fully informed himself as to all that would be involved. Captain Finch especially had warned him of the hardships of a five months' voyage under the latter conditions, assuring him that he could never stand either the work or the companionship that must fall to his lot. But upon examining into details Hudson Taylor found nothing to daunt his faith or courage, and the very fact that it would mean sacrifice to the point of suffering made it seem all the more worth while—for Jesus' sake.

But of this he said little to his mother, dwelling rather upon the rich compensations both in this life and in the life to come.

"I am deeply thankful," he wrote, referring to one of her recent letters, "that you do not wish to recall the offering you made of me to the Lord. Perhaps He means to try our sincerity in this respect sooner than either of us anticipated. If I do not know the intensity of a mother's love, I feel so much the strength of a son's love, a brother's love, of love to friends and brethren in the Lord, that the thought of leaving *all* seems like tearing away part of one's very self. But, praise God, I know something also of a Saviour's love, though but little yet. He is to me a *satisfying* portion, and I can truly say—

> I all on earth forsake,
> Its wisdom, fame and power,
> And Thee my only portion make,
> My Shield and Tower.

" Oh Mother, I cannot tell you how unspeakably happy I was on Sunday afternoon while singing those words ! My soul was overwhelmed with heavenly joys. I felt I had nothing to give up worthy of mention, compared with what I had to receive. I could not refrain from tears of joy as I dedicated myself afresh to the service of Him who has loved us and washed us from our sins in His own precious blood.

" Oh how strong I felt in the joy of the Lord ! . . . He soon, however, made me realise that my strength is in Him and of Him only. I was feeling as if, for Him, I could leave all. But this thought followed quickly : ' It is no use talking and thinking about what you *could* do. What *will* you do ? Peter thought he could do this and that, but when the test came he denied his Lord.' Yes, I should fail as he did if I tried in my own strength. But the Holy Spirit can work in us ' *to will and to do*.' Our sufficiency is of Him. I feel I am helpless in myself, but ' God is the strength of my heart and my portion forever.' "

That he was deeply feeling the reality of all this is evident from a second letter to his sister that accompanied the above, dated March 12.

" We dwell too much on the things that are seen and temporal," he wrote, " and far too little on those that are unseen and eternal. . . . Only let us keep these things in view, and the cares and pleasures of this world will not affect us much. . . . Oh, my dear Sister, let us live for eternity ! Let us seek to be near the throne. What if for this we have to pass, as we undoubtedly shall, through great tribulation ? Does He not promise, ' I will never leave thee nor forsake thee ' ? So that we may boldly say ' The Lord is my helper : I will not fear what man shall do unto me.' Praise His holy name ! . . .

" Oh for more grace and love, a love like His, who counted not His life dear unto Himself that He might redeem us ! He sought not ease and comfort, that He might secure eternal happiness and heavenly rest for us. The value of a soul—how immense, incalculable ! The precious blood of Christ was the only price at which it could be purchased, and that was not withheld. If we really believe these things and have received the blessings that flow from His sacrifice, shall we withhold ourselves, our loved ones from Him ? . . . Shall we fear to enter on His service because it will lessen our comforts ? Shall we count even our lives dear, if we may perchance win souls for Jesus ? No, a thousand times no ! If we do, how dwelleth the love of God in us ? . . .

"Dear, dear Sister, let us live for God and for Him only. Let us seek to know *all* His will and to do it, whatever the cost. And may God, from whom all good desires arise and through whom alone they can be carried out, pour on you and on me ' the healthful spirit of His grace,' that having no desire save to do His will we may be enabled to perform it, and that in us He may be glorified."

But ready though he was for the sacrifice involved, Hudson Taylor was not to work his way out to China before the mast. " He was not to be tried thus far," wrote his mother, recalling with thankfulness the guidance given in answer to their prayers. For it was evident to those whose opinion he valued most that the time had not yet come for him to go forward. He was too young as yet. Further training was needed and experience in the things of God. It was well, no doubt, that it was in his heart to leave all and follow wherever the Master led. But was He leading just at that time to China ? To his parents and friends it seemed not. He had been much in prayer that if it were the Lord's will for him to go without delay, they might recognise it and bid him God-speed. But all advised against it. He could not have taken the step without disregarding the counsel of Christian friends in Hull as well as of his own circle in Barnsley. And this he would not do ; for he was dealing with God, who can overrule second causes.

He gathered therefore that the Lord's time had not yet come. It might be that He was leading to some other step in preparation for the future, but evidently it was not His purpose that he should leave immediately for China. The conclusion was not come to lightly. It was hard to give up his carefully thought-out plans, and he learned that there may be self-will even in what looks like devotion. It was an opportunity, however, for putting into practice the important principle, " To obey is better than sacrifice," and he embraced it cheerfully, handing over all results to the Lord. After taking time to assure himself that he was being led of God, he wrote to his mother on March 22 :

As to my going to China—in accordance with the unanimous advice of those I have consulted here and with your own opinion, I intend, *D.V.*, to remain in Hull another year and wait upon the Lord for guidance. I was much pleased with your judgment, as I had prayed the Lord, to whom all hearts are open, to bring us definitely to one mind. If it be His will for me to go sooner, He can thrust me out or open the way unmistakably. The Lord does answer prayer and make good His promises. I long to see you all again, and do not anticipate a lengthened delay now.

Sunday last was, I think, the happiest day I ever spent, and still I feel the peace that passes all understanding : peace flowing like a river, deep and still, . . . perfect rest in Him who is the Rock of Ages. Praise the Lord, He is ever near us !

> His presence makes our paradise,
> And where He is, is heaven.

A week spent at home in the lovely month of April, while it brought untold refreshment, made the dreariness of Drainside on his return all the more apparent. But inwardly he was rejoicing in the Lord, and though " rather unhinged at first," as he wrote to his sister, soon settled down to hard work and solitude once more. It was like him, as the days lengthened, to turn to good account the strip of waste land in front of the cottage for the benefit of Mrs. Finch and her family. His love of plants and nature generally was so great that even mustard and cress growing outside his window was better than nothing, and his efforts at gardening, though confined within utilitarian limits, afforded him much satisfaction.

That was a precious summer, spent in working, thinking, praying, and in diligent study of the Word of God. Time seemed all too short for the many duties crowded into it, and he was learning how much more can be accomplished in a day from which an hour is deliberately taken for prayer, than in the same time wholly given to one's ordinary occupations.

" I am finding it a good plan," he wrote to his sister in July, " not to attempt anything in my own strength, but to look to the Lord for all. . . . I would earnestly recommend you never to read your Bible, much less any other book, . . . nor even attempt to write a letter, without first lifting your heart to the Lord, that He may guide, enlighten, and teach you . . . delivering you from the snares of the evil one and in all things giving you His blessing. Try it, and you will find it no vain thing to wait upon the Lord."

He was deeply feeling at this time his need of a wisdom higher than his own, his friend and employer having put before him proposals of a generous nature with regard to the completion of his medical studies. Twelve months' work together had convinced Dr. Hardey that he had found no ordinary assistant. He valued his services highly, and was interested in the lad not merely on his own account but because of the missionary future he kept so stedfastly in view. The plan he suggested, however, involved a contract of the nature of an apprenticeship for several years. This was a serious consideration with Hudson Taylor, and finally led to his declining the offer. It was not easy to take this step, eager as he was to become a medical man ; but the more he prayed over it the more he felt he dared not bind himself by any such agreement, not knowing when or how the Lord might open his way to China.

Ever since his visit to Barnsley the conviction had been growing upon him that the time had come for some step in that direction. He was now twenty years of age, and realised the importance of making the best use of the little while that might remain to him in England. London attracted him because of its advantages for medical study. He had not forgotten the help proffered by Mr. Pearse and the Chinese Evangelisation Society, before he came to Hull. They had then been willing to bear the expense of his fees at the London Hospital if he could obtain employment that would leave him time for study, or otherwise provide his board and lodging. Did that offer still hold good, he wondered, and, if so, could he avail himself of it ?

Gradually as he prayed over the matter it became clear to him that he ought not to remain in Hull much longer. He had learned all he could from Dr. Hardey under present conditions, and to stay on meant loss of time, as far as preparation for China was concerned. Yes, go he ought and must, in faithfulness to his future service. But how was it to be accomplished ?

And just then a test of faith was permitted that, coming suddenly, found him unprepared. His father at home in Barnsley had for some time been more or less unsettled in his business. He was still an active man of only five-and-forty, and something, it may be his son's missionary spirit, had stirred in him longings for a wider field of usefulness. He had no doubt thought and prayed over Hudson's suggestion that he should go as an evangelist to China, but many circumstances combined to make this impracticable. A further thought had grown out of it, however, that for a time influenced him strongly. Might there not be in the new world of Canada or the United States opportunities for carrying on his business, and even bettering the family fortunes, in a far more needy sphere than Barnsley and its neighbourhood afforded? The more he considered it the stronger became his desire to go and see ; and the mother was deputed accordingly to find out from Hudson what he would think of taking charge at home for the next two years.

Filled with surprise and almost consternation, the latter hardly gave due weight to the wishes of his parents. Gladly would he have gone home for two years, or ten, to liberate his father for work in China. But a business journey to America, even though combined with an evangelistic purpose, seemed to him a very different proposition. To his mother he wrote freely, dwelling on all that it would mean to abandon at such a time the little preparation he could make for his life-work. Did he forget for the moment that that life with all that concerned it was in the hands of God ? If so he was quickly recalled to the real rest of his soul, and made to realise that his point of view had been selfish and wrong. How true was his repentance may be seen from the following :

HULL, *July* 9, 1852.

MY DEAR FATHER—I cannot come to you, and so write to say in the language of the prodigal, " I have sinned against heaven and in thy sight, and am no more worthy to be called thy son." Conscience has repeatedly troubled me about the answer I sent to your inquiry as to whether I was willing to come home for two years, should you go

L

abroad, and I can no longer rest without . . . entreating your for-giveness.

Though I mentioned the sacrifices I should have to make in coming home, I said nothing about those you have so willingly made for me—the sleepless hours, the anxious thoughts, the expense to which you have been put, the education you have given me by which I am able to procure all the comforts I now enjoy.　And this is the return I have made for all these kindnesses.　I have written of the sacrifices I should have to make in undertaking to manage for a short time the business at which you have toiled for twenty years for my benefit.　Father, I have been an ungrateful son. . . . I am deeply sorry.　Will you forgive me ?

I will earnestly endeavour, by the grace of God, to be more dutiful in future, and if you still wish me to come home for two years I will do so willingly, nay with pleasure, as it will give me an opportunity of showing the sincerity of my repentance.　Then afterwards, if the Lord will, I shall hope to engage in His work in China. . . .—Believe me, dear Father, your affectionate son,

James Hudson Taylor.

But again in the providence of God the sacrifice he was ready to make was not required.　For the father abandoned the idea of going abroad, and soon settled down as before to his useful, honoured life in Barnsley.　Thus Hudson was free to reconsider his own movements and the question of going to London.

And now came a time long to be remembered in his experience, a time that would have been one of painful anxiety had not the grace of God turned it all to joy and peace.　For the clearer became his conviction of what the Lord would have him do, the greater seemed the difficulties in the way of carrying it out.　He felt quite sure that the right thing was to give notice to Dr. Hardey without delay, and go forward to his medical studies in London.　But all his efforts to find suitable employment proved unavailing. With no means to fall back upon, save the small sum laid by to provide an outfit for China ; with few friends in the great city, and no home open to him there, he might well have been discouraged.　But the very reverse was the case. Instead of wasting time and strength in anxious thought, he was enabled to leave it all in the hands of God, praying

with childlike trust, " Make *Thy* way plain before my face."
How things would work out for him he could not tell ; but
he gave himself the more to prayer, confident that at the
right time guidance would be given.

All through July and August this faith was growing
stronger, and he was delighting in the promises of the
thirty-seventh Psalm.

Trust in the Lord and do good, so shalt thou dwell in the land and
verily thou shalt be fed.   Delight thyself also in the Lord, and He shall
give thee the desires of thine heart.   Commit thy way unto the Lord,
trust also in Him, and He shall bring it to pass. . . . Rest in the Lord
and wait patiently for Him. . . . The steps of a good man are ordered
by the Lord, and He delighteth in his way.

As he thought upon these assurances, so full and so
explicit, an unlooked-for change came over everything, and
he began to see in the light that only shines from the Unseen.
What was he really waiting for ?   He was not poor and in
difficulties, but rich—rich as all the promises of God.   Was
it his duty to go forward ?   What though there seemed no
solid ground to tread upon !   Was his Master there' upon
the unknown sea before him ?   Was it His voice heard
across the waters ?   Then he could leave the little boat
without hesitation and go to Jesus.   If it be Thou, Lord,
" if it be Thou, bid me come."   And the answer was in
tones he could not doubt.

" I think I have never enjoyed such peace of mind as lately," he
wrote to his mother on August 27.   " And the reason is that instead of
looking at circumstances I leave myself in the hands of God.   What
a wonderful Psalm the 37th is.   Oh, the rich feasts laid up for us in
the precious Word !   . .

" With regard to London : when I returned here from Barnsley, I
began prayerfully to consider *why* I desired to take the step contem-
plated ; and I believe my only object is that I may be enabled to serve
the Lord better and be more useful in the advancement of His Kingdom.
This step I have every ground for thinking will be a valuable preparation
for China.   Then why do I not take it ?   Simply because I am in
doubt about the wherewithal.   If my earthly father had offered to
send me five or ten pounds in case of need, I should have resigned my
position here without hesitation.   How much more should I go forward
trusting in Him who says : ' Take no thought saying, What shall we

eat ? or What shall we drink ? or Wherewithal shall we be clothed ?
. . . Your heavenly Father knoweth that ye have need of all these
things.' 'Trust in the Lord and do good, so shalt thou dwell in the
land and verily thou shalt be fed.'

"To go on depending on circumstances seems to me like doubting
the Lord. Consequently I gave notice to Dr. Hardey on Saturday
last, and shall go up to London whether I obtain a situation or not,
trusting in the Lord. I have heard of one to-day and shall write about
it, though I do not think it will suit me on account of distance from
the Hospital. As to getting a salary, that is quite out of the question.
If I can find a position that will allow six or eight hours a day for
lectures, that is all I can expect.

"I am indeed proving the truth of that word : 'Thou wilt keep him
in perfect peace whose mind is stayed on Thee, because he trusteth in
Thee.' My mind is quite as much at rest, nay more than it would be
if I had a hundred pounds in my pocket. May He keep me ever thus,
simply depending on Him for every blessing, temporal as well as
spiritual, for Jesus' sake."

This decision arrived at, Hudson was not afraid to burn
his bridges behind him. He wrote at once to his cousin
who was still in Barnsley, suggesting that he should apply
to Dr. Hardey for the post he was himself vacating. John
Hodson had been truly converted during his apprenticeship
through the helpful influence of his relatives, and was now
seeking a situation that would facilitate his medical studies.
He had been in considerable anxiety about the future, and
no one rejoiced more when Dr. Hardey gave him the appoint-
ment than the cousin whose place he was taking. But
Hudson's interest in his welfare went deeper than these
outward things, and very earnestly he sought to make use
of the position in which they found themselves to strengthen
his faith in God.

"Forgive me, dear John," he wrote, "if I urge you to study the
Bible more and pray more for the Holy Spirit . . . to give you more
light and love and more faith in it day by day ; then the unsettled-
ness you have been feeling with regard to your future prospects will
pass away. If you have had enough to make you unsettled, what
about me ? And yet through the grace of God my mind has been and
is kept 'in perfect peace' because stayed upon Him. . . .

"You ask what I shall do if no situation turns up. I shall go, D.V.,
to London ; endeavour to 'trust in the Lord and do good' and in all

my ways to acknowledge Him, . . . and He will care for my needs. At the same time He expects us to pray about these things. 'Ask, and it *shall* be given you.'

"Dear John, it is sweet to depend on Jesus only. I have not heard of a likely situation yet, nor am I anxious to do so if He would have me wait. I received a note from Uncle Benjamin yesterday, offering to take me in as his guest until I can find suitable employment . . . and I shall probably go there. You and I see a providence in these things."

A few lines to his sister written the same day, September 4, show that he was not insensible to the difficulty of his position. He was feeling the uncertainty keenly, but was willing to be tried in this or any other way that was for his good and the glory of God.

No situation has turned up in London that will suit me. But I am not concerned about it, as He is "the same, yesterday, to-day and forever." His love is unfailing, His word is unchangeable, His power is ever the same ; therefore the heart that trusts in Him is kept in *perfect peace.* . . . I know He only tries me to increase my faith, and that it is all in love. Well, if He is glorified I am content. Pray for me, dear Sister, that He who alone can keep us from falling . . . may strengthen my faith and perfect me in love.

Shortly after these letters were written, the way began to clear before him. His uncle in London had already offered a temporary home ; the Chinese Evangelisation Society renewed their arrangement with regard to his hospital fees ; and the Meeting he attended in Hull gave him introductions to a few Christian friends who would be accessible from his Soho quarters. Other offers of help reached him which though not accepted confirmed his assurance that he was being guided aright. Full of thankfulness he wrote to his sister in the middle of September :

Oh the love of God, the goodness of my Father and your Father, my God and your God ! How kind of Him to keep me in such perfect peace and full of joy and happiness when outwardly in the most difficult position. Had I left the question " Shall I go or stay ? " to be settled by circumstances, how uncertain I should have been, and how uncertain John would have been. But as the Lord enabled me to take the step without hesitation, because it was for His glory, leaving everything in *His* hands, my mind has been just as peaceful as it would otherwise have been unsettled. In all probability I should not have been able to sleep properly, and what with that and my business, which fully occupies time and strength, I should have been thoroughly knocked up.

Praise the Lord for His goodness ! He has provided, so far, all that is necessary. Now I have a home to go to, money to pay the fees of the Ophthalmic Hospital as well as the course at the London . . . and some Christian friends. When He sees fit, *if* He sees fit, He will find me a suitable situation, and if not, He will provide for and occupy me as seems best to Him. I leave it all in His hands, for I see plainly that it is the best way for peace and safety. He can manage these matters much better than we can. Last autumn I was fretting and stewing, reckoning and puzzling about how to manage this and that— like a person in water who cannot swim, or a fish out of it. But it all came to nothing. Now, when the Lord opens the way, though everything seems adverse, He first removes one difficulty and then another, plainly saying " Be still and know that I am God."

" Thou art my King, O God : command deliverance for Jacob. . . . ' I will *not* trust in my bow, neither shall my sword save me. . . . In God we boast all the day long, and praise Thy name forever.' "

I know I cannot guide or keep myself, even in temporal matters, but I know that He will guide me by His counsel and afterwards receive me to glory. . . . Why should we be anxious, and for what ? For temporal blessings? He knows that we have need of " all these things." For spiritual blessings ?   In Him there is fulness for every need.   Poor, weak, failing as we are, *Jesus is ours*.   " In Him dwelleth all the fulness of the Godhead bodily " : and we are " complete in Him."

And now, Lord, what wait I for ?
My hope is in Thee.

PART III

PREPARATION FOR CHINA, IN LONDON AND ON THE VOYAGE

1852–1854. AET. 20–21.

I know not if or dark or bright
    Shall be my lot,
If that wherein my hopes delight
    Is best or not.

My bark is wafted to the strand
    By breath divine,
And on the helm there rests a Hand
    Other than mine

One who has known in storms to sail
    I have on board ·
Above the raging of the gale
    I hear my Lord.

He holds me when the billows smite;
    I shall not fall :
If sharp, 'tis short, if long, 'tis light—
    He tempers all

Safe to the Land, safe to the Land—
    The end is this :
And then with Him go hand in hand
    Far into bliss

                HENRY ALFORD

CHAPTER XII

SEPTEMBER AND OCTOBER 1852. AET. 20.

FOG-HORNS were sounding on every hand when a coasting-steamer plying between Hull and London made her way slowly up the Thames. It was Saturday evening, September 25, and Hudson Taylor amongst others was expecting to land that night. But the pall of mist only gathered more and more heavily over the great city, until there was nothing for it but to cast anchor and wait till morning. By noon it was possible to reach the Tower, and most of the passengers went ashore. A quiet Sunday followed for those who remained on board, of which Hudson Taylor was specially thankful in view of the new phase of life opening before him.

How new it was and how great his need of the strength that comes from God alone no one had any idea but himself. Not to his mother, or even to the sister who spent the last days with him at Drainside had he spoken of the decision taken before leaving Hull that now filled his mind as he paced the deck. His friends and parents knew that he was going up to London to support himself, if possible, while completing his medical studies. They knew that the Chinese Evangelisation Society had offered financial help, and concluded that as he had declined similar offers from home he must be sufficiently provided for. And so he was— by nothing more and nothing less than all the promises of God. He had a little money in his pocket and a few pounds laid by toward an outfit for China. He had a promise also of help with his hospital fees, and an invitation to be the guest for a few days or weeks of his bachelor uncle, while looking for a situation. But beyond this there was nothing, humanly speaking, between him and want in the great city in which he was almost a stranger.

Yet this caused him no anxiety as he faced the coming winter. For the future, near as well as distant, he had one all-sufficient confidence. If that could fail, it were better to make the discovery in London than far away in China. Deliberately and of his own free will he had cut himself off from possible sources of supply that he might make full proof, under difficult circumstances, of the promised care of God alone. It was God, the living God he needed; a stronger faith to grasp His faithfulness, and more experience of the practicability of dealing with Him directly about every need. Comfort or discomfort in London, means or the lack of means, seemed to him a small matter compared with deeper knowledge of the One on whom everything depended. And now had come an unexpected opportunity for putting that knowledge to the test, and he was going forward strong in the assurance that the Lord who had already responded so graciously to his little faith would see and would provide.

Of the way in which he had been led to this position just before leaving Drainside the following is his own account:

By-and-by the time drew near when it was thought desirable that I should leave Hull to attend the medical course of the London Hospital. A little while spent there, and then I had every reason to believe that my life-work in China would commence. But much as I had rejoiced at the willingness of God to hear and answer prayer and to help His half-trusting, half-timid child, I felt that I could not go to China without having still further developed and tested my power to rest upon His faithfulness; and a marked opportunity for doing so was providentially afforded me.

My dear father had offered to bear all the expense of my stay in London. I knew, however, that, owing to recent losses, it would mean a considerable sacrifice for him to undertake this just when it seemed necessary for me to go forward. I had recently become acquainted with the Committee of the Chinese Evangelisation Society, in connection with which I ultimately left for China, and especially with its secretary, my esteemed and much-loved friend Mr. George Pearse, then of the Stock Exchange, but now and for many years himself a missionary. Not knowing of my father's proposition, the Committee also kindly offered to bear my expenses while in London. When these proposals were first made to me, I was not quite clear as to what I ought to do, and in writing to my father and the secretaries, told them that I would take a few days to pray about the matter before deciding any course of action. I mentioned to my father that I had had this offer from the Society, and told the secretaries also of his proffered aid.

Subsequently, while waiting upon God in prayer for guidance, it became clear to my mind that I could without difficulty decline both offers. The secretaries of the Society would not know that I had cast myself wholly on God for supplies, and my father would conclude that I had accepted the other offer. I therefore wrote declining both, and felt that without any one having either care or anxiety on my account I was simply in the hands of God, and that He who knew my heart, if He wished to encourage me to go to China, would bless my effort to depend upon Him alone at home.

> Enough, that God my Father knows !
> Nothing this faith can dim :
> He gives the very best to those
> Who leave the choice with Him.

And so Hudson Taylor was to find it, although his London experiences were not to be unmixed with trial.

It was with a brave heart, therefore, that he presented himself at Mr. Ruffles' boarding-house near Soho Square, early on Monday morning. Here lived his uncle, Benjamin Hudson, and a cousin from Barton-on-Humber who was apprenticed to Mr. Ruffles, a builder and decorator by trade. The uncle, a bright, genial man, was not only a skilful portrait-painter, he was something of a poet also, and a clever *raconteur* with a remarkable memory for " good stories." [1] He was decidedly popular in the boarding-house and among a large circle of acquaintances, including more than one medical man to whom he was willing to introduce his nephew with a view to an apprenticeship.

[1] This uncle, a brother of Mrs. James Taylor's, was the seventh and youngest child of the Rev. Benjamin Hudson. He went to Calcutta, shortly after this period, and made quite a fortune by painting Indian princes and officials, entertaining them the while with amusing stories.

The cousin too was friendly, offering to share his room with the new-comer and so lessen expenses, if he decided to remain in Soho.   This arrangement Hudson gladly availed himself of, for it was a comfort to belong to some one, and Tom seemed almost like a breath of home.[1]   Three long flights of stairs led to this attic-chamber, for part of which he had to pay as much as for the little room at Mrs. Finch's that now seemed so quiet and homelike by contrast.   But it was a footing in London, a shelter in the big, busy city that he might call his own.

What a drop in the ocean he felt amid the tides of life now surging around him.   All was so new and strange !   He was in anything but a religious circle, surrounded by people who moved in a world of which he knew next to nothing.   Business, politics and pleasure-seeking absorbed their attention, and his uncle and cousin did their best to draw him into the same sort of life.   They had quite approved his coming to London to study medicine, and were ready in their own way to give him a helping hand.   But his point of view annoyed while it perplexed them.

" Talk about trusting God," his cousin would exclaim, " one must trust one's own exertions too ! "   Which meant, " Do as everybody else does, and lose no time about it."

Then his unwillingness to bind himself by an ordinary apprenticeship on account of a call to missionary work in China was something they could not understand, especially when it seemed that the Society to which he was looking was more than indifferent about the matter.   And this to Hudson Taylor was the most painful surprise of all.

From his own relatives he had not expected sympathy in these things, but Mr. Pearse, with whom he had been in correspondence for more than two years, understood his position and would be ready with counsel and aid.   As soon, therefore, as possible he set out from Soho to find the office of the Society, little anticipating the disappointment that awaited him.

---

[1] It was Tom's elder brother, John Hodson, who had been apprenticed to Hudson Taylor's father in Barnsley for three years, and was now in Hull with Dr. Hardey

For the Hon. Secretary, as it happened, was much occupied that day and could with difficulty spare time to see him.[1] No, nothing definite was arranged as yet. They were awaiting his arrival. Now that he was ready to begin work at the hospital the matter must be laid before the Committee. This would take time of course. Would he not come to Hackney for a Sunday before long, and talk over things more at leisure?

Well was it for Hudson Taylor as he returned to his lodgings that he really was depending on God and knew something of His unfailing care. From a helper in the office he had learned that nothing definite could be done until a formal application was laid before the Committee. In all probability the Society would help, as he had been led to expect, but everything must be done in a certain order. The best thing if there were any urgency would be to send in his application at once, so that it might not miss the next Committee meeting on October 7, for they only gathered once a fortnight.

October 7! and it was not yet the end of September. If his case could not be dealt with at the first meeting, he would have to wait another two weeks, and perhaps another. Meanwhile he could take no position; his store of savings was diminishing; and what would they say at the boarding-house where his indefiniteness was a source of amusement already?

If he had known all this in Hull! And yet what difference did it really make? He had not come to London depending on his own resources or on the help of man. If the winds and waves were boisterous, was there not One beside him whose hand was strong to uphold as His word to bring peace? He knew the end from the beginning; and since He had been Alpha would surely be Omega, and everything between.

So the application was sent in, and while waiting the

[1] Mr. Pearse, it should be remembered, while acting as Hon. Secretary to the Chinese Evangelisation Society, was at the same time much engrossed in business. It was no lack of interest that made him dismiss Hudson Taylor so curtly, but simply the pressure of other claims, and a failure to realise what this coming to London meant to his young friend.

issue Hudson Taylor settled down to study as well as he could in the room shared with his cousin. The latter's occupation allowed him to be frequently at home, and his criticisms however good-natured were not a help to quietness of mind. But there is something better than outward ease and comfort, and in entirely new surroundings Hudson Taylor was learning the old lesson—to rest in the Lord and wait patiently for Him.

"As to your inquiries," he wrote to his mother on October 2, "I will try to answer them as well as I can. But really you know almost as much of my plans as I do. For there is nothing certain yet, except—'*I will never leave thee nor forsake thee.*'

"I have no situation and am not seeking one. I question whether I shall for some months at any rate. But I have commenced study at home. In accordance with Mr. M.'s advice I have written to the Committee formally requesting them to authorise me to attend the London Hospital practice and lectures. But they will have to meet in regular course before I can know the result. . . .

"London seems to me a trying place. There is so much noise and bustle, so much to distract one all the time. You can have no idea of the difference it makes to be among light, thoughtless, worldly-minded people after the quiet I have enjoyed lately. But it is sweet to realise that we are 'kept by the power of God', to be enabled to say with the Apostle, 'Nay, in all these things we are more than conquerors through Him that loved us.'

"I am altogether in the Lord's hands, and He will direct me."

But the uncertainty was not over when the Committee met. Strangely enough, they seem to have considered it necessary to inform themselves further about him ; and all the action taken was the passing of a resolution requesting him to procure an elaborate set of testimonials to be laid before them at their next meeting. It was Hudson Taylor's first experience of the working of a fully-organised Society, and though he subsequently came to understand the need for a certain amount of "red tape" in such affairs it was an experience he never forgot in his own dealings with would-be missionaries.

That he was feeling the position keenly may be judged from a letter to his mother on hearing of the above requirements :

How sweet it is to be dependent on the Lord for everything. . . . All, all is best as He sees fit to guide. And He does guide and provide, both in temporal and spiritual matters, as long as we trust in Him. . . .

Never mind results. . . . Let us leave them all to Him Never mind if like Abraham of old we have to go out, not knowing whither. *He* knows. While unbelief sees only the difficulties, faith sees God between itself and them. . . .

As to my prospects, I cannot tell you much as yet. The Committee met on Thursday and considered my application, and on Friday night I received a note from Mr. Bird containing a resolution desiring me to procure certain testimonials *by next Thursday week* for their further consideration. Now this is a very serious delay, and I intend to see Mr. Pearse to-day, if possible, and talk with him about it. The required testimonials I do not quite understand, and if they are all considered necessary I shall thank the Committee for their kindness and trouble them no further, as I do not see them consistent with my views. Thank God, I am quite as willing to lose as to gain their assistance. If I have time after seeing Mr. Pearse I will add a few lines, if not I will write by a later post.

" Let not your heart be troubled," dear mother. He who has hitherto provided for, protected and guided me, still keeps my mind in perfect peace . . . and will do all things well. How sweet it is to be enabled to trust in Him for *all*. May He ever use us for His glory.

Surely his faith was growing, under these searching tests ! Apart from the Chinese Evangelisation Society what hope had he, humanly speaking, of completing his medical studies or entering upon his life-work ? No other door was open to him, after long years of prayer and waiting. To have been dropped by the Society or compelled to " trouble them no further " might have meant being stranded in London with nothing before him but to take a situation and indefinitely defer going to China. Yet he was " quite as willing to lose as to gain their assistance," if that were the will of God.

He had decided, however, to see Mr. Pearse and come to an understanding about the testimonials. Accordingly he was up early the following morning and went over to Hackney in time to catch the busy secretary before he left for the Stock Exchange. As he explained his difficulties, Mr. Pearse seems to have understood at last. The result was that the testimonials were seen to be superfluous and only a letter or two required from those who knew him best.

Even so another ten days had to elapse before the meeting of the Committee, and during that time an opening that must have had many attractions was put before him. His father, concerned at the ordeal through which he was passing, wrote offering to take him into partnership with himself— that he might have a home and " something to depend on." How easy it would have been, with the justification of this letter, to turn aside to an easier pathway ! But his purpose never wavered. Holding simply to what he believed to be the guidance of God he waited as those alone can whose expectation is from Him And before the end of the month faith was richly rewarded.

" I am happy to say that things seem to be assuming a more settled appearance," he wrote on October 24, " and I expect all being well to commence work at the hospital to-morrow. . . . Please thank Father for his generous offer . . . but those whose trust is in the Lord *always have something to depend on.*"

This was not the only answer to his prayers, however, that filled his heart with thanksgiving. Studying as well as he could in that little attic-chamber, he was unconscious that the one who shared it with him was being drawn in spite of himself to the only source of abiding joy and peace. Yet so it was. Tom Hodson, keenly watching his cousin's experiences, found himself face to face with conclusions he could neither escape nor gainsay. Nothing else, perhaps, would ever have made him feel his own distance from God and need of something more real and satisfying than he had ever possessed. But this did. And before the close of the year Hudson had the joy of seeing him brought to " like precious faith " in Christ, and openly taking his stand in the boarding-house as a Christian.

CHAPTER XIII

OCTOBER–DECEMBER 1852. AET. 20.

THE hospital at last! It was now the end of October 1852, three years almost from the December day that had brought Hudson Taylor his definite call to China. Ever since that time he had had medical study in view as the best preparation he could make for future usefulness. With little help and in spite of many obstacles he had persevered, making considerable progress with the practical side of his work. But now the broad highway lay open before him—the lectures, the wards, and all the advantages of a city hospital.

Not that " The London " of those days, on its broad expanse of Mile End Waste, was anything to compare with the noble institution that stands there now. Still, it could accommodate even then from three to four hundred in-patients, and its students had the benefit of an unusually large practice among the teeming population of the East End. It was a new world indeed to the north-country lad, and one in which no little courage was needed to maintain the standing of a consistent Christian.

But it is not so much with his outward experiences we are concerned, during this period in London, as with the development of his inward life—the growth of both faith and faithfulness amid the circumstances of his providential way.

That his temporal needs were met is manifest, for he was able to live on at Soho even after his little store of savings had been expended.

" I must not now attempt to detail," he wrote, " the way in which the Lord was pleased, often to my surprise as well as delight, to help me from time to time."

Many answers to prayer were given that are not recorded, and from this point of view the winter was a rich one, although we have it on his own authority that his spiritual life was not as bright as it had been in Hull. But, though there was less joy in the Lord, apparently, and less consciousness of His presence, the wonderful *reality* did not fail.

Owing to heavy rains, the season was specially depressing Much of the East End was flooded, with serious results for those who lived near the river or whose employment kept them in the damp, foggy streets. And Hudson Taylor, for a considerable part of every day, was among their number. Lodging at Soho for the sake of remaining with his cousin, he was fully four miles from the hospital in which most of his work was done. This meant a walk of at least two hours daily—from Oxford Street to Whitechapel, and back across the City to Oxford Street again. There was no " Tube " or " Underground " available. The only public conveyance was the old-fashioned omnibus with its three-penny fare each way, a price that was quite prohibitive. So there was nothing for it but to walk.

For the young medical student was economising very strictly. How far this was necessary or desirable, it is not for us to say. He was inexperienced as yet in a life of faith, and felt it a matter of conscience to deny himself everything that could be done without, partly with a view to helping others.

" To lessen expenses," he wrote, " I shared a room with a cousin, four miles from the hospital, providing my own board ; and after various experiments I found that the most economical way was to live almost exclusively on brown bread and water. Thus I was able to make the means that God gave me last as long as possible. Some of my expenses I could not diminish, but my board was largely in my own control. A large twopenny loaf of brown bread, purchased daily on my long walk from the hospital, furnished me with supper and breakfast ; and on this diet with a few apples for lunch I managed to walk eight or nine miles a day, besides being a good deal on foot attending the practice of the hospital. . . ."

Remember it was winter, the month of November, just the most cheerless time of all the year. Trudging home long after dark, how tempting the restaurants would look to the tired, hungry student who had had no dinner for many a day! Did the baker guess, who sold that large twopenny loaf of brown bread, why his customer always waited to have it cut in half? Only half could be taken that night for supper : the remainder had to suffice for the morrow, and experience had proved how very hard it was to make such a division impartially. When at first he tried it for himself, supper had so much the advantage of breakfast that the lad often went hungry the following day. The baker, however, was disinterested, and laid him under obligation by settling the question on the spot.

Brown bread, apples and water, at a cost of threepence a day—a diet worthy of a Bedouin Arab, minus the fragrant coffee, and more suited to his tranquil surroundings. But for a delicate lad amid the stress and strain of London life it left much to be desired.

And all the while it was the greatness of the inward way that told upon him most. Hunger and weariness of body were of little moment compared with the longing of his soul. It was the end in view that meant so much—China in its unutterable need, and what he could do to meet it ; God and His purposes of blessing, to be apprehended only by faith and prayer.

Meanwhile he was getting on well with his work in the hospital.

"No," he wrote in reply to his mother's inquiries, " my health does not suffer. On the contrary, every one says how well I look, and some even that I am getting fat! Though this, I believe, can only be perceived by rather a brilliant imagination. The walks do not fatigue me as they did at first. But the profane conversation of some of the students is utterly sickening, and I need all your prayers.

"How precious the assurance, ' Having loved His own which were in the world, He loved them unto the end ' ! He never forgets, He never tires. . . . The future, as you say, is all in His hands, and where else would we wish it ? "

Yet even as he wrote the words he was in a position that

might well have given rise to anxiety, and was entering on
a period of trial more severe than any he had previously
known. As a background to this experience with which
the year terminated, and of which he wrote as follows,
precious indeed was the assurance, " He never forgets, He
never tires."

One incident I cannot but refer to, that took place about this time.
The husband of my former landlady in Hull was chief officer of a ship
that sailed from London, and by receiving his half-pay monthly and
remitting it to her I was able to save her the cost of a commission.
This I had been doing for two or three months, when she wrote requesting that I would obtain the next payment as early as possible, as
her rent was almost due, and she depended upon that sum to meet it.
The request came at an inconvenient time. I was working hard for
an examination, in the hope of obtaining a scholarship which would
be of service to me, and felt that I could ill afford the time to go during
the busiest part of the day to the city and procure the money. I had
sufficient of my own in hand to enable me to send the required sum,
and made the remittance therefore, purposing as soon as the examination was over to go and draw the regular allowance with which to
refund myself.

Before the time of examination the medical school was closed for
a day on account of the funeral of the Duke of Wellington, and I had
an opportunity of going at once to the office, which was situated in a
street off Cheapside, and applying for the due amount. To my
surprise and dismay the clerk told me that he could not pay it, as the
officer in question had run away from his ship and gone to the gold
diggings.

" Well," I remarked, " that is very inconvenient for me, as I have
already advanced the money and I know his wife will have no means
of repaying it."

The clerk said he was very sorry, but could of course only act
according to orders. So there was no help for me in that direction !
A little more time and thought, however, brought the comforting
conclusion to my mind that as I was depending on the Lord for everything, and His means were not limited, it was a small matter to be
brought a little sooner or later into the position of needing fresh
supplies from Him. So the joy and peace were not long interrupted.

Very soon after this, possibly the same evening, while sewing
together some sheets of paper on which to take notes of lectures, I
accidentally pricked the first finger of my right hand, and in a few
moments forgot all about it. The next day at the hospital I continued
dissecting as before. The body was that of a person who had died

of fever, and was more than usually disagreeable and dangerous. I need scarcely say that those of us who were at work upon it dissected with special care, knowing that the slightest scratch might cost our lives. Before the morning was far advanced I began to feel weary, and while going through the surgical wards at noon was obliged to run out, being suddenly very sick—a most unusual circumstance with me, as I took but little food and nothing that could disagree with me. After feeling faint for some time, a draught of cold water revived me and I was able to rejoin the students. I became more and more unwell, however, and during the afternoon lecture on surgery found it impossible to hold the pencil and continue taking notes. By the time the next lecture was over, my whole arm and right side were full of pain and I was both looking and feeling very ill.

Finding that I could not resume work, I went into the dissecting-room to bind up the portion I was engaged upon and put away my apparatus, and said to the demonstrator, who was a skilful surgeon:

"I cannot think what has come over me," describing the symptoms.

"Why," said he, "what has happened is clear enough. You must have cut yourself in dissecting, and you know that this is a case of malignant fever."

I assured him that I had been most careful and was quite certain that I had no cut or scratch.

"Well," he replied, "you certainly must have had one"; and he closely scrutinised my hand to find it, but in vain.

All at once it occurred to me that I had pricked my finger the night before, and I asked him if it were possible that a prick from a needle at that time could have been still unclosed. His opinion was that this was probably the cause of the trouble, and he advised me to get a hansom, drive home as fast as I could and arrange my affairs forthwith:

"For," said he, "you are a dead man."

My first thought was one of sorrow that I could not go to China; but very soon came the feeling, "Unless I am greatly mistaken, I have work to do in China and shall not die." I was glad, however, to take the opportunity of speaking to my medical friend, who was a confirmed sceptic, of the joy that the prospect of soon being with my Master gave me, telling him at the same time that I did not think I should die, as unless I were much mistaken I had work to do in China, and if so, however severe the struggle, I must be brought through.

"That is all very well," he answered, "but get a hansom and drive home as fast as you can. You have no time to lose, for you will soon be incapable of winding up your affairs."

I smiled a little at the idea of driving home in a hansom, for by this time my means were too exhausted to allow of such a proceeding, and I set out to walk the distance if possible. Before long, however, my strength gave way, and I felt it was no use to attempt to reach home by walking. Availing myself of an omnibus from Whitechapel Church to Farringdon Street, and another from Farringdon Street onwards, I reached, in great suffering, the neighbourhood of Soho Square, behind which I lived. On going into the house I got some hot water from the servant, and charging her very earnestly—literally as a dying man—to accept eternal life as the gift of God through Jesus Christ, I bathed my hand and lanced the finger, hoping to let out some of the poisoned blood. The pain was very severe. I fainted away, and was so long unconscious that when I came to myself I found I had been carried to bed.

An uncle of mine who lived near at hand had come in, and sent for his own medical man, an assistant surgeon at the Westminster Hospital. I assured my uncle that medical help would be of no service to me, and that I did not wish to go to the expense involved. He quieted me on this score, however, saying that he had sent for his own doctor and that the bill would be charged to himself. When the surgeon came and learned all particulars, he said,

" Well, if you have been living moderately you may pull through, but if you have been going in for beer and that sort of thing there is no manner of chance for you."

I thought that if sober living was to do anything, few could have a better chance, as little but bread and water had been my diet for a good while past. I told him I had lived abstemiously and found that it helped me to study.

" But now," he said, " you must keep up your strength, for it will be a pretty hard struggle." And he ordered me a bottle of port wine every day and as many chops as I could consume.

Again I smiled inwardly, having no means for the purchase of such luxuries. This difficulty, however, was also met by my kind uncle, who sent me at once all that was needed.

I was much concerned, notwithstanding the agony I suffered, that my dear parents should not be made acquainted with my state. Thought and prayer had satisfied me that I was not going to die, but that there was indeed a work for me to do in China. If my dear parents should come up and find me in that condition, I must lose the opportunity of seeing how God was going to work for me now that my money was almost come to an end. So, after prayer for guidance, I obtained a promise from my uncle and cousin not to write to my parents, but to leave me to communicate with them myself. I felt it a very distinct answer to prayer when they gave me this promise, and I took care to defer all communication with Barnsley until the worst was over. At home they knew that I was working hard for an examination and did not wonder at my silence.

Days and nights of suffering passed slowly by ; but at length,

after several weeks, I was sufficiently restored to leave my room,
and then I learned that two men, though not from the London Hospital,
who had had dissection wounds at the same time as myself, had both
succumbed, while I was spared in answer to prayer to work for God
in China.

One day the doctor coming in found me on the sofa, and was
surprised to learn that with assistance I had walked downstairs.

" Now," he said, " the best thing you can do is to get off to the
country as soon as you feel equal to the journey.   You must rusticate
until you have recovered a fair amount of strength, for if you begin
your work too soon the consequences may still be serious."

When he had left, as I lay very exhausted on the couch, I just told
the Lord all about it, and that I was refraining from making my
circumstances known to those who would delight to meet my need
in order that my faith might be strengthened by receiving help from
Himself in answer to prayer alone.   What was I to do ?   And I waited
for His answer.

It seemed to me as if He were directing my mind to the conclusion
to go again to the shipping office and inquire about the wages I had
been unable to draw.   I reminded the Lord that I could not afford to
take a conveyance, and that it did not seem at all likely I should
succeed in getting the money, and asked whether this impulse were
not a mere clutching at a straw, some mental process of my own rather
than His guidance and teaching.   After prayer, however, and renewed
waiting upon God, I was confirmed in my belief that He Himself was
directing me to go to the office.

The next question was, " How am I to go ? "   I had had to seek
help in coming downstairs, and the place was at least two miles away.
The assurance was brought vividly home to me that whatever I asked
of God in the name of Christ would be done, that the Father might
be glorified in the Son ; that what I had to do was to seek strength
for the long walk, to receive it by faith, and set out upon it.   Un-
hesitatingly I told the Lord that I was quite willing to take the walk
if He would give the strength.   I asked in the name of Christ that the
strength might immediately be given ; and sending the servant up
to my room for my hat and stick, I set out, not to *attempt* to walk,
but *to walk* to Cheapside.

Although undoubtedly strengthened by faith, I never took so much
interest in shop windows as I did upon that journey.   At every second
or third shop I was glad to lean a little against the plate glass, and
take time to examine the contents of the window before passing on.
It needed a special effort of faith when I got to the bottom of Farringdon
Street to attempt the toilsome ascent of Snow Hill ; but there was no
Holborn Viaduct in those days, and it had to be done.   God did
wonderfully help me, and in due time I reached Cheapside, turned

into the by-street in which the office was found, and sat down much exhausted on the steps leading to the first floor, which was my destina-tion. I felt my position to be a little peculiar, sitting there on the steps so evidently spent, and the gentlemen who rushed up and downstairs looked at me with an inquiring gaze. After a little rest, however, and a further season of prayer, I succeeded in climbing the staircase, and to my comfort found in the office the clerk with whom I had hitherto dealt in the matter. Seeing me looking pale and exhausted he kindly inquired as to my health, and I told him that I had had a serious illness and was ordered to the country, but thought it well to call first and make further inquiry, lest there should have been any mistake about the mate having run off to the gold diggings

" Oh," he said, " I am so glad you have come, for it turns out that it was an able seaman of the same name that ran away. The mate is still on board ; the ship has just reached Gravesend and will be up very soon. I shall be glad to give you the half-pay up to date, for doubtless it will reach his wife more safely through you. We all know what temptations beset the men when they arrive at home after a voyage."

But before giving me the sum of money, he insisted on my coming inside and sharing his lunch. I felt it was the Lord indeed who was providing for me, and accepted his offer with thankfulness. When I was refreshed and rested, he gave me a sheet of paper to write a few lines to the wife, telling her of the circumstances. On my way back I procured in Cheapside a money-order for the balance due to her, and posted it ; and returning home again felt myself now quite justified in taking an omnibus as far as it would serve me.

Very much better the next morning, I made my way to the surgery of the doctor who had attended me, feeling that although my uncle was prepared to pay the bill it was right for me now that I had money in hand to ask for the account myself. The kind surgeon refused to allow me as a medical student to pay anything for his attendance, but he had supplied me with quinine which he allowed me to pay for to the extent of eight shillings. When that was settled, I saw that the sum left was just sufficient to take me home , and to my mind the whole thing seemed a wonderful interposition of God on my behalf.

I knew that the surgeon was sceptical, and told him that I should very much like to speak to him freely, if I might do so without offence ; that I felt that under God I owed my life to his care, and wished very earnestly that he himself might become a partaker of the same precious faith that I possessed. So I told him my reason for being in London, and about my circumstances, and why I had declined the help of both my father and the officers of the Society in connection with which it was probable that I should go to China. I told him of the recent providential dealings of God with me, and how apparently hopeless my position had been the day before when he had ordered me to go to the country, unless I would reveal my need, which I had determined not to do. I described to him the mental exercises I had gone through ; but when I added that I had actually got up from the sofa and walked to Cheapside, he looked at me incredulously and said,

" Impossible ! Why, I left you lying there more like a ghost than a man."

And I had to assure him again and again that, strengthened by faith, the walk had really been taken.

I told him also what money was left to me and what payments there had been to make, and showed him that just sufficient remained to take me home to Yorkshire, providing for needful refreshment on the way and the omnibus journey at the end.

My kind friend was completely broken down, and said with tears in his eyes,

" I would give all the world for a faith like yours."

I on the other hand had the joy of telling him that it was to be obtained without money and without price.

We never met again. When I came back to town restored to health and strength I found that he had had a stroke and left for the country, and I subsequently learned that he never rallied. I was able to gain no information as to his state of mind when taken away, but I have always felt very thankful that I had the opportunity, and embraced it, of bearing that testimony for God. I cannot but enter-tain the hope that the Master Himself was speaking to him through His dealings with me, and that I shall meet him again in the Better Land. It would be no small joy to be welcomed by him when my own service is over.

The next day found me in my dear parents' home. My joy in the Lord's help and deliverance was so great that I was unable to keep it to myself, and before my return to London my dear mother knew the secret of my life for some time past. I need scarcely say that when I went up again to town I was not allowed to live, as indeed I was not fit to live, on the same economical lines as before my illness. I needed more now, and the Lord did provide.

CHAPTER XIV

LIGHT AT LAST

JANUARY–JUNE 1853. AET. 20–21.

THE joy of these experiences was very great and had much to do with Hudson Taylor's return to a fuller consciousness of fellowship with God. His early months in London had not been helpful spiritually, but now as winter passed away a springtide of blessing seemed to awaken in his soul.

"I do not need to be told that you have been praying for me," he wrote to his mother in February. "I have been sure of it. For though at times the heavens have seemed as brass and I have felt myself left and forsaken, I have been enabled to cling to the promises by simple, 'naked faith,' as father calls it . . . and never have I enjoyed more happy seasons than of late."

He had been passing through deep waters since his return to London, not in connection with financial matters, but through the mistakes and suffering of some dear to him that cost him more than words can say. But by Easter these troubles were beginning to pass away, and he was rejoicing once more in inward and outward deliverance.

His Sunday visits to Tottenham were very helpful at this time, especially the hours spent at Bruce Grove and with Miss Stacey. The latter had a way all her own of finding out what people needed, and the young medical student with his bright face, spare figure, well-worn clothes and burning love for China told a story that touched her heart.

In her garden stood a fine old cedar, a landmark in the

neighbourhood and a delightful retreat on sunny days, and the library indoors was of the same restful character, a place seemingly apart from the hurry and care of life. Miss Stacey lived alone, and was quite mistress of the situation even when surrounded as she frequently was with visitors. Hudson Taylor needed rest : she would have him left quiet. So it became an understood thing whenever he was in the house that the library and cedar tree were not invaded save by this privileged but most unconscious guest.[1]

A change in his circumstances too proved helpful, when after six months at Soho he obtained a position as assistant to a surgeon in the City.

It was good to be at work again under experienced super-vision, and a matter for thankfulness to have only a mile and a quarter to walk to the hospital, instead of four. He seems to have been living with his employer, Mr. Thomas Brown of St. Mary Axe, near Finsbury Circus, and it is comforting to read of family meals, including tea and supper ! His life was necessarily a strenuous one—attending the hospital all the morning and working for Mr. Brown until

[1] " It has been one of the privileges of my life," wrote Miss Elizabeth Wilson of Kendal, " to have known so much of your beloved and honoured father. The first time I ever met him was when as a young girl I was on a visit to Miss Stacey   He came for one of the little rests he so much needed and that Miss Stacey rejoiced to give him, leaving him the run of the garden and library and protecting him from much company or con-versation.   He was then a medical student and living I think on very little.   For years after, when I asked him how he had been able to afford the omnibus so often, he replied, ' Miss Stacey was not one who would forget details of that sort.   She never let me pay my fare.'   So no doubt the excellent dinners now and then did him good, as well as the ministry of the Tottenham meeting."

Little could Miss Wilson have imagined at that time that she too would be called to China, and used as one of the most devoted pioneers of the Inland Mission.

Another friend of those days, though still a lad at school, was Theodore Howard, son of Mr and Mrs. Robert Howard of Bruce Grove : now and for many years Home Director of the China Inland Mission.   " I do certainly think," he wrote concerning Mr. Taylor's visits to Tottenham, " that the intercourse he had with friends there must have considerably influenced his views of Christian faith, doctrine, and practice   Those were palmy days (among Brethren) in which there was much of the Holy Spirit's teaching, and I believe they have left their mark on many branches of the Evangelical Church.   And they were followed by the blessed gatherings at Barnet and Mildmay, through which the same truths became the heritage of an ever-widening circle of believers.   Thank God that light has never died away, but has grown brighter and brighter amid the darkness of sacerdotalism, ritualism, and scientific criticism in these days of ' modern thought ' "

nine o'clock at night, after which the time was his own for
study. But his heart was at rest in God. The depression
of spirits from which he had been suffering passed away,
and after fifteen months of " boarding himself " on next
to nothing, the change was in every way beneficial.

China was much on his heart this spring, and his outlook
upon the life-work awaiting him there was becoming more
definite. Previously, in Barnsley and in Hull, he had
rather taken it for granted that the difficulties connected
with his future would all vanish if some Society could be
found to send him out. It was a youthful way of looking
at things, and now with more experience he began to see
that the very opposite might be the case. In London he
had come to understand something of the working of a
Society with its necessary rules and regulations, and he
could not but see that to be under the direction of a Committee, while it would secure him a salary and other
advantages, might greatly curtail his freedom of action, and
in this way increase rather than lessen his trials.

At the same time events were transpiring in China that
deepened his longing to give himself to work in the interior.
This had always been his desire, in spite of the fact that inland
China was inaccessible to foreign missionaries. Gutzlaff's
effort to send the Gospel to the distant provinces had proved
a signal failure, and Protestant Missions were still confined,
and that very strictly, to the Treaty Ports. But for Hudson
Taylor, the vast, dark, waiting interior, with its millions
who had never heard of a Saviour's love, called with a claim
and insistence that could not be disregarded. And now,
through the amazing trend of events within that great
Empire itself, it seemed as though his desire might be nearer
accomplishment than he could ever have anticipated.

For wonderful news was slowly filtering its way from the
inland provinces, news that filled the Western world with
astonishment. The Tai-ping Rebellion, first recognised
in 1850, had not only attained remarkable proportions
under the leadership of Hung Siu-ts'üen. Arising in
southern China, it had swept over the central provinces

A REMARKABLE TABLET ERECTED AT NAN-KING BY THE TAI-PING
"EMPEROR," HUNG SIU-TS'ÜEN.

The small characters above are a quotation of the Beatitudes from Matthew v., while the
large *Fuh* below is the character for happiness or blessedness.

To face page 178.

and was now in possession of the larger part of the Yangtze Valley, including the famous city of Nanking. There, in the former capital of the Empire, the new ruler had established his seat of government, and with a conquered country behind him had rallied his forces for the march upon Peking. But it was not only the success attending this movement that made it a matter of such extraordinary interest in Christian lands. There was about it a character such as no analogous events in history had ever possessed before.

Arising among a heathen people, entirely apart from foreign influence, this mighty upheaval, as far as it had yet developed, appeared to be a crusade upon distinctively Christian lines. Its basis was the Bible ; but little understood, alas, in its spiritual teachings ! The Ten Commandments formed the moral code of the new kingdom. Idolatry in all its phases was abolished with unsparing hand, and the worship of the true and living God substituted, in purpose at any rate. The Christian Sabbath was recognised as a day of rest and prayer, and all restrictions were removed from the preaching of the Gospel.

" I have promulgated the Ten Commandments," wrote the Taiping leader to the only missionary of his acquaintance,[1] " throughout the army and the rest of the population, and have taught them all to pray, morning and evening. Still those who understand the Gospel are not many. Therefore I deem it right to send the messenger in person to wish you peace, and to request you, Elder Brother, if you are not disposed to abandon me, to (come and) bring with you many teachers to help in making known the Truth and to administer the ordinance of baptism. . . .

" Hereafter, when my enterprise is successfully terminated, I will

---

[1] This was the Rev. F. J Roberts of the American Baptist Missionary Union. Hung Siu-ts'uen, founder and leader of the Tai-ping movement, first learned the Truth from a tract given him during a literary examination in Canton, by Liang A-fah, one of Morrison's converts Subsequently he returned to Canton to hear more of the New Doctrine, and spent two or three months in studying the Scriptures under the direction of Mr. Roberts. Though he did not remain long enough to be baptized and received into Church fellowship, he had learned enough of the spirit and teaching of Christianity to make him a missionary to his own people on his return to Kwang-si, the province in which his fervent propaganda began. It was not until bitter persecution from the Chinese authorities had driven his followers to arms, that the movement took on a revolutionary character.

disseminate the Doctrine throughout the whole Empire, that all may
return to the one Lord and worship the true God only. This is what
my heart earnestly desires."

Scarcely less surprising was their attitude toward Western
nations. Opium-smoking was utterly prohibited, and T'ien-
teh [1] made no secret of his purpose to stop the importation
from abroad. But for foreigners as such, their Christian
" brothers " from across the seas, they expressed a cordiality
of feeling wholly contrary to Chinese pride and prejudice.

" The great God," they said, " is the universal Father of all under
Heaven. China is under His government and care. Foreign nations
are equally so. There are many men under heaven, but all are
brethren. Many women are under heaven, but all are sisters. Why
should we continue the selfish practice of regarding a boundary here
or a limit there ? Why indulge the wish to devour and consume one
another ? "

In a word, it seemed as though the hoary exclusiveness
of China as well as its heathen systems would soon be swept
away before Christian light and teaching, and the whole
country thrown open to the influence of the Gospel.[2] From
every standpoint the prospect was inspiring, and Christian
hearts could not but beat high with hope and expectation.
No wonder Hudson Taylor with many others saw in all this
the moving of God's providence. What kings and govern-
ments could never have accomplished, was not He in His
own wonderful way rapidly bringing to pass ? But how
immense the responsibility thus imposed upon the Church,
and how little prepared was she to meet it !

No wonder also in view of all these happenings that
though he was studying medicine Hudson Taylor felt no

[1] The title taken by the Tai-ping leader or " Emperor "

[2] T'ien-teh was probably the only aspirant to a throne who ever made
it a chief object to print and circulate the Christian Scriptures. So eager
was he that his people should possess the Word of God that he kept *four
hundred men* employed in Nanking, under his own supervision, printing and
binding various books of both the Old and New Testament. The version
used was that of Dr. Gutzlaff, which thus found its way in actual fact to
the remotest part of the empire. The title-page of every copy bore the
inscription : " A new edition, published in the third year of the Tai-ping
Dynasty." Around the title itself, the imperial arms were emblazoned,
and a large red stamp, four inches square, stated that the book was sent
out on the authority of the new emperor, the man before whom Peking
itself trembled.

inclination to tie himself down to distinctively medical work. His desire was to use his knowledge rather as an aid to evangelisation in districts that had never yet been reached. This was the work to which the Lord had called him ; deep down in his own soul he knew it beyond a doubt. But whether the Chinese Evangelisation Society would approve was quite another question.

To judge from their Rules and Regulations they would expect, at any rate, to maintain absolute control over the movements of their representatives. These were spoken of as Agents, and were expected to subscribe to by-laws that perplexed him with their detailed requirements ; and over against all this was his growing conviction about the work to which he personally was called. The hand of God was upon him. So far as he was concerned, this was the great fact, the chief consideration. And if the rightful authority of the Committee in London had to be considered as well, how would the two fit in ?

" There is one point about which I have not yet made up my mind," he wrote to his mother on April 5. " If at the expense of the Society I pass my examinations, take one or more degrees, go out to China and commence hospital work, how could I feel myself at liberty to sever the connection and go into the interior if called to do so ?

" It certainly does not seem to me that permanent work in one place, medical or otherwise, has been the way most used of God in the conversion of multitudes. Paul and the apostles of old, Wesley, Whitfield, and others largely used in modern times have been travelling preachers , and I do not feel at all sure that I should be right in binding myself to a different course of action. I shall be thankful to have your opinion on these points, and your prayers for Divine guidance in all my ways.

" That the Rules I mention," he continued a little later, " are reasonable and necessary for the Society, I do not doubt. I see also that after three years and a half I might be legally free to act independently, if I so desired. But I put it to you, Mother, would it be honourable, would you like me to take advantage of such a situation ? After the Society had borne the expense of my medical education and of sending me to China, and I had been there long enough to begin to be useful, would you approve my leaving them just as soon as I could do so legally ?

" And since it is my decided opinion that such would be my course, how can I honestly accept their aid ? Where is the probability that

I should ever be able to refund such an expenditure ? These difficulties seem to me insurmountable."

He was acting, certainly, on principles the Master commended—sitting down to count the cost before beginning to
build. Well would it be if all intending missionaries would
do the same to-day. And as he prayed and pondered he
began to see that even his present position was compromising.
The Society was already bearing, in part, the expense of
his medical education. If he went on and completed it,
it would cost them over a hundred pounds. Already he
was letting himself be involved in obligations he might not
be able to discharge without unfaithfulness to the most
binding thing in all his life, the will of God.

This was a serious situation, and one that called for
immediate consideration. Should he go on as he was,
allowing the Society to misunderstand to some extent his
intentions ? Or should he explain all, and run the risk of
losing their aid ? Must he abandon his medical studies now,
when he really seemed on the way to completing them, and
work his way out to China as a self-supporting missionary ?

It is easy enough in these very different days to smile at
what may seem over-conscientious scruples, but to Hudson
Taylor it was a more perplexing position than we can readily
understand. Missionary agencies were comparatively few
and far between, and he knew of only this one with which
he as an unordained man could become connected. Individuals did not then send out and support their own
representatives, nor was he in fellowship with any Church
that could sustain him. Practically it meant that he must
either become an agent of the C.E.S., subject to all their
regulations, or else go out in faith, looking to the Lord to
supply his needs or provide him with employment in which
he could be self-supporting. And the choice had to be made
immediately.

From early April till the end of May these problems
exercised his mind. He could not let things drift, but still
less could he act before he was sure of the guidance of God.
Full many a prayer in those lovely spring days might have

been measured by the mile, as he went up and down between the hospital and St. Mary Axe, but when the time came to go forward he did so without hesitation.

"With regard to my passing the College of Surgeons," he wrote to his mother in May, "I have written to Mr. Bird stating the reasons that appear to me as obstacles to my entering at their expense. It is necessary for the well-being of the Society that its missionaries should be subject to the Board of Management. . . . Their rules are no doubt reasonable and essential for such an organisation. But to me, to be educated at their expense and of course subject to these regulations would be like removing myself from the direct and personal leading of God, because I should become the servant of the Society. Having no money I could not release myself honourably, and in any case, for nine months at least (the period required as notice) I should be unable to act. Now, it is possible to pay too dearly even for great advantages, and this is more than my conscience allows me to do.

"If I am guided by God in going out, He will open the way and provide the means required. If a degree is necessary, He will supply the means for that also. If it is not necessary, it will be better for the time and money to be otherwise employed. And if I am not called to go, far better for all concerned that I should not leave England.

"But do not think from my using this form of expression that I am at all doubtful, for I never have had a doubt on the subject. My mind is kept in perfect peace, stayed on Him who is the Rock of Ages; and I am willing either to take a degree or not, as He sees fit to order. . . . I have been enjoying great rest of heart lately . . . and often feel the goodness of God in a way that cannot be expressed. . . .

"If in the time required to make me an M D. or M.R.C.S., or both, I am instrumental in leading any poor Chinese to the feet of Jesus, how much better would that appear in the eternal ages! Oh for grace really to live out that beautiful verse:

> I all on earth forsake,
> Its wisdom, fame and power;
> And Him my only Portion make,
> My Shield and Tower

"How very little many considerations that weigh with us now will appear as we look back upon them from the eternal ages! Then we shall reckon indeed that 'the sufferings of this present time' were 'not worthy to be compared' with the glory that was to follow. Would that we always did so here and now."

N

But all this preoccupation with important matters was not allowed to interfere with daily duties and with thoughtfulness for those around him.[1] Like Dr. Hardey in Hull, Mr. Brown soon discovered that he had a valuable assistant, and among the patients for whom Hudson Taylor cared more than one had reason to thank God for his solicitude for soul as well as body. For he did not attempt to evade or to defer the supreme duty of leading men to Christ. The unsaved at home were just as much a burden on his heart as the unsaved in China. Always and everywhere he was a soul-winner.

One among Mr. Brown's patients, for example, caused him no little concern at this time. He had been a hard drinker, and now in middle-life was suffering the bitter consequences of sin. His condition was serious, and his hatred of everything to do with religion so intense that it seemed hopeless to try to influence him.

" The Lord had given me the joy of winning souls before," wrote Hudson Taylor, recalling this experience, " but never in surroundings of such peculiar difficulty. With God, however, all things are possible, and no conversion ever takes place save by the almighty power of the Holy Ghost. The great need of every Christian worker is to *know* God. . . . I was now to prove His willingness to answer prayer for spiritual blessing under most unpromising circumstances, and thus to gain an increased acquaintance with the prayer-answering God as One ' mighty to save.'

" A short time before leaving for China it became my daily duty to dress the foot of a patient suffering from senile gangrene. The

---

[1] The impression made by the young assistant upon those with whom he lived at this time may be judged from the following recollections, kindly communicated to the writers more than fifty years later by a member of Mr. Brown's family.

" Early in 1853, Mr. Hudson Taylor went to assist Mr. Thomas Brown, Surgeon, who then resided at the corner of St. Mary Axe and Camomile Street, London. Mr. Brown's youngest child was a baby of a year old. Dr. Brown did not approve of perambulators for children living in the city, so on week-days the baby went out in his father's carriage On Sundays, however, Dr. Brown never took any of the children with him on his necessary rounds. As little Henry was too heavy for his nurse to carry, he would have had to remain indoors all Sunday, if Mr Taylor had not taken compassion on him. But he was fond of children, and before church time on Sunday used to carry the little fellow in his arms around Finsbury Circus which was near at hand Soon after Mr. Taylor left for China, Dr. Brown and his family moved to Finsbury Circus, where one of his sons still practises.—MARY E. BROWN "

disease commenced as usual insidiously, and the patient had little idea that he was a doomed man and probably had not long to live. I was not the first to attend him, but when the case was transferred to me I naturally became very anxious about his soul. The family with whom he lived were Christians, and from them I learned that he was an avowed atheist and very antagonistic to anything religious. They had without asking his consent invited a Scripture reader to visit him, but in great passion he had ordered him from the room. The Vicar of the district had also called, hoping to help him, but he had spit in his face and refused to allow him to speak. His temper was described to me as very violent, and altogether the case seemed as hopeless as could well be imagined.

"Upon first commencing to attend him I prayed much about it, but for two or three days said nothing of a religious nature. By special care in dressing his diseased limb I was able considerably to lessen his sufferings, and he soon began to manifest appreciation of my services. One day with a trembling heart I took advantage of his grateful acknowledgments to tell him what was the spring of my action, and to speak of his solemn position and need of God's mercy through Christ. It was evidently only a powerful effort of self-restraint that kept his lips closed. He turned over in bed with his back to me, and uttered no word.

"I could not get the poor man out of my mind, and very often through each day I pleaded with God, by His Spirit, to save him ere He took him hence. After dressing the wound and relieving the pain, I never failed to say a few words to him which I hoped the Lord would bless. He always turned his back looking annoyed, but never made any reply.

"After continuing this for some time my heart sank. It seemed to me that I was not only doing no good but perhaps really hardening him and increasing his guilt. One day after dressing his limb and washing my hands, instead of returning to the bedside, I went to the door and stood hesitating a moment with the thought in my mind, 'Ephraim is joined to his idols, let him alone.' Looking at my patient I saw his surprise, as it was the first time since opening the subject that I had attempted to leave without saying a few words for my Master.

"I could bear it no longer. Bursting into tears, I crossed the room and said: 'My friend, whether you will hear or whether you will forbear, I *must* deliver my soul,' and went on to speak very earnestly, telling him how much I wished that he would let me pray with him. To my unspeakable joy he did not turn away, but replied:

"'If it will be a relief to you, do.'

"I need scarcely say that falling upon my knees I poured out my soul to God on his behalf. Then and there, I believe, the Lord wrought a change in his soul. He was never afterwards unwilling to be spoken to and prayed with, and within a few days he definitely accepted Christ as his Saviour.

" Oh the joy it was to me to see that dear man rejoicing in hope of the glory of God ! He told me that for forty years he had never darkened the door of a church or chapel, and that then, forty years ago, he had only entered a place of worship to be married, and could not be persuaded to go inside when his wife was buried. Now, thank God, his sin-stained soul I had every reason to believe was washed, was sanctified, was ' justified, in the Name of the Lord Jesus and by the Spirit of our God.' Often in my early work in China, when circumstances rendered me almost hopeless of success, I have thought of this man's conversion and have been encouraged to persevere in speaking the Word, whether men would hear or whether they would forbear.

" The now happy sufferer lived for some time after this change, and was never tired of bearing testimony to the grace of God. Though his condition was most distressing, the alteration in his character and behaviour made the previously painful duty of attending him one of real pleasure. I have often thought since in connection with this case and the work of God generally of the words, ' He that goeth forth *weeping*, bearing precious seed, shall doubtless come again rejoicing, bringing his sheaves with him.' Perhaps if there were more of that intense distress for souls that leads to tears, we should more frequently see the results we desire. Sometimes it may be that while we are complaining of the hardness of the hearts of those we are seeking to benefit, the hardness of our own hearts and our own feeble apprehension of the solemn reality of eternal things may be the true cause of our want of success "

Very shortly after this the way cleared suddenly for Hudson Taylor. All had seemed uncertain before him, and especially since his letter to Mr. Bird about discontinuing his studies he had scarcely been able to see a step ahead. Very earnestly had he been in prayer for guidance, longing with all his heart to know and do the will of God. And now the light shone suddenly, and in the way he had least expected · because the time had come, and there is behind events, as the old prophet tells us, "a God . . . which worketh for him that waiteth for Him." [1]

In the room of the C.E.S. sat one of the secretaries writing a letter. It was June 4, and events had succeeded one

[1] Isaiah lxiv. 4, R.V.

another in China with startling rapidity. Since their conquest of Nanking in March, the Tai-pings had carried all before them, sweeping over the central and northern provinces until Peking itself was almost within their grasp. Nothing, it seemed, could save the tottering dynasty, unless foreign powers could be persuaded to intervene. Sir George Bonham, the British Representative, after a visit to Nanking had brought back a report very favourable to the Tai-pings. "The insurgents are Christians," wrote the *North China Herald* for May 7; and the religious aspect of the movement seemed to keep pace with the increase of their power.[1]

This could mean but one thing if Peking surrendered, the seclusion of ages was at an end and China would forthwith be thrown open to the Gospel. The very possibility, imminent as it was, proved a powerful stimulus to missionary effort. Christian hearts everywhere were aflame. Something must be done and done at once to meet so great a crisis! And for a time, money poured into the treasuries.[2]

In the light of these new developments the Committee of the C.E.S. had been reconsidering their position. The only representative they had in China was the German missionary Lobscheid, labouring near Canton. They had long wished to supply him with a fellow-worker, and now decided to send two men to Shanghai also to be ready for pending developments. Money was not the difficulty, their income having considerably increased within the last few months, but men, suitable men, would not be easy to find.

Thus it was that early in June, as we have seen, Mr Bird

[1] What the Tai-ping propaganda might have become, had it retained its earlier characteristics, who can say? Success, as is so often the case, led to dissension and decline From the zenith of its triumphant advance on Peking commenced this summer (1853), it degenerated into a corrupt political movement, deluging the country with blood and sufferings untold during the eleven remaining years of its course Even so the Imperial Government was powerless to bring it to an end until succoured by Western Powers. England, in the person of General Gordon, Chinese Gordon as he is still appreciatively called, delivered the empire at last from what had become an intolerable evil. Nanking fell before General Gordon in 1864.

[2] So great was the interest in the Tai-ping Rebellion and the hope that by the sympathetic co-operation of Christian nations it might lead to the conversion of multitudes to Christianity, that in September of this year (1853) the British and Foreign Bible Society decided to celebrate its Jubilee by printing *a million New Testaments* for use in that country, an undertaking almost incredibly great in those days

sat in his office writing as follows to one in whom they had every confidence, the young medical student, Hudson Taylor.

17 RED LION SQUARE,
June 4, 1853.

MY DEAR SIR—As you have fully made up your mind to go to China, and also not to qualify as a Surgeon, I would affectionately suggest that you lose no time in preparing to start. At this time we want really devoted men, and I believe your heart is right before God and your motives pure, so that you need not hesitate in offering.

I think you will find a difficulty in carrying out your plan [of self-support], as even Mr. Lobscheid could not get a free passage. It is a very difficult thing to obtain. The expense for a single man is about £60. Might not the time you want to spend in acquiring a knowledge of Ophthalmics be spent more profitably in China?

If you think it right to offer yourself, I shall be most happy to lay your application before the Board. It is an important step, and much earnest prayer is needed. But guidance will be given. Do all with thy might, and speedily.—I am, my dear sir, very truly yours,

CHARLES BIRD.

It was Saturday afternoon and the letter still lay on the desk, when a knock came, and the young man to whom it was addressed quietly entered.

" Why," exclaimed the Secretary, " I have just been writing to you ! The letter is not yet posted."

Long and earnest was the conversation that followed, for the suggestion made was a great surprise to Hudson Taylor. Constantly as China had been before his mind for three and a half years, it seemed rather overwhelming to think of sailing as soon as a vessel could be found. Besides, there were all those questions about the future and his uncertainty as to whether he ought to connect himself with any Society. Mr. Bird was evidently sympathetic and helpful, and the younger man went home with much to lay before the Lord.

How strange the difference that had come over everything as he retraced his steps toward St. Mary Axe. The same June sunlight shone on London streets, the same birds twittered in the open spaces, but he walked as in a new world—that far vista opening before him. Could it be possible that all that had hitherto blocked his way to China had indeed vanished ; that the Society was not only willing but anxious to send him out ? Then God's time surely must have come, and he could not hold back.

" Mr. Bird has removed most of the objections and difficulties I have been feeling," he wrote to his mother the following day, " and I think it will be well to comply with his suggestions and at once propose myself to the Committee. I shall await your answer, however, and rely upon your prayers. If I should be accepted to go at once, would you advise me to come home before sailing ? I long to be with you once more, and I know you would naturally wish to see me ; but I almost think it would be easier for us not to meet, than having met to part again forever. No, not forever !

> A little while : 'twill soon be past !
>   Why should we shun the promised cross ?
> Oh let us in His footsteps haste,
>   Counting for Him all else but loss :
> Then, how will recompense His smile
> The sufferings of this little while !

" I cannot write more, but hope to hear from you as soon as possible. Pray much for me. It is easy to talk of leaving all for Christ, but when it comes to the proof—it is only as we stand ' complete in Him ' we can go through with it.

" God be with you and bless you, my own dear, dear mother, and give you so to realise *the preciousness of Jesus* that you may wish for nothing but ' to know Him ' . . . even in ' the fellowship of His sufferings.' "

" ' Pray for me, dear Amelia,' he continued later, ' that He who has promised to meet all our need may be with me in this painful though long-expected hour.'

" When we look at ourselves—at the littleness of our love, the barrenness of our service, and the small progress we make toward perfection—how soul-refreshing it is to turn and gaze on Him ; to plunge afresh in ' the fountain opened for sin and for uncleanness ' ; to remember that we are ' accepted in the Beloved ' . . . ' who of God is made unto us wisdom and righteousness and sanctification and redemption.' Oh the fulness of Christ *the fulness of Christ* ! "

CHAPTER XV

SEPTEMBER 1853–MARCH 1854. AET. 21.

MOORED at her landing in a Liverpool dock lay the double-masted sailing-ship *Dumfries*, bound for China. A little vessel of barely four hundred and seventy tons, she was carrying but one passenger, so there were few well-wishers to see her off. Repairs that had delayed her sailing had just been hurried to completion, and the crew were still busy getting the cargo on board. But in the stern cabin, amid the din and hubbub, all was peace as Hudson Taylor knelt in prayer for the last time with his mother.

Hardly could they realise that it was indeed the last time for so long. Since the decision of the Committee there had been much to do and think of, and they had had little time to dwell upon the meaning of it all. And now the parting had come. After a visit to Barnsley where he took leave of his sisters, and meetings at Tottenham and in London commending him to God,[1] the outgoing missionary had come

---

[1] The following paragraph gives all the notice that appeared in *The Gleaner* of Hudson Taylor's departure for China :

"On Friday, the 9th of September, a meeting was held at the rooms of the Chinese Evangelisation Society at 7 o'clock in the evening, for the purpose of commending to the protection and blessing of God, Mr. James Hudson Taylor, on going out as a missionary to China. Mr. J H Taylor embarked on the *Dumfries*, Captain A. Morris, for Shanghai. The vessel left Liverpool on the 19th of September"

It is interesting to notice that the same day witnessed also the departure for China of the Rev. J L. Nevius (of the American Presbyterian Mission) with his bride. They sailed from Boston "in a small, old, unseaworthy vessel," and after a trying voyage round Cape Horn arrived in Shanghai just three weeks later than Mr. Hudson Taylor. These

on to Liverpool, where he had been joined by his mother.
His father too had been there, and Mr. Pearse representing
the Chinese Evangelisation Society, but on account of delays
in the sailing of the ship they had been obliged to return.
So the mother and son were much alone as the time drew
near, and her account of the parting written for those at
home is of special interest.

On Sunday, September 18, Hudson was much blessed through
the services of the day. His soul was filled with the love of God, and
in the evening he wrote a few farewell letters to relatives and friends,
full of affection, and bearing such testimony to the sustaining power
of grace as made it evident that he could freely and cheerfully leave
all, to carry the light of the knowledge of God to those regions of
spiritual darkness so long the object of his desires, and for which he
had studied, laboured and prayed.

Seeing me in tears, he said :

" Oh mother, do not grieve ! I am so happy, I cannot ! I'll tell
you what I think is the difference between us. You dwell on the
parting ; I look on to the meeting : " alluding to their reunion in the
Better Land.

Before retiring for the night he read aloud part of the fourteenth
chapter of John, " Let not your heart be troubled," and engaged in
prayer. The throne of grace was easy of access ; and while offering
thanks for mercies received and imploring continued blessings for
himself, for those he was leaving, for the Church and for the world
yet lying in the arms of the wicked one, it was evident that to him
this was no strange work.

Next morning he went to breakfast at the house of a friend with
Mr. Arthur Taylor (no relative) who was to embark a fortnight later
for Hong-kong—a fellow-missionary also sent out by the Chinese
Evangelisation Society. About ten o'clock we met in the cabin of
the *Dumfries*, and were shortly afterwards joined by Mr. Plunkett,

---

distinguished missionaries became, and continued through life, sincere and
valued friends of Mr Taylor's

But September 19 is chiefly memorable as the day upon which the
following decision was reached by the British and Foreign Bible Society.

" The attention of the British and Foreign Bible Society having been
directed to the unprecedented movement in China, and to the hopeful
prospects thereby presented for the wider introduction of the Sacred
Scriptures into that extensive and densely populated empire, it was
resolved, September 19, 1853, ' that the Committee, relying upon the
sympathy of the British public in this desirable object, are prepared to take
upon themselves all measures necessary for printing, with the least practic-
able delay, one million copies of the Chinese New Testament '

" ROBERT FROST, GEORGE BROWN, *Secretaries* "

an aged minister with whom we had become acquainted during our stay in Liverpool.

After a little conversation, singing and prayer were proposed, and Hudson gave out in a firm, clear voice, the beautiful hymn :

> How sweet the name of Jesus sounds
> In a believer's ear !
> It soothes his sorrows, heals his wounds,
> And drives away his fear.

The good old tune " Devizes " was struck up, and he sang with the utmost composure through the whole hymn. Mr. Plunkett prayed for us all as believers in one common Saviour, and for his two young friends in particular, just going out as ambassadors for the Prince of Peace.

Dear Hudson then engaged in prayer, and a stranger would little have thought that the firm tone, composed manner and joyous expressions were those of a youth who in a few minutes was to bid adieu to parents, sisters, friends, home and country. But his heart was strong in the mighty God of Jacob, therefore his spirit quailed not. Only once was there a slight falter, while commending the objects of his love to the care of his Heavenly Father—a momentary struggle, and all was calm again. Yet he did not forget that he was entering upon a course of trial, difficulty and danger ; but looking forward to it all he exclaimed, " None of these things move me, neither count I my life dear unto myself, so that I might finish my course with joy, and the ministry which I have received of the Lord Jesus, to testify the Gospel of the grace of God." It was a time ever to be remembered.

After Mr. Arthur Taylor had offered prayer, we rose from our knees and Hudson read a Psalm. Soon after we went on deck, intending to go ashore, when to our surprise we found that the vessel had left her moorings and was nearly out of dock. . . .

Then came my moment of trial—the farewell blessing, the parting embrace. A kind hand was extended from the shore. I stepped off the vessel, scarce knowing what I did, and was seated on a piece of timber lying close at hand. A chill came over me and I trembled from head to foot. But a warm arm was quickly round my neck and I was once more pressed to his loving breast. Seeing my distress he had leaped ashore to breathe words of consolation.

" Dear Mother," he said, " do not weep. It is but for a little while, and we shall meet again. Think of the glorious object I have in leaving you ! It is not for wealth or fame, but to try to bring the poor Chinese to the knowledge of Jesus."

As the vessel was receding he was obliged to return, and we lost sight of him for a minute. He had run to his cabin, and hastily writing in pencil on the blank leaf of a pocket Bible, " *The love of God which passeth knowledge*—J. H. T." came back and threw it to me on the pier.

By-and-by the vessel neared again to receive the mate, who shook us warmly by the hand :

" Keep a brave heart," he said, " I will bring good news back again."

Once more our Dear One reached out his hand which was eagerly grasped. Another " Farewell, God bless you " was reciprocated, and the deep waters of the Mersey became a separating gulf between us.

While we still waved our handkerchiefs, watching the departing ship, he took his stand at its head and afterwards climbed into the rigging, waving his hat, and looking more like a victorious hero than a stripling just entering the battlefield. Then his figure became less and less distinct, and in a few minutes passenger and ship were lost to sight.

His own recollections of that parting, recorded long after, show how deeply the son too shared its cost.

After being set apart with many prayers for the ministry of God's Word among the heathen, I left London for Liverpool, and on the 19th of September 1853 a little service was held in the stern cabin of the *Dumfries* which had been secured for me by the Chinese Evangelisation Society, under whose auspices I was going to China.

My beloved, now sainted mother, had come over to Liverpool to see me off. Never shall I forget that day, nor how she went with me into the cabin that was to be my home for nearly six long months. With a mother's loving hand she smoothed the little bed. She sat by my side and joined in the last hymn we should sing together before parting. We knelt down and she prayed—the last mother's prayer I was to hear before leaving for China. Then notice was given that we must separate, and we had to say good-bye, never expecting to meet on earth again.

For my sake she restrained her feelings as much as possible. We parted, and she went ashore giving me her blessing. I stood alone on deck, and she followed the ship as we moved toward the dock-gates. As we passed through the gates and the separation really commenced, never shall I forget the cry of anguish wrung from that mother's heart. It went through me like a knife. I never knew so fully, until then, what " God *so* loved the world " meant. And I am quite sure my precious mother learned more of the love of God for the perishing in that one hour than in all her life before.

Oh how it must grieve the heart of God when He sees His children indifferent to the needs of that wide world for which His beloved, His only Son suffered and died.

The voyage thus begun proved a time of blessing to the solitary passenger on board the *Dumfries*. It was long and tedious in some ways, five and a half months during which they touched nowhere and heard no tidings of the rest of the world. But it was a health-giving, enjoyable experience on the whole, after the first terrible days were over.

For never surely did vessel weather worse perils than this little sailing ship before she could reach the open sea. It almost seemed as though the great enemy, " the prince of the power of the air," knowing something of the possibilities enfolded in one young life on board, were doing his utmost to send her to the bottom. For twelve long days they beat about the Channel, alternately sighting Ireland and the dangerous Welsh coast. During the first week they were almost continuously in the teeth of an equinoctial gale, until driven into Carnarvon Bay they were within two boats' length of being dashed to pieces on the rocks. That midnight scene amid the foaming breakers, and the way in which they were delivered when all hope seemed gone made so profound an impression upon Hudson Taylor that some account of this part of the voyage must be culled from his journal and letters.

" With heartfelt gratitude," he wrote on Monday, September 26, " I record the mercy of God. He and He alone has snatched us from the jaws of death. May our spared lives be spent entirely in His service and for His glory.

" All day on Saturday [the 24th] the barometer kept falling, and as darkness came on the wind began to freshen. The sailors had a hard night of it, so the Captain did not call them aft as is his custom to read prayers on Sunday morning. At noon it was blowing hard and we took in all possible sail, leaving only just as much as would keep the ship steady. I distributed some tracts among the crew and then came down to my cabin, as the increased motion was making me sick. . . .

" The barometer was still falling, and the wind increased until it was a perfect hurricane. The Captain and Mate said they had never seen a wilder sea. Between two and three in the afternoon I managed to get on deck, though the pitching made it difficult. . . . The scene I shall never forget. It was grand beyond description. The sea, lashing itself into fury, was white with foam. There was a large ship astern of us and a brig to our weather side. The ship gained on us,

but drifted more. The waves, like hills on either side, seemed as if
they might swamp us at any moment . . . but the ship bore up
bravely. On account of the heavy sea we were making little or no
headway, and the wind being from the west we were drifting quickly,
irresistibly, toward a lee-shore.

"'Unless God help us,' said the Captain, 'there is no hope.'

"I asked how far we might be from the Welsh coast.

"'Fifteen to sixteen miles,' was his reply   'We can do nothing
but carry all possible sail. The more we carry the less we drift. It is
for our lives. God grant the timbers may bear it.'

"He then had two sails set on each mast.

"It was a fearful time. The wind was blowing terrifically, and
we were tearing along at a frightful rate—one moment high in the air
and the next plunging head foremost into the trough of the sea as if
about to go to the bottom. The windward side of the ship was fearfully elevated, the lee side being as much depressed ; indeed the sea
at times poured over her lee bulwarks.

"Thus the sun set, and I watched it ardently.

"'To-morrow thou wilt rise as usual,' I thought, 'but unless the
Lord work miraculously on our behalf a few broken timbers will be
all that is left of us and our ship ' . . . .

"The night was cold, the wind biting, and the seas we shipped
continually, with foam and spray, wet us through and through."

Earlier in the afternoon he had had a remarkable experience of "great joy and peace," in spite of their desperate
situation, but now as the sun went down a sense of loneliness
and desolation began to come over him, so that for a time
he was "much tried and very anxious." He thought of
the sorrow involved to his loved ones should the *Dumfries*
be lost ; of the expense to the Society, his passage and
outfit having cost little short of a hundred pounds ; of the
unprepared state of the crew, as well as of "the coldness of
the water and the struggle of death." About his eternal
happiness he had not a moment's doubt. Death itself was
not dreaded. But death under such circumstances ! No
one who has not faced it can begin to realise its terrors.

"I went below," the journal continues simply, "read a hymn or
two, some Psalms and John xiii.-xv., and was comforted ; so much so
that I fell asleep and slept for an hour. We then looked at the
barometer and found it rising. We had passed the Bardsey Island
Lighthouse, between Cardigan and Carnarvon Bays (running up the

Channel) and I asked the Captain whether we could clear Holyhead or not.

"'If we make no lee-way,' he replied, 'we may just do it. But if we drift, God help us!'

"And we did drift. . . .

"First the Holyhead light was ahead of us, and then on our outside. Our fate now seemed sealed. I asked if we were sure of two more hours. The Captain could not say we were. The barometer was still rising, but too slowly to give much hope. I thought of my dear father and mother, sisters and special friends . . . and the tears would start. . . . The Captain was calm and courageous, trusting in the Lord for his soul's salvation. The steward said he knew that he was nothing, but Christ was all. I felt thankful for them, but I did pray earnestly that God would have mercy on us and spare us for the sake of the unconverted crew . . . as well as for His own glory as the God who hears and answers prayer. This passage was then brought to my mind: 'Call upon Me in the day of trouble; I will deliver thee, and thou shalt glorify Me': and very earnestly I pleaded the promise, in submission to His will.

"Our position was now truly awful. The night was very light, the moon being unclouded, and we could just see land ahead. I went below. The barometer was improving, but the wind in no way abated. I took out my pocket-book and wrote in it my name and home-address, in case my body should be found. I also tied a few things in a hamper which I thought would float and perhaps help me or some one else to land. Then commending my soul to God my Father, and my friends and *all* to His care, with one prayer that if it were possible this cup might pass from us, I went on deck.

"Satan now tempted me greatly and I had a fearful struggle. But the Lord again calmed my mind, which from that time was so stayed upon Him that I was kept in peace.

"I asked the Captain whether boats could live in such a sea. He answered, 'No.' Could we not lash the loose spars together and make some sort of raft? He said we should probably not have time.

"The water was now becoming white. Land was just ahead. . . .

"'We must try to turn her and tack,' said the Captain, 'or all is over. The sea may sweep the deck in turning and wash everything overboard . . . but we must try.'

"This was a moment to make the stoutest heart tremble. He gave the word and we tried to turn outwardly, but in vain. This would have saved us room. He then tried the other way, and with God's blessing succeeded, clearing the rocks by not more than two ships' length. Just as we did so, the wind most providentially veered two points in our favour, and we were able to beat out of the Bay.

"Had not the Lord thus helped us, all our efforts must have been in vain. Truly His mercy is unfailing. 'Oh that men would praise the Lord for His goodness and for His wonderful works to the children of men.'" [1]

Safe for the present, it was with unspeakable thankfulness they saw the sun rise on Monday morning and the storm gradually pass away.

A week later they were in the Bay of Biscay and there also came in for rough weather, one heavy sea carrying away the fore skylight and seeming almost to swamp the ship. Three weeks from the day of sailing, however, saw them in calmer waters, the worst of their dangers past. During all that time it had been cold and wet, and everything on board seemed either damp or soaking, which meant constant discomfort.

"These things make one long for fine, dry weather," runs the journal for October 5. "Most of my belongings are damp, the floors are wet, and all our boots and shoes are saturated with water. The poor steward's cabin is soaking, the sea having poured into it, and now mine is the only one that has not been flooded. . . . But how thankful I ought to be that it was not the after skylight that gave

---

[1] "One thing was a great trouble to me that night. I was a very young believer, and had not sufficient faith in God to see Him in and through the use of means. I had felt it a duty to comply with the earnest wish of my beloved and honoured mother, and for her sake to procure a swimming-belt. But in my own soul I felt as if I could not simply trust in God while I had this swimming-belt, and my heart had no rest until on that night, after all hope of being saved was gone, I had given it away. Then I had perfect peace, and strange to say put several light things together, likely to float at the time we struck, without any thought of inconsistency or scruple.

"Ever since, I have seen clearly the mistake I made ; a mistake that is very common in these days, when erroneous teaching on faith-healing does much harm, misleading some as to the purposes of God, shaking the faith of others and distressing the minds of many The use of means ought not to lessen our faith in God, and our faith in God ought not to hinder our using whatever means He has given us for the accomplishment of His own purposes

"For years after this I always took a swimming-belt with me and never had any trouble about it , for after the storm was over, the question was settled for me through the prayerful study of the Scriptures. God gave me then to see my mistake, probably to deliver me from a great deal of trouble on similar questions now so constantly raised. When in medical or surgical charge of any case, I have never thought of neglecting to ask God's guidance and blessing in the use of appropriate means, nor yet of omitting to give thanks for answered prayer and restored health. But to me it would appear as presumptuous and wrong to neglect the use of those measures which He Himself has put within our reach, as to neglect to take daily food, and suppose that life and health might be maintained by prayer alone" (from Mr. Taylor's *Retrospect*),

way, for then all my clothes, books and papers would have been deluged.

" And they had no means of drying them."

It was with no little satisfaction, therefore, that favourable winds were welcomed, bearing them to warmer latitudes. But the earlier stages of the voyage had not been lost. Even in the Bay of Biscay, Hudson Taylor had discovered that there was one more earnest Christian on board, the Swedish carpenter, and assured of his help had asked the Captain's permission to commence regular services among the crew. And now in the hot, still days that found them becalmed near the Equator these were continued with much acceptance.

Whole-heartedly the young missionary threw himself into this work. He had been reading the life of Hewitson since coming on board, and had found it stimulating both to faith and zeal.

" How he seems to have fed on the Lamb," he wrote, " and to have ministered the Spirit. Oh for more of the love of God, that out of a full heart I might proclaim it !

" This evening [Sunday, October 9] we had a good attendance at our little service. . . . We began with a hymn, and good it was to hear them sing ! Then I asked the Lord's blessing with great liberty, for He was indeed present. After a short address, I read the fourth chapter of Romans, and explained the way of salvation by faith, dwelling on the love of the Father and the Son, the value of a soul, and the necessity for flying at once for mercy to ' the Lamb of God that taketh away the sin of the world ' Then the steward prayed and we concluded the meeting.

" It was encouraging afterwards to hear that some of the men had been much affected, tears chasing down the weather-beaten faces of one or two. May God, who alone giveth the increase, bless His Word and use it for His glory."

Sixty times during the remainder of the voyage such meetings were held, Hudson Taylor giving unwearied prayer and preparation to this ministry. It was a great blessing to him personally and did much to save him from the spiritual declension that so often accompanies life at sea with its lack of helpful influences. To him the journey was a time of marked blessing, his only sorrow being that so little permanent change was found in the lives of the men. They were interested, and would come to him at times for private talk and prayer. But though some were very near the Kingdom, none of them came out fully on the side of Christ. This was a keen disappointment and cast him much on God. No doubt in some ways the experience was useful, preparing him to " sow beside all waters," even when for a long time no fruit appeared.

Much more might be said about that five months at sea, did space permit.[1] The journal is full of the variety and interest, the occasional excitements and more frequent monotony of twenty-three consecutive weeks on a sailing ship without touching land. There are glimpses of moon-lit nights in the tropics ; of illuminating seas gemmed with trails of light from innumerable Acephalae ; of exciting situations over the capture of a shark or albatross, and perilous ones when becalmed in southern waters they were borne by unseen currents towards sunken reefs or more dangerous cannibal islands.

Still more the journal is taken up with the inner life that meant so much more than outward surroundings. Side by side with his prayers and efforts for the good of the crew went deepened longings for a closer walk himself with God, and entries such as the following abound :

Oct. 30 : Have been much blessed to-day. The Lord is indeed precious to me. Oh that I loved Him more !

Nov. 1 : Another month has been spent, how unprofitably ! How little to the honour of that glorious Being in whom we live and move and have our being. May the next be used more faithfully in His service and to His glory.

Dec. 26 : Enjoying sweet fellowship with the Lord Jesus, and great liberty of access to the throne of grace.

> What is earth with all its treasures
> To the joy our Saviour brings ?
> Well may we resign its pleasures,
> Satisfied with better things.
> All His people
> Draw from Heaven's eternal springs

---

[1] They rounded the Cape of Good Hope early in December, and soon after Christmas Day " began to make northing," having run 14,500 miles since leaving the Mersey. On January 5 they reached the nearest point to

Oh to be ever seeking " the things that are above," as risen indeed with Christ; ever standing on the watch-tower, ready to welcome the glad word, " Behold the Bridegroom cometh."

Dec. 31 : On reviewing the mercies of the year and the goodness of God to me in it, I am lost in wonder, love and praise. . . . Here then I raise my " Eben-ezer " : " Hitherto hath the Lord helped me " . . .

> And since my soul hath known His love,
> What mercies He has made me prove !
> Mercies that do all praise excel :
> My Jesus hath done all things well.

Spent the last moments of the year in prayer . . . and found the Lord present and very precious.

There were times in his solitude when home seemed far away and the longing for those he loved became intense.

" How widely we are separated," he wrote, " who last year were so near. . . Praised be God, He is unchangeable ; His mercy never fails. . . .

" Found in a book lent me by Captain Morris, *The Hebrew Mother*, and was much affected by it. Never shall I forget the last time I heard it. Mother was present, my dearest—played it, and when we came to the lines :

> I give thee to thy God,
> The God that gave thee—

Mother broke down, and clasping me in her arms wept aloud at the thought of parting. May the Lord bless her and comfort her heart day by day. . . .

" Jesus *is* precious. His service is perfect freedom. His yoke is easy and His burden light. Joy and peace His people have indeed. Absent from home, friends, and country even, Jesus is with me. . . . He is all, and more than all. Much as my heart yearns to see them, the love of Christ is stronger, more constraining."

This love then for the souls of men, the love of Christ in him, did not fail under the test of pain and loss. If anything it was deepening, face to face with facts that had been only hearsay before. The lonely inhabitants of many an island, for example, between Java and the Philippines drew forth his compassion. They had already sighted land

---

Western Australia, only 120 miles away, and thence steered a perilous course through the East Indian Islands to the Pacific Ocean and the China Sea, dropping anchor at Woo-sung, in the mouth of the Shanghai River on March 1, 1854.

some weeks before, in rounding the Cape of Good Hope, but not until the nearest point to Australia was reached did they begin to enter the Archipelago lying between the Indian and Pacific Oceans.   This proved a region of fascinating interest, though not without its special dangers.   For almost a month from January 12, when they first hailed with delight the green hills and valleys of Sandal Wood Isle, until they looked their last on the sandy beach of Angour (Pelew Group) shining in the sun, they were hardly ever out of sight of beautiful, fertile, populous islands, in which no witness for the dying, undying love of Calvary was found.

"Oh what work for the missionary!" wrote Hudson Taylor. "Island after island, many almost unknown, some densely peopled, but no light, no Jesus, no hope full of bliss! My heart yearns over them.   Can it be that Christian men and women will stay comfortably at home and leave these souls to perish? Can it be that faith has no longer power to constrain to sacrifice for His sake who gave His life for the world's redemption? . . .

> Shall we whose souls are lighted
> With wisdom from on high,
> Shall we to men benighted
> The lamp of Life deny?

"Shall we think ourselves free from responsibility to obey the plain command, ' Go ye into all the world and preach the Gospel to every creature ' ? Is that word of our Saviour no longer true, ' As My Father hath sent Me . . . even so send I you ' ? Oh that I could get to them ! Oh that I had a thousand tongues to proclaim in every land the riches of God's grace ! Lord, raise up labourers, and thrust them forth into Thy harvest."

A little later no small stir was occasioned when, in passing close to one of these islands at night, a light was seen ashore. More than sixteen weeks had elapsed since the beacons of St. George's Channel had faded from sight, and in all that time no sign had been seen of a human habitation. But that light, that little moving light in Dampier Strait told of fellow-men near at hand, and aroused sensations that were indescribable.

Becalmed next day within reach of Waygion, they

attracted the attention of a few poor islanders who put off
in their canoes to make trade with the foreign ship.   But
the fresh cocoa-nuts, shells, parrots, and even the bird-of-
paradise they offered had little interest for the missionary
compared with the sight of those faces—gentle, intelligent,
appealing—and the sound of their soft speech in an unknown
tongue.

" The men seemed very poor," he wrote, " and those in the last
two boats, timid.   They had probably been taken in by previous
travellers.   They were a little lighter in colour than burnt coffee-bean,
and but for a narrow cloth around their loins were entirely naked.
Their faces, however, were intelligent and pleasing. . . .

" What would I not have given to be able to tell them of a Saviour's
love !   I longed to go and live among them, poor and degraded as
they are, and lead them to that blissful home where sin and sorrow
are no more. . . . Let us pray the Lord to send them missionaries
who shall be willing to sacrifice earthly comforts that they may win
souls to Christ."

But with all its interests the voyage seemed tedious
toward the close, especially in the frequent calms of this
Eastern Archipelago.   Only for a single day during that
month among the Islands had they a steady wind, and more
than once their log did not exceed seven miles in the twenty-
four hours.   Such experiences were more than trying, they
were accompanied with serious danger.

" Never," as Hudson Taylor put it, " is one more helpless than in
a sailing ship with a total absence of wind and the presence of a strong
current setting toward a dangerous coast.   In a storm the ship is to
some extent manageable, but becalmed one can do nothing ; the Lord
must do all."

One definite answer to prayer under such circumstances
was a great encouragement to his faith.   They had just come
through the Dampier Strait but were not yet out of sight
of the islands.   Usually a breeze would spring up after
sunset and last until about dawn.   The utmost use was
made of it, but during the day they lay still with flapping
sails, often drifting back and losing a good deal of the
advantage gained at night.

This happened notably on one occasion when we were in dangerous proximity to the north of New Guinea. Saturday night had brought us to a point some thirty miles off the land, and during the Sunday morning service which was held on deck I could not fail to see that the Captain looked troubled and frequently went over to the side of the ship. When the service was ended I learnt from him the cause : a four-knot current was carrying us toward some sunken reefs, and we were already so near that it seemed improbable that we should get through the afternoon in safety. After dinner the long-boat was put out and all hands endeavoured, without success, to turn the ship's head from the shore.

After standing together on the deck for some time in silence, the Captain said to me :

" Well, we have done everything that can be done. We can only await the result."

A thought occurred to me, and I replied :

" No, there is one thing we have not done yet."

" What is that ? " he queried.

" Four of us on board are Christians. Let us each retire to his own cabin, and in agreed prayer ask the Lord to give us immediately a breeze. He can as easily send it now as at sunset."

The Captain complied with this proposal. I went and spoke to the other two men, and after prayer with the carpenter we all four retired to wait upon God. I had a good but very brief season in prayer, and then felt so satisfied that our request was granted that I could not continue asking, and very soon went up again on deck. The first officer, a godless man, was in charge. I went over and asked him to let down the clews or corners of the mainsail, which had been drawn up in order to lessen the useless flapping of the sail against the rigging.

" What would be the good of that ? " he answered roughly.

I told him we had been asking a wind from God , that it was coming immediately ; and we were so near the reef by this time that there was not a minute to lose.

With an oath and a look of contempt, he said he would rather see a wind than hear of it.

But while he was speaking I watched his eye, following it up to the royal, and there sure enough the corner of the topmost sail was beginning to tremble in the breeze.

" Don't you see the wind is coming ? Look at the royal ! " I exclaimed.

" No, it is only a cat's paw," he rejoined (a mere puff of wind).

" Cat's paw or not," I cried, " pray let down the mainsail and give us the benefit."

This he was not slow to do. In another minute the heavy tread of the men on deck brought up the Captain from his cabin to see what was the matter. The breeze had indeed come ! In a few minutes we were

ploughing our way at six or seven knots an hour through the water . . .
and though the wind was sometimes unsteady we did not altogether
lose it until after passing the Pelew Islands.

Thus God encouraged me ere landing on China's shores to bring
every variety of need to Him in prayer, and to expect that He would
honour the name of the Lord Jesus and give the help each emergency
required.

PART IV

SHANGHAI AND EARLY ITINERATIONS

1854–1855. AET. 22–23.

O Thou, by long experience tried,
Near whom no grief can long abide ,
My Lord, how full of sweet content,
I pass my years of banishment.

All scenes alike engaging prove
To souls impress'd with sacred love !
Where'er they dwell, they dwell in Thee ,
In heaven, on earth, or on the sea

To me remains nor place nor time,
My country is in every clime ;
I can be calm and free from care
On any shore, since God is there.

While place we seek or place we shun,
The soul finds happiness in none ,
But with my God to guide my way
'Tis equal joy to go or stay.

Could I be cast where Thou art not,
That were, indeed, a dreadful thought ;
But regions none remote I call,
Secure of finding God in all

MADAME GUYON

CHAPTER XVI

ARRIVAL AND FIRST EXPERIENCES

MARCH 1854. AET. 21.

IT was a foggy Sunday off Gutzlaff Island, cold with occasional rain, as might be expected at the end of February, and the *Dumfries* lay at anchor waiting for a pilot to take her up to Shanghai. Through stormy weather she had held her way up the China Sea, driven out of her course by westerly gales, caught in a cyclone and blinding snowstorms, but now the last stage of her long journey was reached, and the yellow, turbid water surging around her told that they were already in the estuary of a great river.

Muffled in his heaviest wraps Hudson Taylor paced the deck, doing his best to keep warm and be patient. It was a strange Sunday, this last at sea. For days he had been packed and ready to leave the ship, and hindered by storm and cold from other occupations had given the more time to thought and prayer.

" What peculiar feelings," he wrote, " arise at the prospect of soon landing in an unknown country, in the midst of strangers—a country now to be my home and sphere of labour. ' Lo, I am with you alway.' ' I will never leave thee nor forsake thee.' Sweet promises ! I have nothing to fear, with Jesus on my side.

" Great changes probably have taken place since last we heard from China. And what news shall I receive from England ? Where shall I go, and how shall I live at first ? These and a thousand other questions engage the mind. . . . But the most important question of all is, ' Am I now living as near to God as possible ? ' Alas ! I am not. My wayward heart, so easily occupied with the things of time and sense, needs continually leading back to the fold from whence it strays. Oh ! that my ' rejoicing ' may be ' more abundant in Christ Jesus,' and my ' conversation ' ever · as becometh the Gospel of Christ.' "

As afternoon wore on, what were those boats in the distance—looming toward them through the mist ? One beat its way up before long, eagerly watched from the *Dumfries*. Yes, there was no mistaking that picturesque sail and curiously painted hull, nor the faces of the men as they came into sight. There they were, twelve or fourteen of them, blue-garbed, dark-eyed, vociferating in an unknown tongue—the first Chinese Hudson Taylor had ever seen. And how his heart went out to them ! Behind the strange, uncouth exterior he saw the treasure he had come so far to seek—the souls for which Christ died.

" I did long," he wrote, " to be able to tell them the Glad Tidings."

A little later the English pilot came on board and received a hearty welcome. There was no hope of reaching Woo-sung that day, still less Shanghai, fifteen miles farther up the tidal river ; but there was much he could tell them, while waiting for the fog to clear, of the long winter's doings since they had left England.

From him they learned, for example, of the troubles between Russia and Turkey that within a few weeks were to lead to the Crimean War.[1] The allied fleets of England and France had already reached the scene of conflict, and nothing it was feared could avert the serious issue. But startling though it was to hear of war-clouds hanging over Europe, it was scarcely as great a shock as the news from China itself, and especially from the port at which they were about to land. Not only was the Tai-ping Rebellion still devastating province after province in its progress toward Peking , Shanghai close at hand, both the native city and the foreign Settlement, was plunged in all the horrors of war. A local band of rebels known as the " Red Turbans " had obtained possession of the city, around

[1] This war, which was to cost England twenty-four thousand men, and to add forty-one millions sterling to the national debt, commenced on March 27, 1854, and was not concluded until two years later.

which was now encamped an Imperial army of forty to fifty thousand men, the latter proving a more serious menace to the European community than even the rebels themselves.

For the rest, bad as their passage had been they had arrived ahead of vessels that set out before them, but just too late for the February mail. They must be prepared, moreover, to find everything at famine prices, for the dollar had risen from four shillings, its ordinary value, to six or seven, and would soon be higher : a discouraging outlook for one with a small income in English money !

All this and more the pilot told them, and they had time to think over his communications. Monday was still so foggy that they could not proceed, and though they weighed anchor on Tuesday morning it was only to beat up against the wind a few miles nearer to Woo-sung. But that night the fog lifted, and the young missionary pacing the deck caught sight of a low-lying shore, running far to north and south, that was *no island*. How it arrested him ! His prayers were answered ; the dream of years come true. He was looking on China at last, under the evening sky.

Not until 5 P.M. next day, however (Wednesday, March 1), was he able to land in Shanghai ; and then it was quite alone, the *Dumfries* being still detained by adverse winds.

" My feelings on stepping ashore," he wrote, " I cannot attempt to describe. My heart felt as though it had not room and must burst its bonds, while tears of gratitude and thankfulness fell from my eyes."

Then a deep sense of the loneliness of his position began to come over him ; not a friend or acquaintance anywhere , not a single hand held out to welcome him, or any one who even knew his name.

Mingled with thankfulness for deliverance from many dangers and joy at finding myself at last on Chinese soil came a vivid realisation of the great distance between me and those I loved, and that I was a stranger in a strange land.

I had three letters of introduction, however, and counted on advice and help from one especially, to whom I had been commended by mutual friends, whom I knew well and highly valued. Of course I inquired for him at once, only to learn that he had been buried a month or two previously, having died of fever while we were at sea.

Saddened by these tidings I asked the whereabouts of a missionary to whom another of my introductions was addressed, but only to meet with further disappointment. He had recently left for America. The third letter remained ; but it had been given me by a comparative stranger, and I expected less from it than from the others. It proved, however, to be God's channel of help.

This letter then in hand, he left the British Consulate near the river to find the London Mission compound at some distance across the Settlement. On every side strange sights, sounds and smells now greeted him, especially when the European houses gave place to Chinese shops and dwellings. Here nothing but Chinese was to be heard, and few if any but Chinese were to be seen. The streets grew narrower and more crowded, and overhanging balconies above rows of swinging signboards almost hid the sky. How he found his way for a mile or more does not appear ; but at length a mission-chapel came in sight, and with an upward look for guidance Hudson Taylor turned in at the ever-open gateway of *Ma-ka-k'uen*.[1]

Several buildings stood before him, including a hospital and dwelling-houses, at the first of which he enquired for Dr. Medhurst to whom his letter was addressed. Sensitive and reserved by nature, it was no small ordeal to Hudson Taylor to have to introduce himself to so important a person, the pioneer as well as founder (with Dr. Lockhart) of Protestant missionary effort in this part of China, and it was almost with relief he heard that Dr. Medhurst was no longer living on the compound. He too, it seemed, had gone away !

More than this Hudson Taylor was unable to make out, as the Chinese servants could not speak English, nor could he understand a word of their dialect. It was a perplexing situation until a European came in sight, to whom the new arrival quickly made himself known. To his relief he found he was talking with Mr. Edkins, one of the junior

[1] The name of the London Mission Compound on Shantung Road, familiar and beloved The three characters mean, " Medhurst Family Enclosure."

missionaries, who welcomed him kindly and explained that Dr. and Mrs. Medhurst had moved to the British Consulate, as the premises they had occupied were within sight and sound of constant fighting at the North Gate of the city.   Dr. Lockhart, however, remained ; and while he went to find him, Mr. Edkins invited the stranger into one of the Mission-houses.

It was quite an event in those days for an Englishman and especially a missionary to appear in Shanghai un- announced.   Most people came by the regular mail-steamers once a month, whose arrival caused general excitement. None was expected then, and even the *Dumfries* was not yet in port ; so that when another of the L.M.S. people came in, during Mr. Edkin's absence, Hudson Taylor had to explain all over again who and what he was.   But Alexander Wylie soon set the shy lad at ease, and enter- tained him until Mr. Edkins returned with Dr. Lockhart.

It did not take long for these new friends to understand the situation, and then there was nothing for it but to receive the young missionary into one of their own houses. They could not leave him without a home, and the Settle- ment was so crowded that lodgings were not to be had at any price.   Dr. Lockhart, happily, had a room at his disposal. He was living alone, Mrs. Lockhart having been obliged to return to England, and with genuine kindness welcomed Hudson Taylor as his guest, permitting him to pay a moderate sum to cover board-expenses.

This arrangement made, Mr. Edkins took him to see Mr. and Mrs. Muirhead, who completed the L.M.S. staff in Shanghai, and introduced him also to Mr. and Mrs. Burdon of the Church Missionary Society, who had rented an unoccupied house (belonging possibly to Dr. Medhurst) on the same compound.   The Burdons invited him to dinner that evening.   They were young and newly married, hav- ing only been a year or two in China, and from the first were drawn to Hudson Taylor in a sympathy he warmly reciprocated.

" The fireside looked so homelike, their company was so pleasant and all the news they had to tell," he wrote, " so full of interest that it was most refreshing. After prayer at ten o'clock I returned to Dr. Lockhart's, who kindly gave me a room and made me quite at home to enjoy once more a bed on shore." [1]

Here then was an answer to many prayers, the solution of many ponderings. For the moment he was provided for under favourable circumstances, and though he could not long trespass upon the doctor's hospitality, it would afford

[1] It is a matter of no little interest to think of Hudson Taylor on his arrival as welcomed by this group of distinguished missionaries. "There were giants . . in those days," and certainly the L M.S. had their share ! Among the honoured names on the long roll of its missionaries few take a higher place than Medhurst, Lockhart, Wylie, Muirhead, Edkins, and Griffith John who joined them a few months later

"Most of the large cities in Kiang-su and North Cheh-kiang first heard the Word of Life from this band of devoted young men . . . who in the years before 1860 were associated with the pioneer evangelist to central China, Dr. Medhurst" (*A Century of Missions in China*, p 7).

Of Dr. Lockhart it need only be said that he was the first medical-missionary from England to China. He landed in Canton four years after Dr. Peter Parker from America, and accompanied Dr. Medhurst when, in 1843, he commenced missionary operations in central China

At the time of Hudson Taylor's arrival, Dr. Medhurst and Dr. Lockhart had already been eleven years in Shanghai. Both were in middle life, Dr. Medhurst being fifty-eight and Dr. Lockhart forty-three years of age. Mr. Wylie was a man of thirty-nine, and a widower. Messrs. Edkins and Muirhead were thirty-one and thirty-two respectively, and had been in Shanghai already six and seven years : the important centre in which they were still to be fellow-labourers after more than half a century had gone by.

The literary as well as evangelistic labours of these men were most remarkable. Dr. Medhurst was proficient in eight or ten languages, and published fifty-nine works in Chinese, six in Malay, and twenty-seven in English Dr. Lockhart wrote and translated valuable books on medicine and medical-missions. Alexander Wylie "acquired French, Russian, German, and the Manchu and Mongol languages while in charge of the L.M.S. Press in Shanghai, and published numerous works of great value both in English and Chinese." The venerable and beloved Dr. Muirhead, during his fifty-three years of incessant evangelistic and pastoral labours, "translated the first considerable work on Geography ever published in Chinese . . . and was the author also of many theological works, and a member of the Bible Revision Committee." While the well-known Dr. Edkins, who survived them all, with "an extraordinary gift for languages and a profound knowledge of Chinese," was one of the leading sinologues of his day.

The Rev. J. S. Burdon also continued for nearly half a century in missionary labours in China He was the first representative of the Church Missionary Society to commence work in Peking, which became his head-quarters for eleven years. "He translated the Prayer Book and a Bible History, and published several lesser works, besides aiding in the translation of the Scriptures" In 1873 he was consecrated third Bishop of Victoria, Hong-kong, which responsible office he held for more than twenty years.

A remarkable group of men, reinforced by a remarkable addition in the coming among them of Hudson Taylor.

Photograph.   By a Chinese.

PAGODA IN THE IMMEDIATE NEIGHBOURHOOD OF SHANGHAI.

To face page 207.

him at any rate a little while in which to look about and make permanent arrangements. With good courage, therefore, he arose next morning to see what could be done. The *Dumfries* would be coming in and he must have his luggage brought ashore, then procure necessary books and a teacher to commence as soon as possible the study of the language. It was his first whole day in China.

" My pleasure on awakening," he wrote to his sister, " and hearing the cheerful song of birds may be better imagined than described. The green corn waving in the fields, budding plants in the garden, and sweetly perfumed blossoms on some of the trees were indeed delightful after so long at sea."

Breakfast over he went to the Consulate, and though disappointed to find only one letter (on which he had to pay no less than two shillings postage) it was a letter from home, containing enclosures from both mother and sisters.

"Never did I pay two shillings more willingly in my life," he assured them, " than for that letter."

Soon the *Dumfries* was reported, and with a Chinese helper he managed to get his things brought up to Dr. Lockhart's. It was a peculiar sensation to be marching at the head of a procession of coolies through the crowded streets, all his belongings swinging from bamboo poles across their shoulders, while at every step they sang or shouted " Ou-ah Ou-ay " in varying tones, some a third above the rest. They were not really in pain or distress, although it sounded like it ; and by the time some of the copper cash he had received in exchange for a Mexican dollar had been distributed amongst them, he had had his first lesson in business dealings with the Chinese.

Then came the daily service in the hospital, conducted on this occasion by Dr. Medhurst, and Hudson Taylor listened for the first time to Gospel preaching in the tongue with which he was to become so familiar. In conversation afterwards, Dr. Medhurst advised him to commence his studies with the Mandarin dialect, the most widely spoken in China, and undertook to procure a teacher. Evening brought the weekly prayer-meeting, when Hudson Taylor was introduced to others of the missionary community, thus ending with united waiting upon God a day full of interest and encouragement.

But before the week closed he began to see another side of Shanghai life. The journal tells of guns firing all night, and the city wall not half a mile away covered with sentry lights ; of sharp fighting seen from his windows, in which men were killed and wounded under his very eyes ; of a patient search for rooms in the Chinese part of the Settlement, only emphasising the fact that there were none to be had ; of his first contact with heathenism ; and of scenes of suffering in the native city which made an indelible impression of horror upon his mind.

Of some of these experiences he wrote to his sister ten days after his arrival :

On Saturday [March 4] I took a walk through the Market, and such a muddy, dirty place as Shanghai I never did see ! The ground is all mud ; dry in dry weather, but one hour's rain makes it like walking through a clay-field. It scarcely is walking—but wading ! I found that there was no probability of getting a house or even apartments, and felt cast down in spirit.

The following day, Sunday, I attended two services at the L.M.S., and in the afternoon went into the city with Mr. Wylie. You have never seen a city in a state of siege, or been at the seat of war. God grant you never may ! We walked some distance round the wall, and sad it was to see the wreck of rows upon rows of houses near the city. Burnt down, blown down, battered to pieces—in all stages of ruin they were ! And the misery of those who once inhabited them, and now at this inclement season are driven from house, home and everything, is terrible to think of.

At length we came upon a ladder let down from the wall, by which provisions were being conveyed into the city. We entered also . . . and had a little conversation with the soldiers on guard who offered us no opposition. For a long time we wandered through the city, Mr. Wylie talking with people here and there, and giving them tracts. We went into some of the temples and had conversation with the priests, who also received tracts from us. Everywhere we seemed welcome. . . .

As we passed the West Gate, we saw that the mud with which it had been blocked was cleared away. Hundreds of the Rebel soldiery were assembled there, and we met many more going in that direction.

They were about to make a sally upon the Imperialists, who would not be expecting it from that quarter.

We then proceeded to the L.M.S. Chapel, and found it crammed with people. Dr. Medhurst was preaching, after which six bags of rice were distributed among the poor creatures, many of whom must perish but for this assistance, rendered daily, as they can do nothing now to earn a living. Some of the windows smashed in the Chapel, and the lamps broken by passing bullets tell of the deadly work that is going on. . . .

By the time we came to the North Gate they were fighting fiercely outside the city. One man was brought in dead, another shot through the chest, and a third whose arm I examined seemed in dreadful agony. A ball had gone clean through the arm, breaking the bone in passing. We could do nothing for him unless he would come to the hospital; for, as Dr. Lockhart said, who came up just at the moment, they would only pull our dressings off.

A little farther on we met some men bringing in a small cannon they had captured, and following them were others dragging along by their tails (queues) five wretched prisoners. The poor fellows cried piteously to us to save them, as they were hurried by, but, alas, we could do nothing! They would probably be at once decapitated. It makes one's blood run cold to think of such a thing.

Dr. Medhurst, who left the city first, waited a little while for us to overtake him, and as we did not come, went on alone. Shortly after, a cannon-ball struck two men on the very spot where he had been standing, and wounded them so seriously that I fear one if not both will die. When we reached home we found they had been brought to the hospital, and traces of blood seen on the way were thus explained. It makes one sad indeed to be surrounded by so much misery; to see poor creatures so suffering and distressed, and not be able to relieve them or tell them of Jesus and His love. I can only pray for them. But is not He all-mighty? He is. Thank God we know He is! Let us then pray earnestly that He may help them.

All this was intensely painful to a sensitive nature, and Hudson Taylor doubtless felt it the more that it was so unexpected. Trial and hardship he had looked for, of the kind usually associated with a missionary's lot, but everything was turning out differently from his anticipations. External hardships there were none, save the cold from which he suffered greatly; but distress of mind and heart seemed daily to increase. He could hardly look out of his window, much less take exercise in any direction, without witnessing misery such as he had never dreamed of before.

P

The tortures inflicted by the soldiery of both armies upon unhappy prisoners from whom they hoped to extort money, and the ravages perpetrated as they pillaged the country for supplies, harrowed him unspeakably. And over all hung the dark pall of heathenism, weighing with a heavy oppression upon his spirit. Many of the temples were destroyed in whole or part and the idols damaged, but still the people worshipped them, crying and praying for help that never came. The gods, it was evident, were unable to save. They could not even protect themselves in these times of danger. But in their extremity, rich and poor, high and low, turned to them still, for they had nothing else.

Seeing which, it can be easily imagined how Hudson Taylor longed to tell them of One mighty to save. But not a sentence could he put together so as to be understood. This enforced silence was a keen distress, for he was accustomed to speaking freely of the things of God. Ever since his conversion five years previously he had given himself as fully as possible to the ministry of the Gospel. And now for the first time his lips were sealed, and it seemed as if he never would be able in that appalling tongue to tell out all that was in his heart. This again could not but react on his own spiritual life. The channels of outflow to others were sealed, and it was a little while before he realised that they must be kept all the more clear and open toward God. His eagerness to get hold of the language made him devote every moment to study, even to the neglect of prayer and daily feeding upon the Scriptures. Of course the great enemy took advantage of all this, as may be seen from early letters to his parents in which he unburdened his heart :

"My position is a very difficult one," he wrote soon after his arrival. "Dr. Lockhart has taken me to reside with him for the present, as houses are not to be had for love or money. . . . No one can live in the city, for they are fighting almost continuously. I see the walls from my window . . . and the firing is visible at night. They are fighting now, while I write, and the house shakes with the report of cannon.

"It is so cold that I can hardly think or hold the pen. . . . You will see from my letter to Mr Pearse how perplexed I am   It will be four months before I can hear in reply, and the very kindness of the missionaries who have received me with open arms makes me fear to be burdensome.   Jesus will guide me aright. . . . I love the Chinese more than ever.   Oh to be useful among them ! "

To Mr. Pearse he had written about his arrival, and continued on March 3 :

I felt very much disappointed on finding no letter from you, but I hope to receive one by next mail.   Shanghai is in a very unsettled state, the Rebels and Imperialists fighting continually.   This morning a cannon fired near us awoke me before daybreak, shaking the house and making the windows rattle violently.

There is not a house to be obtained here, or even part of one ; those not occupied by Europeans are filled with Chinese merchants who have left the city   The Pilot told me they will give for only three rooms as much as thirty dollars a month, and in some instances more. The missionaries who were living in the city have had to leave, and are residing with others here in the Settlement at present ; so that had it not been for the kindness of Dr Lockhart I should have been quite nonplussed.   As it is I scarcely know what to do.   How long the present state of things may last it is impossible to say.   If I am to stay here, Dr. Lockhart says that the only plan will be to buy land and build a house.   The land would probably cost from a hundred to a hundred and fifty dollars, and the house three or four hundred more.   If peace were restored, Dr. Lockhart thinks I could rent a house in the city at from two to three hundred dollars per annum. So that in any case the expense of living here must be great.   I do not know whether it would be less at Hong-kong or any other port ? . . .

Please excuse this hasty, disconnected letter with all its faults.   It is so cold just now that I can scarcely feel pen or paper.   Everything is very dear, and fuel costs at times an almost fabulous price.   Owing to new arrivals, coal is now at thirty dollars [nearly £10] a ton.   Once more I must beg you to excuse this letter, . .   and please reply with all possible expedition that I may know what to do.

May the Lord bless and prosper you.   Continue to pray much for me, and may we all, sure of Jesus' love when everything else fails, seek to be more like Him . . . Soon we shall meet where . .   sorrow and trial shall be no more.   Till then may we be willing to bear the cross, and not only to do but to suffer His will.

" The cold was so great and other things so trying," he continued to his parents a week later, " that I scarcely knew what I was doing or saying at first.   Then, what it means to be so far from home, at the seat of war, and not able to understand or be understood by the people was fully realised.   Their utter wretchedness and misery, and my inability to help them or even point them to Jesus, powerfully affected me   Satan came in as a flood ; but there was One who lifted up a standard against him.   Jesus *is* here, and though unknown to the majority and uncared-for by many who might know Him, He is present and precious to His own."

CHAPTER XVII

MAKE IT A PLACE OF SPRINGS

April–August 1854.   Aet. 21–22.

It was April 4, a day long to be remembered in Shanghai on account of " the battle of Muddy Flat," an engagement between foreign troops and the Imperial soldiery.   And a regular battle it was, the Chinese force amounting to fifty thousand men.

For some time the attitude of the latter had been increasingly menacing toward Europeans, several of whom, including Dr. Medhurst, had narrowly escaped with their lives. Under cover of operations against the native city, the Imperial Camps had been moved nearer and nearer to the Settlement, until the foreign community with all they possessed was well within range of Chinese guns.   Startled by the danger of their position, the Consuls agreed to require the removal of the camps to a greater distance, and when— the time-limit having expired—their demand was not complied with, felt there was nothing for it but to open fire.

And then it was only too evident that the Chinese were prepared to resist.   A sharp return fire poured upon the attacking force, many of whom fell before it.   Still, superior discipline and arms carried the day, and the handful of Europeans, volunteers and marines from the gun-boats, succeeded in scattering the astonished army and setting fire to the deserted camps.

After this, relations were so strained that it was hardly safe for Europeans to venture beyond the protection of their own guns.   At first, indeed, it seemed as though retaliations would be attempted, and the Settlement was barricaded and an extra gun-boat sent up. But no attack was made. The dislodged soldiery vented their rage upon the poor, defenceless villages instead, and there the matter ended.

All this was not only a keen distress of mind to Hudson Taylor ; it did not a little to add to the trial of his position. For just before the battle of Muddy Flat the way had seemed more hopeful. He had made several excursions with older missionaries in the populous plain around Shanghai, and had been much impressed with the friendliness manifested. Everywhere the foreigners and their message seemed welcome, the distracted villagers finding in their presence some hope of escape from the cruelty of both Rebel and Imperial soldiers. This had encouraged the thought that away altogether from the Settlement he might find a home of his own right among the people. The danger involved would not have deterred him for a moment, and hardships would have been welcome that enabled him to live within his income and be independent. Besides, he longed to be more in touch with the suffering poor around him, and to do what little he could to help them. With his teacher, he might be useful medically and in other ways, and still give a large part of his time to study. His hopes had risen with each fresh visit to the country, and he had been on the look-out for a suitable place in which to settle.

But now all this was at an end, and even preaching excursions had to be discontinued. Foreigners were obliged to remain strictly within the limits of the Settlement, and missionary work was much hampered in consequence. A journey Mr. Edkins had planned, in which Hudson Taylor was to have been his companion, had to be given up, greatly to the disappointment of both missionaries.

" Had we started as we intended," wrote the latter, " or had this affair happened a day or two later, we should probably have been seized and beheaded by the Imperialists in revenge. But God is ever with us. On His watchful protection we rely. He never forgets, never changes. . . .

" It is of course impossible to go at all into the country now, so

there seems no chance of my getting a place of my own at present. . . .
I would give anything for a friend with whom to consult freely.   My
position is so perplexing that if I had not definite promises of Divine
guidance to count upon, I do not know what I should do.   There is,
I fear, no probability of my being able to keep within my salary under
present circumstances.   If I had quarters of my own I could live on
rice (not bread, that would be too expensive) and drink tea without
milk or sugar, which is cheap enough here.   But that I cannot do
now.   Things are increasing in expense all the while and dollars are
getting dearer.   They were at six and a penny when last I heard, and
if we are involved in further hostilities may rise to double that price—
and yet have no more purchasing value.   Well, He will provide. . . .

" They are building barricades in the Settlement to-day [April 8],
and instead of seven roads into it are going to have only three or four.
I think we are safe . . . but the poor people round us are in a sad
state.   My teacher said yesterday :

" ' I have great fear.   Turning to the right hand I fear the Rebels,
and on the left the Mandarin soldiers fill me with alarm.   Truly these
are hard times to live in.'

" What the poor man says is indeed true. . . . I tried to comfort
him as well as I could.   Nothing gives me so much delight as speaking
even a few words for Jesus, and I hope I shall soon be able to do so
more freely."

It may seem exaggerated, at first sight, to dwell much
upon the trials of Hudson Taylor's position.   True he was
at the seat of war, but as far as circumstances permitted
he was living in safety and even comfort.   He was so well
off, apparently, that one wonders at the undertone of suffering in his letters, until a little consideration reveals another
side of his experiences.   The assistance received from Dr.
Medhurst and other L.M.S. missionaries was of the greatest
value, and yet it gave rise to a distressing situation.   If he
had belonged to their Society and had been preparing to
work with and for them, nothing could have been better
But as it was, he felt almost like an unfledged cuckoo—an
intruder in another bird's nest.   That his companionship
at every meal in solitary *tête-à-tête* was somewhat wearisome
to his generous host, he could not but feel.   Not that he
received anything but kindness from Dr. Lockhart and his
associates.   But he was not as they were, highly educated
and connected with a great denomination and important

work. The preparation providentially ordered for him had
been along different lines, and his religious views made him
singular, while his position as a missionary was isolated
and open to criticism.

He had been sent out, hurried out almost by his Society,
before his medical course was finished, in the hope of
reaching the Rebels at Nanking. Misled by optimistic
reports about the Tai-ping Movement, the Secretaries of
the C.E.S. had taken a position that to practical men on
the field seemed wholly absurd. It is just as natural for
missionaries to be critical, apart from restraining grace, as
for others, and it was not long before Hudson Taylor discovered that the Chinese Evangelisation Society, with its
aims and methods, was the butt of no little ridicule in
Shanghai. It was keenly painful as *The Gleaner* came out
month by month to hear it pulled to pieces in this spirit,
although he could not but acknowledge that many of the
strictures were deserved. This did not make it easier, however, for the Society's representative in that part of China,
especially when for the time being he was dependent upon
those who spoke and felt so strongly.

He realised the weaknesses of the C.E.S., or was coming
to, no less clearly than they did ; but he knew and respected
many members of the Committee, and to some (including
the Secretaries) he was attached with grateful love. This
put matters in a very different light. Fellowship with them
in spiritual things, at Tottenham and elsewhere, could never
be forgotten, and even when feeling their mistakes most
keenly he longed for their atmosphere of prayer, their love
of the Word of God and earnest zeal for souls.

The influence of the world was tremendously strong in
Shanghai, even in missionary circles. It was the heyday
of the Settlement, as regards financial and commercial
opportunities. True, a temporary check had been imposed
by the local rebellion, and it was still a question as to how
long the disturbed state of things might continue. But the
native city once again in the hands of the Imperialists,
business would boom and the price of land go up, carrying
all commercial undertakings forward on a flood-tide of

success. And so it proved before twelve months were over. Many a fortune was to be made in Shanghai in those days, and lavish expenditure on luxury, with its attendant evils, were to be found on every hand. Among the Europeans hardly a man of advanced age was to be seen, for it was a new world to Western enterprise, entered only within the last twelve years.[1]

Those were the good old times when every Englishman in China was youthful, the great firms princely, the hospitality unbounded, and the prospect of achieving fortune with ordinary industry and luck appeared to every young fellow as assured.[2]

Such a state of things was not without its effect on the missionary community. The great expense of living necessitated increased salaries; and it was unavoidable that there should be a good deal of intercourse with government officials, to whom the missionaries were useful as interpreters, and with officers from the gun-boats stationed at Shanghai for the protection of the Settlement. Without finding fault with anything or any one in particular, there was a general spirit of sociability that surprised Hudson Taylor a good deal. It was not what he had expected in missionary life, and fell far short of his ideal.

He himself, on the other hand, did not entirely accord with the current conception of what a missionary should be. He was bright and fairly educated, but had no university or college training, had taken no medical degree, and disclaimed the title Reverend given him at first on all hands. That he

---

[1] The Treaty of Nanking, opening the "Five Ports" to Western commerce, had only been signed twelve years previously, in 1842.

[2] Sir Thomas Sutherland, G C M.G ; article entitled "Far Eastern Shipping, Fifty Years Ago," in *The London and China Express* for November 27, 1908 : Fiftieth Anniversary Number

The next paragraph continues: "Exchange was constant at not less than 4s. 6d. for the dollar and 6s. 8d. for the tael The current rate of interest was twelve per cent per annum. Alas! a change came over the spirit of the dream a few years later, when the telegraph reached China and the centre of gravity in trade was in large measure transferred to Europe No longer could China merchants store their silk and teas in London with the tolerable certainty that if they held their merchandise long enough the price would rise to meet their demands. Following the telegraph, the opening of the Suez Canal and the rapid development of steam-shipping changed completely the character of Eastern trade. But I am anticipating events that were undreamed of in China or India fifty years ago."

was good and earnest could easily be seen ; but he was connected with no particular denomination, nor was he sent out
by any special Church. He expected to do medical work,
but he was not a doctor. He was accustomed, evidently,
to preaching and an almost pastoral care of others, and yet
was not ordained. And strangest perhaps of all, though
he belonged to a Society that seemed well supplied with
funds, his salary was insufficient and his appearance shabby
compared with those by whom he was surrounded.

That Hudson Taylor felt all this, and felt it increasingly
as time went on, is not to be wondered at. He had come
out with such different expectations !   His one longing was
to go inland and live among the people. He wanted to
keep down expenses and continue the simple, self-denying
life he had lived at home. To learn the language that he
might win souls was his one ambition. He cared nothing,
nothing at all about worldly estimates and social pleasures,
though he did long for fellowship in the things of God.
With a salary of eighty pounds a year, he found himself
unable to manage upon twice that sum. So he was really
poor, poor and in serious difficulty before long ; and there
was no one to impress the fact upon the Committee at home
or make them understand the situation.

Then too he was lonely, unavoidably lonely. The
missionaries with whom he lived were all a good deal
older than himself, with the exception of the Burdons who
were fully occupied with their work. He could not trespass
on their kindness too frequently, and having no colleague
of his own found it impossible to speak of many matters
connected with the Society and future developments that
were on his heart. Soon he learned to mention such affairs
as little as possible, but he did long for some one with whom
to bring them before the Throne of Grace.

Much as he felt his position, however, it was well for the
young missionary that he could not hive off just then or
attempt to live on rice and tea minus milk or sugar. He
would have done it had he been his own master. He would
have done anything along lines of self-sacrifice to make the

money given for missionary purposes go as far as possible. But in that unaccustomed and trying climate it would have been a dangerous experiment during the hot season. And more than this—were there not higher purposes in view in the providential limitations imposed upon him at this time ? He longed to be free and independent, and the Lord saw fit to keep him in the very opposite position, letting him learn from experience what it is to be poor and weak and indebted to others even for the necessaries of life. For His own, His well-beloved Son there was no better way ; and there are lessons still that only can be learned in this school.

But for such circumstances early in his missionary career, Hudson Taylor would never have been able to feel for others as it was necessary he should. By nature he was resourceful and independent to a fault. He had sacrificed, as we have seen, the hope and ambition of years, breaking off his medical curriculum before he could obtain a degree, simply that he might be free to follow the guidance of the Lord as it came to him personally, untrammelled by obligations even to the Society with which he was connected. And now at the very opening of his new life in China, he found himself cast upon the generosity of strangers, shut up to a position as little welcome, possibly, to them as to himself, and from which there seemed for a long time to come no hope of escape.

As spring advanced, his journal gave evidence of more trial and depression of spirits than could be attributed to the climate. His eyes, never strong, became inflamed through the sunshine and excessive dust, and he suffered also a great deal from headache. In spite of this he worked at Chinese on an average five hours every day, besides giving time to necessary correspondence. To Mr. Pearse he wrote as fully as possible, trying to supply information that would interest readers of *The Gleaner*, as well as detailed statements of the condition of things around him with a view to the future conduct of the work.

From these letters one sees how much he was beginning to feel the monotony of a young missionary's life, occupied mainly with study. There was little of interest to write

about, now that he was practically restricted to the Settlement, and it is clear that he was passing through that stage
of weariness and disillusionment in which so many, drifting
away from the Lord, lose spiritual usefulness and power.
What missionary does not know the temptation at such a
time to let go higher ideals and sink to the level about one?
Prayer becomes an effort and Bible reading distasteful, and
the longing creeps in for stimulus of some kind—if it be
only that of gossip or novel-reading. Then the way is
open for a fault-finding, critical spirit, for dissatisfaction
and irritability, and gradually for worse backsliding still.
And all this, so often, has its first beginnings in the almost
unendurable monotony from which the young missionary
finds it difficult if not impossible to escape.

" Pray for me, pray earnestly for me," wrote Hudson Taylor to
his mother early in April, " you little know what I may be needing
when you read this."

And to Mr. Pearse a few days later :

May the Lord raise up and send out many labourers into this part
of His vineyard and sustain those who are already here. No amount
of romantic excitement can do that. There is so much that is repugnant to the flesh that nothing but the power of God can uphold
His servants in such a sphere, just as His blessing alone can give them
success.

Thanks to good judgment and sensible home-training,
Hudson Taylor was in less danger than many young missionaries during those months of language study. From early
childhood he had been encouraged, as we have seen, to take
an interest in " nature study," his butterflies and insects
being always housed with consideration though at some
cost to his parents in their limited surroundings. This
stood him in good stead, for now he not only knew the
value of such recreation, but also how to take it up.

" Ordered a cabinet for insects," runs the journal for April 25, " and
worked at Chinese and photography.
" April 28 : Very warm again. Worked at Chinese five hours.
Had a bad headache all day. Caught a few insects as a commencement of my collection.

" April 29 : At Chinese six hours. After dinner took a walk in search of nocturnal insects. Had some difficulty in getting into the Settlement again, the gates being closed."

" To-day," he wrote to his mother in May, " I caught sight of a large black butterfly with swallow-tail wings, the largest living butterfly I have ever seen. . . . At first I thought it must be a small bird, although it seemed to fly so strangely. But when it settled on a tree and I saw the splendid creature, it really took my breath away . . . it was so fine !

" I intend also to collect botanical specimens, but at present have no convenience. . . . There are some trees here that have a strange look to our eyes, being covered with blossoms before a single leaf appears. Among the wild plants I see many old friends—the violet, forget-me-not, buttercup, clover, chickweed, dandelion, hemlock, and several common herbs. There are also wild flowers that are new to me and very pretty."

In addition to working hard at Chinese this summer he was diligently keeping up other studies, medicine and chemistry especially, that he might not lose the benefit of his hospital course. The classics he gave as much time to as possible, and he seems always to have had some useful book on hand dealing with history, biography, or natural science. The following is a typical entry in a journal-letter to his sister :

Before breakfast read Medicine, then Chinese nearly seven hours. After dinner, Greek and Latin exercises, each an hour. After poring over these things till one can scarcely see, it is a comfort to have a fine, clear, large-type Bible, such as Aunt Hardey gave me. It is quite a luxury. Well, all these studies are necessary. Some of them, the classical languages of Europe, ought to have been mastered long ago ; so it is now or never with me. But the sweetest duties of the day are those that lead to Jesus—prayer, reading and meditation upon His precious Word.

Summer was now upon them—those hottest months of the year when one lives in a perpetual Turkish bath, and mosquitoes, prickly-heat, and sleeplessness have to be reckoned with, as well as a temperature that for weeks together scarcely falls below 80° F. at night. It is easy to write about it, but who that has not lived through such days and nights can imagine how much grace it takes to bear the discomfort and distress without irritability, and

keep on steadily with work when all one's courage seems
needed just to endure

All through this trying season, however, Hudson Taylor
kept up his studies, never falling below his average of five
hours at Chinese every day.   Once or twice he went into
the country with Mr. Burdon, risky as it was to attempt it.

" These are troublous times," he wrote, " but we must do something."

And their faith that the Lord would help them was
rewarded by the welcome met with from the village people,
who were only too glad to see them out again.

" I think I may say I have one friend now," he added, telling of a
happy evening with Mr. and Mrs. Burdon after one such excursion.
" But I do not want to go over there too often, as I am only one of his
circle and he has a wife for company.   I feel the want of a companion
very much.   The day is spent with my teacher, but my evenings
generally alone in writing or study."

Letters, of course, were a great comfort, and much time
was given during his first year in China to correspondence.
Strangely enough the months of June and July brought him
the peculiar trial of hearing nothing from home mail after
mail when he was especially longing for news.   How this
happened never quite appeared, for he had been written
to regularly, but the letters never reached him, or if they
did it was out of their proper order and long after they were
due.   This, combined with the great heat and the effects of a
brief but serious illness, tried him to a degree that can only
be understood by those who have been in similar circumstances.

" When last mail came in," he wrote to his mother in the middle
of June, " after walking a mile and a half to the Consulate on a broiling
hot day and waiting nearly two hours, which lost me my ' tiffin ' or mid-
day meal, I had the pleasure of bringing up letters and papers for
every one at the Mission except myself.   When I found there really
was nothing for me, the disappointment was so great that I felt quite
sick and faint and could scarcely manage to walk home, for it was
reported that we should have no other mail for six or eight weeks."

Another trial of those summer months, and one he felt

still more keenly, was his financial position, overlooked
apparently by the Society. The first quarter since his
arrival in China was now at an end, and on making up his
accounts he was more than troubled. His balance in hand
was so small that it would be necessary to draw again very
soon, and he had already spent more than a hundred and
thirty dollars. At that rate his salary would be exhausted
before half the year was over, and what would the Committee
say and think ?

With anxious care he explained to Mr. Pearse every item
in these accounts, the first he ever sent home from China,
revealing touching details as to needs he had not supplied
because of his desire to save expense as far as possible.

" I feel quite oppressed when I think of what a cost I am to the
Society," he wrote, " and yet how little good I am able to accomplish."

And just then, to add to his perplexity, news reached him
in a round-about way that seemed a climax to his troubles.
The Society was sending another missionary to Shanghai, and
not a bachelor like himself, but a married man with a family.
Dr. Parker, a Scotch physician who had applied to the C.E.S.
before Hudson Taylor left England, was already on his way
to join him and might be expected in a few months. Glad
as the young missionary would have been of such tidings
under other circumstances, with Shanghai in the condition
in which it was the outlook was cause indeed for concern.
Dependent himself for shelter upon the generosity of others,
what arrangements could he make for a married couple with
three children ? He hardly dared mention it to those with
whom he was living, and yet the news would soon be the
talk of the Settlement whether he kept silence or not.

Anxiously he awaited letters from the Committee explaining the situation. Surely they would send him notice,
in view of all he had written, of such an addition to their
staff, and instruct him fully how to act. But mail after
mail came in with no reference to Dr. Parker's coming.
Repeated requests for directions as to how to arrange for
himself had as yet received no answer, and before summer

was over Hudson Taylor saw that he must act on his own
initiative.

Meanwhile comments and questions were not wanting
that made the position more trying. " Is it true that a
medical man is about to join you, with a wife and family ?
When did you hear it ?   Why did you not tell us ?   Have
you bought land ?   Why do you not begin to build ? "
And so forth !   To all of which no satisfactory reply was
forthcoming.   At first in his perplexity Hudson Taylor
suffered as only a sensitive nature can ; but when the talk
was at its worst and the summer heat almost unbearable,
the Lord himself drew near and went with him.

" As you know," he wrote to Mr. Pearse in July, " I have been
much tried since coming here, ' pressed beyond measure ' almost at
times.   But the goodness of God is never-failing ; and the last few
days I have enjoyed such a sweet sense of His love, and such a personal
application of some of the promises as though they were written or
spoken directly to me, that the oil of joy has indeed been given me
for mourning.   I feel sure that dear friends in England have been
specially remembering me in prayer, and I am truly grateful.   Oh,
continue to pray for me !   I am so weak that difficulties seem overwhelming, and ofttimes I have to cry with Peter, ' Save, Lord ; I perish.'
But never does that cry go up in vain.   He has a balm for every
wound, and is always ready to calm the troubled waters of the soul.
I long much for the time when I shall be able to spread the knowledge
of His grace among this people in their own tongue.   May that time
be hastened and an effectual door opened before me. . . .

" I hope I may be able to find a home of some kind for Dr. and
Mrs. Parker on their arrival, though I cannot see how or where it will
be.   All the houses seem more than filled already, and new missionaries
are expected out.   I think it seems necessary that you should at once
consider and decide upon the question of building.   If we are to
establish a Mission in Shanghai there is no alternative.   No one can
have a greater objection to building than I have, or see its disadvant-
ages more clearly.   But the question lies at present within narrow
limits.   There is only a given space in which we are permitted to
live, i.e. the Settlement, and in it all the houses are occupied or shortly
will be.   We may or may not find those who, having been at the
expense of building for themselves, are willing to accommodate us for
a time, to their own inconvenience ; but this cannot be a permanent
state of things.   Those who are best able to judge see no hope of a
restoration of peace for years to come ; but we are all very short-
sighted when we look into futurity "

The more he thought over the situation, the more he felt that there was nothing for it but to seek a native house in the Chinese part of the Settlement, in which to receive the travellers who were drawing nearer every day. So in spite of overpowering heat and his lack of a sedan-chair, he set about the weary search once more. It was four or five months now since he had hunted for quarters on his first arrival without finding even a room available, and if anything the conditions seemed worse than before. Nothing he could begin to think of was to be found, and but for a growing rest of heart in God, Hudson Taylor would have been almost in despair. As it was, he was learning precious lessons of his own helplessness—and of Almighty strength.

To Miss Stacey in Tottenham he wrote during those August days .

How sweet is the thought that we have not an High Priest who cannot be " touched with the feeling of our infirmities," but One who was " in all points tempted like as we are, yet without sin." Nothing is more sure than that we are wholly unable to sympathise with those in whose circumstances we have never been placed. How delightful then is the reflection that though our friends can only in part enter into our joys and sorrows, trials and discouragements, there is One ever ready to sympathise to the full ; One to whom we have constant access, and from whom we may receive *present help* in every time of need.

This has been such a comfort to me when thinking and perplexed as to a residence not for myself only but for Dr. and Mrs. Parker. In the present state of Shanghai this is no easy problem, there being neither native nor foreign houses unoccupied. But I have much to be thankful for. Our dear Redeemer had not where to lay His head. I have never yet been placed in that extremity.

One who is really leaning on the Belovéd finds it always possible to say, " I will fear no evil, for Thou art with me." But I am so apt, like Peter, to take my eyes off the one Object and look at the winds and waves. As in that scene, however, the grace and tenderness of Jesus are as apparent as Peter's little faith, so with us to-day : as soon as we turn to Him, " He giveth power to the faint, and to them that have no might He increaseth strength." While we depend entirely on Him we are secure, and prosper in circumstances apparently the most unfavourable. . . .

Oh for more stability ! The reading of the Word and meditation on the promises have been increasingly precious to me of late. At

Q

first I allowed my desire to acquire the language speedily to have undue prominence and a deadening effect on my soul. You see from this how much I need your prayers. But now, in the grace that passes all understanding, the Lord has again caused His face to shine upon me.

And to his sister Amelia he added, two days later :

I have been puzzling my brains again about a house, etc., but to no effect. So I have made it a matter of prayer, and have given it entirely into the Lord's hands, and now I feel quite at peace about it. He will provide and be my Guide in this and every other perplexing step.

" Quite at peace about it "—with such serious difficulties ahead ! A situation he could not meet, needs for which he had no provision and no possibility of making any, a problem he had puzzled over until he was baffled, and to no effect ! " So I have made it a matter of prayer," is the simple, restful conclusion, " and have given it entirely into the Lord's hands He will provide and be my Guide in this as in every other perplexing step."

Yes, that is how it ever has been, ever must be with the people of God. Until we are carried quite out of our depth, beyond all our own wisdom and resources, we are not more than beginners in the school of faith. Only as everything fails us and we fail ourselves, finding out how poor and weak we really are, how ignorant and helpless, do we begin to draw upon abiding strength. " Blessed is the man whose strength is in Thee " ; not partly in Thee and partly in himself. The devil often makes men strong, strong in themselves to do evil—great conquerors, great acquirers of wealth and power. The Lord on the contrary makes His servant weak, puts him in circumstances that will shew him his own nothingness, that he may lean upon the strength that is unfailing. It is a long lesson for most of us ; but it cannot be passed over until deeply learned. And God Himself thinks no trouble too great, no care too costly to teach us this.

Thou shalt remember all the way which the Lord thy God led thee these forty years in the wilderness, to humble thee and to prove thee and to know what was in thine heart, . . . that He might make thee know. . . .

Yes, " all that long, wearisome, painful experience, infinitely well worth while in the sight of the Eternal, if it produced one moral, spiritual trait in the people He was educating :—what a scale of values ! "

At which point in our meditation, fresh light was thrown upon all this from the eighty-fourth Psalm, by an aged saint drawing upon the fulness of his own experience.[1]

" Speaking to my students one day," he said, " I asked them : ' Young men, which is the longest, widest, most populous valley in the world ? ' And they began to summon up all their geographical information to answer me.

" But it was not the valley of the Yangtze, the Congo, or the Mississippi. Nay, this *Jammerthal*, as it is in our German, this valley of Baca, or weeping, exceeds them all. For six thousand years we trace it back, filled all the way with an innumerable multitude. For every life passes at some time into the Vale of Weeping.

" But the point for us is not what do we suffer here, but what do we leave behind us ? What have we made of it, this long, dark Valley, for ourselves and others ? What is our attitude as we pass through its shadows ? Do we desire only, chiefly, the shortest way out ? Or do we seek to find it, to make it, according to His Promise, ' a place of springs ' : here a spring and there a spring, for the blessing of others and the glory of Our God ?

" Thus it is with the man ' whose strength is in Thee.' He has learned the preciousness of this *Jammerthal*, and that these dry, hard places yield the springs for which hearts are thirsting the wide world over.

" So St. Paul in his life. What a long journey he had to make through the Valley of Weeping !

" ' In labours more abundant, in stripes above measure, in prisons more frequent, in deaths oft. Of the Jews five times received I forty stripes save one. Thrice was I beaten with rods, once was I stoned, thrice I suffered shipwreck, a night and a day have I been in the deep. In journeyings often, in perils of waters, in perils of robbers, in perils by mine own countrymen, in perils by the heathen, in perils in the city, in perils of the wilderness, in perils in the sea, in perils among false brethren. In weariness and painfulness, in watchings often, in hunger and thirst, in fastings often, in cold and nakedness. Besides

---

[1] The beloved and now departed Herr Inspektor, C. H. Rappard-Gobat, director of the " Pilgrim Mission " at St. Chrischona, near Basel, himself in early years a missionary.

those things that are without, that which cometh upon me daily, the care of all the churches.'

" A long journey indeed through the Valley of Weeping ; but oh, what springs of blessing ! What rain filling the pools ! We drink of it still to-day."

And is not this the meaning, dear reader, of your life and mine in much that is hard to be understood ? The Lord loves us too well to let us miss the best. He has to weaken our strength in the way, to bring us into the Valley of Weeping, to empty, humble and prove us, that we too may know that our strength, every bit of it, is in Him alone, and learn as Hudson Taylor did to leave ourselves entirely in His hands.

So your Valley of Weeping shall become " a place of springs." Many shall drink of the living water, because you have suffered, trusted, conquered through faith in God. You go on your ways as He has promised, to appear at last in Zion, rejoicing before God ; and in the Valley of Weeping remains for those that follow many a well, still springing up in blessing where your feet have trod.

CHAPTER XVIII

BUILDING IN TROUBLOUS TIMES

AUGUST--NOVEMBER 1854. AET. 22.

IT must have seemed almost too good to be true when only two days after the preceding letter was written Hudson Taylor heard of a house, and before the month was over found himself in possession of premises large enough to accommodate his expected colleagues. Five rooms upstairs and seven down seemed a spacious residence indeed ; and though it was only a native house, built of wood and very ramshackle, it was right among the people, near the North Gate of the Chinese city.

It did not all come about, however, as easily as the statement is made. Between August 9 and 21 he learned many a lesson of patience, for in China these arrangements are compassed with difficulty. The house first heard of was not the one finally obtained, nor was the price first demanded one that he could or would give ; and between the two lay much weary negotiation that had to be carried on through interpreters and deepened the debt he was already under to his missionary friends.

So much labour and difficulty in accomplishing so ordinary a transaction opened his eyes to what really constitutes a large part of the trial of missionary life. He was reading at the time *The Hand of God in History*, and wrote to his sister who had given it him :

What a very different thing it is to review the aggregate success of Missions and missionaries over many years from taking part in the process itself with all its trials and discouragements. But let us be comforted. So will it be for us too at last. One smile from Him we love will repay all the sorrows, and leave a clear balance to the good of whatever has been accomplished.

" Oh Amelia," he continued when difficulties were at their worst, " one needs an anchor for one's faith . . . and thank God we have it ! The promises of God stand sure. ' The Lord knoweth them that are His.' How easy it is to talk about economy, the high salaries of missionaries, and all the rest. But there is more than one missionary here who hardly knows how to manage to make both ends meet. Well, if we want a city, there is one we can turn back to. But no, we will be pilgrims and strangers here, looking for a better home, ' that is an heavenly,' ' whose builder and maker is God.' Oh that those around us had the same hope ! . . .

" You ask how I get over my troubles. This is the way. . . I take them to the Lord. Since writing the above, I have been reading my evening portion. The Old Testament part of it happens to be the 72nd to the 74th Psalms. Read them as I have if you want to see how applicable they are. I don't know how it is, but I seldom can read Scripture now without tears of joy and gratitude. . . .

" I see that to be as I am and have been since my arrival has really been more conducive to improvement and progress than any other position would have been, though in many respects it has been painful and far from what I should have chosen for myself. Oh for more implicit reliance on the wisdom and love of God ! "

But even when the agreement was signed and sealed, much yet remained to be accomplished.

" My house has twelve rooms," he wrote, . . . " doors without end, passages innumerable, outhouses everywhere, and all covered with dust, filth, rubbish and refuse. What all the outhouses have been for I cannot imagine. There are no less than thirty-six of them, none of which I want or shall use. I have been getting a whole batch of doors fastened up, for however well it may suit a Chinaman to have six or eight ways into his house, it does not please me at all just now. I see how to arrange it so that with one pair of gates I can shut off the dwelling itself from all the outhouses Indoors there are two stair-cases of a sort. One of these I am having removed and the trap-door screwed down.

" The five upstair rooms are side by side, each communicating with the others by double doors . . . so that the middle rooms have not much privacy. This set of apartments I shall whitewash and fumigate thoroughly . . . taking one for a bedroom and another for dining-room and study. Once there I must dig away at this fearful Shanghai dialect with its eight tones, for which I shall need a new teacher. He will probably occupy some of the downstair rooms, which not being raised above the ground are of little use for foreigners."

But it was one thing to talk about cleaning the house and going into residence, and quite another to accomplish it, as Hudson Taylor was to prove. He had had no experience so far of the unsupervised Chinese workman, and the discovery of his characteristics was discouraging. On August 22 for example, in spite of overpowering heat, he got a few men to clear the place and remove rubbish enough, as he said, " to have bred a pestilence." Early next day he was on the scene again and discovered his men absorbed in watching the bricklayers, never dreaming of setting to work themselves. Having found them plenty to do, he went to inquire about a box expected from Hong-kong. Returning in an hour, what was his surprise to find one man writing, another smoking and the rest asleep. The third time he came it still seemed as though nothing had been done.

" So I have brought over my desk and a chair," he wrote that afternoon, " to remain on the premises . . . and even so they perpetually relapse into idleness. I say, for instance, ' Now this must be thoroughly washed.' For a while there is a noise of splashing, but soon all is still. I go to see . . . and the man looks quite astonished when I remark that only the outside has been cleaned. ' Oh,' he replies, ' you want within-and-without washing.' ' Yes,' I say, ' I do,' and return to my letter for a few minutes. Amusing though it may seem at first, this kind of thing becomes wearisome, especially when one can get nothing else."

Though trying enough in its way, all this was the least serious part of the new life he was undertaking. The unavoidable outlay weighed on his mind far more. Furnish as sparingly as he might and live as frugally, he seemed to be spending a great deal on himself. At home he had been a collector for Missions, and knew what it was to receive the hardly earned pence of the poor. And now, against all his own inclinations, to be using missionary money in ways that seemed to him so lavish was indeed a trial   He would not have felt it so keenly had he been directly engaged in missionary work, but when he could do nothing but study it was almost more than he could bear.

" To save the expense of a sedan," he wrote to his mother, " I have tried staying indoors altogether during the great heat, or walking out only in the evening ; but several attacks of illness as well as threatenings of ague have warned me to desist. . . . No one, I am sure, can be more anxious to avoid expense than I am ; but if we are to live here at all we must accommodate ourselves to circumstances. . . .

" These things sometimes make me cry with David, ' My flesh and my heart faileth.' But that is not his last word ; and by grace I too can add, ' God is the strength of my heart and my portion for ever.' Though often cast down . . . I am where I would be and as I would be—save for more likeness to Christ and more familiarity with the language."

Still more serious than the question of expense, however, was the danger involved in his intended move. Not only was he leaving the Settlement, to live entirely alone among the Chinese, he was going to a house very near Imperial camps and within range of the guns of both parties. It was a position as he well knew of considerable danger, but no other residence had been procurable and the time had come when something must be done.

" The Chinese house to which I am removing," he wrote to a friend, " is in a dangerous position, being beyond the protection of the Settlement and liable to injury from both Imperialists and Rebels. The former have threatened to burn the street, and the latter have two cannon constantly pointing at it. My teacher who comes from a distance dare not go there, and as I cannot get another who speaks Mandarin at present I shall have to commence the study of the Shanghai dialect. . . . As I can talk with my present teacher tolerably well, it is a trial to lose him and commence again from the beginning. But as there is no hope of being able to go to Mandarin-speaking districts for several years, and the Shanghai dialect I can use as I learn it, this too no doubt is wisely ordered. At any rate I am thankful that my way is hedged up on every side, so that no choice is left me. I am obliged to go forward. . . . And if you hear of my being killed or injured, do not think it a pity that I came, but thank God I was permitted to distribute some Scriptures and tracts and to speak a few words in broken Chinese for Him who died for me."

In this spirit, then, Hudson Taylor bade farewell to the kind host who for six months had afforded him a home, and on August 30, near the North Gate of the native city, set up housekeeping on his own account. In spite of trouble, expense, loneliness and danger, it was good to feel that he could begin a little work on his own account. And the Lord who knew the heart of His servant, responded to his longings after usefulness and blessing, meeting him at the outset of this new pathway with rich compensations of His grace. In the solitude that was now his lot, the soul began to revive again and grow. The blessing of the far-away days at Drainside seemed to come back. He lived his own life as then, the simple self-denying life that made brighter spiritual experience possible.

It was now September, almost a year from the time he had left home, and his joy in being able to do something for the people round him was very great. His new teacher, happily, was an earnest Christian, and able to conduct morning and evening worship to which all who came were made welcome. After this there were patients to see, visitors to entertain and housekeeping to attend to, in all of which Mr. Sī was indispensable. But his pupil was rapidly learning useful terms and polite phrases, as well as carefully chosen sentences in which to convey the Gospel. On Sundays they went out together to distribute tracts and preach in the crowded streets. The dispensary was making many friends, and when a day-school was added both for boys and girls they had no lack of occupation. Before long, Si had to give all his time to these operations, and another teacher was engaged for the language. And then, with everything in working order and his heart full of the blessing of the Lord, Hudson Taylor began to taste some of the real joys of missionary life.

To this period belongs a letter to his parents which shews the cheerful, natural spirit in which he was working.

NORTH GATE, SHANGHAI,
September 20, 1854

MY DEAR FATHER AND MOTHER—Whether you weary of my letters or not, I cannot but write them, . . . and I will take it for granted that this one at any rate will be welcome, as it is to inform you that the experiment made in coming to this house has been so far successful, and that now though not doing much I am at any rate doing something. I am glad also to say that I get on with the Shanghai dialect much better than I at first expected.[1] . . . The only thing that has really troubled me has been the outlay I have had to make and that my current expenses are so great. But this is unavoidable. On first coming here I was disposed to economise at the risk of usefulness and health, but I see now that one cannot do this with impunity ; and as I have no desire to be sent home useless within two or three years, with considerable doubt as to my ever being able to return, I have been led to consider that proper care on these points is in the long run the truest economy.

The Chinese house I am occupying is as good as can be obtained, and though the neighbourhood is undesirable one gets accustomed to it. If I feel lonely or timid at night, I recall some sweet promises of Divine protection, turning them into prayer, and invariably find that they compose my mind and keep it in peace. I do not neglect any precaution for safety ; but keep a light burning all night and have my swimming belt blown up, so that at a moment's notice I could take to the water if necessary—the planks forming the bridge between me and the Settlement being removed at dark. . . .

And now I must tell you what I am doing. First then, I have commenced a day-school with ten boys and five girls. Three more boys are promised and will be coming shortly. The teacher, Si, is a Christian and very useful, as he preaches well in the local dialect. The school opens and closes with a Scripture lesson and prayer. At present I cannot do much with the children, but every day increases my power to make myself understood. As I sit in my study and hear their voices chanting over their lessons, it fills me with thankfulness I cannot begin to express. . . . I often wish Amelia were here to take charge of the girls and gather in others. There are plenty to be found who are by no means improved by being at liberty in this neighbourhood, young as they are, for it is a bad one. On this account, if I have to go out after dark, I always take a servant and lantern.

Secondly, the dispensary. I have not laid myself out for medical work, but every day brings some patients. To-day for example, being wet, only ten have come. I am gradually learning Chinese terms for ordinary diseases, symptoms, etc., and the expressions needed in questioning patients and telling them how to take our medicines ; and I find that though the amount of work I get through may seem small, the labour attending it is considerable.

Thirdly, our services. From the very first day in this house, I have had family prayers night and morning. At these times the servants, teachers, Si's family and any others who like to come in are

---

[1] " The idea of commencing a new dialect," he had written a month before (August 18), " is rather overwhelming, *one* being a tolerable dose ! But if you mean to learn Chinese, you must not say, ' Can I do it ?' but ' I *can* and *will*, by the blessing of God.' "

present. We have had as many as twenty. To-day we had nine in the morning and ten at night. Those who can read do so, verse about, and yesterday (the anniversary of my sailing from Liverpool) I commenced joining them. Of course I make blunders, and so do one or two others, but the teachers are there to correct, and by and by I shall do better. On several occasions also, Si has accompanied me into the city to distribute tracts and Scriptures. At these times, when we have gathered a few people together, Si has read a portion and explained it in a way that all could understand, . . . so you see he is very useful.

All these engagements take time, and with Chinese study occupy most of the day. I also find it necessary to do some reading in medicine, surgery or *materia medica* every day . . . and what with domestic matters and keeping a careful watch over everybody and everything, I can assure you I do not spend much time in bed—as I never go till I can keep awake no longer.

The other day I had an interesting excursion to Woo-sung with Mr. Edkins and a young American missionary named Quaterman. We went by boat . . . arriving there at noon, with a large supply of Scriptures and tracts. These we distributed on many junks going northward, receiving promises from not a few captains and others that they would read them and pass them on to friends in the ports to which they were travelling.

Returning home in the evening well pleased with our excursion, we were puzzled to know how we should pass the Imperial fleet in safety. They are somewhat random with their fire after dark, and might easily have taken us for natives if not Rebel spies. Mr. Edkins came to the rescue, proposing that we should sing as we passed them, that they might know we were foreigners. The suggestion seemed good and the boatmen were pleased with the idea, the only objection being that as we had already been singing a good deal we had exhausted all the hymns and tunes we had in common and were more than ready for a rest.

Having perfected our arrangements, we approached some ships we took to be the fleet, and passed them singing lustily. But just as we were about to congratulate one another on our success, the boatmen shouted to us to recommence, as we had been mistaken in what we supposed to have been the fleet and were just coming within range of their guns.

So we had to tune up again without delay, and sang " The spacious firmament on high," to that beautiful tune *Creation*. Unfortunately we concluded just opposite the largest ship of the fleet. It was now quite dusk.

" What next ? " cried Mr. Edkins, as the alarm-gong struck on board the ship, " there is not a moment to lose."

He then commenced singing I know not what. Quaterman struck up a truly American tune to " Blow ye the trumpet, blow ! " while I at the same moment raised a third with all the voice I could command. The men on the warship were shouting loudly, our boat's crew outdoing them if possible, and the whole thing was so ludicrous that I could control myself no longer and burst into a fit of laughter most inappropriate to the occasion.

" Who goes there ? " was shouted from the Imperial ship.

" *Peh-kuei* " (white devils), yelled our men, while we cried simultaneously, " *Ta Ing-kueh* " (Great English Nation) and " *Hua-chu-kueh*," which means Flowery Flag Country, or America.

After a little further explanation we were allowed to pass, upon which my companions began to lecture the boatmen for having called us " White Devils." The poor men who had not yet received their day's pay were very penitent, and explained that they had been so frightened that they really did not know what they were saying and would be most careful to refrain from such expressions in future. As soon as we landed I set off for home, and found them just going to draw the last plank across the creek. Happily I got over in time, for I was fearfully hungry and tired.

My eyes, the lamp and paper alike inform me that I must be drawing to a close. But I must not forget to tell you that the other day a Sung-kiang man presented me with a couple of valuable crickets in a glass box. They require two freshly boiled grains of rice daily, and are kept on account of their song, which is quite different from the sound made by English crickets, and very pleasant.

And now Good-night, or rather Good-morning.—Ever my dear Parents, your affectionate son,

J. HUDSON TAYLOR.

Mingled with joy in his new work, however, came unexpected trials, great and small — difficulties of household management, quarrels between his servants and the neighbours, anxiety about his cook who was laid up with typhus fever, disappointment with the second teacher who had to be dismissed, great discouragement about the language, and repeated attacks of illness that left him low-spirited and unfit to bear the strain of constant skirmishing so close at hand.

" There has been a great deal of fighting for several days," he wrote in the middle of September, " and the Rebels have been gathering at the bottom of this street. Of them I have little fear, but I hope there may be no counter-move on the part of the Imperialists. . . .

Several cannon-balls have passed so near these premises as to make me feel some trepidation for the moment. It is easy to tell whether a gun is loaded or not, as the ball makes a *whizz* which once heard is not likely to be forgotten."

He was in real sorrow too over the illness of Mrs. Burdon, who had suffered a great deal since the birth of her little daughter three months before. Her husband was worn out with anxiety and nursing, and for them both Hudson Taylor felt deeply concerned. Mrs. Burdon had been his chief counsellor in beginning housekeeping. The very last time she went out she had helped him with necessary purchases, full of interest in all that concerned his moving to the North Gate. And now it seemed that she could not recover. Her love for those she was leaving and perfect submission to the will of God touched him unspeakably ; and as often as possible he went over to relieve Mr. Burdon, entering with a brother's sympathy into the anguish through which he was passing.

Beside all this, he was increasingly burdened about money matters, not knowing even yet how the Society would respond to his letters. Obliged to exceed his salary for the necessaries of life, he had made use of a Letter of Credit provided against emergencies, but was still uncertain as to how far his bills would be honoured. It was a painful position, and one that cost him many a wakeful night as well as many a prayer.

Thus September ended, and looking back upon it he could say :

Though in some ways I never passed a more anxious month in my life, I have never felt before so conscious of God's presence with me. I begin to enjoy the sweet, peaceful rest in the Lord and in His promises experienced first in Hull. That was the brightest part of my spiritual life, and how poor at the best ! Since then I have been in a declining state, but the Lord has brought me back ; and as there is no standing still in these things, I trust to go on to apprehend heights and depths, lengths and breadths of love divine far exceeding anything I have yet entered into. May God grant it, for Jesus' sake.

One cannot but be impressed in reading the letters of this period with the sacred ambition of Hudson Taylor's prayers ; a subject worth pondering, if it be true that prayer moulds the life and not circumstances, and that as are our deepest desires before God so will the trend of our outward experiences be. Certainly nothing is more significant in the life before us than the longing for usefulness and likeness to the Lord he loved. Not honour or success, but usefulness, "widespread usefulness," was his constant prayer. Would he have drawn back could he have foreseen that the only way to its fulfilment was through the furnace seven times heated ?

For much preparatory work had yet to be done. His prayers were indeed to be answered beyond anything he asked or thought ; but he must pray with yet fuller meaning, and go through with all the training needed at the Master's hands. The iron must be tempered to steel, and his heart made stronger and more tender than others, through having loved and suffered more, with God. He was pioneering a way in China, little as he or any one else could imagine it, for hundreds who were to follow. Every burden must be his, every trial known as only experience can teach it. He who was to be used of God to dry so many tears, must himself weep. He who was to encourage thousands in a life of child-like trust, must learn in his own case deep lessons of a Father's loving care. So difficulties were permitted to gather about him, especially at first when every impression was vivid and lasting, difficulties attended by many a deliverance to cheer him on his way.

As much of his usefulness later on was to consist in helping and providing for young missionaries, it is not to be wondered at that a large part of his preparation at this time had to do with financial matters and the unintentional mismanagement of the home Committee. He had to learn how to do and how *not* to do for those who on the human side would be dependent on him ; a lesson of vital importance, lying at the very foundation of his future work. Hence all this trial about a small, settled income and large uncertain needs ; about irregularity of mails and long-unanswered letters ; about rapidly-changing opportunities of service on the field, and the slow-moving ideas and inaccessibility of Committees at home.   He did his best, and the inexperienced Secretaries in London did their best also, as faithful men of God.   But something, somehow, was wanting ; and just what it was Hudson Taylor had to discover, and later on to remedy. Seen in this light it need hardly be said a special significance attaches to his financial cares ; and the letters in which he tells at times so touchingly of the exercise of mind through which he was passing have an interest all their own.   The iron—one sees it—was entering into his very soul ; but from this long endurance was to spring heart's-ease for many another.

At the risk of some repetition, the following letter is quoted for its value in this connection, and as showing how keenly he continued to feel the circumstances in which he was placed :

NORTH GATE, SHANGHAI,
October 17, 1854

MY DEAR PARENTS—You wish to know all about my pecuniary as well as other affairs, so I am enclosing a copy of a list of expenses I am just forwarding to Mr. Pearse.   As you will perceive, they so largely exceed the sum we were led to suppose would be sufficient (£80 per annum) that I am sending full details, so that the Secretaries can see for themselves.   I shall have to draw again this year, probably next month.   I am not sure that I can get credit, for my authorisation from the Society does not exceed forty pounds a quarter, and if the agents here knew that I had just received a copy of the Committee's Resolution stating that they will not accept bills for more than that amount, of course it would be refused.

You will not wonder that anxiety about expenses and as to whether my bills will be honoured or not, added to the dangers of my present position, has proved rather much for me lately. . . . I have been very poorly for a fortnight . . . but am better now, though distressingly weak as yet.   My cook has been ill with typhus fever for three weeks or more.   I hope he is improving.   He was better some days ago, but threw himself back by going contrary to explicit orders.

You will wonder what all those " discounts " in my list of expenses mean.   They were paid on the Ferdinand dollars with which I was supplied in England, and that are not in regular circulation here. Chair-coolies, another item, are indispensable in the hottest weather. Their services were mostly required in seeking a house, and running to and fro from Dr. Lockhart's before I could get one.   The water-jars are for drinking-water, which has to be fetched from the river and being very muddy has to settle and have the organic matter precipitated by alum before it is fit for use. Of chairs I have only six, the cheapest usable ones I could get. The tables are second-hand. New, they would have cost much more. Crockery is the dearest item. The whole lot in England would hardly fetch ten shillings, for they are of many different patterns. The cups and saucers do not match, nor do the dishes and plates, while the vegetable dishes are again dissimilar. I had to take what I could get, and was thankful they were odd, for no one would have broken into a set. . . . As to fuel, how would you like to be paying six and sixpence a week for barely enough for the simplest cooking, the fire being put out as soon as done with, and have the prospect of the thermometer going down to 15° F. within two months?

Everything is dear in Shanghai now, Chinese as well as foreign goods. Just to think that in seven months I have spent more than a hundred pounds! Is it not frightful? Two hundred pounds per annum will barely cover my expenses, unless the exchange falls, and other things too. The Church Missionary Society allows single men seven hundred dollars (about £210 at the present rate of exchange) beside paying rent, medical expenses, and a sum sufficient for Chinese teacher and books. . . .

Saturday, Oct. 21. It is very cold to-day. I am better than I was earlier in the week, but still far from well. . . Fortunately I have been able to buy a second-hand stove for ten dollars that will burn wood. A new one would have cost thirty. And now having had another month's expenses to settle, I have only twelve dollars left. What can I do? I must draw soon. And even if I can get a bill accepted here, I am in terror of its being refused by the Committee, which would put me in a pretty fix. I think and study night and day, and cannot tell what to do.

Last Wednesday night, a fire that seemed very near awoke me at three o'clock in the morning. Dressing hastily, I climbed on to the roof to ascertain if it were coming this way. Chinese houses like these, built only of wood, burn very quickly on a windy night. It was an anxious moment, for in the darkness I fancied the burning building was only four or five doors away. Just then, as I was praying earnestly for protection, it began to rain. The wind fell, for which I was most thankful, and gradually the fire smouldered down. But it was after five before I dared go to bed again.

While there on the roof, several bullets struck the buildings round me, and two or three seemed to fall on the tiles of my own house. At last a heavy ball struck the ridge of the opposite roof, carrying away a lot of tiles, the fragments of which fell around me, and itself flew off obliquely. You may be sure I did not wait up there for another. . . . The day before a ball of that size, evidently spent, struck the roof of this house, broke some tiles, and fell at the feet of my teacher's child who was standing in a doorway. Had he been half a yard further out, it must have killed him. That was at noon.

I have never passed, as you will well believe, such a trying time in my life. But it is all necessary, and I feel is being made a blessing to me. I may have to leave here suddenly. . . . But whatever happens, I do not regret coming to this house, and would do it again under similar circumstances. Our Society must provide better, however, for its missionaries. This sort of thing will not do.

I must now conclude, trusting that the Lord, who is precious to me in my extremity, is proving Himself near also to you.—With love . . . believe me, your ever affectionate son,

J. HUDSON TAYLOR.

That Resolution of the Committee not to honour bills exceeding forty pounds a quarter caused more pain and perplexity to their solitary representative in Shanghai than they could at all realise.[1] Crisp, sharp autumn weather had now set in, forecasting the bitter cold of winter. His Chinese house was not only unwarmed but unwarmable, draughts sweeping through it mercilessly, from unnumbered cracks and crevices. His blankets, only two in number, were fit for nothing but summer use, and all the clothing he had brought from home was now so shabby that he was ashamed to be seen amongst other foreigners. Yet he had far exceeded his allowance, and dared not spend a penny save for actual necessaries. And to add to his perplexity he was driven to see that the house he had secured with so much difficulty in view of the arrival of the Parkers would not be a place they could come to even for a night.

---

[1] Based as it was upon his own correspondence, it was little wonder that this Resolution produced a painful impression on his mind. It hurt like a wound inflicted by one from whom he had expected sympathy. In a letter to Mr. Pearse of November 2, he expressed himself as follows :

" And lastly, in reference to the Resolution of June 29, 1854 · your Board ought to be very careful how they bind their Secretaries to such a course in present times. Your missionaries are sent into a country in a state of revolution, where it is literally true that they know not what a day or an hour may bring forth. They should be well provided against contingencies before you adopt such an *ultra* measure, a measure that would at once and forever destroy their credit, if they have any, and compared with which their dismissal by the Society would not be severe. At any rate, if not accepted, such bills should not be positively refused before you hear the reasons which led to their being drawn. But more I need not say. Your hearts are in the work as well as ours, and I know you will excuse these remarks when you remember that half the world lies between us."

R

" As to my position," he wrote on October 2, " it certainly is one
of great peril. On two successive nights, recently, bullets have struck
the roof over my head. How little difference in the direction of the
gun might have rendered them fatal to me. But ' as the mountains
are round about Jerusalem ' so the Lord is on every side to protect
and support me and to supply all my need, temporal as well as spiritual.
I can truly say my trust is in Him. When I hear guns fired near me
and the *whizz* of the balls as they pass the house, I do feel alarmed
sometimes ; but a sweet, still voice says inwardly, ' Oh thou of little
faith, wherefore didst thou doubt ? ' Awakened suddenly in the
darkness by the thundering report of guns from the North Gate which
shake the house, and hearing gongs sounding and firearms discharging
close at hand I have felt lonely, and my heart has palpitated painfully
at times, not knowing whether my own house might not be the object
of attack. But ' Lo, I am with you always,' has quieted the troubled
waters and restored peace to my soul. One night I was roused from
sleep by a strong smell of burning, and finding the rooms full of smoke
was not a little alarmed, for I knew the Imperialists had threatened
to burn all the suburbs as far as the creek. But it was only stubble
burning in a field near by, and the windows being open the smoke had
drifted in   Thoroughly ashamed of my fears I returned to rest with
a very sweet sense of the presence of my Protector, the ' Watchman
of Israel.' "

Three weeks later matters were even worse, and he wrote
again to the Secretaries :

There is a great deal of firing going on here now, so much so that
. . . I am seldom able to get half a night's sleep. What Dr. Parker
and his family are to do, I do not know. Their coming here as things
are now is out of the question. This constant anxiety for them as
well as myself, together with another still more trying (the expense
I am unable to avoid) is by no means a desirable addition to the
difficulties of language and climate. . . .
We have heard nothing of the *Swiftsure*, but she is hardly due as
yet. I shall be thankful when Dr. Parker is here and we are able to
consult together about the future. You will find this a much more
expensive Mission, I fear, than was anticipated. . . . I shall have
to draw again this month, and with all possible economy cannot alter
the high rate of prices   The total expense of my first year will be
little under two hundred pounds, and even so I feel confident that
there is no other missionary in Shanghai who will not have cost considerably more. . . .
Pray for me, for I am almost pressed beyond measure, and were

it not that I find the Word of God increasingly precious and feel His presence with me I do not know what I should do.

But the Lord knew, and He had not forgotten His tried servant. At that very moment, when the *Swiftsure* was nearing the end of her long and perilous voyage, the Lord had a home in view into which to receive the Parkers and their children. He was not shut up to the house on the North Gate Street, though Hudson Taylor was ; and just in time, when lessons had been learned that He saw to be needed, the way was opened to a safer residence.

On the London Mission Compound, through the coming of a great sorrow, a little house stood empty that in comparison with Hudson Taylor's quarters offered a haven of security and peace. Shadowed as it was with the suffering of his dearest friends in China, he had not thought of it as other than their home. There he had found them in their early married life, rejoiced with them in the gift of a precious child, and shared the bereavement that in so short a time left her motherless. Then he had helped Mr. Burdon to leave the home from which the light had fled, and take his infant daughter to the care of the Chaplain's household. And still the little house at Ma-ka-k'üen stood empty.

CHAPTER XIX

A WAY OF ESCAPE

IT is put before us as an evidence of the faithfulness of God that for those who trust Him He always has "a way of escape," that no trial may be greater than they can bear. Strong consolation this for the troubled soul ! And Hudson Taylor was to make full proof of it now in his extremity.

For extremity it really was, just after the foregoing letter had been written. Where to go and what to do he knew not, and the Parkers were drawing nearer every day. Without authorisation from the Committee or instructions from Dr. Parker himself, how could he venture upon the expense of Mr. Burdon's house ? And yet it was just what they needed, and might be lost by delay. He had no money to furnish, nor did he know where the rent was coming from ; but at the end of October, looking to the Lord for help and guidance, he obtained at least the refusal of the premises.

Meanwhile the situation of the native city was becoming desperate. The French, in defiance of international law and treaty obligations, were openly taking part in the siege. Their soldiers, "bloodthirsty as tigers," seemed bent on slaughter, and the house at the North Gate daily witnessed scenes of almost fiendish cruelty. It became unendurable at last. The premises next door were deliberately set on fire, with intention to drive the foreigner out, and just at this juncture another offer was made for Mr. Burdon's house. Word was sent to Hudson Taylor that if he wanted it he must take it at once. And so, paying the rent out of his own meagre resources, a home was secured for the family so soon to arrive in the Settlement.

And then, providentially no doubt, he was urged to sublet half the premises. Another missionary was in distress, not knowing where to take his wife and children with safety, and for three rooms was thankful to pay half the rent. True the house was very small for two families, but it was a relief to have his financial obligations lessened and a comfort to be able to help somebody else. So with many regrets at parting from his school-children and neighbours, Hudson Taylor left the scenes in which he had commenced his first direct missionary work, and on Saturday, November 25, returned to a house shared with others on the familiar compound of the London Mission.

Two days later he was again at the North Gate to remove the last of his belongings, when he was recalled by a message from Dr. Lockhart. Hurrying back with many conjectures as to what the summons might mean, he found the doctor at lunch with a pleasant-looking stranger—none other than his own long-expected colleague Dr. Parker. So they had come at last! And he was only just in time with arrangements for their accommodation.

At first in the joy of meeting and all the excitement of bringing up their belongings from the ship, Hudson Taylor had hardly time to realise how the narrowness of their quarters would strike his new-found friends. But when they were all in them, including the little baby whose first appearance had been made at sea, the three rooms seemed even more crowded than he had feared they would be. Strong, sensible Scotch people, the Parkers were quite prepared to put up with hardships, and accommodated themselves to the situation as well as could be expected. But to Hudson Taylor it was a painful experience to have to reveal the pitifulness of his preparations.

If the rooms had been suitably furnished it would have been another matter; but his Chinese bed, two or three square tables, and half a dozen chairs seem to have been all that he possessed. He had only just moved in on Saturday night, and had not had time to get into working order, and now the sudden advent of a family with all their paraphernalia made confusion worse confounded, and the despair of a thrifty housewife with three little children to provide for may be better imagined than described.

Oh, the trying, difficult days that followed, could they ever be forgotten ! For to make matters worse, the Shanghai community began to call upon the new arrivals, and those with whom Hudson Taylor was acquainted were not sparing in their comments upon what seemed his negligence.

It was all very well for him to live in Chinese style if he liked, and put up with a hundred and one discomforts. But people who knew what was what could not be expected to fall in with such ways. Why had he not furnished their rooms properly, and provided warm carpets and curtains ? Did he not know that children must be protected from the bitter cold of winter ? Had he no stoves in readiness, no proper supply of fuel ? Had he not written to tell them that they would need warm clothes and bedding on their arrival in November ? And as to unpacking and getting settled, how could it be done without shelves or cupboards, chests of drawers or book-cases in which to bestow their belongings ?

All of which was true, no doubt, and unanswerable ; for how could the young missionary let it be known that he had gone far beyond the limits of authorised expenditure in taking the house at all—that he had done it entirely on his own responsibility, and that after paying the first instalment of rent he had been left with only two or three dollars in hand, not enough to cover a week's expenses ?

His hope was, of course, that Dr. Parker would be supplied with all that was necessary, and would be the bearer of instructions from the Society about Mission-headquarters in Shanghai or elsewhere, as well as some more satisfactory arrangement for financial transactions in the future. The very reverse, however, was the case. Dr. Parker had nothing with him but a few dollars for immediate use. He was expecting a Letter of Credit to be awaiting him in Shanghai, understood to have been sent off before he left England. As to supplies, they had abundance of clothing for the Tropics, but had not been at all prepared for cold weather, so that the children were in immediate need of winter outfits. And for the rest, nothing had been said about how they were to live and work in Shanghai, or in what way their salary was to reach them. All this they seem to have taken for granted that Hudson Taylor would be able to arrange.

No special anxiety was felt as yet, however. A large mail was waiting their arrival, and among the letters would doubtless be one containing the document on which so much depended. The Secretaries had assured Dr. Parker while he was still in London that his Letter of Credit, if not already on its way to Shanghai, would be there long before his own arrival. But on going through his mail no trace of it appeared. Carefully they read and reread the letters, but although it was taken for granted that he would be at the end of his journey when they reached him, there was no mention whatever of money-matters, or how his needs were to be supplied. The Letter of Credit had evidently been overlooked and forgotten.

Happily another mail was due within a day or two, and that no doubt would put matters right. In the meanwhile, they were thankful for the little preparation Hudson Taylor had been able to make, and with his few dollars and their own laid in a small supply of what was indispensable.

The mail came in. Yes, there were letters from the Secretaries dated September 15, more than three months after the Parkers had left London. There seemed to be no enclosures; but perhaps they had sent the Letter of Credit direct to their Shanghai Agents, and would mention having done so. No, nothing was said about it. There was positively no allusion to the matter. What could be the meaning of such an omission? To Dr. Parker it seemed inexplicable. But Hudson Taylor, with more experience of the working of things, was not altogether surprised, and found it less easy to be hopeful, though he acceded to the only suggestion that could be made, that they should go at once to the Agents and enquire. Dr. Parker was satisfied that this must bring a conclusion to their difficulties, so with a light heart as far as he was concerned they presented themselves at the office of Messrs. Gibb, Livingston and Co.

Hudson Taylor had had dealings before with the manager of this firm, and though he had found him a friend in need on more than one occasion, it was not possible to forget the sarcasm of some of his remarks, nor the emphasis with which he said, " the management or rather mismanagement of your Society is very bad." It was with some trepidation, therefore, he introduced Dr. Parker and asked if any advice had been received as to his Letter of Credit.

" No," answered the manager promptly, " none."

" Was it possible," queried Dr. Parker, " that they had heard nothing from the Society as to the amount he was entitled to draw ? "

" It was more than possible," replied the manager, " to judge by past experiences " ; though when he saw how this information was received, he was inclined to be more sympathetic.

Painful as the position was in itself, it was rendered still more so by the necessity they were under of explaining matters to this comparative stranger, with his prompt, efficient, business-like ways, upon whom for the time being they were dependent. If he had not seen fit to advance them money upon such evidence of their genuineness as they could afford, they would have been reduced to sore straights indeed. But his friendliness, both then and after, was the Lord's way of answering their prayers, and providing for them in the absence of the Letter of Credit that for long months did not make its appearance.

Dr. Parker said little about all this, but he must have felt it keenly, and probably all the more so as he came to realise the tempting possibilities opened to him as a medical man in China. How easily he could have supported his family in comfort, had he been willing to turn aside from missionary work. But in spite of poverty and many privations, prolonged all through the winter, spring, and following summer, he and Mrs. Parker held on their way with quiet self-sacrifice that never wavered.

From the first Sunday after landing, he went out regularly

with Hudson Taylor to evangelise in the city or surrounding villages, and frequently made longer excursions, giving away tracts and attending to simple ailments, while others more familiar with the language did the talking. And at home in their crowded quarters, he devoted himself assiduously to study. How difficult it was in that small house, shared by another family, no one who has not laboured at Chinese under similar circumstances can begin to imagine. Poor Mrs. Parker did her best to keep the children quiet But there were three of her own, besides those of the American missionaries, and she often had to go downstairs to attend to household affairs or receive visitors. The lower apartment being necessarily devoted to the uses of drawing-room and dining-room in one, there was nowhere for the doctor to study, a difficulty that could only be met by his sharing Hudson Taylor's room next to the nursery. What they did with their Chinese *pundits* does not appear. But if both teachers had to work with their respective pupils in that one small chamber, separated only by a partition from a busy mother and three little children, one can well understand Hudson Taylor's difficulty in preserving an unruffled spirit.

" No one who has not experienced it," he wrote, " can understand the effect of such incessant strain on mind and body.[1] It makes one so nervous and irritable that we sorely need your prayers as well as our own to enable us at all times to manifest a proper spirit.

" How gracious of God thus to keep us from being deluded into supposing that we are free from the evils that belong to fallen nature, and to make us long the more earnestly for the time when we shall see our blessed Master and be perfected in His likeness. Thank the Lord, there *does* remain a rest for us. I am so apt to grow weary and selfishly wish I were there, instead of desiring only to do His will and wait His time ; to follow the footsteps of Jesus and finish all that He will give me to do. Indeed, the work of grace seems only just begun in my heart. I have been an unfruitful branch, and need no small amount of pruning. May these present trials result only in blessing, preparing me for more extensive usefulness here and a crown of rejoicing hereafter."

" The continued strain to which I have been subjected of late,"

---

[1] Though written at the North Gate house just before the arrival of the Parkers, what he said then seems even more applicable a little later.

he wrote in another letter,[1] " has caused a degree of nervous irritability never before experienced, requiring the greatest watchfulness to prevent the manifestation of an unsuitable spirit before those by whom I am surrounded. What a solemn thing it is to be a *witness* for God, sent into the midst of heathen darkness to show forth in our lives all that by our words we teach. . . . Pray for me that I may have more grace, humility and reliance on the power of God, that I may prove henceforth more efficient, by His blessing, in this holy service."

Somewhat different in tone though not less humble in spirit was the first letter addressed to Mr. Pearse after the arrival of Dr. Parker and his family. In addition to their own difficulties about which he had to write, Hudson Taylor was suffering from imprudent statements in *The Gleaner* calculated to give serious offence to the L M.S. missionaries in Shanghai ; " men who," as he put it, " however much you may differ from them in judgment, are more thoughtful for the shelter and support of your missionaries than the Society that sends them out . . . if not more wishful."

" I trust you will not deem it unkind or disrespectful of me," he continued, " to write thus. For though I feel these things and feel them keenly, were it not for the sake of others and the good of the Society I would pass over them in silence. To do this, however, would be unfaithfulness on my part. For not only is it morally wrong and thoughtless in the extreme to act as the Society has acted towards Dr. Parker, but you must surely see that men who can quadruple their salary by professional practice, or double it by taking a clerk's berth will not be likely, if they find themselves totally unprovided for, to continue in the service of the Society. I do not make these remarks with respect to Dr. Parker, who seems thoroughly devoted to the work and by his spirit has encouraged me not a little. But they are true none the less. And I may add that a vacant post at £200 a year, the whole duties of which would not occupy two hours in the evening, did look inviting to me at a time when I had been obliged to incur a responsibility of £120 for rent, and a Resolution upon my last letter to the Committee informed me that missionaries drawing more than was authorised would not have their bills honoured by the Society.

" Dr. Parker arrived on Monday, a week ago to-day, calling forth true gratitude to God for deliverance from the many dangers that

---

[1] To his intimate friend Mr. B. Broomhall, dated November 19, 1854.

had beset their path. Of course he found our half of the house nearly empty, as my few things did not go far in furnishing. The missionaries, when they discovered this lack of preparation, blamed me very much. Could I tell them that having paid nearly twenty pounds for rent I had only three dollars left . . . a sum not sufficient to purchase provisions for a week at the present high rate of prices ?

" Fortunately Dr. Parker had a few dollars, for which, however, we had to give twenty to thirty per cent discount to get them into cash. He was not a little surprised to find that Mr. Bird's communication contained no Letter of Credit nor allusion to one. And when I learned that he had none with him, I was no less astonished that my last letter from the Society did not bring it, as you expressed the expectation that by the time of its arrival he would be here.

" The following day we were cheered by receiving another letter from you, dated September 15, but the . . . expectation that it contained the all-important document was soon turned to dismay when it proved that hope deferred was all there was to live on Now you cannot but see, I am sure, what evidence this is of gross neglect. We do, at any rate. And while we both cherish the warmest and most affectionate regard for many members of the Committee personally, and especially for its Secretaries, we cannot but feel that the Society had acted disgracefully.

" We went to Messrs. Gibb, Livingston and Co., for Dr. Parker felt sure that you had communicated with them, as Mr. Bird promised to do (if it were not already done) when he asked for his Letter of Credit. But they had heard nothing of it, and we could get no money. I asked if any alteration had taken place in my Letter of Credit since the Society augmented my quarterly allowance, but was informed that they had heard nothing of it. To relieve us of our painful embarrassment, Mr. —— offered on his own responsibility to cash a Bill for my extra £20, if I would write requesting him to do so, enclosing a copy of that part of your letter which authorised it, and get the extract signed by two merchants. This I have done. He also promised on our producing evidence from the Society's letters or magazines, to cash a Bill for Dr. Parker, endorsed by me, if I would assure him that it was right to do so. But when we went with the necessary papers we found them so busy that they could not attend to us until Tuesday (to-morrow).

" The weather is now exceedingly cold, and not having been led to expect it the Parkers needed an immediate supply of warm clothing. Beds and other articles of furniture were also necessary, as well as food and firing, all of which run into a considerable sum. Though he has said little, I am sure Dr. Parker has felt it keenly. I do trust that you will avoid such occurrences in future, that your missionaries may be spared unnecessary suffering."

Difficulties notwithstanding, they tackled their work bravely, and between long, busy Sundays among the people, settled down as well as they could to study. It was almost impossible to concentrate attention upon the language at this time, for the condition of the people around them was heart-rending. Hundreds were dying of cold and starvation, and there seemed no hope of relief until one side or other could win a decisive victory.

For still the Rebels would not yield, although the French in violation of their promised neutrality were taking sides more and more against them. A French frigate and steamer stationed opposite the native city deliberately cut off supplies that might have come to it by water, while on land the same end was served by a massive wall built and guarded by French forces. All this, it was becoming evident, was part of a Jesuit policy bent on supporting the reigning dynasty. For the Tai-pings and other insurgents were confessedly hostile not only to idolatry in all its forms, but to Roman priestcraft and image-worship, and to the growing habit of opium-smoking. If success crowned their long and desperate struggle, Romanism as well as opium and idolatry were bound to fall before them, and this was known at the Vatican as well as at the Court of St. James. First the French, therefore, and later on the English lent efficient aid to the Imperial cause, and the activity of the former in Shanghai at this time was the beginning of the foreign interference which ultimately led to the suppression of the Tai-ping movement. Whether this was on the whole a benefit to China is a question beyond the scope of these pages, but what does concern us here is the added misery and suffering that Hudson Taylor and his colleagues were compelled to witness :

"From the present aspect of affairs," wrote the former, " I think it all but certain that the French will shell and take the city before long. . . . If they do it will be an awful affair, for there are thousands of innocent people in the city who will suffer with the guiltiest of the Rebels. It is heart-rending to see and hear what we must from day to day ; and to think of the horrors yet to be endured makes one sick and faint. Oh, when will Jesus come and put an end to all this sin and misery ! "

One opportunity Hudson Taylor had of trying to avert the final catastrophy. He had gone into the city to obtain permission for his teacher Sï to bring out some members of his wife's family, and was talking with the Rebel leader, Chin A-lin, when a letter was brought in from the English and American Consular authorities. The letter was read aloud and interpreted to the general in the young missionary's presence. It urged upon him the duty of saving the lives of the helpless and innocent people for whom he was responsible, and offered to undertake to have matters peaceably settled on condition of an immediate capitulation upon the best terms the Imperial party could be prevailed upon to make. Hudson Taylor seems to have been the only foreigner present, and realising the issues at stake he did his best to persuade the irate general to consider the letter favourably.

"I had a great deal of conversation with him," he wrote on the day in question, December 11, "and endeavoured to induce him to accept the mediation proposed. . . . But he seemed desperate, and would not hear of capitulation, declaring that he would fight to the last and die if need be, but not alone. Dusk compelled me to leave the city, as there seemed no hope of influencing him for the better."

Ever since the arrival of Dr. Parker, this open interference on the part of the French had been rousing the hatred of the Rebel soldiery. Their attitude was becoming menacing, and the Chinese who favoured their cause, both in and around the Settlement, were plotting revenge upon the whole European community. This made evangelistic work both difficult and dangerous, and might not unreasonably have formed an excuse for lessened activity for the time being. But as far as the missionaries on the L.M.S. compound were concerned it had no such effect. Dr. Medhurst and his colleagues still planned and carried out their excursions to the interior, as well as constant evangelisation in the neighbourhood of Shanghai; and Dr. Parker made many visits in company with Hudson Taylor to towns and villages within a radius of ten or fifteen miles. Down the Hwang-pu River they went, and up the creeks and canals where shipping congregated, everywhere searching out serious and intelligent persons with whom to leave Scriptures and tracts. In this way in the month of December alone they distributed many hundreds of New Testaments and Gospels, together with a still larger number of tracts explaining the way of life.[1]

"These have been given with all possible care," wrote Hudson Taylor to the Committee, "and in most cases to men whom we knew were able to read. A considerable number were taken on junks travelling to the northern provinces."

But before the year closed an opportunity came for more aggressive efforts. Mr. Edkins was about to pay his long-deferred visit to Ka-shing, and renewed the invitation to his young friend to accompany him. Eight months previously they had been stopped by the Battle of Muddy Flat, but now the way seemed open, and in spite of the threatening aspect of Shanghai affairs they determined to set out at any rate, and see what could be done.

[1] During October, November and the first part of December, Hudson Taylor distributed, with help from Dr. Parker, more than eighteen hundred New Testaments and Scripture portions and two thousand two hundred Christian books and tracts

CHAPTER XX

IT was with no little interest, as may well be imagined, that Hudson Taylor made preparation for this first inland journey. In addition to clothes and bedding, a good supply of drugs and instruments had to be packed, for there was no knowing what demands might be made upon him as a medical man. Then there were food-baskets to be stored with provisions ; a stove, cooking utensils, and fuel to be provided ; and last but not least, an ample assortment of books and tracts. The native house-boat engaged by Mr. Edkins was happily large and clean. It had one tall mast with a sail in proportion, and a cabin " capable of affording considerable shelter from wind and rain, without causing its occupants any concern as to want of ventilation." Here, then, their belongings were arranged as conveniently as possible, and commending themselves to the care and blessing of God an early start was made on Saturday, December 16.

They were absent the whole of the following week, and in city after city had wonderful opportunities for preaching the Gospel. Everything about their experiences, it need hardly be said, was memorable to Hudson Taylor—from the crowds that thronged them to the least detail of life upon the water, and the look of the low-lying country as it glided by, with its innumerable homes of the living and grave-mounds of the dead.

But that first night on the river had an interest all its

own. Anchored amid a fleet of other boats, for mutual
protection, they were out among the people at last as he
had so often longed to be. Each boat had its family as
well as crew, and cheerful was the clatter that went on
while the evening meal was in preparation. Then came
the little service in their cabin, when the dim light fell on
faces full of interest in the old, old story. Born, brought
up and married on the water, many among the boat-people
never live ashore, and three generations may well have been
represented in that evening meeting. Of the talk that
followed we know nothing, save that it cannot have been
much prolonged. Rising before daylight means retiring
early, and soon the young missionary would hear nothing
on all the boats around them but an occasional voice or
movement and the gong of the night-watchman above
the soft lapping of water along the shore.

With the turn of the tide after midnight, a stir began on
the boats. Anchors were drawn up, sails hoisted, and
junks got under way. As it was still dark our travellers
slept on, awakening to find themselves within sight of
Sung-kiang, a Fu city [1] some forty miles south of Shanghai.

Of their work in this place and others *en route* for Ka-
shing we must not attempt to tell much in detail. A few
scenes, however, may be touched upon as showing how the
busy days were passed.

In a Buddhist monastery in the first city visited a poor
recluse was living, a " holy man," walled up in a tiny
chamber in which he had been practically buried alive
for years. In the temple-courtyard a great crowd was
gathered, listening to some strange religious teachers in the
dress of Western lands. They were giving away books as
well as preaching, and not until their supply was exhausted
did they make a move to pass on. Some of the brother-
hood then pressed forward, inviting them to rest awhile in
the monastery, and especially to visit the " holy man."

---

[1] A Fu is the governing city of a prefecture (or group of counties), seven
to fourteen of which go to make up a province The word is also applied
to the prefect himself and to the district he governs. So that the Sung-
kiang Fu (mandarin) resides in Sung-kiang Fu (the city) and from that
centre controls the entire Sung-kiang Fu (prefecture).

Photograph   By a Chinese.

WATERWAYS NEAR SHANGHAI.

Many of which Mr. Taylor visited in his early evangelistic journeys.

To face page 256.

Thus it was that Hudson Taylor saw for the first time one of these unhappy beings. Surrounded by the yellow-robed, shaven-headed priests, the missionaries were escorted to the cell. The only access to the poor devotee was a small opening left when the wall was in process of building, through which a man could scarcely pass his hand. There, almost without light or motion, unwashed, unkempt, and alone, the "holy man" passed his days and nights of silence. How strange must have seemed to him those voices with their foreign accent, and the pale faces of which he caught a glimpse through that little opening, his one point of contact with the outer world. Mr. Edkins, happily, could speak a dialect with which he was familiar, and very earnest were their prayers that the "glad tidings of great joy," heard under these circumstances for the first time, might bring light and salvation to his soul.

In the same city a very different experience awaited them, and one that made them appreciate the eighty-nine stone bridges to be found within its walls. Followed by a noisy rabble as they were seeking their boat, the visitors turned down a side street leading to a landing-stage, which they took to be that of the public ferry. To their dismay it was a private wharf protected by a pair of gates they had hardly noticed in passing. To return by the way they had come was impossible, for the narrow street was filled with an uproarious crowd, who, to prevent escape in that direction, swung to the gates and swarmed all over them, watching between the bars for the next move of the strangers. The position was far from pleasant in an unknown city, with the crowd growing larger and more noisy all the time, and no bridge in sight. But the missionaries quietly looked to the Lord in prayer, and kept their wits about them.

"There were plenty of boats at hand," wrote Mr. Taylor, "but none of them would take us. We called to several, to the great amusement of the crowd, but in vain. . . . At length seeing that something must be done I took 'French leave,' jumped into a boat that was passing, and pulled it to the side for Mr. Edkins. Taken by surprise the men made no objection, and off we went to the chagrin of our tormentors who opened the gates and rushed to the waterside shouting tumultuously."

s

A first experience of trying crowds ; and he was to meet so many !

Before leaving the city that night, a second or third supply of literature being all distributed, a turn in the road brought them suddenly on the base of the Square Pagoda. Grey and imposing the massive structure rose before them that for nine hundred years had been the glory of Sung-kiang. The priest in charge consented to admit them, and soon the crowding of the streets gave place to the sombre quiet of the old pagoda and the view to be seen from a gallery near the top.

Long and silently they stood looking down upon the myriad homes outspread before them. Far reached the ancient wall enclosing its hundreds of thousands, and beyond it the tent-like roofs still stretched away toward the setting sun. And this was only one great centre. All about it lay the rich, level country, dotted as far as eye could see with villages and hamlets, while distant pagodas and temples told of other cities within easy reach.

It was the first time Hudson Taylor had looked out on such a scene, and the fact of China's immense population began to assume new meaning from that hour. In the quiet of their boat that evening he was thinking of it still, pen in hand,

" I think you will join me sooner or later," he wrote to his friend Mr. Broomhall. " Consider the use you could be out here. Oh, for the sake of Him who loved you even unto death, leave all, follow Him, come out and engage in this all-important work."

More important than ever did their work appear next morning when the city of Ka-shan was reached. Could the young missionary ever forget the crowd that awaited them in one of its temple courts ? Having unintentionally disturbed a group of ladies engaged in idol-worship, the missionaries had retired to the pagoda, and upon returning found a sea of faces filling the courtyard, men of all sorts and ages eager to see and hear. For a long time Mr. Edkins held their attention, reasoning with them of sin, righteousness and judgment to come, while Hudson Taylor beside him laboured fervently in prayer.

The address finished and their books distributed, Mr. Edkins asked the crowd to make way for them to leave the temple, and they had just reached the main entrance when an imposing cavalcade arrived. To their surprise it soon transpired that the handsome, dignified official who stepped from his chair, and came down the avenue of soldiers to meet them, was no less a person than the Mayor of the city, intent upon turning back the foreigners. An anxious hour followed, but by explaining their object fully and promising not to go beyond the next prefectural city, the missionaries obtained permission to continue their journey.

"Your books are good," he admitted, "and you may take them as far as Ka-shing, provided some of my attendants accompany you."

And to this requirement he held firm, pointing out the men who were to "shadow" the foreigners. But it does not appear that their presence proved any drawback to the work in hand.

The sun was setting on the fourth day of their journey when at length the city for which they were bound came in sight. Far reached its suburbs along the river-bank, following the grey line of the turreted wall. Informed already as to its history, the travellers knew that Ka-shing Fu was far more ancient and important than any of the places yet visited. Dating from a dynasty that flourished twenty centuries before the Christian era, it had been contemporaneous in its early history with the cities of Abraham's time. Not until A.D. 888, however, had its present wall been built, four miles in circumference, with the moat that surrounds it still.

Despite its long history and many changes, Ka-shing at the time of this visit was a notable centre of wealth and learning. Printing and publishing employed many of its people, but the manufacture of silk and cotton, and a variety of articles in copper and brass, were also among its special industries. The population was vast, but in common with all other places removed by any distance from the Treaty Ports, it was wholly destitute of the Gospel.

Unspeakably thankful to have been able to reach a

point so far in the " interior," the missionaries realised that
great tact and caution would be needed in making the
most of their opportunity. They had learned something
already of the difficulties that might arise from showing
themselves too freely on the crowded streets, and determined to work in the extensive suburbs rather than enter
the city itself. Their presence would soon become known,
and those who wished to obtain books or see them personally
would have no difficulty in finding out their junk.

Immediately upon arrival, therefore, they went ashore,
and before people had awakened to the fact that foreigners
had appeared outside the West Gate, they had distributed
a large number of tracts. But even so,

" Returning to our boat," wrote Mr. Taylor, " we unintentionally
gratified hundreds of spectators   . including many ladies, elegantly
dressed. But soon the gathering shades of evening emptied the
windows and closed the doors. Boats ceased coming for tracts, the
people went home for the night, and we ourselves were glad of a little
rest."

Next morning they were up betimes, and even before
breakfast made a good beginning in the Liu-li-Kiai, or Two-
Mile Street, bordering the Grand Canal. Whenever a
crowd collected they passed on in their boat to another
part of the river-bank, their movements being so quick
that they were able to leave tracts along the whole length
of this suburb before it became prudent to absent themselves for a time. This they did by poling round to the
south side of the city, where a wide expanse of water and
some picturesque islands formed a favourite pleasure-
resort. Here they were accessible to any who wished to
follow them, and even if the crowds were large business
would not be interrupted, nor the shopkeepers annoyed.

Little were they prepared, however, for the invasion of
the Yen-yü Leo (Mansion of Smoke and Rain) that followed.
Out in the middle of the lake, this attractive island was
the place chosen by the Emperor K'ien-lung of the present
dynasty for a summer residence, and the beautiful building
and gardens preserved a romantic interest, though falling
somewhat into decay. Mooring their boat near the palace,

now used as a temple, Mr. Edkins and his companion went
ashore to see what was to be seen.   But they themselves
were the sight of supreme interest, as they soon discovered.

Before we had finished looking round we observed a number of
boats putting off in our direction, and soon a regular ferry was established between the island and the opposite suburb.   The people came
in multitudes, and those who could read were quickly supplied with
tracts.   When a large number had collected, Mr. Edkins preached,
and afterwards I had a long talk with some who gathered round me
for books.   By this time the numbers who had come were so great
that we were obliged to go on board our boat, from which Mr. Edkins
again addressed the people, to many of whom tracts were given.

As the crowd was continually receiving accessions, we thought it
wiser to put off a little from the island, to prevent those who were
behind from pushing the foremost into the water in their eagerness
to see and hear.   Immediately, however, the people followed us, and
in the middle of the lake we were surrounded by boats and kept hard
at work supplying the newcomers with portions of Scripture and
tracts.   As fast as one boat was supplied it pushed off and another
took its place.   It must have been a paying business for the boat-
people !   The boats were a better class than those commonly seen
about Shanghai, and almost without exception they were skulled by
women.   Supplying tracts and talking without intermission proved
tiring work as the afternoon wore on.   But what joy it was to remember the promise that cannot be broken, " My Word shall not
return unto Me void," and to think that not a few around us might
shine forever like the stars of heaven in the Kingdom of our Lord.

Later in the day visits were received from several intelligent men who wanted to know more about the contents
of the books they had received.   Some were strangers
from a distance, others Mandarins awaiting office, and one
an Inspector of Grain in the Ka-shing district.   These
persons engaged Mr Edkins in prolonged conversation,
while Hudson Taylor continued supplying tracts from the
deck.   Not until evening was there any cessation in this
work, and then boat-people and foreigners were alike
weary and thankful for rest.

The following morning found them again near the Two-
Mile Street, as the island would not have been a safe
anchorage for the night.   After breakfast, and united
prayer for blessing, they visited several smaller suburbs

before moving off to the South Lake as before. Here the people began coming at once, and much of the day was occupied in preaching and seeing patients as well as in supplying literature, for which there was a great demand.

"We found no difficulty," wrote Mr. Edkins of the entire journey, "in distributing a full share of the Million Chinese Testaments."

In the course of the afternoon they spent an hour or two in a famous temple containing several idols of twenty to thirty feet in height. A most impressive view was obtained from the pagoda near at hand, and the brief respite for prayer that it afforded sent them back refreshed to the crowd below. Until evening they were again the centre of a busily-plying ferry-system on the South Lake, for only when dusk was falling did the last of their visitors row away.

A stormy night followed, ushering in a change of weather that put a stop to their work for the time being ; but not before one rainy day had been spent in conversation with specially-interested callers.

"Your words are true and your books are true," said some of these on leaving. "It is a good doctrine."

CHAPTER XXI

OUR PLANS OF USEFULNESS

INCLUDING SECOND, THIRD, AND FOURTH JOURNEYS.
DECEMBER 1854–MARCH 1855. AET. 22.

USEFULNESS was what they desired most of all, and it was natural that as the year drew to a close they should consult together and work out careful plans to this end. Dr. Parker, an able, experienced man, had a family to think of, and Hudson Taylor, young as he was, was becoming an efficient missionary. Nothing had yet been heard of the missing Letter of Credit, so that their perplexity with regard to money matters was extreme, and tidings that new missionaries of the L M.S. were about to sail for China reminded them that even the premises they now occupied would have to be vacated before long. This it was that gave urgency and definiteness to their consultations, and resulted in several letters setting forth " plans of usefulness," that for the next few months largely occupied their thoughts.

" We who are on the field," wrote Hudson Taylor at the end of December, " desire to be as efficient as possible ; and while relying on the blessing of God alone for success, we wish to employ every means in our power to attain it. In this I know you are heartily with us, and I trust that by united prayer and effort and above all through the influence of the Holy Spirit we shall not be disappointed."

And then he went on to outline to the Committee the thoughts they had worked out.

To begin with, a permanent centre was needed and must be obtained without delay. Of the five Treaty Ports open to the residence of foreigners, none was more suitable than Shanghai—within reach of many important cities, and holding a strategic position with regard to mid-China. In Shanghai, therefore, their headquarters should be located And the next step was equally plain : in Shanghai they must have suitable premises, and that at once.

This again necessitated a certain adequacy of method and equipment, for other missions were there before them, and had established precedents that could not be ignored. Plan as simply as they might, they would at least require a doctor's house and a school-building, in addition to hospital and dispensary. For a chapel they could wait, using meanwhile the receiving-room of the hospital, specially adapted for meetings. From this central station, their plan was to visit the surrounding country and establish branch-schools and dispensaries wherever possible. These would be regularly supervised by one or other of the missionaries, and would become in their turn centres of Christian effort.

It was all admirable no doubt, and the estimate of a thousand pounds for land and buildings was not immoderate. But it was based upon conclusions that in their case were misleading, and just because the good is often the enemy of the best would have thwarted their real life-usefulness, fore-ordained in the purposes of God.

But the letters were sent off, and the New Year given to prayer with these thoughts specially in mind. It was now the depth of winter and exceptionally cold. Hudson Taylor had bought a native boat for half its value, and on frequent excursions to the country was able to purchase fuel and provisions at a lower rate than in Shanghai. This with Mrs. Parker's thrifty housekeeping made such means as they had last as long as possible, but even so it was with difficulty that they could keep one room warm enough for study. Hudson Taylor was working hard at two dialects, a Shanghai teacher coming to him in the daytime, and his Mandarin-speaking pundit at night. He was also carrying on a school, encouraged to find himself well understood by the children.

" I trust that by the time I have been here a year," he wrote, " I shall be able to preach both in Mandarin and in the Shanghai dialect. . . . I should have been further advanced in the latter, of course, had I commenced it on arrival. But I begin to think that I was directed by a higher Wisdom in taking up Mandarin first, and trust that though some delay has been occasioned in getting into work, I shall in the end be fitted for more extensive usefulness."

Eager as he was to make progress with his studies, it was all the more remarkable that the need of the un-evangelised regions round about should press so heavily upon his heart. Certainly it was not the season of the year that tempted him to another journey, nor was it pleasant companionship, for he had to go alone. The condition of affairs, politically, might in itself have been sufficient to hold him back, for a crisis could not long be delayed in the siege of the native city. But little as he realised what it foreshadowed, Hudson Taylor found himself unable to disregard the appeal of the unreached. The ice was broken. He had been on one evangelistic tour already, and had seen how such work could be done. Perhaps it was this that drew him on ? Perhaps it was something deeper, more significant.

Second Journey *January* 1855

At any rate he set out on January 25, travelling in his own boat. A few miles south of Shanghai, a tributary stream was reached, leading to a district little known to foreigners. Lying between the Hwang-poo river and the coast, the region was one infested with smugglers, and even its larger centres of population had rarely if ever been visited with the Gospel. It was a favourite resort of desperate characters throughout that borderland between two provinces,[1] and might well have been avoided by the solitary evangelist had he desired an easy task. Travelling on far into the night, however, he was conscious of a Presence

---

[1] The province of Kiang-su in which Shanghai is situated, and the province of Cheh-kiang immediately to the south, with Hang-chow and Ning-po among its well-known cities

that precluded fear, and robbed the unknown of its possible terrors.

Far from promising must have seemed the awakening when they found themselves next morning frozen in between high, snow-covered banks, the water covered with a thick coating of ice. To the uninitiated it may sound interesting enough to pole one's way along such a river, breaking a channel for the boat a foot at a time. But any one who has spent long days and nights on a leaky junk, under similar conditions, will not be anxious to repeat the experiment, except for the ends Hudson Taylor had in view.

And these ends were in no wise hindered by the slow progress that was all they could make. Accompanied by a servant to carry books, the young missionary went ashore and walked from hamlet to hamlet. His dress, speech and occupation everywhere aroused the intensest interest, and great was the eagerness to obtain his beautifully bound and printed books.[1] That he was giving these away was not the least part of the wonder, and as village after village turned out to meet him, the schoolmaster or some promising student was put forward to secure as many as possible. It was casting bread indeed " upon the waters," but very definite was his faith in the promise, " It shall accomplish that which I please and . . . prosper in the thing whereto I sent it."

Two governing cities were visited on this journey, besides many villages, and a market-town whose population equalled that of both cities combined. It was lonely, trying work, for the people were rough, and the crowding dangerous, and in reading the journal one is surprised at the thoroughness with which it was done. Every street in Chwan-sha was visited, for example, and in each of the suburbs ; all the reading men he could find being supplied with Gospels and tracts. In several temples also addresses were delivered. There was no companion to fall back upon, and unless he

---

[1] *Pah-ko ts'ien ih pun*, " Eight cash a copy," is a phrase that early becomes familiar to the missionary who in *these* days presents his Scriptures for sale rather than free distribution And certainly they are a wonder at the price (one farthing), printed in clear, large type, and attractively bound in tinted paper covers.

preached himself the people might never hear. So looking to the Lord for help, Hudson Taylor made the most of his few sentences, following up long days ashore with hours of medical work and private conversation on the boat at night.

In Nan-hwei,[1] the crowds were especially turbulent, and a Sunday spent there was memorable both to himself and the local authorities. Alarmed at the news that a foreigner was approaching, orders had been issued to close the principal gate of the city, and keep it locked and barred until after he had withdrawn. Knowing nothing of this defensive movement, Hudson Taylor spent the night outside a gate of secondary importance, unnoticed in his little boat, and early on Sunday morning passed in and went about his work. Meanwhile a sharp look-out was kept on the opposite side of the city, and it was a crestfallen messenger who bore tidings to the Ya-men [2] that the foreigner was already within its walls. Greatly taken aback, the Mandarin sent to learn all he could about the intruder ; and when it proved that he was alone and unarmed, a well-behaved person whose stay would be of short duration, his fears were dispelled, and the East Gate shortly after was reopened to traffic.

The excitement of the people, however, was not so easily allayed, and after a brave attempt at preaching Hudson Taylor had to retire before overwhelming crowds. Knowing that those who were interested would follow him, he took refuge on his boat at a little distance from the city. And a busy day he had of it—receiving the hundreds who came, supplying all who could read with Christian literature, giving medicines to the sick, telling over and over again the main facts of the Gospel, and answering endless questions as to personal matters. Several educated men paid him a visit, two of whom warned the boatmen that it was not safe for a foreigner to be in that district alone and unprotected. But Hudson Taylor, overhearing the conversation, assured them that he had no fear, for the Great God,

[1] Nan-hwei " Hsien," the latter word standing for a county-town or governing city next in importance to a "Fu."
[2] The Ya-men is the residence of the local Mandarin.

Creator and Upholder of Heaven and earth, never fails to keep watch over those who put their trust in Him.

So real was this faith that he did not even hesitate, the following day, when urged to go he knew not whither to visit a dying woman. He had just completed a morning's work in the city, and upon reaching the boat found several men from a distance, one of whom had brought a chair and bearers to carry him back to see his suffering wife. They were all earnest in their entreaties that he would accompany them, so in spite of the risk involved in going off with entire strangers, the young missionary set out.

Mile after mile they hurried over the frozen paths until almost benumbed with cold he wondered whether it would be possible to get back that night. Even so he seems to have had no fear. Yet how easily the whole thing might have been a trap! In that lawless part of the province, with the country in the disturbed state in which it was, nothing was more likely than that he should be seized and held to ransom, or even tortured and killed as a hated foreigner. But, as he had written home the night before : '

I knew that I was where duty had placed me, unworthy as I am of such a position, and felt that though solitary I was not alone.

The visit proved interesting when their destination was reached. The poor woman was suffering from dropsy, and though great relief could have been afforded under suitable circumstances, it was not possible to operate where she was. Mr. Taylor urged her husband to take her to Shanghai, regretting that he had no hospital into which he could promise to receive her ; and after making what arrangements he could for her comfort, he explained to them simply and fully the message he had come so far to bring. Of course all the village and surrounding hamlets turned out to look and listen, so that his audience was considerable, nor had they ever heard the tidings of redeeming love.

As he was leaving, the husband came up with a fine fowl tied by the legs, which he presented to the " foreign doctor," with many apologies for the insufficiency of his offering. And it was his turn to be surprised when the stranger begged him to set it free, saying with many thanks, that his medicine, like his message, was " without money and without price." Tired though he was on reaching the boat, he had the joy of knowing that in one more home and district the name of Jesus was as ointment poured forth—a sweet fragrance at any rate to God.

Two days later, on the last of January, he was leaving the market-town of Chow-pu, anxious to reach Shanghai that night. But though the boatmen travelled on till nearly morning, it was not until late on February 1 they dropped anchor at their starting-point. Then there were provisions to unload and carry home to replenish Mrs. Parker's supplies before Hudson Taylor could give attention to a matter that was specially on his heart.

A few weeks previously, three men of his acquaintance had been seized in the North Gate house, dragged out of bed in the middle of the night, and handed over as rebels to the local authorities. Upon hearing of it the young missionary had at once sought their release. But though assured that they would soon be at liberty, no charge having been proved against them, the poor fellows were only hurried from prison to prison, everywhere starved and tortured to make them confess alleged crimes. Again and again Hudson Taylor had appealed on their behalf, but as long as there was any chance of extorting money the case seemed hopeless. Now, returning encouraged from his journey, he went once more and to his great joy was successful. The men still lived, and before long he had the satisfaction of seeing them in such comfort as their homes could afford.

But how small a thing it seemed to relieve the sufferings of one group of people amid all the horrors that were going on ! Shanghai was in a worse condition than ever, if that were possible. After more than a year of desultory fighting, the Imperial forces seemed roused at length to take the city. A large new camp quite near the Settlement had cut off the last hope of relief on the landward side, and among the beleaguered garrison famine and disease were doing their

deadly work. Terrible indeed was the strain of those days
for foreigners and natives alike, for it was only too evident
that a wholesale massacre would be the end of the tragedy
before their eyes.

Even in the Settlement the position was one of danger.
The attempts of the French to take the city had been
unsuccessful, and by their manifest futility had impaired
the prestige of all the European forces.

" It is openly announced," wrote Hudson Taylor on February 3,
" that foreigners are no longer to be feared. . . . Added to this, the
Imperial soldiers are nearer and more numerous than ever, their new
Camp being hardly more than a stone's throw from this house. Dr.
Parker has already told you of a ball and shell thrown into our compound. . . . So you see we are safe only as protected by Him who is
the Shield as well as Sun of His people."

Still more threatening in some ways was the attitude of
the rebel party. Their indignation at French interference
knew no bounds, and had resulted in a Secret Society for
purposes of revenge in which no distinction would be possible
between one nationality and another. Alarming rumours
were afloat of an attack to be made on the Settlement, and
it was well known that should such plans be carried out no
help could be relied upon from the Government soldiery,
who would gladly see the foreigners massacred that they
might share the spoils.

So they were anxious times indeed after Hudson Taylor's
return from this second journey, and might well have
hindered further aggressive work. But in the midst of it
all he was quietly planning another preaching tour, to be
taken in company with older missionaries.

THIRD JOURNEY: *February to March* 1855

Proceeding in a westerly direction, the little party seems
to have travelled as far as Tsing-pu on their way to the Soo-
chow Lake. Only the briefest record remains of this
itineration, probably because it was curtailed by the fall
of the doomed city. For they had not been absent many
days when they saw from the top of a hill the smoke of an

immense conflagration. So great a fire in that direction could mean but one thing. Shanghai was in flames ! And what of their families in the foreign Settlement ?

Setting out at once to return, their apprehensions were confirmed by Rebel soldiers who came seeking protection. This, of course, the missionaries, themselves defenceless, were unable to afford ; and shortly after the poor fellows were taken and beheaded before their eyes. Sadly continuing their journey, they soon came upon abundant traces of the catastrophe that had taken place, and as they passed the native city had to turn away from sights of horror on every hand. But the Settlement was in peace. The uprising of the Triad Society had been averted, and the Imperialists, satiated with slaughter, were too exultant over their achievements to pay much attention to foreigners.

Thus ended in a holocaust of human lives the sufferings of the siege that had been in progress ever since Hudson Taylor's arrival in China, twelve months previously.

" Shanghai is now in peace," he wrote on March 4, " but it is like the peace of death. Two thousand people at the very least have perished, and the tortures some of the victims have undergone cannot have been exceeded by the worst barbarities of the Inquisition. The city is little more than a mass of ruins, and many of the wretched objects who have survived are piteous to behold. . . .

" How dreadful is war ! From the South to the North Gate of Shanghai, on one side only, sixty-six heads and several bodies are exposed by the sanguinary Imperialists, including those of old men with white hair, besides women and children. . . . These terrible sights are now so common that they do not upset one as they did at first. But it is impossible to witness them without feelings of intense abhorrence for the Government that permits and even perpetrates such atrocities."

Still the worst was over, and relieved from the strain of that terrible winter the missionaries looked forward to largely increasing their work. Surely now had come the moment for advance. Before the energy of the population round them, a new Shanghai would soon arise upon the ruins. Thousands of people would be flocking in to share the prosperity that enterprise and commerce would create.

As far as possible they must purchase land before it was taken up, enlarge their schools, open preaching halls, found hospitals, and take a front rank among the builders of the new time.

All this, it goes without saying, stirred the hearts of Hudson Taylor and his colleague, still anxiously waiting the reply of the Committee. Three months had now elapsed since their plans had been laid before the Society, and communications that had crossed their own had not been encouraging. Old objections had been raised against building in the Treaty Ports, and arguments reiterated in favour of opening new fields to the Gospel. But how they were to live and work until this was possible the letters did not suggest. The missionaries themselves could not believe that this point of view was unalterable. They had stated the case so clearly that its importance *must* be felt, and surely when their well-considered scheme was laid before the Committee it would be seen to forward the very ends they had themselves in view.

Meanwhile it was more and more difficult to wait on in uncertainty. The American missionary who shared their little house was building premises of his own, but with no hope of completing them before summer. Dr. Parker's Letter of Credit had not come, nor did the Society seem to remember that he had any financial needs. If their privations through the winter had been severe, what would the hot season mean—the dreaded months of summer—in those crowded rooms ?

When all these circumstances are considered, and it is further taken into account that missionaries, even the most devoted, are only human after all, it will not be wondered at that some things were said and felt that hardly seem in keeping with Hudson Taylor's simple faith in God. He was passing through a period of peril for his spiritual usefulness, and was under the influence of friends called to a line of things entirely different from his own. But though carried away for the time, as may be seen from his letters, he was not allowed to involve himself in responsibilities that would have hindered his life-work.

"You *are* going to have a fine Chapel in Barnsley!" he wrote to his parents in March. "I wish some wealthy friend would send us a thousand pounds to put up our hospital, school, and other premises, for we are in a shocking position now With only three rooms to live in, we are obliged to set apart one for callers . . . so that my bedroom has to do duty as study for both Dr. Parker and myself, and I have no place to which I can retire for a moment's privacy from morning till night. . . What we are to do when the hot weather comes, I cannot imagine.

"We have written to the Society laying a definite plan before them, and if they do not take it up we mean to try and carry it through without their aid. If they oppose it, as contrary to their principle of not working in the Ports, we must try to have the principle modified. And if they will not alter and we cannot find other better means of working, it may become a question as to which we shall dispense with—the Society, or our plans of usefulness.

"But you need be under no apprehension on this score. Our plans will be formed with prudence, in the fear of the Lord, and not without seeking His direction. But useful we must and will be, if the Lord bless us, at any cost.

"Do you think a Bazaar could be got up anywhere, to assist us in the purchase of ground and erection of suitable buildings? . . . If you could get the ladies interested, it would be sure to succeed. The sum we want is really so trifling that a few good collections would soon raise either the whole or the greater part."

But side by side with this, which one cannot but see was unlike him, went another, very different development. Strangely the currents mingled at this time—one drawing him to the settled life of the Ports, the other carrying him far afield, to regions beyond any that had yet been reached. He could not even wait for the expected reply of the Committee, so eager was he to set out upon another evangelistic journey. The local Rebellion was at an end, Dr. Parker needed change from study, their boat was lying in the Creek —was it not just the opportunity for a preaching-tour which should include a good deal of medical work?

FOURTH JOURNEY · *March* 1855

Deeply interesting was the week that followed. Leaving Shanghai by the Soo-chow Creek they travelled north and

T

west to the county-town of Kia-ting. Many busy places
were passed *en route*, and remarkable openings found for
the Gospel ; but limits of space will only admit of our
dwelling upon the visit to the *Hsien* itself, where a novel
experience awaited them.

Accustomed as they were to large, excited crowds, they
hardly knew what to make of it when grown-up people as
well as children fled in terror, so that the streets were
literally cleared at their approach. Yet this was what
happened in Kia-ting. No one would venture near them,
and it was strange to see people of all classes hurrying to
the nearest buildings as if for protection from imminent
danger.

" Even men," remarked Dr. Parker with grave amusement, " took
refuge in their houses as we drew near, hastily shutting the doors ;
to which, however, they crowded to look after us as soon as we had
passed."

So strong were these unreasoning fears, due to the
" bogy stories " in circulation about foreigners, that it is
doubtful whether any entrance could have been gained for
more favourable impressions but for the influence of the
medical work. They were there to heal the sick as well as
preach the Gospel, and were wise enough to put it in this
order until the hearts of the people were won.

Realising that in all probability they were the first
foreigners to visit the city, Dr. Parker and his companion
let themselves be seen as much and as openly as possible.
They made it known that they were physicians, " able to
prescribe for both external and internal complaints," and
that on the morrow they would *k'an-ping*, or " investigate
diseases," providing each patient gratuitously with the
appropriate remedy. This seemed to turn the tide of
popular feeling, and as they went about the streets and
made the circuit of the city-wall they heard many remarks
as to their being *shan-ren*, or " doers of good deeds." The
crowds that followed them, still at a respectful distance, so
increased that shop-fronts were in danger and the goods
exposed for sale were trampled under foot. By retiring to
more open parts of the city they were able to save the

business-people annoyance, and at the close of a tiring day had the satisfaction of feeling that not a little prejudice had been overcome.

"Long before breakfast," wrote Dr. Parker of the following morning, " the banks of the river were crowded with persons desiring medical aid. . . . After working hard until 3 P.M , finding we could not possibly see them all, Mr. Taylor selected the more urgent cases and brought them on board the boat. No sooner were those attended to than we were taken to see patients in their own homes who were unable to come to us, and were much gratified to find that we had access to and were welcomed in some of the very houses the doors of which had been shut against us the day before."

What a turning of the tables in favour of the missionary ! and all due to ointments, pills, and powders, prescribed with sympathy and prayer. After this there was nothing but friendliness as they walked through the city, and they had all they could do during the remainder of the day to supply books to those who came for them. In a temple near the West Gate, a parting address was given to a large concourse of people, many of whom would gladly have detained the visitors. But time and experience alike warned them to leave while they were still welcome, in the hope of repeating the visit later. Even then they were not too weary to land at a neighbouring village before nightfall and seek out those who could read ; after which, travelling slowly on till morning, they were lulled to sleep by the monotonous rhythm of the oar.

Throughout the remainder of their journey the value of the medicine-chest as an aid to evangelisation was still further proved in a variety of ways. This encouraged Dr. Parker not a little, as did also the eagerness of the people to obtain books and the relative number of those who could read. At one important city the missionaries were kept busy all day long handing Gospels and tracts from the boat to a steady stream of applicants.

"Never have I seen or imagined," wrote the Scotch physician, " such opportunities for giving the Word of Life to those who seem anxious to obtain it."

Amongst others who came to them in boats were not a

few scholarly men and officials, drawn through interest in the medical work. These visitors were in many cases friendly, and stayed long enough to gain a clear idea of what the missionaries were teaching.

. . . . .

In his report of this journey Mr. Taylor stated that with Dr. Parker's help he had distributed since the beginning of the year,[1] three thousand New Testaments and Scripture portions, and more than seven thousand other books and tracts.

" The excursion from which we have just returned," he continued, " was particularly interesting on account of unusually good opportunities for seeing patients as well as scattering the good seed of the Kingdom, and for the illustration it afforded of the scarcely to be exaggerated value of medical work as an aid to missionary labour. . . .

" The crying need for a hospital was brought home to us afresh by cases in which life or limb could have been saved and chronic diseases relieved had we been able to care for the sufferers. . . . I sincerely trust that funds for this purpose, and instructions to purchase land and build without delay, are on the way to us ; for we could easily carry on efficient medical work without interfering with our present operations. . . . The door is widely open and no man can shut it. . . . May our united prayers and efforts result in abundant blessings."

But though these accounts and others of later journeys aroused much interest at home, the thousand pounds needed was not forthcoming. Great indeed was the trial of this long waiting and uncertainty ! But the Lord Who understood all that it meant to His servants did not leave them without tokens for good, two of which taking the form of financial help were especially encouraging.

Of these gifts in aid of the work, one was handed to Dr. Parker by a resident, and consisted of fifty dollars toward the purchase of land for a hospital. The other, received by Hudson Taylor himself, had a special interest as being the first that ever came to him apart from the Society for the cause so dear to his heart.

And when one records the name of the donor—Mr W. T. Berger of Saint Hill, near London—what a vista is opened

[1] A period of only three months : January-March 1855.

up into the province of God ! Mr. Berger, a frequent visitor at the Tottenham Meeting, had met the young missionary on one or more occasions before he sailed for China. From his friends the Howards of Bruce Grove and from Miss Stacey he would hear sufficient to awaken interest in the Yorkshire lad, an interest Hudson Taylor's letters from Shanghai could not fail to deepen. The result was this gift of ten pounds, thankfully appropriated toward the support of a child the missionaries were anxious to adopt ; a first step, as they hoped, toward a permanent boarding-school.

But how much more was in the plan of the Great Giver ! Could Hudson Taylor have foreseen how many hundreds, even thousands of pounds would come to him through the same channel, and the still more important gifts of counsel, sympathy, and brotherly love in the work he and Mr. Berger were to do together for the Lord, how amazed and over-whelmed he would have been ! But all this, and far, far more was being brought to pass by Him Who even then was working out His own purposes in the life of His servant, as in our lives to-day.

CHAPTER XXII

NOT WHERE CHRIST WAS NAMED

FIFTH JOURNEY. APRIL 1855   AET. 22

SPRINGTIME was drawing on apace, a season to be made the most of for evangelistic purposes, and the travellers had hardly reached home before Hudson Taylor was planning another journey. In the estuary of the Yangtze distant only thirty miles from Shanghai, lay the great island of Tsung-ming. Sixty miles long by fifteen or twenty broad, it was the home of more than a million people, covered at this time of year with blossoming peach-orchards amid a sea of early wheat. But though so near the foreign Settlement it was off the beaten track, and had never yet been visited by Protestant missionaries. Little wonder it attracted the young evangelist, about to set out with Mr. Burdon on a longer itineration than any he had yet attempted.

FIFTH JOURNEY: *April* 1855

Interesting as it would be to follow them as they crossed the rough waters of the Yangtze, ran up a creek on the landward side of the island, and in spite of alternate deluges of rain and overwhelming crowds carried on their work in the capital and other places, we must content ourselves with a mere outline of those busy days to dwell more at length upon the latter part of the journey.

Their plan on this occasion was to penetrate as far inland as possible, testing what could be done in a good many places rather than spending much time in any one; and the direction chosen was the estuary of the Yangtze river.

Tsung-ming they found singularly open. In the chief city, bearing the same name as the island, they spent several encouraging days. All the principal streets and suburbs were visited, and in four large temples Mr. Burdon addressed the crowds. As inquiries had been made about them from the Ya-men, they felt it desirable to call upon the Mandarin who had probably anything but a favourable impression of foreigners. This official proved to be a grave though rather young man, who received them with courtesy. He accepted copies of the New Testament and other books, and listened attentively while they explained their contents, putting before him the way of salvation through faith in Christ. He made no objection to their visiting the island, and very thankfully they felt that this interview alone would well have repaid their coming to Tsung-ming.

The temple of the city-god was a busy scene during the remainder of that day. Mud or no mud the people came; and while Hudson Taylor did his best to attend to patients in one of the side rooms, Mr. Burdon occupied the crowd with books and preaching in the open courtyard. Only when his voice gave out was the medical work interrupted; for the greater part of his audience surged over to the improvised dispensary, and no more doctoring was possible.

Then it was Hudson Taylor's turn to take the field, and not being as tall as his companion he looked about for some sort of pulpit from which to see and be seen. The only place that presented itself was a bronze incense-vase of large dimensions, into which he clambered, without apparently giving offence to the temple authorities.

"At the lowest computation," he wrote, "five or six hundred persons must have been present, and I do not think it would be over the mark to say a thousand. As they quieted down, I addressed them at the top of my voice, and a more orderly, attentive audience in the open air one could not wish to see. It was most encouraging to hear one and another call out . . . *puh-ts'o, puh-ts'o*, 'not wrong, not wrong,' as they frequently did when something said met with their approval."

But when it came to distributing literature the missionaries had a more difficult task. They adhered to their principle of giving only to those who could read, though many illiterate persons were bent on getting books. This rougher element in the crowd gave them no little trouble, and both tact and patience were needed to avoid an unpleasant scene. Public opinion was on their side, however, and though some tracts and Gospels were snatched away, they succeeded in getting most into the right hands.

Heavy and continued rains made it difficult to keep on with such work. One whole day had to be spent in the little boat shared with their teachers—the mat roof leaking all over, and the low, windowless cabin affording neither room to stand nor even sit in comfort. It would have been useless to go ashore, for streets are empty and doors all shut during such a downpour. Yet a few people waded through mud and slush to get to them, carrying back a clearer understanding of the Gospel than they would have been likely to obtain but for this persistent rain.

Before leaving Tsung-ming city, one interesting morning was spent in looking up the principal schools, to leave Christian literature with both scholars and teachers. Thirteen schools and a college were visited, the pupils varying in number from nine to twenty-five. The teachers were in many cases intelligent men, able to give information as to the chief centres of population on the island. Followed as usual by a noisy crowd, one of the visitors had to stay outside to keep the excitement within bounds. But the other, seated in the place of honour within, had a comparatively quiet opportunity for laying the main facts of the Gospel before a small but influential audience.

After this it was a comfort as they went on their journey to fall in with an empty boat willing to travel with them. To this they transferred their books and Chinese helpers, which gave them room to take a little rest between excursions on shore wherever people were to be found. One busy place named K'iao-t'eo had an unusually large proportion of reading men, and in several schools and temples they were helped in delivering their message.

Rounding the north-west corner of the island a little later, they put into a creek in time for a quiet talk before nightfall. It was a beautiful evening, and the freshness and silence about them were grateful after the experiences of the past few days. Scattered homesteads here and there stood among cypress and willow trees, the park-like country stretching away without wall or fence to the horizon. Even the grave-mounds, usually so marked a feature of a Chinese landscape, were few and far between, being replaced by simple earthenware jars containing human bones. A million living. How many millions dead? And yet Tsung-ming, as far as they could learn, had never before heard the glad tidings of Salvation.

"We went back to our boats," wrote Hudson Taylor, " rejoicing that we had been privileged to bring the word of God . . . to the people of this fertile island. . . . We determined also to sail round it, to ascertain as much as we could as to the facilities for missionary work, and to leave New Testaments if possible in every important place."

With these ends in view, they instructed the boatmen to proceed next morning in an easterly direction, following the line of the shore. But this to their surprise met with the strongest disapproval. The further side of the island might have been beset with unimaginable dangers, from all the boatmen had to say of it ; and soon their employers gathered that it would be necessary to keep a sharp lookout if they intended to have their orders obeyed. Accordingly when the anchor was weighed before daybreak Hudson Taylor roused himself to speak to the men, and for some time watched the compass to see that they kept the right course.

And then a very Chinesey thing happened. The boatmen, alarmed at the prospect before them, had made up their minds that the east coast of Tsung-ming should remain an unexplored region as far as they were concerned. Opium was a necessity of their lives, and in those out-of-the-way places who could tell at what price it was to be had. The foreigners were tired, and soon would sleep again. They would follow their instructions to begin with, and when all was quiet—please themselves. Accordingly the coast-line was kept well in sight for an hour or more ; after which, there being no remonstrance from within, the boat's head was turned northward, and with the help of a good breeze Tsung-ming soon faded from sight.

Still the weary missionaries slept on, and it was not until they were nearing what is now the north shore of the Yangtze that Hudson Taylor awoke in a double sense to the situation.

" It was no use then to be angry or scold the men," he wisely concluded, " for they would only have enjoyed that the more. The island we had left was already thirty or thirty-five miles behind us, and we should have lost a day in endeavouring to beat back to it. We therefore entered the first stream that presented itself . . . and learning that there were plenty of towns and villages on this island also, determined to do what we could in a short time."

Tuh-shan on which they thus found themselves is not to be seen on any of the maps of to-day. Great areas of alluvial deposit have long since united it with the mainland, where the city of Hai-men now appears. At that time, however, it was cut off by water ; an island reproducing on a smaller scale the natural features of Tsung-ming, which it also resembled in the primitive state of its roads, and its wholly unevangelised condition.

Inquiring for some sort of conveyance by which to visit as many places as possible, the missionaries found the only means of transportation to be the heavy, cumbersome wheelbarrow whose strident squeak is still measured by the mile in almost every part of China. Engaging two of these vehicles they set out, their books on one and them-selves on the other, carefully balanced on either side of the wheel.[1]

A couple of miles of this laborious travelling brought them to the village of U-kioh-shan, a place of a thousand or more inhabitants, many of whom seemed intelligent and were able to read. Here it was a joy to give their

[1] Should there be only one traveller, and no luggage or corresponding burden on the other side, the barrow is simply tilted till his weight is well over the wheel, and in this seemingly precarious position he is trundled from behind.

message, and it was not until many books had been distributed that they passed on to the neighbouring town of Huang-shan.

The demand for books at this latter place exhausted their supply, and the attention with which they were listened to made them forget weariness and hunger. The only drawback was that they were obliged to return to their boats for more literature before proceeding to Hai-men itself, the capital of the island.

The sun was almost setting when the latter place was reached, but the long spring evening gave time for a good deal of work in the principal streets, which proved to be those of a large and busy city. Here to their surprise the missionaries were taken for Chinese from one of the southern provinces, Fu-kien men and probably rebels, which roused a good deal of excitement. But when Mr. Burdon explained that they were from a far western country, religious teachers who had come to heal the sick, and bring a message of love and pardon from the one true God, against Whom all have sinned, the people were satisfied and listened with attention.

" Before leaving," wrote Mr. Taylor, " I addressed the crowd, asking if we should come again. . . . The reply was an eager affirmative, and many wanted to know when they might expect us."

Candles and lanterns having now appeared, the missionaries set out on their return journey. Every book they had brought with them had been given away, and ten times as many might easily have been disposed of. Thus their visit, though brief, had accomplished something, and tired as they were they trundled cheerfully through drenching rain to reach their boats at ten o'clock at night, thankful for the openings found on this large island also.[1]

Before daylight next morning a favourable wind and tide had carried them far up the Yangtze, and when the sun

[1] Six months later, two wealthy men, brothers, sent a servant all the way to Shanghai to invite the missionaries to return to Hai-men. They had obtained books, it appeared, on the occasion of this first visit, and were anxious to have " the foreign teachers " make a long stay in their home. Unfortunately it was not possible to accept the invitation in person See Chap. XXVII. p. 341, footnote.

rose upon a cloudless sky they found themselves nearing the sacred mountains that command the north and south banks of the river, just where its estuary narrows away from the sea. It was a day of unusual beauty, and their voices being sadly in need of rest they decided to make the ascent of the northern range, and learn all they could of the lie of the land around them. Directing the boatmen therefore to enter the nearest tributary stream and await their return in the latter part of the day, the young men set out full of expectancy.

"The country was delightfully fertile," wrote Hudson Taylor, " and the breeze fragrant from blowing over fields of peas and beans in flower. As we approached the hills,[1] the scene became beautiful beyond description. Of the five summits the central one was the highest, crowned by a fine pagoda, evidently newly painted and repaired. At the foot of this hill and running up its side was the T'ai-shan t'ang, a Buddhist temple and monastery so extensive that at a little distance we mistook it for a village.

"The hill itself was steep, with bare declivitous rocks, and soil sparsely covered with grass and flowers. The ascent was by means of stone steps here and there among the trees . . . some of which were very fine and had seen many summers. Varying shades of foliage, from the deep, gloomy cypress to the light, graceful willow, mingled with orange, tallow, and other trees, gave a lively and interesting variety to the scene, and each turn of the path, revealing new shrines and pavilions, only increased the charm. . . . Anything more beautiful I have never seen.

"Entering the temple itself, we found it undergoing repairs. Some parts, apparently just finished, were in process of painting and gilding. Scores if not hundreds of men were at work, and from the amount and style of the decorations the expense must have been and will be enormous. Strangely enough, nothing could have been more timely than our visit, for the day happened to be a festival, and thousands of persons of all classes were gathered to join in the ceremonies. . . . Here were the rich and learned as well as the poor and wretched, here the gaily-apparelled and the meanly-clad, all victims of the same heathen superstitions, servants of the same master. Nothing could be more evident than that idolatry was here a *living* system, flourishing unmolested by soldiers of the Cross. . . . Here was one single institution, swarming with priests and those in training for that office, its idols to be numbered by hundreds . . . all richly

---

[1] The *Lang-shan* group, facing the heights of Fu-shan on the opposite side of the river.

painted, as was every part of the establishment, and gilding in profusion lavished upon them. Nothing was omitted and no expense spared that the eye might be charmed and the beholder captivated, and to the thousands present, no doubt, the idolatrous ritual was of the most imposing kind. . . .

" Ascending from height to height, we passed shrine after shrine, and everywhere the same scene was repeated—idols, priests, worshippers. Heavy fumes of incense filled the air ; and the clinking of cash, as the passers-by threw their coins into baskets placed before the idols mingled with strains of music, the buzz of conversation and tramp of passing feet. Upon reaching the summit we entered the halls connected with the pagoda, named from the temple T'ai-shan t'ah,—the hideous figures of the idols, seen through smoke and flames from burning paper,[1] making it seem like . . . a place where Satan's seat is.

" Turning sadly away we mounted the pagoda, and what a contrast was the scene outspread before our eyes ! Here nature seemed to be offering that worship to her Creator which man refused, and with surprise and delight we involuntarily exclaimed, ' How beautiful!' No words can describe the landscape, and the more one looked the more fresh beauties lay revealed. The day was so clear that with the telescope the most distant objects were well-defined, and the brilliant sunlight threw an air of gladness over everything. The hill on which we stood was between four others . . . two on our right and two on our left, presenting innumerable objects of interest to our view. The country below, covered with early crops and tended like a garden, was of the brightest hue, owing to recent rains. Streams intersected it in every direction, bordered with drooping willows. Farm-houses with their fruit trees and neat willow-fences, cemeteries here and there, cypress-shaded, and numerous villages and hamlets dotted the foreground. Beyond these lay the magnificent Yangtze, fifteen to twenty miles broad, its great northerly sweep looking calm as a lake and bearing on its sunny waters many a boat and junk with graceful sails, some snowy white, some brown or black with age. Beyond again rose the ' sacred mountains' of the southern shore, crowned with their monasteries and temples, . . . and other ranges of more distant hills. The opposite side of the square pagoda presented an entirely different view. There to the north-west lay the great city of Tung-chow surrounded by a populous plain ; and several little lakes shining like molten silver put a finishing touch to the beauty of the scene."

With hearts greatly moved by this panorama, they stood long and silently—looking out as Moses over the promised

---

[1] Offerings of money and other objects made in paper, expressly for burning before the idols.

land. Yes, this was China, seen at last, away from the narrow limits of a Treaty Port. How great it was, how far-reaching! And here at their very feet what darkness, superstition, and sin! Shanghai and its surroundings began to dwindle in importance, in view of all this. So many lights seemed gathered there—as they thought of all the Missions. After the appeal of unreached Tsungming, unreached Hai-men—this told. It was a sight to change a life, and Hudson Taylor's life was changed. From this time onward he swung free from influences that had held him, returning more and more in heart to his earlier position, his first sense of call to preach the Gospel, " Not where Christ was named. . . . But, as it is written, they shall see to whom no tidings of Him come, and they that have not heard shall understand."

Still throbbing with great though unspoken longings, they came down from the pagoda to make their way back to the boats, when in one of the courts below Hudson Taylor was stopped by a priest who requested him to bow before his Buddha and burn incense, with the usual offering of money. Stirred to the depths he could refrain no longer, and mounting the stool he had been desired to kneel on he addressed the throng about him in Mandarin, setting forth " the folly and sin of idolatry and the love of God in Christ which passes knowledge."

" When I had concluded," his journal continues, " Mr. Burdon followed in the Shanghai dialect. . . . It was evident that we were understood and that many felt the force of our message, amongst whom were some of the priests. When they saw the turn things were taking, however, they requested us to leave. This we would not do until we had finished, and when they began to go away themselves Mr. Burdon requested one or two to remain, that they might reprove us if we advanced anything contrary to the truth. I believe we were much assisted from above, and also that we were guided here by Providence to reach these multitudes who had never heard the precious truths of the Gospel. They gave us the most patient hearing, and listened with remarkable attention.

" Descending the hill we passed some stalls at which we purchased a few curiosities. We also witnessed scenes the very mention of which would outrage propriety, but were glad that we had thus an opportunity of seeing what tendencies these Buddhist festivals really have.   While such iniquities are practised in the face of heaven and on the very ground belonging to the temples, who will say that despite all its moral teachings and fair outward profession Buddhism is not polluting ?

" After leaving the temple we distributed the Scriptures and tracts we had with us, and feeling sincerely thankful that we had been permitted to bear testimony against these abominations and to dispense the Word of Life, we set off for our boats, a walk of two or three miles.   It was not until we reached them and had time to rest that we found our sore throats, which in the excitement of the day had been forgotten, had not particularly benefited by the strain they had unexpectedly sustained."

But tired throats could not deter them from the work of the following day.   Their purpose now was to visit Tung-chow, the city seen from the pagoda, whose unenviable reputation had already reached them.   It might be months, years even, before other evangelists would reach it, and they could not bear the responsibility of leaving its vast population any longer in ignorance of the way of Life.   If nothing more were possible, they could at any rate distribute their remaining Scriptures within its walls, praying that the good seed might bring forth fruit to life eternal.

" After breakfast we commended ourselves to the care of our Heavenly Father," wrote Mr. Taylor, " and sought His blessing before proceeding to this great city.   The day was dull and wet, the very opposite of yesterday.   We both felt persuaded that Satan would not allow us to assail his kingdom without raising serious opposition ; but we were also fully assured that it was the will of God that we should preach Christ in this city and distribute the Word of Truth among its people.   We were sorry that we had but few books left for such an important place.   The result, however, proved that this also was providential.

" Our native teachers did their best to persuade us not to go, but we determined that by God's help nothing should hinder us.   We directed them to remain in their boat, and if we did not return to learn whatever they could respecting our fate, and make all possible haste to Shanghai with the information.   We also arranged that the other boat should wait for us, even if we could not get back that night, so that we might not be detained for want of a boat in case of returning later.   We then put our books in two bags, and, with a servant who always accompanied us on these occasions, set off for the city, distant

about seven miles   Walking was out of the question from the state
of the roads, so we availed ourselves of wheelbarrows, the only
conveyance to be had   . .

" We had not gone far before our servant requested permission to
go back, as he was thoroughly frightened by reports concerning the
native soldiery. Of course we at once consented, not wishing to
involve another in trouble, and determined to carry the books ourselves and look for physical as well as spiritual strength to Him who
had promised to supply *all* our need.

" At this point a respectable man came up and earnestly warned us
against proceeding, saying that if we did so we should find to our
sorrow what the Tung-chow militia were like. We thanked him for
his advice, but could not act upon it, as our hearts were fixed. Whether
it were for bonds, imprisonment, and death, or whether to return in
safety we knew not, but we were determined, by the grace of God, not
to leave Tung-chow any longer without the Gospel. . . .

" After this my wheelbarrow man would proceed no farther and I
had to seek another, fortunately not difficult to find. As we went on
the ride was anything but agreeable in the mud and rain, and we
could not help feeling the danger of our position—though wavering
not for a moment. At intervals we encouraged one another with
promises from Scripture and verses of hymns . . . which were very
comforting

" On our way we passed through one small town of about a thousand
inhabitants, and here in the Mandarin dialect I preached Jesus to a
good number of people. Never was I so happy in speaking of the
love of God and the atonement of Jesus Christ. My own soul was
richly blessed and I was enabled to speak with unusual freedom.
And how happy I was afterwards when one of our hearers repeated to
the newcomers, in the local dialect, the truths upon which I had been
dwelling. Oh, how thankful I felt to hear a Chinaman, of his own
accord, telling his fellow-countrymen that God loved them, that they
were sinners, but that Jesus had died instead of them and paid the
penalty of their guilt. That one moment repaid me for all the trials
we had passed through, and I felt that if the Lord should grant His
Holy Spirit to change the heart of that man, we had not come in vain.

" We distributed a few Testaments and tracts, for the people were
able to read. It was well we did so, for when we reached Tung-chow
we had quite as many left as we had strength to carry.

" Nearing the western suburb of the city, the prayer of the early
Christians when persecution was commencing came to my mind,
' And now, Lord, behold their threatenings, and grant unto Thy
servants that with all boldness they may speak Thy Word ' : a petition
in which we most heartily united. Before entering the suburb we
laid our plans so as to act in concert, and told our barrow-men where

to await us, that they might not be involved in trouble on our account. Then, looking up to our Heavenly Father, we committed ourselves to His keeping, took our books and set off for the city.

"For some distance we walked along the principal street leading to the West Gate unmolested, and were amused at the unusual title *Heh-kwei-tsi* (black devils) which was applied to us. We wondered about it at the time, but afterwards found that it was our clothes, not our complexions, that gave rise to it. As we passed several of the soldiers, I remarked to Mr. Burdon that these were the men we had heard so much about, and that they seemed willing to receive us quietly enough.

"Long before we reached the gate, however, a tall powerful man, made tenfold fiercer by partial intoxication, let us know that all the militia were not so peaceably inclined, by seizing Mr. Burdon by the shoulders. My companion endeavoured to shake him off. I turned to see what was the matter, and in almost no time we were surrounded by a dozen or more of his companions, and were being hurried on to the city at a fearful pace.

"My bag now began to feel heavy. I could not change hands to relieve myself, and was soon in a profuse perspiration and scarcely able to keep up with them. We demanded to be taken before the chief magistrate, but were told, with the most insulting epithets, that they knew where to take us and what to do. The man who first seized Mr. Burdon soon afterwards left him for me, and became my principal tormentor, for I was neither so tall nor so strong as my friend and was less able to resist him. He all but knocked me down again and again, seized me by the hair, took hold of my collar so as almost to choke me, and grasped my arms and shoulders, making them black and blue. Had this continued much longer I must have fainted. All but exhausted, how refreshing was the remembrance of a verse quoted by my dear mother in one of my last home letters :

> We speak of the realms of the blest,
>   That country so bright and so fair,
> And oft are its glories confessed :
>   But what must it be to be there !

To be absent from the body . . . present with the Lord . . . free from sin. . . . And this is the end of the worst that man's malice can ever bring upon us.

"As we were being hurried along, Mr. Burdon tried to give away a few books that were under his arm, not knowing whether we might have another opportunity. But the fearful rage of the soldier . . . and the way he insisted on manacles being brought, which fortunately were not at hand, convinced us that in our present position it was

U

useless to attempt such work. There was nothing to be done but quietly to submit and go along with our captors.

"Once or twice a quarrel arose as to how we should be dealt with, the more mild of our conductors saying that we ought to be taken to the Ya-men, but others wishing to kill us at once without appeal to any authority. Our minds were kept in perfect peace, and when thrown together on one of these occasions we reminded each other that the Apostles rejoiced that they were counted *worthy* to suffer in the cause of Christ. Having succeeded in getting a hand into my pocket, I produced a Chinese card (if the large red paper bearing one's name may be so called) and after this was treated with more civility. I demanded that it should be given to the chief official of the place, and that we should be led to his office. Before this we had been unable, say what we would, to persuade them that we were foreigners, although we were both in English attire.

"Oh the long weary streets we were dragged through ! I thought they would never end ; and seldom have I felt more thankful than when we stopped at a place where we were told a Mandarin resided. Quite exhausted, bathed in perspiration and with my tongue cleaving to the roof of my mouth, I leaned against the wall, and saw that Mr. Burdon was in much the same state. I requested them to bring us chairs, but they told us to wait, and when I begged them to give us some tea, received only the same answer. Round the doorway a large crowd had gathered, and Mr. Burdon, collecting his remaining strength, preached Jesus Christ to them. Our cards and books had been taken in to the Mandarin, but he proved to be one of low rank, and after keeping us waiting for some time referred us to his superior in office.

"Upon hearing this and finding it was their purpose to turn us out again into the crowded streets, we positively refused to move a single step and insisted on chairs being brought. After some demur this was done, and we were carried off. On the way we felt so glad of the rest the chairs afforded and so thankful for having been enabled to preach the Gospel in spite of Satan's malice, that our joy was depicted on our countenances, and as we passed along we heard some say that we did not look like bad men, while others seemed to pity us. When we arrived at the Ya-men I wondered where we were being taken, for though we passed through some great gates that looked like those of the city wall, we were still evidently within the city. A second pair of gates suggested that it was a prison into which we were being carried. But when we came in sight of a large tablet with the inscription *Min-chï fu-mu* (the Father and Mother of the people) we felt more at ease, for this is the title assumed by civil magistrates.

"Our cards were again sent in, and after a short delay we were ushered into the presence of Ch'en Ta Lao-ie (The Great Venerable

Grandfather Ch‘en), who, as it proved, had formerly been Tao-tai in Shanghai and knew the importance of treating foreigners with civility. Coming before him some of the people fell on their knees and bowed down to the ground, and my conductor motioned me to do the same, but without success. This Mandarin who seemed to be the highest authority in Tung-chow and wore an opaque blue button on his cap, came out to meet us with every possible token of respect. He took us to an inner apartment, a more private room, followed by a large number of writers, runners, and semi-officials. I explained the object of our visit and begged permission to give him copies of our books, for which he thanked me. As I handed him the New Testament with part of the Old (from Genesis to Ruth), and some tracts, I tried to say a little about them, and also to give him a brief summary of our teachings. . . . He listened very attentively, as of course did all the others. He then ordered refreshments to be brought, which were very welcome, and himself partook of them with us.

" After a long stay, we asked permission to see something of the city and to distribute the books we had with us before returning. To this he kindly consented. We then mentioned that we had been most disrespectfully treated as we came in, but did not attach much importance to the fact, being aware that the rough soldiery knew no better. Not desiring, however, to have such experiences repeated, we requested him to give orders that we were not to be further molested. This also he acceded to, and, with every possible token of respect, accompanied us to the door of his ya-men, sending several ' runners ' to see that no trouble arose. . . . We distributed our books well and quickly, and after visiting the Confucian temple left the city quite in state. It was amusing to see the use the ' runners ' made of their tails. When the way was blocked by the crowd they turned them into whips and laid them about the people's shoulders to right and left !

" We had a little trouble in finding our wheel-barrows, but eventually succeeding, we paid off the chair-coolies, mounted our humble vehicles and returned to the river, accompanied for fully half the distance by an attendant from the Ya-men. . . . Early in the evening we got back to the boats in safety, sincerely thankful to our Heavenly Father for His gracious protection and aid."

Thus the vision was clenched with suffering, and Hudson Taylor's first sight of the great unreached interior was immediately followed by his first experience of danger to life itself at the hands of those he sought to help and bless. What could be more calculated to deepen, while at the same time it tempered his life-purpose ? Love first, then suffering, then a deeper love—thus only can God's work be done.

CHAPTER XXIII

A VISION OF HIS LIFE-WORK

THE joy of preaching Christ where He had never before been named had now laid hold of Hudson Taylor. Of the five journeys hitherto undertaken, the last two at any rate had been over untrodden ground. Both with Dr. Parker and Mr. Burdon he had found willing hearers for the Gospel where, as far as they could tell, it had never yet been proclaimed. It was a new experience, and to the young, devoted missionary a great experience, weaning his heart away from other, less-important things. Plans and hopes as regards settled work in Shanghai that for months had occupied him began to take a secondary place. He had tasted the wondrous sweetness of bringing tidings of the Saviour's love to those who but for him might never have heard, and this henceforth was the work that claimed him more and more.

Not that he no longer wished to settle somewhere. The strain of such frequent journeys made him increasingly conscious of the need for suitable headquarters. But he was beginning to hope that it might be away from a Treaty Port, among those who had no one else to lead them in the heavenward way.

It was now early summer in Shanghai, and beginning to be hot. No answer had yet been received from the Committee as to the plans laid before them, so that, as far as the Society was concerned, matters were somewhat at a standstill. This made it all the more natural that Hudson Taylor should be drawn in the one direction that was providentially open, that of evangelistic journeys. His fitness for this work was becoming so evident that the British and Foreign Bible Society was willing not only to supply him with as many Scriptures as he could distribute but also to meet the larger part of his travelling expenses. Thus while his hands were tied in one way, and plans for local work kept in abeyance, openings of an important kind were not lacking in other directions.

" I hope to go inland again in a few days," he wrote to Mr. Pearse scarcely a week after his return from Tung-chow. " You will join us in thanking the Lord for His protection in recent dangers. The Rebellion, especially since foreigners have enlisted themselves on both sides, has made access to the interior no easy matter. But the Word of God *must* go. And we must not be hindered by slight obstacles in the way of its dissemination. . . .

" I trust you will be much in prayer for us. We have many trials, and Satan does not let off easily those who attack his strongholds. Pray that we may be kept from harm spiritually as well as physically, and that the one intense desire of our hearts may be granted, that we may be made useful."

SIXTH JOURNEY: *May* 1855

Ten days at home had barely given time to write up his journal, attend to letters and prepare for another journey, before the young evangelist set out upon a longer absence than any he had previously undertaken. This time he was alone, and with growing experience was able to strike out on lines more characteristically his own. He seems to have had in view a long-cherished hope, the purpose, in fact, with which he had been sent to China, of penetrating inland as far as Nan-king, the headquarters of the Tai-ping Rebellion. Be that as it may, he steered his course up the Yangtze, exploring the southern shore with its principal tributary streams about two hundred miles   He was absent altogether twenty-five days, during which time he made known the Gospel in no fewer than fifty-eight cities, towns and larger villages, *fifty-one* of which had never before been visited by a Protestant missionary.

Starting on May 8 he did not reach home again until June 1, having made a careful investigation of the openings for such work up to within sixty miles of Chin-kiang, where the rebel forces were established, travelling in all a distance of four or five hundred miles.

It was a lonely journey and a courageous one with Tung-chow experiences fresh in mind. At any point he might have been seized, tortured, and even put to death as a rebel or foreign spy. And short of this he was exceeding the most liberal interpretation of treaty rights, and could claim no protection either from his own Consul or from the local authorities. Serious indeed was the possible danger from excited crowds in places where European dress had never yet been seen. But these and all other complications he handed over to the One best able to deal with them, in the consciousness of whose presence he could be calm and free from care.

And the Lord was not only with him amid those lonely labours. He did more than protect His servant, and supply needed grace. It was, if one may say so reverently, His opportunity. And He drew very near revealing Himself and His purposes as He only can perhaps when one is much alone.

Long, long years after, on another journey—the last he ever took up that great river—pacing the deck of the steamer in company with the writers, he paused again and again, looking with misty eyes towards the hills that here and there break the level of that southern shore. It was somewhere near Green Grass Island that he said at length, " I wish I could tell you about it. It was over there. But I cannot remember just the spot."

Seeing him moved by some recollection, we waited silently to hear more. But fifty years had passed since that day—the remembrance of which still brought so deep a joy and awe. He could not put it into words. He tried, but could tell us little of what had been between his soul and God. But there, over there on those more distant heights, it had come to him. Some revelation of his future work perhaps. Some call to utmost self-surrender for the life to which the Lord was leading. And its influence remained.

.   .   .   .

Time would fail to follow in any detail the varied activities of this journey, but some idea of its general character must be given. On the banks of tidal rivers running into the wide estuary of the Yangtze, the traveller found himself within reach of numerous towns and villages. The more important of these were visited as he worked his way up the main river. Here and there cities were found, and busy market-places, in which many Scriptures could be distributed. But in the countless villages between the reading population was small, and Hudson Taylor began to realise how large a part in the evangelisation of China must be taken by simple preaching and individual instruction in the Truth.

The first three days after leaving Woo-sung were spent opposite Tsung-ming Island, where the boat, overtaken by a storm, was nearly wrecked before they could reach the shelter of the Liu river. Putting into this stream they found themselves in the neighbourhood of a city and several towns, one of which had a population of forty thousand. Here Hudson Taylor could not have desired better opportunities for the work he had at heart, and in the temple of the " Mother of Heaven " as well as among the junks crowded along the water-frontage many listeners were eager to obtain books and learn more about his message.

His journal for the days that followed spent on another tributary stream gives an impression of unremitting labour, and reveals also something of what it meant to be alone amid such overwhelming needs.

Friday, May 11, 1855 : Got off at 6 A.M.. and with the tide ran up the Yangtze till we reached the Pah-miao kiang or Creek of the Eight Temples, which we entered. Here, after seeking the Lord's blessing, I landed, and was quickly surrounded by sixty or eighty people who had never seen a foreigner before. To them I preached the glad tidings of salvation before proceeding to a town called Liu-ho-chen. The road was miserably dirty, and though the distance was only two miles it seemed like four at least.

On arrival I found that it contained a good many respectable shops and intelligent people. As usual the demand for books was great. . . . The population of this place cannot be less than twenty thousand, and they had never heard before of the Word of the Living God. Here I distributed many portions of Scripture and tracts, and would willingly have stayed longer but that time did not permit.

On the way to the next town, Huang-king, I could not help feeling sad and downcast. Wherever one goes—cities, towns and villages just teeming with inhabitants, few of whom have ever heard the only Name " under heaven given among men whereby we must be saved." Just to visit them, give away portions of Scripture and tracts, and after preaching a few times pass on to other places, seem almost like doing nothing for the people. And yet unless this course is adopted *how are those further on ever to hear at all ?* It is the Word of God we leave behind us, living seed that cannot be fruitless, for He from whom it comes has said, " My word . . . shall not return unto Me void, but it shall accomplish that which I please, and it shall prosper in the thing whereto I sent it."

We see no fruit at present, and it needs strong faith to keep one's heart from sinking ; besides which I have felt a degree of nervousness since we were so roughly treated in Tung-chow which is quite a new experience, a feeling that is not lessened by being quite alone. I remember, however, His faithful promise, " They that sow in tears shall reap in joy," and " He that goeth forth and weepeth, bearing precious seed, shall doubtless come again with rejoicing, bringing his sheaves with him."

Faint and weary, having had no food since breakfast, I arrived at Huang-king at 4 P.M., and prayed God to enable me to distribute my books to the best advantage and to give me a word to speak to the people.

The prayer was indeed answered, and I found the place so large that had I had four times as many books with me they would have been barely enough to supply all the applicants who could read. . . . When I had finished the work of distribution I went into the temple in which the pagoda stands and found it full of cases of newly-made incense laid out to dry. Connected with the temple is a nunnery, and one of the nuns, a superior-looking woman, came out to meet me and seemed vastly amused at my costume. People followed me into the courtyard, and when some hundreds were assembled I asked them if they would like me to address them ; upon which a stool was brought, and mounting it I preached " Jesus, and Him crucified." They listened with the utmost attention, and when I concluded many asked for books containing these doctrines and eagerly inquired when I would return and bring more. I could only recommend them to borrow from one another and pray that God would enable them to understand and believe in what they had already heard.

As I left the place many persons accompanied me with every manifestation of friendly feeling. I could not but be struck with the contrast between my arrival and departure, for when I first entered the town, people ran away as from a wild animal ! . . . It was gratifying to see a friendly feeling so soon established, and to know that two towns now possessed the Gospel of the grace of God which until that morning had never received it. As we repassed Liu-ho-chen, a good many people came out and we had a little conversation, after which we went on, reaching our boat about 8 P.M. very tired and ready for dinner.

Saturday, May 12 : One of the hottest days we have had this year. Having arranged my books and prepared a good selection to take with me, I set out to visit several more towns in the neighbourhood. The first place I went to was the " Dragon Emperor's Temple," a little town in which I was told a Mandarin resided. I found it quite a small place, consisting of a few houses, the largest of which was occupied by a Revenue Officer of the name of Li. Calling upon him I was courteously received, and left in his possession a New Testament, part of the Old, and several tracts. After this we went on and in due time reached the " Shrine of the Chang Family " (Chang-kia-sï), a town of about four thousand inhabitants, where for the first time the Word of God was distributed and a foreigner seen and heard.

At first the people were frightened, but this soon wore off, and men, women and children seemed to be intensely interested. Their astonishment was great when they found that I could understand their language, and it was most amusing to hear their remarks about many things. When I took out my watch to look at the time, one grown-up person exclaimed that never before had he seen such spectacles ! Another promptly corrected him, informing the company that it was nothing less than a telescope I had in my pocket, and that western men were celebrated for making them. Upon which a third chimed in : No, he knew better than that ; the wonderful object they had seen was a clock, which told the hour by striking a bell ; and what I was wearing on my nose was a telescope, and not a pair of spectacles as some had ignorantly suggested !

A short distance beyond this place was a group of houses looking like the beginning of another little town, to which I next directed my steps. I found it to be a private residence, the home of a fine old gentleman, eighty years of age, who had formerly been a Mandarin at Soo-chow. Taken to the guest-hall, I noticed over the entrance this inscription, " Act morally and you will obtain Happiness." I took the lowest chair of course, nearest the door, but in a little while the master of the house appeared and with much ceremony insisted on my moving to a higher seat.

When I offered him a selection of our books, he told me he also had books to give, and made me a present of three works of his own, in ten volumes, beautifully got up and treating of almost every imaginable subject. There was a little astronomy, a little meteorology, a little geography, some mathematics, and so on. But he said he had one superlative idea which he was delighted to have the opportunity of imparting to me.

Three great kingdoms existed in the world he said, England, Russia and China, but his discovery was as yet unknown in any of them. Confucius himself was ignorant of it, and likewise all the Sages. In short it was known to but one person—himself; and he was now eighty years of age. This long prelude and the importance of his manner made me wonder what could be coming, and it was hard to repress a smile when it proved to be that the sun stood still and the earth travelled round it. . . .

This gentleman seemed to be a close observer of nature, for amongst other things he wrote out for me a list of climbing plants arranged in two columns according as they turned to the right hand, in growing, or to the left After an interesting visit I went a few miles further and found another town (Teng-chow-si) of about a thousand inhabitants. Here also I distributed Scriptures and tracts, and preached to about two hundred people in the open air. Then as the sun was low we set off for our boat with all speed, but were caught in torrents of rain and did not arrive till long after dark.

Sunday, May 13: Enjoyed some quiet hours of reading and prayer in my boat, after which . . . I distributed Scriptures and tracts in the Town of the "Eight Temples." Thence we went on to the "Shrine of the Heng Family," a place of some eight thousand inhabitants. There in the principal temple I preached to two or three hundred people, distributing afterwards many Testaments and other books.

We then made our way again to the "Chang Family Shrine," and after conversation with several others I revisited the old Mandarin seen yesterday. When our talk took a religious turn he made the common remark, "Jesus is your Sage, Confucius ours," and was much astonished when I told him that the Lord Jesus was not an Englishman; that though born a Jew He was no mere man, but perfect God and perfect man in one; and in proof of His deity adduced His miracles and the fact of the resurrection. He told me he intended coming to Shanghai in a few weeks and would return my call, promising in the meanwhile to look into my books and desiring me to read those he had given me. After this we returned to our boat, again arriving long after dark; and having supplied medicine to a man who had followed us four miles to get it, I closed another Lord's day with prayer to God for His blessing.

Thus he worked his way up the main river until on May 15 the hills of Lang-shan and Fu-shan again came in sight. The temples crowning the former he had visited already, so it was to the latter, the sacred mountain of Fu-shan with the city of the same name at its base, that Hudson Taylor now turned his attention. In and around this city several days were spent and in ascending the tributary stream to another famous pilgrim resort, the city and hills of Chang-shu. Very interesting is his account of work done in these places, in which his preaching was so well understood that people said " The foreign-devil language is almost the same as our own."

One more Sunday on a creek still farther up, and the young missionary reached Green Grass Island, lying in the first, great westward bend of the Yangtze. Here on his birthday (May 21) two towns and a large village were visited and the Gospel preached to many willing hearers. As evening was drawing in he was taken to see a sick person, to whom he gave some simple remedies. The news soon spread, and before he could reach his boat, a hundred or more people had assembled, fully half of whom were suffering in ways he could relieve. Tired and hungry though he was he gladly set to work to dispense medicines, and before supper that evening had treated between forty and fifty patients.

This, of course, opened his way to many homes and hearts, and the rest of the week was fully occupied either on the island itself or on the mainland opposite. Of the day following his birthday he wrote :

Tuesday, May 22 : Left the island early this morning, and after a pleasant sail of seven miles entered a creek running in toward some high hills. Here I landed, took as many books as our bags would hold and set off for the country. On the way we passed through a small town, in which I distributed a few Testaments and other books, and was as usual an object of wonder to the people, who had never seen a foreigner before.

Thence we went on to the city of Yang-shae, entering by the North Gate, and distributed a good many Scriptures and tracts. I then addressed the people in the temple of the City-God, but the noise was so great that only those nearest me can have heard. After this, and a walk on the wall which gave one a good view of the city, we left by the South Gate and continued our work of distribution in the suburb.

Though only small in size, Yang-shae might well be called a model city. Its walls are in perfect repair, not a brick wanting nor a battlement injured. . . . Its houses and shops are good, its streets clean and people respectable, though they can make a hubbub ! a thing not to be wondered at when the exciting cause is remembered. An Englishman in foreign dress, distributing religious books and preaching in the very temple of the presiding deity of the city, was enough to upset their composure. . . .

From Yang-shae I walked out to the " Pebble " or " Grave Mountain," the highest elevation I have yet seen in China. The view from the top was very fine. With the aid of the telescope I counted no fewer than fifty-four distinct hills, some at a distance of quite as many miles. In an easterly direction, north of the Yangtze, rose the Lang-shan group with their pagodas and temples, and opposite across the river the heights of Fu-shan and Chang-shu. South of the hill on which I stood was the large town of Hwa-shih with its pagoda in excellent repair, and south-by-west the hill and city of Wu-sih on the Grand Canal. Southward still, quite in the distance, were the mountains near the Great Lake and beyond Soo-chow. Westward lay the hill and city of Kiang-yin, some distance up the Yangtze. To the north Green Grass Island was well in sight, and the mighty river hidden here and there by the hills along its bank . . . completed a view well worth the toilsome ascent it had cost.

How long he stayed there in the welcome silence the journal does not say, nor what were the thoughts and feelings that filled his mind. It was a wonderful outlook, and could not but draw forth his sympathies for the great land that lay beyond on every side. Was it at this time and in this place the vision of his life-work came to him ? We do not know : the records do not tell us. But he was quite alone, only just twenty-three, and already launched on pioneering labours the trend of which he often longed to understand. It was an occasion at any rate for fresh consecration to the work and to the Lord he loved ; and it is more than likely that in view of needs so overwhelming, deeper longings and more earnest prayer would rise within him—" great thoughts, calm thoughts, thoughts lasting to the end."

Certainly many of the principles of later years can be

seen in embryo on this journey, and the spirit of it all is specially characteristic, read between the lines of his brief, simple journal. Of two long, hot days on Green Grass Island, for example, he wrote as follows :

Thursday, May 24 : Set off early this morning with books, and spent the whole day going from house, hamlet and village, to house, hamlet and village. In this way more than a dozen schoolmasters were supplied with books, and readers wherever they were found. . . . On this island the towns seem to be neither large nor numerous. The people live mostly in hamlets of from one to three hundred, with here and there a larger village. In the afternoon we reached one place, Nian-feng-kiai, with about six hundred inhabitants. Here I finished the distribution of my books, and visited one or two sick people who were unable to come to us. We then set off on the return journey and reached our boat at about 5 P.M. very tired with the long walk. Many persons, however, had followed us, wanting medicines either for themselves or their friends, some indeed having come two, three or more miles. So I told them of Jesus, found out about their symptoms and supplied them with medicines, removed a tumour from a young man's neck, and was thus employed till some time after dark. Then my visitors left me. I got my things put away, had some dinner, for which I was more than ready, and finished the day with writing.

Friday, May 25 : Saw a few patients, then left for the mainland, where we went ashore with books for distribution. After supplying the little town of K'ian-t'u we visited not a few villages, and put the Word of God into the hands of every teacher we could find. Getting back to the boat again at 6 P.M. I saw several patients, after which we left with the tide. During the day while walking from place to place, tired and bathed in perspiration, I was much refreshed in spirit by the thought that the Lord Jesus, doubtless, had often felt the same ; for He too went about in a hot country. We made good progress after leaving, wind and tide both favouring us, and shortly after dark anchored out on the river.

Yes, He too lived amid crowds of sick and suffering people, and could not escape dirt, discomfort, weariness, and all the monotony and discouragement of a missionary's lot. And He knew loneliness, the solitude of a life that had no sympathy as regards its deepest needs, its highest aspirations. Not one tear you shed, not one pang you feel is unknown to Him. It is all, every ache of it, " fellowship

with His sufferings." Does not that transfigure the darkest
moment, rob the bitterest humiliation of its sting ? Think,
He has felt the same　and to all eternity there shall be
that closer sympathy between your heart and His. He
shares with you something deeper, more wonderful than
His glory, His joy. He shares with you just all that these
experiences mean, all that it ever must mean to be the
Saviour of the World : and is there anything more sacred
even in the heart of God than this ?

And then the Lord who knows His servant's need brings
in some moment of relief—a day of tropical rain it may be,
when it is useless to go out ; an attack of illness, giving
time for rest and prayer ; a swollen river that cannot be
crossed, or a Sunday in some quiet spot upon your journey—
and in the brief respite comes soul-renewing fellowship
with Him.

Thus it was for Hudson Taylor the day after the above
entry in his journal. Passing the extremity of Green Grass
Island the wind turned against them and the channel was
too narrow to admit of tacking. For nine hours they had
to wait, the wind meanwhile increasing to a perfect hurricane.
Travelling late on Saturday in consequence, they were again
obliged to anchor in mid-stream. There Sunday morning
found them (May 27), a lovely summer day after the storm,
and who can tell the refreshment to the weary missionary
of a few quiet hours before they went ashore ?

"Very much enjoyed reading and prayer," he wrote, "in my
cabin, and felt renewed confidence in Him who has brought us
hitherto."

Whatever may have been his intention on leaving
Shanghai, he seems to have felt it wiser not to continue his
journey much beyond this point. It may be that the boatmen were unwilling to venture farther up the Yangtze on
account of the Insurgents at Chin-kiang. It may be he
himself thought it better to be satisfied with what was
already accomplished, without running into needless danger.
He had been wonderfully preserved so far, and was now
nearly two hundred miles from home. Three weeks was

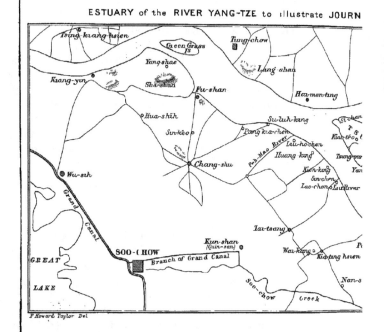

ESTUARY of the RIVER YANG-TZE to illustrate JOURN

Tsing-kiang-hsien

Green Grass
IS

Tung-chow

Yangshae

Lang-shan

Kiang-yin

Sha-shan

Fu-shan

Hai-men-ting

Hua-shih

Su-luh-kang

St-chan

Sin-kéo

Pang-kia-chen

Kian-téo

Liu-ho-chen

Huang-king

Tsing-par

Chang-shu

Kien-kong

Yan

Wu-sih

Sin-chen

Lao-chen Liu River

Grand
Canal

Tai-tsang

Kun-shan
(Quin-san)

Wai-kiang

Kia-ting-hsien

SOO-CHOW

Branch of Grand Canal

GREAT

P

LAKE

Soo-chow

Creek

Nan-s

F. Howard Taylor Del

an unusually long absence from a foreign Settlement in those days, and he was coming to an end of his supplies. He distributed his remaining books, therefore, in Kiang-yin with its extensive surburbs and in a city seen from the neighbouring hills (Tsing-kiang), and on Tuesday, May 29, commenced the return journey.

Two days later, about midnight, they succeeded in reaching Shanghai in spite of serious gales, very thankful for renewed preservation from shipwreck, and for having been enabled to distribute in peace and safety over two thousand seven hundred Scripture portions and tracts.

CHAPTER XXIV

EMPTIED FROM VESSEL TO VESSEL

INCLUDING SEVENTH JOURNEY. JUNE–AUGUST 1855. AET. 23

SUMMER was now in possession of the Settlement, and it
was a warm welcome Hudson Taylor received in more ways
than one on his return to Ma-ka-k'üen. The little house
was still as crowded as ever, and there seemed no prospect
of relief for this season at any rate ; but grace was found
sufficient for the daily needs, even when these extended
into long, breathless nights, when sleep was well-nigh impossible for the heat. If only the rats had not been so
lively the nights would have been less trying. But whether
the temperature excited them or not, they were aggressive
in the extreme, running all over the room and even jumping
on the beds in their nocturnal carousals.

Yet, how thankful Hudson Taylor and his fellow-workers
were for the shelter of even these indifferent quarters !
Anything better, indeed anything they could live in at all
was still unattainable, in spite of the reconstruction that
was going on apace. So that worse than staying on in
those three rooms all summer would be having to leave
them when they were needed for reinforcements expected
by the L.M.S. This could not be for several months
however, and meanwhile provision would surely be made
for mission-premises of their own Hope deferred, they
found, was but poor diet for cheerfulness under the circumstances ; but the Committee was slow in replying to their
communications of the previous December, and there was
nothing for it but to wait on, working in such ways as were

open to them through the hot season. All through July
and August, while travelling was impracticable, Hudson
Taylor carried on a daily service in the Shanghai dialect
for their teachers, servants and others who wished to join
them. This opportunity of giving regular instruction to
the same set of people was a great joy to him, and all the
more so when it seemed to be bearing fruit. A sudden
death occurring in the neighbourhood from cholera, he made
the most of the opportunity to urge the importance of
immediate salvation from sin and its eternal consequences.
A few days later he alluded to the circumstances again,
asking if any of his hearers had definitely come to God for
pardon through faith in Jesus Christ. Pausing a moment,
perhaps hardly expecting an answer, what was his thankfulness when Kuei-hua the young cook said earnestly, " I
have."

This open confession before his fellow-servants meant
a great deal.

" I do hope," wrote Hudson Taylor, " that he is under the influence
of the Holy Spirit. Though not without faults, he is greatly changed
for the better. For some months we have not detected him in false-
hood or dishonesty of any kind, which is saying a good deal." [1]

The school meanwhile was also doing well, though their
adopted pupil was still the only boarder. On his return
from the Yang-tze Mr. Taylor had found a room to let in
the native city, in a quarter where no missionary work was
being carried on. This he gladly rented, moving the school
from the Settlement early in June. Now, with an excellent
teacher, it was exercising an influence for good amid the
large population of the South Gate and its busy suburb.

On Sunday, when the ordinary routine was suspended,
the schoolroom was well filled for a Gospel service, and
several times through the week Dr. Parker came down to
see patients and dispense medicines. Both there and in
a room he had secured across the river,[2] the medical work

[1] This young man, a brother of the pupil they had adopted on the
strength of Mr Berger's gift, proved increasingly satisfactory as time went
on, and was the first convert Mr. Taylor baptized in China.
[2] This dispensary and " outstation " Dr. Parker opened in May, when
he had been about six months in China. It was in the town of Yang-king,
across the Hwang-poo river, a few miles east of Shanghai.

X

brought large numbers of people round them and afforded excellent opportunities for preaching. These Mr. Taylor supplemented with excursions to the surrounding country, often walking many miles from village to village and preaching four or five times in the open air. All this in addition to language-study made it necessary somewhat to curtail his correspondence as compared with the previous summer, but on Sunday evenings when the work of the day was done he still found time for letters that revealed much of his inner life.

"I have been spending an hour," he wrote one close evening in August, "in happy communion with Him whose wondrous grace has called and numbered me with His people. The more I see of myself and the more I learn of Him, the more I am astonished that He can ever have given me a place among His children. It is only at the foot of the cross we see ourselves, the world, and God in the true light. . . . There alone can we form true impressions . . . and how far short they still fall of the reality ! But I must conclude. My walking to-day (about six miles) and three services, with the thermometer at 90° F. in the shade, has made me feel worn out."

And on a later Sunday : "I do indeed *need* your prayers. To work on without seeing results takes much faith, and mine is so weak. What a beautiful hymn that is of Wesley's,

> Give to the winds thy fears ;
> Hope and be undismayed :
> God hears thy sighs, and counts thy tears ;
> God shall lift up thy head.[1]

"What I need is more faith, more intimate communion with God. . . . We can impart that only which we first receive. The disciples could make the people sit down, but Jesus must bless the bread and give it to them ere they could break it to the multitude. Oh that we may be much with Jesus; may be enabled to feed many with the Bread of Life, and finally have an abundant entrance into the abode where holiness ever reigns."

But all the while he was carrying on this settled work in and around Shanghai, Hudson Taylor was longing to be farther afield. Only the heat of summer that made travelling dangerous kept him so in Shanghai, for all he had seen and experienced on recent journeys was calling with the claim of a greater need.

[1] Paul Gerhardt; translated by John Wesley.

One itineration indeed had been attempted since the beginning of June, which though cut short by illness was to have an important bearing on his future as well as on that of Dr. Parker. Accompanied by Mr. Burdon they had set out on a preaching tour that was to include a visit to Ning-po for partial rest and change. Missionaries of several societies were at work in that important city, and the blessing of God was manifestly resting upon their labours. Hudson Taylor and his colleague looked forward therefore to much help from this visit, far though they were from realising all it was to bring into their lives.

SEVENTH JOURNEY: *June* 11-25

On the way down to Ning-po, four governing cities and a number of towns were visited. Forty miles south of Shanghai they reached the coast at Che-lin, a deserted *Hsien*. Pirates swarmed in the neighbourhood, and people had taken refuge further back from the seashore.

Next day, at the border of the Cheh-kiang province, Mr. Taylor separated from his companions in order to visit on foot several places to which the boat could not take them. This gave him an opportunity of climbing the Cha-pu hills, from which an extensive view was obtained over Hang-chow Bay, with its beautiful islands. Reaching the city of Cha-pu some hours before sunset, he preached in the temple of the Mother of Heaven, the sailor's special divinity, and distributed his remaining books.

A comfortless night followed, for he missed his friends and was not able to get back to the boat. Having no bedding or luggage, he might have hunted in vain for an inn that would receive him, and it is more than likely that he and his servant would have had to spend the night in the streets but for the kindness of an elderly woman who had compassion on them. It was already late when she took them into her house, the first Chinese home to welcome the young missionary, and glad enough he was of the rice-gruel and straw bed that was all it could afford.

After a long hunt, his missing companions were found

the following morning, and together they spent the day in preaching and tract-distribution throughout the city. Cha-pu, a large and busy place, was protected from pirates by a garrison of Manchu soldiers, and the trade carried on in salted fish and such-like commodities was considerable. It was the point of embarkation also for Ning-po and other great cities, and was well supplied in consequence with sea-going junks.

Engaging one of these to take them across the Bay, the missionaries went on board in the evening to find the cabin they had expected to occupy full already with passengers, and that more were crowding in. This was disconcerting, and it did not mend matters when the captain, siding with the majority, declared that his boat was a passenger-boat, although the missionary party had paid for all the accommodation. Finally a compromise was arranged. As many as could find room enough to lie down were allowed to remain, including the foreigners, and the rest were turned away without compunction. It was Hudson Taylor's first night on a passenger-boat—first of so many !

Starting at midnight, they found themselves at Ha-pu the following morning, and all that day was spent in rowing up one of the many streams by which Ning-po is reached. Twilight fell upon the guardian hills as the travellers made their way through the multitudinous craft that line the chief approaches to the city, and from the darkness of the narrow streets it was good to be welcomed in the hospitable mission-house to which Mr. Burdon led the way.

Here as guests of Mr. and Mrs. Cobbold the next few days were spent, days which to the visitors were full of interest, introducing them to a peculiarly united community in which they were received with great kindness. Eleven foreigners in all represented several English and American Societies, and there was in addition an excellent school carried on by a lady of independent means,[1] assisted by

[1] Miss Aldersey, an English lady who six years before China was opened to the residence of foreigners had settled in Java to work among Chinese women there. After the Treaty of Nanking in 1842 she was the first to commence a school for girls on Chinese soil—coming to Ning-po in 1843 as one of the pioneer missionaries to settle in that city.

the orphan daughters of the Rev. Samuel Dyer. His had
been a much-loved name among the earliest group of
missionaries to the Chinese, and these young ladies though
only eighteen and twenty years of age were already fluent
in the language and very useful in the work to which their
lives were given.

One thing only seemed lacking to the all-round development of the Ning-po Missions. There was no hospital.
The missionaries felt this drawback keenly, and as they
came to know something of Dr. Parker a new hope sprang
up which resulted in a unanimous invitation to the Scotch
physician to join them. But this was not until he and his
companions had returned to Shanghai, greatly benefited
by their change, and linked for the future, little as they
suspected it, with lives in Ning-po that had touched their
own.

The return journey was to have been given to further
evangelisation ; but hardly had they left the city when a
messenger overtook them, bringing news of the serious
illness of Mr. Burdon's only child. It was not yet a year
since the young mother had been taken, and the thought
of the little one suffering and perhaps dying in his absence
was too much for the father's heart. He felt he must
hasten back at once, and his friends decided to accompany
him. It was well they did, for Hudson Taylor had already
been very poorly in Ning-po, and further illness was only
warded off until Shanghai was reached, showing that he
was in no condition for travelling during the hot season.

The next two months were spent, therefore, as we have
seen, in and around the Settlement. But though this
temporary work was encouraging and full of promise, it
was accompanied by no little trial as to their position and
prospects. Gradually it was becoming evident that the
Society was not prepared to endorse their suggestion with
regard to mission headquarters in any of the Treaty Ports.
It was a matter of principle with the Committee not to
put money into bricks and mortar, even though it seemed
that their representatives could be housed in no other way.

But their veto upon the carefully thought-out scheme laid before them did not come all at once ; and meanwhile the far-away missionaries were not forgotten by Him who sees the end from the beginning.

It is easy enough now for us to realise that the Shanghai idea, as far as they were concerned, was a mistaken one, but it was anything but easy for them. Dr. Parker had not yet received the invitation to Ning-po, and Hudson Taylor, eager though he was to go inland, knew all too well the seriousness of such an undertaking and the need for a good home base.

"It is hard to be ever on the move," he had written to his sister after their return from Ning-po,[1] "and to have no settled dwelling. I have some thought of buying a set of Chinese garments soon, and seeing how I could get on with them. If I could get a little place somewhere in the interior, perhaps I might settle down and be useful. As things are at present, we cannot hope to *see* much fruit—for we have no station, no chapel, no hospital, no house even of our own. . . .

"The future is in the hands of God. . . . There we must leave it. . . . Pray for me, for I am very weak and unworthy, and have been a good deal tried of late."

And no wonder, when one considers the conditions under which they were living, and the exhausting heat of summer ! But the point specially worthy of notice is the changed attitude of the writer since his last letter on the subject three months previously.[2] Then it had been—Our plans are laid before the Society : if they do nothing, we mean to try and carry them out ourselves : if they oppose, it may become a question as to which we shall dispense with, the Society, or our plans of usefulness. Now it was— Chinese dress, a little place somewhere in the interior, and, above all, a future left in the hands of God. How great a difference ! The Lord had had time to work. And as always in His providence, the moulding force came not only from outward circumstances, but from the development of His life within.

Do we not need to remind ourselves in these days,

---

[1] In a letter dated June 28, 1855.
[2] See Chap XXI. p 273.

especially in connection with His service, of the danger of impatience and taking things too much into our own hands ? If we are really waiting on God and doing His will, hindrances that are not removed are safeguards, keeping us from mistaken courses, and bringing about the preparation of spirit necessary in ourselves before His best can be given.

It does not always seem so. How little could Hudson Taylor have imagined that, even before the answer to those January letters could be received, his own outlook would be so changed that he would no longer cling to what had then seemed desirable ? How little could Dr. Parker have foreseen that before summer was over he would be called to a more important and congenial sphere ? And how little can we tell all we are being delivered from by our very limitations, or the wider service to which the Lord is leading in ways beyond our ken ? So let us thank God from our hearts for trials that are not removed, though brought before Him in believing prayer, and praise Him for answers that seem long in coming, knowing the delay is needed to make us ready to receive them.

Thus Hudson Taylor and his colleague were being really led of God, though August only seemed to bring a climax to their difficulties. What was the Lord's guidance in it all ? That was the question.

" Many reasons," wrote Hudson Taylor,[1] " make me desire to go to Ning-po with the Parkers, but there are also many against it. There are already fourteen missionaries there, . . . and they are working the field well and in much peace and unity. Shanghai is not nearly so well worked, with more than double the number of missionaries. The Ning-po dialect, I must confess, is no attraction, though once learned it would no doubt increase my opportunities of usefulness. There may be something of laziness in it, but I do feel this is an objection against going to a new district. . . . Expenses are less there than in Shanghai. If I stay here I shall certainly have to move, for our co-tenants are leaving in about a month (their new house is just finished), and the whole rent of these premises would be far more than I can afford.

" So you see that I am as unsettled as to my future prospects as

[1] A letter to his parents dated July 24, 1855.

the first day I landed in China. I am waiting on the Lord for guidance. Meanwhile, my thought is to stay on here in Shanghai if possible, at any rate for the present. I feel as if my work here were not done. But eventually I may go to Ning-po, if my efforts to obtain a footing in the interior should fail in this district. It does seem as if I never should be settled ! I do long for a helpful companion with whom I could take counsel and have real sympathy of mind and feeling, and to be fixed somewhere in good, regular work."

But there was something more important still, if his prayers for usefulness were to be answered as fully as the Lord was able and willing to answer them. Moab, we are told, was " at ease from his youth, . . . settled on his lees, . . . not emptied from vessel to vessel "—a poor, inferior quality of wine of which nothing could be made. " Therefore, his taste remained in him and his scent is not changed." [1] But the life that was to be made a blessing the wide world over must pass through a very different process, including much of that emptying and re-emptying " from vessel to vessel," so painful to the lower nature, from which we are being refined.

> Leave to His sovereign sway
> To choose and to command ;
> So shalt thou wondering own His way,
> How wise, how strong His hand.

> Far, far above thy thought
> His counsel shall appear,
> When fully He the work hath wrought
> That caused thy needless fear.

It was August 6 when the long-expected came at length, and Hudson Taylor and his colleague received notice that the house they were occupying must be vacated by the end of September. Two new missionaries were on the way from England and would require the premises.

And just then, strangely enough, further letters from their own Committee put a final veto upon their plans for Shanghai as a permanent centre. No, they were not to build, though permission was given Dr. Parker to rent rooms for a dispensary. How or where they were to live was left

---

[1] Jeremiah xlviii. 11.

a matter of uncertainty, the Committee apparently having no suggestion to make.[1] Well was it for the much-tried missionaries that the Lord had not overlooked this important detail, but was caring for His workers as well as for the best interests of His work.

Another letter, also received early in August, gave full proof of this. Several weeks previously the unanimous invitation of the missionaries in Ning-po had reached Dr. Parker, earnestly requesting that he would go and settle among them. He had replied that he could not feel justified in doing so unless assured that it would open to him a wider door of usefulness. For a home and practice of his own, no matter how attractive, he could not sacrifice missionary work. But if in connection with such a position he could see his way to the support of a hospital for the Chinese, the expense of which would be at least eight hundred dollars per annum, the matter might look very different. And now the answer reached him. Just when he was ready for it—eight months in the country having given him some familiarity with the people and language—then, and not before, the opening came that was to determine his life-work.

" You will be glad, I am sure, to learn," he wrote to his Committee on August 22, " that the friends in Ning-po have become surety for the amount required, and rejoice in the prospect of a missionary hospital there—the only Treaty Port without one.

" This, of course, shuts me up to taking this step, unless I set at nought the plain indications of Providence. And as I believe it to be God's will, I have resolved to go, and to do so at once."

The resolution come to thus opportunely, while it cleared the way for Dr. Parker and his family, only left Hudson Taylor the more cast upon God. Now he would be lonely indeed, bereft of companionship as well as home. Feeling,

[1] On September 7, writing to his mother, Hudson Taylor alluded to their disappointment as follows :
" The hospital project for here, as you will see, is over. The Society's objection is not, ' We *cannot* do it.' . . . Had that been all, I believe we here *could*. But they say, ' Our professed intentions are not to work in the five Ports, but in the interior. We do not wish our representatives to spend money in Shanghai.' "

as he did, so definitely that his work in Shanghai was not yet finished, he had at once to set about seeking quarters to which he might remove his belongings. But, as before, the search proved useless. Nothing was to be had at a price within his means.

Day after day went by in weary trampings up and down the city, and at the end of three weeks the hope of finding what he needed seemed farther off than ever. Many thoughts had been in his mind during this time, some idea of which may be gathered from a note to his sister of August 19 :

Dr. Parker has accepted the invitation to Ning-po, and will be going down in a few days to arrange accommodation for his family. Nearly the whole of last week I spent in seeking a house to move into here myself, but I have not found one. They all want heavy deposits that I am not able to pay. It is wearisome work, and if I do not succeed soon I shall adopt Chinese dress and seek a place in the country. . . , These changes are not easy. Do pray much for me.

Chinese dress and a home somewhere in the country— the thought was becoming familiar. But it was an expedient almost unheard of in those days. Sometimes on inland journeys a missionary would wear the native costume as a precautionary measure, and Dr. Medhurst himself had suggested to Hudson Taylor that he might find it helpful. But it was invariably discarded on the traveller's return, and he would have been careless of public opinion indeed who would have ventured to wear it always, and in the Settlement.

But it was nothing less than this that the young missionary was meditating, driven to it by his longing to identify himself with the people and by the force of outward circumstances. If he could not find quarters in Shanghai he *must* go to the interior, and why add to his difficulties and hinder the work he most desired to accomplish by emphasising the fact that he was a foreigner ?

Another week went by in almost incessant house-hunting, and the time drew near when Dr. Parker was to leave for Ning-po. Hudson Taylor had promised to escort him as far as Hang-chow Bay, to see him through the more difficult part of the journey. They were to start on Friday morning the 24th, and up to Thursday afternoon the search for premises had been in vain.

Yes, it was growing clearer. For him, probably, the right thing was a closer identification with the people ; Chinese dress at all times and the externals of Chinese life, including chop-sticks and native cookery. How much it would simplify travelling in the interior ! Already he had purchased an outfit of native clothing. If, after all the prayer there had been about it, he really could not get accommodation in Shanghai, it must be that the Lord had other purposes. He would send his few things down to Ning-po with Dr. Parker, who had offered to store them, and living on boats would give himself to evangelistic work until his way opened up somewhere in the interior.

Thursday night came, and Dr. Parker was to leave the following morning. It was useless to seek premises any longer, so Hudson Taylor went down to engage the junk that was to take them to Hang-chow Bay with their belongings. His Chinese dress was ready for the following morning when he expected to begin a pilgrim life indeed.

And this, apparently, was the point to which it had been necessary to lead him. He had followed faithfully. It was enough. And now on these new lines could be given the answer to weeks and months of prayer.

As he was on his way to make arrangements for their journey, a man met him. Did he want a house in the Chinese city ? Would a small one do, with only five rooms ? Because near the South Gate there was such a house, only it was not quite finished building. The owner had run short of money and hardly knew how to complete the work. If it suited the Foreign Teacher, no deposit would be asked : it could be had in all probability for an advance of six months' rent.

Feeling as though in a dream, Hudson Taylor followed his guide to the southern quarter of the city, and there found a small, compact house, perfectly new and clean, with two rooms upstairs and two down, and a fifth across the courtyard for the servants—just the very thing he needed, in the locality that suited him best, and all for the moderate sum of ten pounds to cover a half-year's rent.

What it must have been to him to pay the money over that night, and secure the premises, is more easily imagined than described. The Lord had indeed worked on his behalf. Prayer was being answered. He had not missed or mistaken the guidance for which he had waited so long. It almost seemed as if the Lord had broken silence, to confirm and encourage His servant at this critical time. And best of all was the wondering consciousness that He Himself had done it when, humanly speaking, it seemed impossible : " I being in the way, the Lord led me."

That night he took the step he had been prayerfully considering—called in a barber, and had himself so transformed in appearance that his own mother could hardly have known him. To put on Chinese dress without shaving the head is comparatively a simple matter ; but Hudson Taylor went all lengths, leaving only enough of the fair, curly hair to grow into the *queue* of the Chinaman. He had prepared a dye, moreover, with which he darkened this remaining hair, to match the long, black braid that at first must do duty for his own. Then in the morning he put on as best he might the loose, unaccustomed garments, and appeared for the first time in the gown and satin shoes of a " Teacher," or man of the scholarly class.

CHAPTER XXV

SOME BETTER THING

INCLUDING EIGHTH JOURNEY. AUGUST–OCTOBER 1855.
AET. 23.

How it all opened up after this step had been taken! Returning alone from Hang-chow Bay, Hudson Taylor hardly
knew himself for the same person who had so often been
tried by the petty annoyances and more serious hindrances
to his work by curious and excited crowds. Plenty of
people still followed him whenever he became known as a
foreigner, and it was not difficult to gather an audience to
listen to the Gospel. But the rowdy element seemed somehow to have disappeared with his European dress, and if
he wished to pass unnoticed he was able to do so, even in
the busiest streets. This, of course, greatly lessened the
strain of being much alone among the people, and at the
same time gave him access to a more respectable, serious-
minded class.

Not suspected even of being a European until his speech
betrayed him, he had a far truer, more natural point of
view from which to study conditions round him, and found
himself coming into touch in a new way with people and
things Chinese. It was natural now to adopt their point
of view as he could not before, and instinctively he began
to identify himself with those toward whom he had hitherto
occupied the position of a foreigner. Now he was one of
them in all outward respects—dressing, living, eating as
they did, and greatly lessening the cost and difficulty of
providing for his needs by doing so. Altogether the change

was one for which he found himself increasingly thankful, and that made this August journey one of peculiar interest.

EIGHTH JOURNEY: *August* 24-31

Working his way back by places he had not hitherto visited, he saw a good deal of new country, and was able to observe more closely its character and needs.

" I parted from Dr. Parker last night," he wrote on August 28,[1] " and am now alone for the first time in the interior in Chinese costume. . . . I have been travelling through beautiful scenery to-day, and among some rough people. How I wish you could have seen their gratitude for medical aid ! Men and women, old and young, all seemed thankful to receive it, and much groundless suspicion against foreigners must have been removed. Of course I am known to be a foreigner by my accent as soon as I begin to speak. . . .

" As you may suppose I am not yet quite at home in my new dress . . . the turned-up shoes being especially uncomfortable ; but I shall get used to them soon. The worst inconvenience is the head being uncovered, as the Chinese wear no cap at this time of year. . . .[2]

" I do not think I told you that the very evening before we left Shanghai I obtained a house in the native city for quite a moderate rent. From repeated disappointments I had quite given up the hope of getting one, . . . when just as I was preparing to send my things to Ning-po with Dr. Parker, the Lord providentially opened my way. I have every reason to be thankful for this, for I thought I was going to be houseless and homeless for the time being. How true it is that ' Man's extremity is God's opportunity.' . . .

" The change from a large household, two families besides myself, to living quite alone will no doubt have its trials, but I hope to be rewarded by increasing fluency in the language, leading to greater usefulness. Will you join me in constant prayer for more close and abiding communion with Him who never forsakes His own ? . . . May He fulfil His gracious promise, and bless my efforts to the conversion of sinners. Oh, to walk blameless in love before Him myself, and to be used in turning many from their idols ' to serve the living and true God, and to wait for His Son from heaven.' "

As to the discomforts of Chinese dress, of which he was fully conscious, he was enabled from the first to make light

[1] A letter to a friend in Hull.
[2] For protection from sunstroke Mr. Taylor carried a native umbrella.

of them, as may be seen from a letter to his sister written just after parting from Dr. Parker:

HAI-YEN CITY,
August 28, 1855.

MY DEAR AMELIA—By way of surprise I mean to write you a letter—for I know you have never received one before from a man with a long tail and shaven head! But lest your head should be bewildered with conjectures, I had better tell you at once that on Thursday last at 11 P.M. I resigned my locks to the barber, dyed my hair a good black, and in the morning had a proper *queue* plaited in with my own, and a quantity of heavy silk to lengthen it out according to Chinese custom. Then, in Chinese dress, I set out with Dr. Parker, accompanying him about a hundred miles on his way to Ning-po. This journey we made an occasion for evangelistic work, and now that I am returning alone I hope to have even better facilities for book-distribution and preaching.

But I have not commenced the recital of my tribulations, and as there is some doubt as to whether they will all go into a single letter, the sooner I begin the better.

First then, it is a very sore thing to have one's head shaved for the first time, especially if the skin is irritable with prickly heat. And I can assure you that the subsequent application of hair-dye for five or six hours, (Litharge 1 part; quick lime, freshly slaked, 3 parts; water enough to make a cream) does not do much to soothe the irritation. But when it comes to combing out the remaining hair which has been allowed to grow longer than usual, the climax is reached! But there are no gains without pains, and certainly if suffering for a thing makes it dearer, I shall regard my *queue* when I attain one with no small amount of pride and affection.

Secondly, when you proceed to your toilet, you no longer wonder that many Chinese in the employ of Europeans wear foreign shoes and stockings as soon as they can get them. For native socks are made of calico and of course are not elastic . . . , and average toes decidedly object to be squeezed out of shape, nor do one's heels appreciate their low position in perfectly flat-soled shoes. Next come the breeches— but oh, what unheard-of garments! Mine are two feet too wide for me round the waist, which amplitude is laid in a fold in front, and kept in place by a strong girdle. The legs are short, not coming much below the knee, and wide in proportion with the waist measurement. Tucked into the long, white socks, they have a bloomer-like fulness capable, as Dr. Parker remarked, of storing a fortnight's provisions! No shirt is worn. But a white, washing-jacket, with sleeves as wide as ladies affected twenty years ago, supplies its place. And over all goes a heavy silk gown of some rich or delicate colour, with sleeves equally wide and reaching twelve or fifteen inches beyond the tips of one's fingers—folded back of course when the hands are in use. Unfortunately no cap or hat is used at this season of the year, except on state occasions, which is trying as the sun is awfully hot.

Wednesday, August 29.—I do not know, dear Amelia, whether you are weary of these details. But I have no time for more upon the subject, so will dismiss it with only a mention of the shampooing I got from the barber the other day. I thought I had better go in for it as part of the proceedings, for I might be in difficulty some day if found to be uninitiated. So I bore with an outrageous tickling as long as I could, and then the beating commenced ! And my back was really sore in places before it was over. On the next occasion, however, I stood it better, and I hope to acquit myself creditably in time with regard to this phase of the barber's art.

While still with Dr. Parker on the way to Hang-chow Bay I was frequently recognised as a foreigner, because of having to speak to him in English, but to-day in going about Hai-yen City no one even guessed that such a being was near. It was not until I began to distribute books and see patients that I became known. Then of course my men were asked where I came from, and the news soon spread. Dressed in this way one is not so much respected at first sight as one might be in foreign clothing. But a little medical work soon puts that all right, and it is evidently to be one's chief help for the interior. Women and children, it seems to me, manifest more readiness to come for medical aid now than they did before . . . and in this way too, I think the native costume will be of service.

Thus he returned to Shanghai as summer merged into autumn, to take up in the old surroundings a very different life. For the change he had made after so much prayer was soon found to affect more than his outward appearance. The Chinese felt it, Europeans felt it, and above all he felt it himself—putting an intangible barrier between him and foreign associations, and throwing him back as never before upon the people of his adoption. This, while he rejoiced in it for his work's sake, was not without its sting.

The covert sneer or undisguised contempt of the European community he found less difficult to bear than the disapproval of fellow-missionaries. But this also had to be faced, for he was practically alone in his convictions, and certainly the only one to carry them into effect. The more he suffered for them, however, the more they deepened ; and the more he gave himself to the Chinese in consequence, the more a new and wonderful joy in the Lord flooded his soul.

"The future is a ravelled maze," he wrote to his mother early in September, "but my path has always been made plain just one step at a time. I must wait on God and trust in Him, and all will be well. I think I do love Him more than ever, and long increasingly to serve Him as He directs. I have had some wonderful seasons of soul-refreshing lately, unworthy of them as I have been."

And to his sister a few days later :

The love of God is indeed wonderful to contemplate. His long-suffering how unbounded ! If ever there was one who deserved eternal banishment from His presence, it is I ; and yet I have had such melting seasons in prayer, such manifestations of His love, and such strong faith and confidence in Him of late that I have been quite astonished at His abounding grace to one so lukewarm and unfaithful. His grace even exceeds our unworthiness. Can we say more than this ? What a happy day it will be when, seeing Him as He is, we shall be made like Him—free from sin and perfect in purity !

And these experiences only deepened when he left the Settlement, parting from the friends with whom he had lived for months.

"Dr. Parker is in Ning-po," he wrote a little later,[1] "but I am not alone. I have such a *sensible* presence of God with me as I never before experienced, and such drawings to prayer and watchfulness as are very blessed and necessary."

Yet his surroundings were far from attractive within the walls of the native city, and his arrangements of the simplest, providing only for the bare necessaries of life. Chinese food and cooking were something of a trial at first, especially while the weather continued warm, and so were the sights and smells that could not be avoided amid that teeming population devoid of the most elementary ideas of sanitation. But the principal remains the same throughout the ages : "As the sufferings of Christ abound in us, so our consolation also aboundeth by Christ" : and the consolation, or "encouragement," as it may be read, far exceeds the loneliness and sacrifice.

---

[1] A letter to his sister Amelia, dated October 3.

Y

It was Monday, September 17, when he resumed upon
moving into his new quarters a solitary life, and only three
weeks later he wrote to tell his mother of the sweetest joy
he had ever known. For those three weeks had told. It
is always " overflow that blesses," and a heart so full of the
love of God could not but awaken in others a hunger for
more than they had known. The boys in the school felt
it ; the enquirers felt it, coming daily to the meetings ;
patients crowding the little dispensary felt it, and stayed
to hear what " the foreign doctor " had to say ; and above
all Kuei-hua felt it, his own faithful servant and friend.

Fully instructed in the truths of the Gospel, the latter
had for some time been a sincere believer, but now he could
no longer refrain from confessing his master's God. Early
one morning, therefore, he sought the young missionary,
with the earnest request that he might be baptized. The
day that followed was a busy one, but Hudson Taylor could
not let it pass without communicating so great a joy.

" This morning," he wrote just as the mail was leaving, " my heart
was gladdened by the request of Kuei-hua (my adopted pupil's brother)
to be baptized. The Lord has been working a manifest change in
him of late . . . but not until to-day has he asked to be admitted
into church membership. I cannot tell you the joy this has brought
me. . . . ' My soul doth magnify the Lord, and my spirit hath rejoiced
in God my Saviour.' Were my work ended here, I feel I could say
with Simeon, 'Lord now lettest Thou Thy servant depart in peace . . .
for mine eyes have seen Thy salvation.' If one soul is worth worlds,
mother, am I not abundantly repaid ? And are not you too ? "

But this was not the only encouragement of which he
had to tell before the month was over. For that October
mail brought another letter from Mr. Berger. Satisfied
with the use made of his first gift of ten pounds, this kind
friend now repeated it, undertaking to do so every half
year, and thus provide entirely for Han-pan's education.
But more than this, he wrote " a very affectionate letter,"
urging the young missionary to expect great things from
God, and enclosing a further sum of forty pounds to be used
as he thought best in the interests of the work.

It seems to have been with an almost solemnised sense

of the goodness of God that Hudson Taylor pondered all this in the light of the past, and in its relation to the future. How long he had looked forward to the joy of winning his first convert among the heathen ! How keenly he had felt lack of means properly to develop the work ! Now souls were being given, not Kuei-hua only, but one or two other promising enquirers ; and this generous friend in England was being drawn more and more into sympathy with the line of things to which he felt himself called. It was all so wonderful, so like God !

What the future held he could not tell. But already the Lord was more than making up for plans they had had to abandon, and for all the trials undergone. And straight to his heart came the message of Mr. Berger's letter :

" Open thy mouth wide, and I will fill it." Oh yes ! God is not straightened ! If we expect much from Him, He surely will not disappoint us.

PART V

SEVEN MONTHS WITH WILLIAM BURNS

1855–1856. AET. 23–24.

Surely one star above all souls shall brighten,
  Leading for ever where the Lord is laid ;
One revelation thro' all years enlighten
  Steps of bewilderment and eyes afraid.

Us with no other gospel thou ensnarest,
  Fiend from beneath or angel from above !
Knowing one thing the sacredest and fairest,—
  Knowing there is not anything but Love.

Ay, and when Prophecy her tale hath finished,
  Knowledge hath withered from the trembling tongue,
Love shall survive and Love be undiminished,
  Love be imperishable, Love be young.

Love that bent low beneath his brother's burden,
  How shall he soar and find all sorrows flown !
Love that ne'er asked for answer or for guerdon,
  How shall he meet eyes sweeter than his own !

Love was believing,—and the best is truest ;
  Love would hope ever,—and the trust was gain ;
Love that endured shall learn that thou renewest
  Love, even thine, O Master ! with thy pain.

Not in soft speech is told the earthly story,
  Love of all Loves, that showed thee for an hour ;
Shame was thy kingdom, and reproach thy glory,
  Death thine eternity, the Cross thy power.

                    FREDERIC W. H. MYERS.

CHAPTER XXVI

A PARISH OF A MILLION

OCTOBER–NOVEMBER 1855.   AET. 23.

COULD it be really true ?   A home of his own in the interior, and he himself in Chinese dress quietly living among the people, a day's journey from the nearest Treaty Port ? Often during those autumn days it must have seemed like a dream.   Yet the dream lasted, with most encouraging results.

It was all in answer to prayer no doubt, but the Chinese dress he was wearing had had a great deal to do with it. As soon as he could leave the South Gate house in charge of Teacher Si he had set out on another evangelistic journey, which was to include a second visit to the island of Tsung-ming.   But he had got no further than the first place at which he landed, for there within two or three days of his arrival he found himself in possession of this little house of his own.

The people simply would not hear of his leaving.   Clothed like themselves and living much as they did, he did not seem a foreigner ; and when they heard that he must have an upstairs room to sleep in, on account of the dampness of the locality, they said, " Let him live in the temple, if no other upper room can be found."

And quite willingly the young missionary would have done so, if the semi-discarded idols could have been cleared out of one of the silent, dusty chambers looking down upon the court.   But in this the priests foresaw a difficulty. Most of the idols, they said, were old and unimportant ; but

327

there were some, even upstairs, that it would not do to interfere with. Could not the Foreign Teacher allow them to remain ? But when he explained that it was a question of his God—the true and living God, Creator of earth and Heaven, who could not be asked to company with idols, the work of men's hands, and dependent for power, if they had any, upon the presence of evil spirits—both priests and people saw the reasonableness of his position. But even so they dared not dispossess certain of those idols.

What made them want so much to have him does not appear. Perhaps it was the medicine chest. Perhaps it was the preaching. At any rate there was nothing in his outward appearance to frighten them away, and the difference between this experience and anything he had met with on previous journeys taught him afresh the value of Chinese dress.

The second day of his stay there was a Sunday, and already a house had been discovered with some sort of an upper story whose owner was quite willing to receive the missionary. Indeed he could rent the entire premises, if they pleased him, for a moderate sum. But keen as he was to secure the place Hudson Taylor would not go to see it on Sunday, and the people watching him received their first impressions of the day God calls His own.

The delay did but forward Hudson Taylor's interests, however ; and before Monday was half over the agreement was concluded that gave him possession of his first home in " inland China."

Busy indeed were the days that followed—one of the hardest-worked and happiest times the young missionary had ever known in his life. The house needed cleaning, not to speak of furnishing, before it could be considered habitable even from a Chinese point of view. But more important than all this was the stream of visitors who had to be received with courtesy—gentlemen from the town and country, patients eager for medicine, and neighbours who seemed never weary of dropping in to watch and listen to all that was going on. His servant Kuei-hua and an earnest inquirer from the South Gate named Ts'ien were invaluable in helping him to preach the Gospel, morning, noon and night. But even so he finished up the week with an attack of ague, due to over-weariness and the change to autumn weather

All that was necessary, however, had been accomplished. The curiosity of the neighbourhood was satisfied, visitors had for the most part carried away favourable impressions, the house was whitewashed and sufficiently set in order, forms were ready for " the Chapel," and best of all, the conviction had gone abroad that the young missionary had come to Tsung-ming not for pleasure and comfort merely,[1] but to do good, to relieve suffering and to tell them something everybody ought to know.

After that things settled down to a regular routine. Patients were seen and daily meetings held, and to the thankfulness of the missionary and his helpers a few inquirers began to gather about them. One of these was a blacksmith named Chang, and another an assistant in a grocery store, men of good standing in the town " whose hearts the Lord opened." Ts'ien was invaluable in helping these beginners and in receiving guests, and both he and Kuei-hua were so eager to learn more themselves that they made the most of the little while Mr. Taylor could give them at night when outsiders had all gone home.

And all about them stretched the populous island—a parish of a million, every one of whom he longed to reach. The town itself contained only twenty to thirty thousand, but villages were numerous in every direction, and the medical work was making friends. Wherever Mr. Taylor and his helpers went they found somebody ready to welcome them, and as frequently as possible they spent a day in the country preaching the Gospel.

" It is almost too much to expect," he wrote at the beginning of

---

[1] It is a common impression among the Chinese, especially in places new to missionary work, that the attractions of their native land must be great in order to induce foreigners to travel so far to settle among them. Clearly they can have nothing so beautiful at home, or they would not leave it ! Material comfort especially, they conclude, must be immeasurably greater among themselves than anything " outside barbarians " know. This of course only applies in the present day to districts remote from the coast.

this work,[1] " that I shall be allowed to remain on without molestation, so I must use every effort to sow the good seed of the Kingdom while I may, and be earnest in prayer for blessing. Should it please the Lord to establish me in this place and raise up a band of believers, it seems to me that by making a circuit somewhat on the Wesleyan plan we should be enabled to do the greatest amount of good. . . .

" Pray for me. I sometimes feel a sense of responsibility that is quite oppressive—the only light-bearer among so many. But this is wrong. It is Jesus who is to shine in me . . . I am not left to my own resources. The two native Christians are a great comfort. May I be enabled to help them by life as well as teaching, and see them continually grow in grace."

It seemed a matter for regret that after three weeks of this happy work supplies began to run short and Mr. Taylor had to return to Shanghai for money and medicines. Not anticipating a long absence, he arranged for the meetings to go on without him, and leaving Ts'ien in charge sailed for the mainland on Tuesday evening, November 5. Next day he wrote from the South Gate :

MY DEAR MOTHER—I have returned here in safety, and the mail leaving to-day gives me an opportunity for answering your welcome letters. . . .

Last week on the island, to which I return as soon as possible, I saw more than two hundred patients and frequently preached the Gospel. But for a slight cold I am quite well, and am also very happy. . . . Kuei-hua is with me, but Ts'ien is left on the island to preach daily and carry on meetings with the inquirers. . . . The Lord be with and bless him. I hardly liked to leave so young a Christian in such a responsible position. But what was to be done ? . . . Do pray that he may be kept faithful and may be much used in the dissemination of the Truth.

Eager though Mr. Taylor was to go back at once he found it necessary to wait while a fresh outfit of Chinese clothing was prepared for the winter season. So far he had only used unlined garments, but now it was a question of wadded coats, shoes and trousers, not to speak of a gown lined with lamb-skins and a big red hood to cover head

[1] In a letter to an uncle by marriage, the Rev. Edward King, dated October 23, 1855, in which Mr Taylor also says : " That I have succeeded in renting a house here so easily is due no doubt to my having adopted the native costume, not losing sight of the fact that the hearts of all are in the Lord's hands, to be moved by Him as He will "

and shoulders. All this took time, and while the things were being made Mr. Taylor found he could fit in a visit to Sung-kiang to look up an inquirer in whom Ts'ien was interested. Sunday, November 11, was spent in his company, and then the young missionary hastened back to Shanghai on his return journey.

He had been absent little more than a week from the island, but much may happen in that time as he learned from the news awaiting him. A storm was brewing at Sin-k'ai-ho. Ts'ien had come over hurriedly, and finding no one at the South Gate had returned to his post leaving letters to explain the situation. Amid many exciting rumours one clear fact emerged : a proclamation had been issued to the effect that the foreigner who had unwarrantably taken up his abode on Tsung-ming was to be sent back to Shanghai at once where he would suffer the severest penalty, and that all persons who had aided his presumptuous action would also be punished after the strictest letter of the law.

All this seemed very serious, and it was with a heavy heart Mr. Taylor returned to the island as quickly as possible.

" I left my things on board the junk," he wrote to his parents a fortnight later,[1] " and went up to see what was happening. After hearing all Ts'ien had to say I concluded to dismiss the junk, and now must tell you what has taken place as far as I have been able to gather it.

" Well, it seems that the two doctors and four druggists of this town have begun to find me rather a serious rival. Bad legs of many years' standing have been cured in a few days. Eye-medicine exceeding theirs in potency can be obtained for nothing. A whole host of itch cases, regular customers for plasters (!) have in some way disappeared. Ague patients are saying that the doctors are without talent, and asthmatics are loud in praise of foreign cough-powders. What was to be the end of it all ? That was the question.

" So the fraternity met together, took tea, tobacco and counsel, and sent twelve dollars to the Mandarin to have the intruder expelled. I believe, however, that none of it ever reached him. It is much more likely to have been seized by rapacious underlings who forthwith took the matter into their own hands. But of this I have no positive

---

[1] Written from Sin-k'ai-ho at the end of November

proof Here was a foreigner anxious to settle on the island; the landlord, middle-man, and Elder of the town who had received him would doubtless be squeezable by threats of punishment; while the doctors and druggists would be sure to give more, if necessary, to get rid of their rival. So down they came and soon managed to frighten the parties concerned, but not to get any money. . . .

" Again they came, hoping I might have returned, this time bringing a writ sealed with the Mandarin's seal, though I believe from subsequent events that this also was without his knowledge. The tenor of the document was that I was to be handed over at once to the Taotai in Shanghai, who with the British Consul would most severely punish me; and that the Chinese, one and all, were to be brought before the Mandarin in Tsung-ming city and made to suffer according to their deserts.

" Ts'ien, fearing this might be serious, made a copy of the writ and came over to Shanghai, but as I was not to be found he went back at once. The messengers then came a third time, saying they had discovered my objects to be wholly virtuous, and if I would pay expenses (a sum of thirteen dollars) they would hush up the matter and there would be an end of it.

" On my return I felt a little anxious, not for my own sake but on account of those who would be implicated if trouble were to arise. But finally the ' runners,' after lowering their demand to ten dollars and then to three, finding that I would not give them a cash, managed to squeeze thirteen dollars out of the doctors and druggists and came no more. All then seemed over. I continued to see patients as before, going every alternate day to preach in neighbouring towns and villages till Monday the 26th instant, which with yesterday have been days of intense anxiety.

" On Monday morning while we were at breakfast the Mandarin from Tsung-ming city passed by, his attendants making it known that he had come for the double purpose of seizing some pirates at a town below and of examining into our affairs. Ts'ien and Kuei-hua were to be dragged before him, the landlord also, and an old man of over seventy who had acted as go-between; and unless their replies were ' satisfactory ' they would be beaten from three hundred to a thousand blows each. We had morning worship, specially praying for protection, and then preached and saw patients as usual. . . . Toward the close of the afternoon we were told that the Mandarin had gone to seize the pirates first, and would deal with our matters on his return journey.

" Next day I kept all who were concerned in the house, that none might be taken without my knowledge. We saw patients, some having come many miles, . . . and preached as usual. In the afternoon, as I was operating on the eye of a woman, who should pass but the

Mandarin with all his followers. It was well that the operation was over, or I should have found it difficult to complete it, for I was trembling with excitement. It was not until two hours later that we definitely learned that he had gone on to the capital without stopping. Then our prayers were turned into praise indeed ! It may be that he is not even aware of my presence . . . and that the whole story was a further attempt to extort money on the part of his underlings. If so, finding it unsuccessful, I hope they will not repeat it.

"From that time to this, November 29, we have had no trouble. To-day I have been at a village seven miles away containing about four hundred inhabitants. We preached at some length and left a few tracts and Gospels, but I doubt whether more than one person in the place is able to understand what he reads. . . . The truth is China must be evangelised like other heathen countries by the Word *preached* as well as written. So we need men, more men willing to deny themselves the pleasures of society and of the table, to live among the people and make the Gospel widely known. There is a blacksmith here who as far as I can judge is truly converted, thank God ! "

Thus in spite of persecution and threatened danger, the good work went on. Six weeks was a long time to have been enabled to reside in one place, preaching the Gospel daily, forty miles from the nearest Treaty Port. And now that the storm had blown over, the young missionary was more than ever earnest in making the most of his opportunities. To see the inquirers growing in grace and in the knowledge of the Lord was a joy no words could express. The blacksmith, Chang, now closed his shop on Sundays, and both he and Sung openly declared themselves Christians. The change that had come over them awakened not a little interest among their fellow-townsmen, several of whom were attending the services regularly. So that the blow when it fell was all the more painful for being unexpected— and it came from an unforeseen quarter.

It was December 1, and Hudson Taylor had gone over to Shanghai to obtain money and send off letters. To his surprise an important-looking document was awaiting him at the South Gate, which read as follows :

BRITISH CONSULATE, SHANGHAI,
November 23, 1855.

British Consul to Mr. J. H. Taylor.

SIR—I am directed by Her Majesty's Consul to inform you that information has been lodged at this office by His Excellency the

Intendant of Circuit, to the effect that you have rented a house from a Chinese named Si Sung-an, at a place called Sin-k'ai-ho in the island of Tsung-ming, and opened this house as a physician's establishment in charge of one of your servants named Lew Yang-tsuen,[1] you yourself visiting it occasionally. His Excellency refers to a former complaint lodged against you for visiting Ts'ing-kiang, upon which subject you appeared before Her Majesty's Consul.[2] His Excellency also reports that Lew Yang-tsuen, Si Sung-an and Ts'ien Hai-yae have been arrested.[3]

Her Majesty's Consul has therefore to call upon you to appear at this office without delay, in order that he may investigate the matter above referred to.—I am, Sir, your most obedient servant,

FREDERICK HARVEY (*Vice-Consul*).

Of course he went at once and explained the true facts of the case, which were listened to with interest. But his plea to be allowed to remain on at Sin-k'ai-ho where all now seemed peaceful and friendly was in vain. The Consul reminded him that the British Treaty only provided for residence in the five ports, and that if he attempted to settle elsewhere he rendered himself liable to a fine of five hundred dollars.[4] But there was a supplementary treaty, as the young missionary well knew, in which it was stipulated that all immunities and privileges granted to other nations should apply to British subjects also. Roman Catholic priests, Frenchmen, were living on the island supported by the authority of their Government, and why should he be forbidden the same consideration?

Yes, replied the Consul, that was undoubtedly a point, and if he wished to appeal for a higher decision, Her Majesty's representative (Sir John Bowring) would be arriving in Shanghai before long. But as far as his own jurisdiction went, the matter was at an end. Mr. Taylor must return

---

[1] Presumably Kuei-hua's full literary name

[2] This was in the summer after Mr. Taylor's return from his long journey up the Yang-tze. In a letter to his mother dated July 29 he referred to the circumstance as follows :

" The Chinese authorities have had me up before the Consul for violating the treaty with England by travelling in the interior. He said very little, not more than he was obliged to, but told me that if I continued to exceed treaty rights his position admitted of no respect of persons ; he must punish me as he would a merchant."

[3] This was happily incorrect : no one had been arrested.

[4] Worth at that time considerably over a hundred pounds.

to Tsung-ming at once, give up his house, remove his belongings to Shanghai, and understand that he was liable to a fine of five hundred dollars if he again attempted residence in the interior.

Well was it that next day was Sunday and he had time to lay it all before the Lord. Little by little as it came over him, and he began to realise that all the happy, encouraging work at Sin-k'ai-ho must be suddenly abandoned, it seemed almost more than he could bear. Those young inquirers, Chang, Sung and the others, what was to become of them ? Were they not his own children in the faith ? How could he leave them with no help and so little knowledge in the things of God ? And yet the Lord had permitted it. The work was His. He would not fail nor forsake them. But for himself, the sorrow and disappointment were overwhelming.

" My dear mother," he wrote that evening (December 2), " my heart is sad, sad, sad. I came over to Shanghai last Friday . . . and found a letter awaiting me from the Consul, dated a week or more previously. I lost no time in seeing him, and have been prohibited from residing any longer on Tsung-ming. I do not know what to think. If I disobey, I incur a fine of $500, and may bring my Chinese friends into trouble. All I can do is to give up the house and pray over my future course. . . .

" I leave to-night at 1 A.M. for the island. . . . Pray for me. I need more grace, and live far below my privileges. Oh to feel more as Moses did when he said, ' Forgive their sin, forgive it, . . . and if not, blot me I pray thee out of Thy book ' (Conquest's Version) . . . or as the Lord Jesus when He said, ' I lay down my life for the sheep.' I do not want to be as a hireling who flees when the wolf is near, nor would I lightly run into danger when much may be accomplished in safety. I want to know the Lord's will and have grace to do it, even if it results in expatriation. ' Now is my soul troubled, and what shall I say ? . . . Father, glorify Thy Name.' Pray for me that I may be a follower of Christ not in word only, but in deed and in truth."

The last days on Tsung-ming, however, were not wholly sad. It was hard to pack up and send everything to the boat ; hard to answer the interrogations of neighbours and bid farewell to the old landlord and many friends. But the very parting brought with it elements of comfort.

Could he ever forget, for example, that last evening spent with the inquirers ?

" My heart will be truly sorrowful," said the blacksmith, " when I can no longer join you in the daily meetings."

" But you will worship in your own family," replied his friend. " Still shut your shop on Sunday, for God is here whether I am or not. Get some one to read for you, and gather your neighbours in to hear the Gospel."

" I know but very little," put in Sung, " and when I read I by no means understand all the characters. My heart is grieved because you have to leave us ; but I do thank God He ever sent you to this place. My sins once so heavy are all laid on Jesus, and He daily gives me joy and peace."

" Come again, come again, Tai Sien-seng," the neighbours called the following morning. " The sooner you return the better ! We shall miss the good doctor and the Heavenly Words."

" It is hard indeed to leave them," he wrote in the freshness of his sorrow, " for I had hoped a good work would be done there, Much seed has been sown, and many books are in the hands of the people. It rests with the Lord to give the increase. May He watch over them, for Jesus' sake."

CHAPTER XXVII

AS RIVERS OF WATER IN A DRY PLACE

DECEMBER 1855. AET. 23.

" AND a man shall be as a hiding-place from the wind, and a covert from the tempest ; as rivers of water in a dry place, as the shadow of a great rock in a weary land." Spoken primarily of the Lord and wholly true of Him alone, yet how often these words find a limited and human but very blessed fulfilment in an earthly friendship through which He comes to us in time of need. Thus it was for Hudson Taylor in the friendship of William Burns.

Alone, perplexed and disappointed, he had indeed come to a time of need. The restrictions imposed upon him as a Protestant missionary, compared with the liberty granted to priests of the Romish Church, opened up a difficulty he had not anticipated in his evangelistic work. And how formidable it might prove !

" Forbidden to reside on the island," he had written to Mr. Pearse on his return journey from Tsung-ming, " and finding that even travelling into the country and remaining for a short time is an infringement of the Treaty which may be visited by a fine of five hundred dollars, I have thought it best to write privately and enquire whether, in case I should be fined . . . the Society would be responsible for the sum ? Also whether, if circumstances should make it possible for me to go to the interior, *giving up all claim to Consular protection,* you would approve my doing so ? Should I be left free to follow this course ? Or would the Society object to one of their missionaries adopting such a position ?

" Although the attempt to rent a house and reside in Tsung-ming has met with failure, we must be very thankful for what has been accomplished I have every reason to hope that three of those who profess to believe in the Lord Jesus are sincere, and if so the results will last to all eternity. May God watch over them and bless them. At the same time it makes it all the harder to give up the work. Also I cannot hide from myself that the results to the landlord and others for having received us may be serious in the extreme. . . . All we can do is to pray for their protection. 'It is better to trust in the Lord than to put confidence in man. It is better to trust in the Lord than to put confidence in princes.' God grant that in this we may not be confounded, for should any who are not believers suffer on our account, it would indeed be grievous.

"Pray for me—pray for me ! I greatly *need* your prayers. I do not want on the one hand to flee from danger, nor on the other to court troubles, or from lack of patience to hinder future usefulness. I do need more grace, more of the spirit of my Master, more entire resignation to the will of God, and greater boldness too. These Mandarins are for the most part treacherous and cruel in the extreme. . . . It will need no small faith to go amongst them without hope of protection, save from Him to Whom ' all power ' is given I know we ought to desire no more. Would I were living in that state of grace."

The British Minister was expected shortly, but Hudson Taylor was in uncertainty about bringing the case before him. Sir John Bowring was not likely to be in sympathy with aggressive missionary effort, and should he confirm the Consul's action it would only add to the difficulties of a situation already trying enough. And yet what was to be done ? Stay in Shanghai he could not, where so many, comparatively, were occupying the field. But to travel or attempt to live in the interior had become a serious matter.

"I shall probably appeal against the Consular decision," he continued a few days later.[1] "I feel the importance of this case in many respects It will test the footing on which Protestant missionaries really stand, and if I am still forbidden to reside in the interior will at any rate prevent its being said that while Romish priests deny themselves the pleasures of society, etc., to live among the Chinese, we are not willing to do so.

"The Gospel *must* be preached among this people, and if owned of God the opposition of Satan is sure to be roused May the Lord

---

[1] A letter from the South Gate to Mr. Pearse, dated December 7, 1855.

give us grace and boldness to do our duty regardless of consequences, and at the same time wisdom to avoid unnecessary dangers."

But Sir John Bowring was unaccountably delayed just then. He did not arrive by the mail-steamer on which he was expected, nor by the next. This gave time for further thought and prayer; and meanwhile Hudson Taylor was brought into contact with the one prepared of God to help him.

Beloved all over Scotland by those to whom he had been made a blessing, the name of William Burns was in the best sense a household word. For where in town or country was there a Christian household that did not recall with thankfulness the Revival of 1839 ? The young evangelist of those days, moving in Pentecostal power from place to place, everywhere accompanied by marvellous tokens of the divine presence and blessing, had become the toil-worn missionary—his hair already tinged with grey, his spirit more mellow though no less fervent, his sympathies enlarged through experience and deeper fellowship with the sufferings of Christ.[1]

Just returned to China after his first and only furlough, Mr. Burns had not resumed, as might have been expected, his former successful work. Others were caring for the little flock in the neighbourhood of Amoy, and prayerful interest would never be lacking for so encouraging a field. If difficulties arose he could at once return; but failing any special need, he felt strongly drawn to the Yang-tze Valley and a service no one had as yet been able to render.

Nan-king was on his heart, and the unknown leaders of the Tai-ping movement in whose hands the future of China still seemed to lie. No missionary had hitherto succeeded in reaching them, though the rebel king had earnestly pleaded for Christian teachers to aid in the great work of national regeneration upon which he thought himself embarked. Certainly if any one in China could have strengthened him for this hopeless task it would have

[1] For details of this truly Apostolic life, see *Memoir of the Rev. William Burns, M.A.*, by his brother, the Rev. Islay Burns, D.D.

been William Burns, with his easy mastery of the language, intense force of character and deeply prayerful spirit. But as events had already proved, this was not the purpose for which he had been brought to central China.

Unsuccessful in his attempt to reach Nan-king, Mr. Burns had returned to Shanghai by the southern reaches of the Grand Canal, much impressed with the need and accessibility of that part of the country. With the concurrence of the local missionaries, all too few to meet the overwhelming needs, he had devoted himself for several months to its evangelisation—living on boats in very simple style, and travelling up and down the endless waterways spread like a network over the vast alluvial plain. Thus it was that in the providence of God he was still in that locality when Hudson Taylor returned from Tsung-ming, and engaged in the very work so dear to the younger missionary's heart.

Where and how they met does not appear, but one can readily believe that they were drawn together by sympathies of no ordinary kind. The grave, keen-eyed Scotsman soon detected in the English missionary a kindred spirit, and one sorely in need of help that he might give. The attraction was mutual. Each was without a companion, and before long they had arranged to join forces in the work to which both felt specially called.

In a little house at the South Gate or on Mr. Burns's boat almost the first subject they would discuss would be the difficulty about Tsung-ming with its bearing on the future, and it was not long before the spiritual point of view of the older man seemed to change the whole situation. It was not a question really of standing on one's rights, or claiming what it might be justifiable to claim. Why deal with second causes? Nothing would have been easier for the Master to Whom " All power " is given than to have established His servant permanently on the island, had He so desired it. And of what use was it, if He had other plans, to attempt to carry the thing through on the strength of Government help? No, " the servant of the Lord must not strive," but must be willing to be led by just such indications of the divine will, relying not on the help of

Photograph

By a Chinese.

WATERWAYS IN KIANG-SU.

Such as Mr. Burns and Mr. Taylor traversed on their evangelistic journeys.

To face page 841.

man to accomplish a work of his own choosing, but on the
unfailing guidance, resources and purposes of God.

And so, very thankfully, Hudson Taylor came to realise
that all was well. A measure of trial had been allowed, over
which perhaps he had felt unduly discouraged. But all
was in wise and loving hands. Nothing the Lord permitted could lastingly hinder His own work. And all the
while had He not been preparing for His servant this
unexpected blessing, by far the most helpful companionship
he had ever known ?

TENTH JOURNEY: *December–January* 1856

It was the middle of December when Hudson Taylor
left Shanghai once more, setting out on his tenth evangelistic journey, the first with Mr. Burns.[1] Travelling in two
boats, each with their Chinese helpers and a good supply
of literature, they were at the same time independent and a
comfort to one another.[2] Practical and methodical in all
his ways, Mr. Burns had a line of his own in such work
that his companion was glad to follow.

Choosing an important centre, in this case the town of
Nan-zin, just south of the Great Lake, in Cheh-kiang, they
remained there eighteen days, including Christmas and the
New Year. Every morning they set out early with a
definite plan, sometimes working together and sometimes
separating to visit different parts of the town. Mr. Burns
believed in beginning quietly on the outskirts of a place
in which foreigners had rarely if ever been seen, and working
his way by degrees to the more crowded quarters. Accordingly they gave some days to the suburban streets, preaching
whenever a number of people collected and giving away
Gospels and tracts. This was repeated in all the quieter

[1] Residence on Tsung-ming had been forbidden, but he saw no reason
why he should not accompany another missionary to whose itinerations
no objection had been raised.

[2] Mr. Taylor had his teacher with him, but Ts'ien and Kvei-hua had
been sent to the island of Hai-men in response to an urgent invitation
from two gentlemen, brothers, who had received books on Mr. Taylor's
visit with Mr Burdon (see Chap. xxii. p. 283), and desired to learn more
of the way of Salvation. They rejoined Mr. Taylor at Nan-zin just after
the New Year.

parts of the town, gradually approaching its centre, until at length they could pass along the busiest streets without endangering the shopkeepers' tempers as well as their wares.

Then they visited temples, schools and tea-shops, returning regularly to the most suitable places for preaching. These were usually tea-shops on quiet thoroughfares, on open spaces left by demolished buildings. Announcing after each meeting when they would come again, they had the satisfaction of seeing the same faces frequently, and interested hearers could be invited to the boats for private conversation.

Of those busy days, always begun and ended with prayer with their Chinese helpers, many details are given in Mr. Taylor's letters, including the following glimpse into a tea-shop, showing how their evenings were spent.

It was December 28, and after addressing large, attentive audiences in the earlier part of the day, the afternoon had been given to visitors who sought them out on their boats. Darkness had fallen before they could think of supper, after which lighting their lanterns they sallied forth into the winter night. It was not far to the tea-shops at which they were expected, and an unseen Friend must have been present with them, for Mr. Taylor's journal simply records "We were greatly blessed."

"I wish I could picture the scene," he continues. "Imagine a large dimly lighted room, on a level with the ground, filled with square tables and narrow forms, so arranged that eight persons might be seated at each table. . . . Scattered about the room, a number of working men were drinking tea and smoking long bamboo pipes with brass heads, while a boy with a copper kettle went to and fro from the fireplace with boiling water.

"Hardly had we entered before Mr. Burns's lantern began to attract attention. It was an ordinary lantern such as one often sees in England, with glass on three sides and a plated mirror to reflect the light, but quite a curiosity here. Around us soon gathered a group of questioners, some of whom were educated, and the rest workmen of more or less intelligence. . . . I was in native dress of course, and Mr. Burns had on a Chinese gown that hid all but his collar, shoes, and a cap the peak of which he had taken off, so there was not much about him to look at.

"Before long the conversation became interesting. We did not have to make a way so to speak for the Gospel, it was drawn from us by their own questions. One asked, ' Are all the idols false ? ' and another, ' What benefits arise from believing in Jesus ? ' ' If Jesus is in heaven, how can we worship Him here ? ' was a very natural question ; while one who had not understood much said earnestly, ' Take me to see God and Jesus, and then I can believe on them.' The boy, too, as he went about filling the cups, would put his kettle down upon the table, and folding his arms over it listen to what was being said.

"Some present urged Mr. Burns to have his head shaved (in front) and wear a Chinese cap as I did. They were sure he would look much better so ! And one man who has followed us from place to place insisted on paying for our tea, a sum equal nearly to a penny. . . .

" We were enabled to speak plainly on many topics, and best of all our Master was with us." [1]

The hint given in the tea-shop was not without effect, though other more important considerations decided Mr. Burns upon the step of which he tells in the following letter. Ever since leaving Shanghai he had not failed to notice the benefit derived by his companion from wearing Chinese dress. Although so much younger and in every way less experienced, Mr. Taylor had the more attentive hearers and was occasionally asked into private houses, he himself being requested to wait outside, as the disturbance occasioned by his presence would make attention impossible. The riff-raff of the crowd always seemed to gather round the preacher in foreign dress, while those who wished to hear what was being said followed his less noticeable friend. The result was a conclusion come to that night if not previously, and communicated to his mother a few weeks later ·

TWENTY-FIVE MILES FROM SHANGHAI,
January 26, 1856.

Taking advantage of a rainy day which confines me to my boat, I pen a few lines in addition to a letter to Dundee containing particulars which I need not repeat.

It is now forty-one days since I left Shanghai on this last occasion. An excellent young English missionary, Mr. Taylor of the Chinese Evangelisation Society, has been my companion, he in his boat and

---

[1] Extracted from Mr Taylor's journal for December 28, 1855, and from a letter of the same date.

I in mine, and we have experienced much mercy, and on some occasions considerable assistance in our work. . . .

I must once more tell the story I have had to tell more than once already, how four weeks ago, on the 29th of December, I put on Chinese dress, which I am now wearing. Mr. Taylor had made this change a few months before, and I found that he was in consequence so much less incommoded in preaching, etc., by the crowd, that I concluded that it was my duty to follow his example. . . .

We have a large, very large, field of labour in this region, though it might be difficult in the meantime for one to establish himself in any particular place. The people listen with attention, but we need the power from on high to convince and convert. Is there any spirit of prayer on our behalf among God's people in Kilsyth ? Or is there any effort to seek this spirit ? How great the need is, and how great the arguments and motives for prayer in this case ! The harvest here is indeed great, and the labourers are few and imperfectly fitted, without much grace, for such a work. And yet grace can make a few, feeble instruments the means of accomplishing great things—things greater even than we can conceive.

This change into Chinese dress was found to have so many advantages that Mr. Burns never again resumed European clothing. Among the people of Nan-zin it was received with cordial favour. Returning from the tea-shop a few days later, both the missionaries were invited by one who had been present to go with him to his home and repeat there the wonderful Story. It was evening, and they had already been preaching for a couple of hours, but such invitations were none too frequent and they gladly accompanied him.

" It was very interesting," wrote Hudson Taylor to one of his sisters, " to see all the family collected . . . that we might speak to them of Him Who died to atone for the sins of the world. Close to me was a bright little girl about ten years of age, her arms crossed upon the table and her head resting on them. Beside her was her brother, an intelligent boy of fourteen. Next came Mr. Burns and on his other side a young man of twenty, and so on. The men sat round the table, while the mother, two older daughters and another woman kept in the background, half out of sight While I was speaking, as I did on their account, of the prayers of my mother and sister before my conversion, I noticed that they were attending closely. Oh, may God give China *Christian mothers and sisters* before long ! Returning to our boats, I could not help tears of joy and thankfulness

that we had been induced to adopt this costume, without which we
could never have such access to the people "

Of the comfort of the dress there could be no doubt.

" It is real winter now," wrote Mr. Taylor on New Year's eve,
" and the north wind is very cutting. But instead of being almost
' starved to death ' as I was last year, I am now, thanks to the Chinese
costume, thoroughly comfortable and as warm as toast.

" Indeed, we have many mercies to be thankful for. A good boat,
costing about two shillings a day, gives me a nice little room to myself ;
one in front for my servant to sleep in, used in the day-time for receiving
guests ; and a cabin behind for my teacher, as well as a place for
cooking, storing books, etc. My tiny room has an oyster-shell window
that gives light while it prevents people from peeping in, . . . a table
at which I write and take meals, . . . a locker on which my bed is
spread at night, . . . and a seat round the remaining space, so that
two visitors, or even three, can be accommodated. For family worship
we open the doors in front and behind my cabin, and then the boat-
people, teachers, servant and Mr. Burns can all join in the service. . . .

" How very differently our Master was lodged ! ' Nowhere to lay
His head.' And this for my sins—amazing thought ! . . . Then I
am no longer my own. Bought with His precious blood . . . Oh,
may I be enabled to glorify *Him* with my whole spirit, soul and body,
which are His."

Deep as his longing had ever been for likeness to and
fellowship with the Lord, Hudson Taylor was increasingly
conscious of this heart-hunger in companionship with
William Burns. He, too, had found how sadly possible it
is to be professedly a witness for Christ amid the darkness
of a heathen land, " and yet breathe little of the love of
God or the grace of the Gospel." Nothing was more real
to him than the fact that a low-level missionary life can,
and too often does, make even " the cross of Christ . . . of
none effect." But great and many though the dangers may
be, and the pressure brought to bear on every missionary to
lower his spiritual standards and draw him away from
living contact with the Lord, Mr. Burns had proved the
faithfulness of that divine Master in coming to the help of
His own.

" I was preaching last Sabbath day," he wrote on one occasion,
" from Matthew xxiv. 12, ' because iniquity shall abound, the love
of many shall wax cold ' ; and alas ! I felt they were solemnly applic-

able to my own state of heart.   Unless the Lord the Spirit continually uphold and quicken, oh how benumbing is daily contact with heathenism !   But the Lord is faithful, and has promised to be ' as rivers of water in a dry place, and as the shadow of a great rock in a weary land.'   May you and all God's professing people in a land more favoured, but alas ! more guilty also, experience much of the Lord's own presence, power and blessing ; and when the enemy comes in as a flood, may the Spirit of the Lord—nay, it is said ' the Spirit of the Lord *shall* lift up a standard against him.' "

Upon such promises he counted, and he had not found them fail.   The presence of the Lord was the one thing real to him in China as it had been at home.   " He did not consider that he had a warrant to proceed in any sacred duty," his biographer tells us, " without a consciousness of that divine presence   Without it, he could not speak even to a handful of little children in a Sunday School ; with it he could stand unabashed before the mightiest and wisest in the land."

Ruled by such a master-principle, it was no wonder there was something about his life that impressed and attracted others even while it inspired a sense of awe.   The brightest lamp will burn dim in an impure or rarefied atmosphere, but William Burns was enabled so to keep himself " in the love of God " that he was but little affected by his surroundings.   Prayer was as natural to him as breathing, and the Word of God his God as necessary as daily food.[1] He was always cheerful, always happy, witnessing to the truth of his own memorable words :

I think I can say, through grace, that God's presence or absence alone distinguishes places to me.

---

[1] " His whole life was literally a life of prayer, and his whole ministry a series of battles fought at the mercy-seat."

" Who among us has the spirit of prayer? " he wrote from Swatow. " They are mighty who have this spirit, and weak who have it not."

" In digging in the field of the Word," said an intimate friend, " he threw up now and then great nuggets which formed part of one's spiritual wealth every after."

" He was mighty in the Scriptures, and his greatest power in preaching was the way in which he used ' the Sword of the Spirit ' upon men's consciences and hearts . . Sometimes one might have thought, in listening to his solemn appeals, that one was hearing a new chapter in the Bible when first spoken by a living prophet "

Quoted from the *Memoir* by the Rev Islay Burns, D D., pp 545, 237, 549.

Simplicity in living was his great delight. " He enjoyed quietness and the luxury of having few things to take care of," and thought the happiest state on earth for a Christian was " that he should have few wants."

" If a man have Christ in his heart," he used to say, " heaven before his eyes, and only as much of temporal blessing as is just needful to carry him safely through life, then pain and sorrow have little to shoot at. . . . To be in union with Him Who is the Shepherd of Israel, to walk very near Him Who is both sun and shield, comprehends all a poor sinner requires to make him happy between this and heaven."[1]

Cultured, genial and overflowing with mother-wit, he was a delightful companion, and the contrast—for those who knew him in China—was very marked between " the mind and thoughts so trained to higher things and the heart so content with that which was lowly." A wonderful fund of varied anecdotes gave charm to his society, and he was generous in recalling his experiences for the benefit of others. Many a time his life had been in danger in Ireland and elsewhere at the hands of a violent mob, and the stories he had to tell could not but encourage faith and zeal, although at times they might provoke a smile.

" *The devil's dead*," shouted one Irish voice above the uproar of a crowd determined to put an end to his street-preaching. It was a perilous moment, for the shower of mud and stones was increasing and there was no possibility of escape should the rougher element prevail. But the quick-witted reply, touched with sarcasm, " *Ah then, you are a poor fatherless bairn !* " not only won the day, but carried home a deeply solemn lesson.

Sacred music was his delight, greatly to the satisfaction of his young companion. Many were the hymns they sang together both in English and Chinese, Hudson Taylor, no doubt, appreciating Mr. Burns's rendering of these into colloquial words and phrases, for the use of the illiterate. Their intercourse with one another was carried on almost entirely in the language of their native helpers. Mr. Burns " lived by choice and habitually in a Chinese element,"

---

[1] Quoted from the *Memoir* by the Rev Islay Burns, D.D., p. 551.

and with this line of things and the courtesy it indicated toward those around them, Hudson Taylor was in fullest sympathy.   The fact that they did not belong to the same missionary society, the same denomination, the same country even, made no difference in their relations.   Burns was far too large-hearted to be narrowed by circumstances or creeds.   " He was at home with all Protestant Christians," and co-operated with missionaries of many societies, German, English and American, with the greatest goodwill and the most Catholic spirit, aiming at the advancement of the Kingdom of God rather than of his own particular cause.

Yet his faithfulness to conviction was unflinching, and his testimony against wrong-doing never withheld.   His denunciations of sin could be terrible, strong men cowering before them, pale and trembling, under an overwhelming sense of the divine presence.   He did not hesitate, for example, on this very journey, to mount the stage of a Chinese theatre in the presence of thousands of people and stop an immoral play in full swing, calling upon the audience gathered under the open heavens to repent of their iniquities and turn to the living God.

But it was toward himself he was most of all severe, in the true apostolic spirit, " We suffer all things, *lest we should hinder* the Gospel of Christ."   There are glimpses in his journal of whole days or nights spent in prayer— " seeking personal holiness, the fundamental requisite for a successful ministry."   Yet he felt himself wholly unworthy to represent the Lord he loved.   " Oh, that I had a martyr's heart," he wrote, " if not a martyr's death and a martyr's crown."

And this man, the friendship of this man with all he was and had been, was the gift and blessing of God at this particular juncture to Hudson Taylor.   Week after week, month after month they lived and travelled together, the exigencies of their work bringing out resources of mind and heart that otherwise might have remained hidden. Such a friendship is one of the crowning blessings of life. Money cannot buy it ; influence cannot command it.   It comes as love unsought, and only to the equal soul. Young and immature as he was, Hudson Taylor had the capacity to appreciate, after long years of loneliness, the preciousness of this gift. Under its influence he grew and expanded, and came to an understanding of himself and his providential position that left its impress on all after-life. William Burns was better to him than a college course with all its advantages, because he lived out before him right there in China the reality of all he most needed to be and know.

But to come back to their first journey together on the waterways of Cheh-kiang. The front room in Mr. Taylor's boat was made good use of during the eighteen days of their stay at Nan-zin, many a conversation being held there with interested guests. Early in their stay, a young man named King called one evening, with a book he had received elsewhere from other foreigners. He was evidently impressed, and told them that he wished to become a Christian. He knew very little of the truth, however, and was surprised to learn that the God of Thunder must be abandoned as well as other idols. Not worship the God of Thunder ? Why, that had seemed so obvious a divinity ! He remained to evening worship, kneeling for the first time in prayer to the true and living God. The following day was Sunday, and the missionaries were encouraged to see him at both services. But on Monday business called him away from the town, and they could but commend him to God and the Word of His Grace, hoping that sometime, somewhere, he might again be brought into touch with Christians.

Hardly had he left them when several visitors came on board, two of whom seemed specially interested. They made particular enquiries about prayer and the proper forms of Christian worship. But when after a good deal of conversation Mr. Taylor proposed to pray with them, one of the two looked very uneasy and declined, saying he was really too ignorant, and moreover was expecting to eat pork on the morrow !

On Christmas eve, a few days later, Mr. Taylor was explaining to some guests the folly and sin of worshipping idols when it is to the one, true and living God we are indebted for every good gift.

"But," said one of his hearers, "surely you are too general in your statement. There are good idols as well as many that are good-for-nothing."

"And which are the good idols?" asked the missionary with interest.

Pointing through the window of the little cabin in the direction of a temple near at hand, "They are in there," he said. "Many years ago two men came to our town with a boat-load of rice to sell. It happened that the time was one of famine. There had been no harvest and the people were in much distress. Seeing this, the strangers took the rice and gave it away among the poorest. Then, of course, they had no face to go home again."

"And why not?" questioned the listener.

"Oh, because they had given away the rice instead of selling it."

"Then it was not their own?"

"No, it belonged to their master. And as they dared not meet him again they both drowned themselves here in the river, and the people said they were gods, made idols to represent them, and built this temple in which they have been worshipped ever since."

"Then your 'good idols,'" said the missionary, "are men, only men to begin with, who stole their master's property and then sinned yet further by taking their own lives."

It was a good starting-point from which to tell of the true and living God Who "gave His only begotten Son that whosoever believeth in Him should not perish but have everlasting life."

Again on the last Sunday in the year they were encouraged by really interested enquirers. Returning to their boats in the twilight after a long day's work ashore, Mr. Taylor found a young man waiting who had called several times previously. He seemed specially earnest that evening, and said:

"I have read seventeen chapters in the first book of the New Testament, and find it very good."

He was soon joined by a friend who had also heard a good deal of the Gospel, and together they listened seriously while Mr. Taylor applied the truth to their own lives. Before leaving they knelt in prayer, and the first of the two at any rate seemed not far from the Kingdom.

On New Year's day a good opportunity was found in the tea-shop of emphasising the difference between Buddhism and Christian faith and experience. Seated as usual at one of the little tables, Mr. Taylor was speaking with a good deal of liberty when a superior sort of man came and sat down beside him.

"Ah," he put in, "your doctrines—as to truth, they are true enough. But these people are Buddhists, and worship their meaningless idols. They will never believe you. Their hearts are in the midst of their internals; who is able to turn them about? It is a pity to waste time and strength on the *ü-min*, the stupid populace." [1]

"Alas," replied the missionary, "what you say is but too true. The religion of Jesus is indeed good, but you are wedded to your idols and cannot turn your hearts about, neither can I change them for you."

He then dwelt for a time upon the evils of Buddhism—which taught men to give to the work of their own hands the adoration due to God alone; which made it meritorious, as in the case of priests, to cease to care about their parents even if they were aged and in want; which forbade the eating of pork, but not the use of opium; prevented marriage, but not adultery; and taught that a bad man's soul might be released from hell if his friends would pay for the performance of certain rites, while a good man would be left to suffer if his family happened to be poor and could not give all the priests demanded.

"But though our sins are heavy," he continued, "and we can do nothing to put them away, the Lord Jesus is able to save to the uttermost, and the Holy Spirit can not only turn but *renew* our hearts. Confucius cannot do this; Buddha cannot do this; but the Lord Jesus can.

---

[1] Confucianists, *i.e.* scholarly men, affect to despise Buddhism and its grosser forms of idolatry, together with many superstitions of the uneducated.

And this is the religion that not only scholars but the poor and unlearned need."

"True, true," said the listeners, many of whom had been following every word, and the self-satisfied first speaker moved silently away.

It was the following day that returning to their boats after dark they met with unexpected encouragement. Accompanied by a group of friendly people Mr. Burns paused on the river-bank, talking with them long and earnestly before parting for the night.

"What do you think of it all?" said one man quietly to another. "Do you believe in this doctrine of Jesus?"

"Believe? I certainly believe!" replied his friend, little thinking of the joy with which Hudson Taylor overheard his answer.

Thus day after day the good seed was scattered, and though there was no immediate ingathering such as Mr. Burns had seen previously in the neighbourhood of Amoy, he and his companion could not but feel that their prayers were being answered for Nan-zin.

"I wish I could tell you of an outpouring of the Holy Spirit on this place," wrote Hudson Taylor to his sister. "The Lord has not been pleased to grant this. But there are many who have learned a good deal of the way of salvation, and some have bowed the knee with us in prayer, confessing that they believed in the truth of our teachings. As yet we have seen no deep conviction of sin, nor evidence of real change of heart. The seed when it is sown, however, rarely springs up at once. It often lies a winter, but harvest comes. So here, though we see not all we could wish at present, we know that our labour is ' not in vain in the Lord.' "

CHAPTER XXVIII

UNDER THE SHADOW OF THE ALMIGHTY

JANUARY 1856. AET. 23.

BLACK TOWN would have been the last place to include in their itinerary had they been considering personal comfort or safety. Half-way between two great cities [1] and near the border of the province it was a refuge for the unruly, many of whom were salt-smugglers of desperate character. But it was close at hand, only one day's journey from Nan-zin, and it had never yet been visited by messengers of the Prince of Peace. This in itself was sufficient to take our travellers thither, and though their visit was cut short by reason of serious danger, they were enabled to learn as well as teach important lessons.

Dropping anchor on Monday, January 7, near this important place (Wu-tien), they commenced work by distributing several hundreds of sheet-tracts in the outlying streets. This aroused considerable interest, and of the crowds that gathered round them Mr. Taylor was able to write: " I never spoke to more attentive audiences, nor saw such seriousness among the Chinese before."

Following the same plan as at Nan-zin, they visited the suburbs on the farther side of the town next morning, and selected a tea-shop for the purposes of a street-chapel. Not far from the boats a great concourse of people was addressed later in the day.

[1] The Fu cities of Hu-chow near the Great Lake and Ka-shing on the Grand Canal.

" The Lord graciously helped us," wrote Mr. Taylor, and we were heard with marked attention. In the evening we went to the tea-shop and found several persons waiting who had come expressly to meet us. Our lips were opened, and people listened with evident interest. . . . Some even seemed to believe, and nearly all approved, or seemed to approve, what we were teaching."

Encouraged by this good beginning the missionaries were looking forward to much blessing, when all unexpectedly troubles arose from which they were delivered only by a series of remarkable providences.

It began quite suddenly through the annoyance of a group of men, afterwards found to be salt-smugglers, who could not obtain all the books they wanted. Tracts and Gospels were given freely to those who could read, but, as elsewhere, they were withheld from wholly unlettered persons. This resulted in an attack upon the boats in which happily no one was injured, though one of the cabins was battered in.

As soon as quiet was somewhat restored, we all met in Mr. Burns' boat and joined in thanksgiving for our preservation, praying for the perpetrators of the mischief and that it might be over-ruled for good.

After lunch we went ashore, and but a few steps from the boats addressed a large concourse of people. We were conscious of being specially helped. Never were we heard with more attention, and not one voice was raised in sympathy with those who had molested us. In the evening the same spirit was manifested in the tea-shop, and some seemed to hear with joy the tidings of salvation through a crucified Redeemer.

Again on the following day (January 11) the Word was in power. Visited by two northern men, Mr. Taylor was greatly helped in telling them of Jesus. One did not pay much attention but the other did, asking question after question that showed the interest he was feeling. After they left him, the young missionary went on shore and in a garden full of mulberry-trees found a company of people to whom Kuei-hua had been speaking.[1]

[1] Ts'ien and Kuei-hua, Mr Taylor's valued helpers, had just rejoined him, having returned from their visit to the island of Hai-men. See Chap. XXVII. p. 341.

" The sun was just setting," he wrote, " and supplied me with a striking simile of life. . . . As I spoke of the uncertainty of its duration and the nearness of the Lord's return, deep seriousness prevailed. A Buddhist priest who was present was constrained afterwards to confess that Buddhism was a system of delusions and could give no peace in death. When I engaged in prayer all were silent and impressed, and my own soul was deeply moved with the solemnity of the scene."

Trouble was at hand, however, for the salt-smugglers were intent on getting more than a few books from the foreigners. On Saturday the 12th, fifty of these desperate characters assembled in a tea-shop near the river and sent one of their number, professing to be a constable, with a written demand for ten dollars and a pound of opium. If this were forthcoming the boats would be left in peace ; if not, fifty men were determined to destroy them before morning.

The day was already drawing in, and the missionaries had gone ashore to visit the farther end of the town. Sung, the teacher, was alone with the boat-people and, like them, not a little alarmed at the turn events were taking. Having no money and of course no opium, all he could do was to go in search of his employers, giving a hint to the boat-people to make the most of any opportunity to get away. Knowing that the missionaries had planned to preach in a tea-shop at the east end of the town, he set off on a walk of two miles or more to find them ; and the constable, quite willing to let him go alone, returned to report progress to those who had sent him.

Meanwhile Mr. Burns and Mr. Taylor had been led to change their plans. As they were going eastward it occurred to them that some interested inquirers might be expecting them at the usual meeting-place, and, under a strong impression that they should return at once, they retraced their steps to the tea-shop nearer the river. Thus Sung was not able to trace them, and while he was occupied in the search the boat-people had an opportunity to move quietly away.

For the night which had been fine and clear now became

intensely dark. Knowing it would be some time before Sung could return, the men who were awaiting the missionaries called for more tea, for which the foreigners were to pay to the extent of three hundred cash, and settled themselves down to smoke and play cards. Unobserved for the moment, and aided by the welcome darkness, the boats weighed anchor and moved off, one in one direction and one in another, so that if either were discovered and attacked the other might afford a refuge for the missionaries. This done the captain went ashore, and, keeping out of sight among the shadows, watched anxiously for his passengers.

And strange to say he had not long to wait. No one had come to the tea-shop to meet the missionaries, and the few people they found there were singularly inattentive. Earlier than usual Mr. Burns proposed returning to the boats, and, leaving Ts'ien and Kuei-hua to talk with any who desired it, they set out for the river, hoping to distribute their remaining tracts by the way. But the night was so dark that few people were on the streets, and for the first time since they arrived in Black Town no one followed them.

Thus when Mr. Burns' lantern appeared, the boatman found to his relief that the missionaries were alone. Going up to them he took the light and blew it out, instead of carrying it on in front as they expected. Surprised at the strangeness of his manner they would have relighted it, seeing which he removed the candle, threw it into the canal, and walked down in silence to the water's edge. Fearful lest he had lost his reason and might drown himself, Mr. Taylor ran forward to restrain him ; but, with a manner that effectually silenced them, the captain said that a number of men were intent on destroying the boats which had moved away to avoid them. He then cautiously led the way to where one of the boats were waiting. Before long Ts'ien and Kuei-hua were brought on board, and Sung also joining them they were able to move off in safety.

The meaning of the mystery was then explained, and with thankfulness each one of the little party realised that the Lord had been thinking upon them in that hour of danger. Sung especially was conscious of His providential care, for on reaching the place where the boats had been moored when he left them, he found a dozen or twenty men searching among the trees, and heard them asking with astonishment what could have become of the foreigners. They even inquired of him, not recognising who he was, and he was just as puzzled as they were to know where the boats could be. Happily he met one of the boatmen a little farther on, who, without word or sign, led him to his companions.

"After a while the boats joined company," wrote Mr. Taylor, "and rowed together quite a distance. It was already late, and to travel by night in that part of the country was not the way to avoid dangers, so the question arose as to what should be done. This we left the boat-people to decide. They had moved off of their own accord, and we felt that whatever we personally might desire, we could not constrain others to remain in a position of danger on our account. We urged them to do quickly whatever they thought of doing, as the morrow was the Lord's Day and we should not wish to travel. We also reminded them that wherever we were we must fulfil our mission, to preach the Gospel. It would make but little difference where we stayed, for even if we passed the night unperceived we were sure to be found out the following morning. Upon this the men concluded that they might as well return to the place from which we had started, a decision with which we fully agreed, and they turned back accordingly. But whether by accident or on purpose, they got into another stream, and rowed on for some time they knew not whither. At last as it was very dark they dropped anchor for the night.

We then called them all together with our native assistants and read the ninety-first Psalm. . . .

He that dwelleth in the secret place of the Most High
Shall abide under the shadow of the Almighty.
I will say of the Lord, He is my refuge and my fortress
My God, in Him will I trust. . . .

Thou shalt not be afraid for the terror by night, nor for the arrow that flieth by day. . . .

Because He hath set His love upon me, therefore will I deliver him.
I will set him on high, because he hath known My name.
He shall call upon Me and I will answer him
I will be with him in trouble :

I will deliver him and honour him.
With long life will I satisfy him, and show him My salvation.

Then committing ourselves to His care and keeping, Who had covered us with thick darkness and enabled us to escape the hand of violent men . . . we passed the night in peace and quietness, realising in some measure the truth of that precious Word, ' He is their help and their shield.'

The following morning I was awakened about 4 A.M. by violent pain in the knee-joint. I had bruised it the day before, and severe inflammation was the result. To my great surprise I heard the rain pouring down in torrents, the weather having previously been particularly fine. On looking out we found ourselves so near our former stopping-place that had nothing happened to prevent it we should have felt it our duty to go into the town to preach as usual. But the rain was so heavy all day long that no one could leave the boats, and much inquiry about us was also prevented. We thus enjoyed a delightful day of rest, such as we had not had for some time. Had the day been fine we should most likely have been discovered even if we had not left the boats ; but as it was we were left to think with wonder and gratitude of the gracious dealings of our God, who had indeed led us apart into a desert-place to rest awhile.

Monday was a cloudless morning and Mr. Burns was preparing to go ashore when one of the assistants, who had been early to fetch some clothing left with a laundress, returned with serious tidings. In spite of the drenching rain of Sunday the salt-smugglers had been seeking them in all directions, and unless they made good their escape the boats would certainly be found and broken to pieces.

Thoroughly alarmed, the boat-people would remain no longer in the neighbourhood of Wu-tien, and Mr. Taylor being quite unable to walk, the missionaries had no choice but to leave with them. This also seemed providential, for by evening it was evident that he was really ill and must return to Shanghai for rest and treatment. They had been absent already more than a month, and much as he regretted leaving Mr. Burns to continue the work alone, he did so in the assurance that :

Ill that God blesses is our good,
And unblest good is ill :
And all is right that seems most wrong,
If it be His sweet will.

CHAPTER XXIX

STEDFAST, UNMOVABLE

FEBRUARY–APRIL 1856   AET. 23.

IT was the middle of February, and Mr. Burns and Mr.
Taylor were again in Shanghai after some weeks' absence.
It had been a keen disappointment to them to leave the
neighbourhood of Wu-tien where the openings had seemed
so promising, and now they had returned from another
journey [1] to obtain fresh supplies and go back if possible
to that part of the country. But the Lord had other
plans in view.

" He was leading us," wrote Mr. Taylor, " by a way that we knew
not : but it was none the less His way."

> O Lord, how happy should we be
> If we would cast our care on Thee,
>   If we from self would rest ;
> And feel at heart that One above
> In perfect wisdom, perfect love,
>   Is working for the best.

Glad to be once more among fellow-missionaries, Mr. Burns
and Mr. Taylor had come up from their boats that wintry
night to the prayer-meeting at Dr. Medhurst's near the
British Consulate. This weekly gathering was a rendezvous
for all in Shanghai who cared about the Lord's work, and
on this occasion a Christian captain was present whose
vessel had just arrived from Swatow.

---

[1] This second campaign with Mr. Burns lasted between two and three
weeks. They left Shanghai for Sung-kiang Fu on January 28 or 29, returning about February 18, 1856. It was Mr. Taylor's Eleventh Evangelistic
Journey since reaching China.

His heart was unspeakably burdened with the condition of things in that southern port to which he carried cargo and passengers from time to time. An important and growing centre of commerce, it was the resort of increasing numbers of people greedy of gain and wholly unscrupulous in their ways of obtaining it. The opium trade and the equally iniquitous "coolie traffic" were carried on with shameless activity. Piracy flourished to such an extent that even Chinese merchants had taken to shipping their goods in foreign vessels that they might obtain the protection of British and other flags. Thus, although Swatow was not an open port and foreigners had no business to be there as far as treaty rights were concerned, quite a European settlement had sprung up, connived at by the local authorities. On Double Island, five miles out of Swatow, captains of opium-ships and other foreigners had bought land and built houses just as they might at Hong-kong, their presence, sad to say, only increasing the vices of this notoriously wicked place. And neither there nor in Swatow itself was there any witness for Christ or any influence that made for righteousness. No missionary, minister, or foreign lady was to be found nearer than Amoy, a hundred and fifty miles away ; and in the absence of family life, as well as the restraints of law and order, the condition of things was as bad as it could be.

From this place Captain Bowers had just come, and he could not but seek prayer on its behalf in the meeting at Dr. Medhurst's. In conversation afterwards, especially with Mr. Burns and Mr. Taylor, he urged the importance of Swatow as a centre for missionary operations. If merchants and traders could live there, of all nationalities, why should not ministers of the Gospel ? But the missionary who would pioneer his way amid such darkness must not be afraid, he said, to cast in his lot with " the off-scourings of Chinese society, congregated there from all the Southern ports." It was Wu-tien truly, but on a more desperate scale !

Silently that evening the friends returned to their boats, thinking of what they had heard. To Hudson Taylor, at any rate, the call of God had come while Captain Bowers was speaking, and he was struggling against rebellion of heart in view of the sacrifice involved.

"Never had I had such a spiritual father as Mr. Burns," he wrote long after; "never had I known such holy, happy intercourse; and I said to myself that it could not be God's will that we should separate."

Thus several days passed by, and he could not escape the conviction that Swatow was where the Lord would have him.

"In great unrest of soul," he continued, "I went with Mr. Burns one evening to visit some American friends near the South Gate of Shanghai [1] After tea, Mrs. Lowrie played over to us 'The Missionary Call.' I had never heard it before, and it greatly affected me. My heart was almost broken before it was finished, and I said to the Lord in the words that had been sung:

And I will go.
I may no longer doubt to give up friends and idol hopes,
And every tie that binds the heart . . .
Henceforth then it matters not if storm or sunshine be my
  earthly lot, bitter or sweet my cup;
I only pray, God make me holy, and my spirit nerve for the
  stern hour of strife.

"Upon leaving, I asked Mr. Burns to come to the little house that was still my headquarters, and there with many tears I told him how the Lord had been leading me, and how rebellious I had been, and unwilling to leave him for this new sphere. He listened with a strange look of surprise and pleasure rather than of pain, and replied that he had determined that very night to tell me that he had heard the Lord's call to Swatow, and that his one regret had been the severance of our happy fellowship."

Thus the Lord not only gave, but gave back, the companionship that meant so much in the life of Hudson Taylor. Together they went next morning to Captain Bowers and told him that the way seemed clear for them both to go to Swatow. So overjoyed was the captain to hear it that he offered them forthwith a free passage on his ship which was returning in a few days. This was gratefully accepted,

[1] The Rev. and Mrs. Robert Lowrie, of the American Presbyterian Mission

and on March 6, two years from Mr. Taylor's first arrival
in Shanghai, they sailed for their new field of labour.

Anchored in a fog that night off Gutzlaff Island, everything must have recalled to Hudson Taylor the February
Sunday when he first reached that spot.[1] Then he had
never seen the shores of China nor looked into the face of
any one belonging to that land. Now how familiar it had
grown! Many and varied had been his experiences, trans-
forming the lad fresh from the old country into a useful
missionary. At home in two dialects, one of which was the
language of four-fifths of China, he was about to learn a
third as an incident of his service. Seasoned as a good
soldier of the Cross by many a trial and hardship, he was
ready to stand alone in a peculiarly difficult sphere. War,
with all its horrors, prolonged distress through insufficient
supplies, the discipline of indebtedness to others, even for a
home, and then of loneliness in his own quarters, sickness,
change, uncertainty; and great discomfort as to material surroundings—all these had schooled his heart to quietness and
patience, and brought a deeper dependence upon God. And
then evangelistic journeys, alone or with other missionaries,
had greatly widened his outlook. Eleven such itinerations
now lay behind him within these first two years. How
much each one had meant, with its necessary exercise of
mind and heart, its strain upon endurance, dangers by
land and water, " perils in the city, . . . perils of robbers,
. . . labour and travail," and all its secret springs of faith
and prayer !

And now encouragement had come—all the more
precious for many a disappointment : some souls brought
into endless blessing through his ministry, nearness to the
people that made up for all the trial involved in wearing
native dress, and a friendship richer and deeper than any
he had given up or ever hoped to know. Freedom also as
to funds was a new and welcome experience. Friends
whom the LORD had raised up now helped so liberally that
for a good many months he had not needed to draw at all
upon the Letter of Credit from his society. Apart from

[1] February 26, 1854.

them, his needs were all supplied in a way that greatly strengthened his faith in God.[1]

In one thing only the years since he came to China seemed to have made no advance · he had still no home, no permanent work, no settled plans ahead. Where or how he was ultimately to labour was no more clear than it had been at the beginning. But the way of faith was clearer, and he had learned to leave the future in the hands of God. One who knew the end from the beginning was guiding and would guide. So a great rest had come about it all, and he was not concerned to make everything fit in. How this visit to Swatow would eventuate for him personally, how it would affect his life-work he could not tell. He only knew the Lord had set before him this open door, and he was growingly content to walk a step at a time.

> And feel at heart that One above
> In perfect wisdom, perfect love,
> Is working for the best.

" As to Swatow," he wrote just before leaving, " we go looking to the Lord for guidance and blessing. . . . As we are led, we shall return sooner or later or not at all. . . . Having no plans, we have none to tell. May the Lord be with us, bless us abundantly, and glorify His own great name. . . . Pray for us ; pray for us. You little know where or how we may be when you receive this note. Oh, pray that we may be kept from sin and used of God in the conversion of sinners."

Thus in prayer and faith they drew near the great province of Kwang-tung, and on March 12 anchored off Double Island a few miles from their destination. It would have been quite possible to settle here among other Europeans, and from comfortable headquarters to visit the

---

[1] " Faith looks to Jesus," he wrote in April of this year, " and walks the troubled sea in spite of winds and waves I understand that the funds of the Chinese Evangelisation Society were much reduced a short time ago, on account, I suppose, of the [Crimean] war It does not affect me, however, . . as I have not needed to draw on my Society for the last two quarters, and have now in hand enough for six months to come. Only by last mail a valued friend and devoted servant of Christ who has sent me one hundred pounds since last October, wrote urging me to tell him of any additional way in which he could forward the work by supplying the means. So as you truly say, if we are in the will of God, difficulty or trial as to circumstances cannot hinder us Nothing can by any means harm us or frustrate His designs."

mainland for their missionary operations. But such a plan had no attractions for either William Burns or Hudson Taylor. Avoiding all connections with the vice and luxury of the Settlement, they went on to Swatow itself, to seek a footing among the people they had come to reach. In this their Chinese dress was of great assistance; and though at first it seemed that not a corner could be found, prayer was again answered and their faith strengthened by one of those "chance providences" so often prepared for the children of God.

Situated on the delta of the Han between two of its principal channels, Swatow has little room to extend save by banking out its water-frontage, an operation in which hundreds of workmen were engaged. Houses were running up as rapidly as possible, for the supply was altogether unequal to the demand; and meanwhile the missionaries almost despaired of finding quarters.

After two days' fruitless search during which they were thankful for Captain Bowers' continued hospitality, they "happened" to meet a Cantonese merchant whom Mr. Burns addressed in his mother-tongue. Delighted at hearing excellent Cantonese from a foreigner, and a foreigner wearing Chinese dress, this gentleman interested himself on their behalf, and through a relative who "happened" to be the highest official in the town succeeded in securing them a lodging. It was not much of a place, it is true, just a single room over an incense-shop in a crowded quarter, but how glad they were to take possession before Captain Bowers had to sail for Singapore!

That it did not meet with their kind friend's approval is hardly to be wondered at. Great was his love and admiration for Mr. Burns, and he could not bear to leave him in such surroundings. Of his visit to the incense-shop he wrote to a mutual friend, Mrs. Barbour of Bonskeid:

Seeking out his wretched lodging in Swatow amongst the degraded of every class, I remarked, "Surely, Mr. Burns, you might find a better place to live in!" He laughingly told me that he was more content in the midst of this people than he would be at home surrounded with every comfort. He said his expenses amounted to ten dollars a month. "Mr. Burns," I exclaimed, "that would not keep me in cigars!" He said it was sufficient for him.

But to the missionaries themselves, ten dollars a month and a single room, into which they had to climb through an opening in the floor, did not seem so bad. It was in touch with the people, that was the chief thing, and they were very conscious that the Lord was with them. The single room they divided as well as they could into three tiny apartments—two running east to west, and one north and south, which included the hole in the floor.

"My bedroom is on the south," Mr. Taylor explained in his first home-letter. "Mr. Burns takes the north side, and the strip on the west we use as our study. The partitions are made of sheets and a few boards. . . . We have only just obtained exclusive possession,[1] a passage having been needed for the landlord's family until alterations were made in the house. We are promised a trap-door next week, and then shall have more privacy.

"Our beds are a few deal boards, and our table the lid of a box supported on two bags of books. We may get a better some day, but nothing of that sort is to be bought ready-made in Swatow. So for the present, at an outlay of two hundred and thirty cash [one shilling and a penny], we have completely furnished the house—with two bamboo stools and a bamboo easy-chair."

Here, then, amongst the worst and lowest, the little seed was planted that was to result in the abundant harvest seen to-day.[2] Years before, a solitary missionary had laboured there in face of overwhelming odds. Driven from place to place he had widely itinerated in the surrounding country, living a life of Christlike patience and love.[3] But

---

[1] Written on March 29, after they had occupied the room for two weeks.

[2] Although in the first five years after Mr. Burns commenced work in Swatow only thirty-nine converts were received into church fellowship, more than 4400 adults have been baptized since that time in connection with the English Presbyterian Mission alone, of whom 2700 are actual communicants to-day (1911). A strong native ministry has been developed which is now entirely supported by the native Church.

[3] This devoted servant of God, the Rev. R. Lechler, was sent out by the Basel Missionary Society in 1846, and with the Rev. Th. Hamburg was the first representative of the Society in China. Mr. Lechler went to Swatow in 1848, and did not retire from that difficult field until obliged to do so in 1852. For more than fifty years he was almost continuously at work in China, witnessing the development of a Church which now numbers, by the blessing of God, over 5700 communicants.

from the time that Mr. Lechler had been driven back to Hong-kong, no one had taken his place, and Swatow had remained without testimony to the Gospel.

His knowledge of Cantonese enabled Mr. Burns to make himself understood from the first, and greatly helped him in acquiring the local speech. For his companion this was a much more serious matter. They had not been long in Swatow, however, before they both felt that so important a centre must never again be left unoccupied, and as the only way to usefulness was to be able to talk freely with the people, Mr. Taylor set himself once more to study.

" There is plenty of work to be done," he wrote to his mother soon after their arrival, " but I cannot do it. It is a great trial after being able to speak freely to begin again in a place where one cannot understand a single sentence. But if only we are used here, what a privilege is ours ! All my previous experience I find of the greatest value, for one without knowledge of Chinese, dressed as a foreigner, and unaccustomed to living as we do among the people would not be able to stay on at all. . . . How gracious the Lord is and how wonderful His ways ! . . . Pray for me, and do not be uneasy about me. The Lord will undertake."

If his mother and friends could have realised the conditions under which he was living, they would have felt more concern at this time than probably they did. For Swatow was a dangerous as well as difficult field. Two great evils already mentioned flourished under the protection of foreigners, and made the very sight of a European odious to the people.

" About two hundred boxes of opium are imported monthly," Mr. Taylor stated in the same letter ; " each box contains forty balls of about four pounds in weight. Thus not less than thirty-two thousand pounds weight of opium enter China every month at this port alone, the cost of which is about a quarter of a million sterling. After this you will not be surprised to learn that the people are wretchedly poor, ignorant, and vicious.

" A cruel slave trade also is carried on under the name of the ' coolie traffic.' The men are engaged (nominally) for a certain term of years, but few live to return. A bounty is paid them, and they are told that they are going to make their fortunes, or they are entrapped by worse means. Once on the ship the agent receives so much a head for the poor fellows who soon find themselves in captivity of the most horrible kind. Some jump overboard in their efforts to escape, but they are generally retaken and flogged. Some ships carry a thousand and others three or four hundred, and very many die before reaching their destination—Cuba, Havanna and Callao. . . . Of one ship with several hundreds on board, I heard the surgeon say that not more than two-thirds would survive the voyage. Poor people ! ONE only is able to help them. Oh, for His blessing ! "

It was little wonder under such circumstances, and with many of the traders of Double Island living lives worse than those of the heathen, that the missionaries endeavouring to obtain a foothold in Swatow should be regarded with hatred, suspicion, and scorn. But it was a painful experience none the less, and as new to Mr. Burns as to Hudson Taylor.

" The people have no love for foreigners," wrote the latter, " and we never go out without being insulted and laughed at.[1] . . . I think I never was in such a wicked place. . . . Pray much for us, that we may have grace and patience, and strength of body and mind to pass through all unharmed and even find it a blessing."

In towns and villages at a little distance a more friendly spirit was manifested, but the same poverty and degradation prevailed, and the people were so turbulent that those who went amongst them had to face constant danger. In their visits to the country the missionaries were liable to be seized at any moment and held to ransom, and they frequently heard the saying that the whole district was " without Emperor, without rulers, and without law." One small town in which they were preaching had recently captured a wealthy man belonging to a neighbouring clan. Refusing to pay the exorbitant sum demanded for his release, he had been subjected to cruel tortures, his ankle-bones finally being smashed with a club, after which his tormentors succeeded in obtaining all they desired.

" There was nothing but the protection of God," wrote Hudson Taylor, " between us and the same sort of treatment. The towns were all walled, many of them containing ten or twelve thousand

---

[1] The usual term " Foreign Devil " was here reinforced by more offensive epithets, " Foreign Dog," " Foreign Pig " and worse, hissed out with bitterest scorn.

people who might be and frequently were at war with a neighbouring town. To be kindly received in one place was often a source of danger in the next. But amid such circumstances the preserving care of our God was the more manifest."

Trusting in His unfailing presence, the missionaries were enabled to go on stedfastly through all, embracing many opportunities for bringing light into the darkness. Mr. Burns frequently visited Double Island, holding services in English that were well attended, and Mr. Taylor, whenever he could spare a day from study, joined him in expeditions to the surrounding country.

One such journey together toward the end of March brought them to a busy place called Hwa-wu, where they came across an old farmer who could read intelligently. Failing any other teacher, they were glad to secure his services, and for the local dialect could hardly have wished a better. Talking and reading with him for several hours daily, Mr. Taylor made such rapid progress that by the middle of April he was able to undertake a little work on his own account.

"The country is very beautiful," he wrote. "Fine ranges of hills enclose fertile valleys, watered by many channels through which the Han empties itself into the sea. I have been out to-day (April 17) with my servant for a little air and exercise. . . . After climbing several hills and getting a good idea of the neighbourhood we went to the first village I have visited alone. Great is the change that has taken place in three and a half weeks! When we first came into this district, I could understand nothing. Now, by the blessing of God, I am able to talk a little as well as understand a good deal. As we had books with us, I asked if there were a teacher in the village and a school.

"'No,' said an elderly man who had just left his work in the fields to join us. 'Last year we had one, but now we are too poor. We have scarcely clothes to cover us.' And he pointed to the only garment he was wearing, a very small and scanty pair of trousers.

"'If you would not smoke opium,' I answered, 'and spend so much money worshipping dead relatives, and the Queen of Heaven and other idols, you would be far better off than you are at present. You hope to be preserved, enriched, and prospered, but evidently you are disappointed. Your idols have eyes, but do they see? They have ears, but can they hear when you pray? They have mouths, but do they speak ? Can they preserve you from robbers, from quarrels, sickness, or disaster ? '

" ' True ! True ! ' some replied. ' They are certainly not much use.'

" I then went on to tell them of the living God, the great Father they ought to worship, who had made heaven, earth, man, and all things, and would forgive their sins, for Jesus' sake, if they would turn to Him. Believing in this precious Saviour, I told them, they would find peace in life or death, and possess a *satisfying* portion.

" Some thirty or forty people, besides children, listened under the shade of a magnificent banyan tree, and seemed friendly. But very few could read. So that had it not been for junks on the river most of my stock of books would have returned with me."

These visits to the country were helpful and refreshing in spite of attendant danger, especially as the heat of summer came on. Even in May it was intensely hot, and Mr. Taylor wrote that sitting quietly at study he had to keep a towel by him to wipe the perspiration streaming from face and hands. Oh, those little rooms under the naked tiles, how they did glow in the pitiless glare of the sun ! They would have been unbearable during the day-time but that Mr. Taylor rigged up a sort of punkah to stir the air a little and give relief. Mr. Burns, already accli-matised to a southern summer, was able to be out at all hours without danger, but his companion suffered seriously. Still, right on into June, he worked with unremitting diligence, eating hardly anything till evening came, when, with the help of a breeze that usually sprang up, they made their evening meal.

But more distressing than the heat, harder to bear than sleepless nights and all the weariness their work involved, was the sin and suffering that surged around them.

" If ever there were a place needing the blessings of the Gospel," Hudson Taylor wrote to his sister, " it is certainly this place. Men are sunk so low in sin as to have lost all sense of shame, . . . lower even than the beasts that perish. The official classes are as bad as the rest, and instead of restraining evil are governed themselves by opium and love of money. And if it be possible to live worse lives than the heathen, then the sailors and others who frequent Double Island carry off the palm. There may be exceptions, so I had better say at once that there probably are, but I do not know of any save Dr. De la Porte [1] who is there just now. . . .

" Sin does indeed reign here, and, as always, those most to be pitied and whose case seems most hopeless are the women. However low men sink in heathen lands, women sink lower. Looked upon as hardly having any soul, girls are sold here for wives or slaves, and are left entirely without education. Married women and families are not numerous in proportion to the population, but the number of unfortunate women is very great. I say unfortunate advisedly, for they are bought and brought up for this very purpose. They are the absolute property of their owners, and have no escape from that which many of them abhor. Only a few nights ago I was distressed by heart-rending screams from two female voices, and, on inquiring, was told that they were most likely newly bought women in a house near by, who were being tortured into submission. ' And that,' added my informant, ' is very common here.' The cries went on for about two hours. Poor things ! poor things !

" This is hardly a fit subject to write to you about, but, unless you know, how can you pity and pray for them ? English women little realise all they owe to the Gospel. And how few have love enough for Christ to come out here and seek to save the perishing ! It does mean sacrifice ; but low as they would have to stoop, Jesus stooped lower."

Here, then, amid such surroundings, he quietly endured week after week, month after month, drawing his strength from God. Frequently separated from Mr. Burns for the work's sake he was much alone. Keenly the people watched him coming and going from the incense-shop, and inquired into every detail of his life and doings. It was an open life, lived within sight of his neighbours all day long—a life whose love and purity told on their sad, dark hearts far more than he had any idea. Three years later in London, at the Annual Meeting of the Society to which Mr. Taylor belonged, Dr. De la Porte from Double Island was one of the speakers.

He had had the pleasure and honour, he said, of an intimate acquaintance with one of the agents of the Society, labouring at the time in Swatow—a Mr. Hudson Taylor, to whose zeal and devotion he could bear the most cordial testimony.

He had seen that young man come home at the close of the day

---

[1] A Christian man, who entertained the warmest friendship for Mr. Taylor and Mr. Burns, and subsequently joined the latter as a medical missionary in Swatow.

footsore and weary, his face covered with blisters from the heat of the sun, and throw himself down to rest in a state of utter exhaustion, only to rise again in a few hours to the toil and hardship of another day. It had been very evident that he enjoyed the highest respect from the Chinese, and was doing a great amount of good among them. His influence was like that of a fragrant flower, diffusing the sweetness of true Christianity around him.

Among the bright spots in his life at Swatow this summer were the red-letter days when the mail arrived from home. Always eagerly welcomed it had now an added value, cut off as they were in large measure from the outside world. Some mails even there would come in without any tidings from those he loved, but others made up for the disappoint-ment by spreading before him a feast that made him forget his surroundings. Such for example was the April day on which he wrote to his sister :

The mail has just arrived from Shanghai, bringing amongst others your letters of two months, one from Mr. Broomhall, two from mother, and one with an enclosure from Mr. Berger.

All letters of special interest.

Those from his mother and sister, as it happened, brought their first comments on his adoption of the native dress, and to his surprise they did not like it. So conscious had he been of its advantages, that he had almost forgotten how it might appear to them. They could not bear to think of his shaven head, blue cotton gown, and Chinese appearance.

" I am sorry that the change is disagreeable to you," he wrote in answer, " but you will regret it very little when you learn that without it we could never have gained a footing in this important place. . . .

" A little thought will, I am sure, enable you to realise that if the Chinese costume seems so barbarous to us, our English dress must be no less so to them, and that it cannot but be a hindrance in going amongst them in the friendly way necessary to securing their confidence and affection. . . . Without it we could not stay on here a single day. That Miss —— does not like it I am very sorry to hear, but that does not make me regret that I have adopted it. It is one of those matters about which I and my devoted companion, Mr. Burns, thank God almost every day "

But his disappointment over their feeling in this matter was soon lost sight of in the all-important news contained in these letters. Could it be—his own dearest sister and friend, in a sense going from him to another, a deeper love ? And yet the thought was not new to him, and there was no one to whom he would more gladly have given her. A letter from Mr. Broomhall made it pretty clear that matters would soon be settled between them, and all the far-away brother could do was to write his heartfelt congratulations.

A little later, he learned that they were not only engaged, but thinking of China, and the hope grew strong that they might become his fellow-workers. He had written to Mr. Broomhall several times already on the subject, and now mentioned it again in a June letter to his sister. The prospect was a delightful one, but knowledge of his own heart taught him how easily they might be misled by natural inclinations.

" I long for you to be working here," he wrote, " not for my sake only, but for Jesus' sake, and for the sake of the poor Chinese. Look to the Lord for guidance, and see your way very clearly as to the will of God before you leave dear mother. If you do come, let it not be to live with or near me. If God grant it we shall be very thankful ; if not we must be submissive. What He is training me for I cannot tell. May it be for His glory. You will not imagine from this that my love to you is in any way lessened. What I do want you to do is—to give up all to the Lord. And the more fully you do that the more He will give you back again, yes, more by far than you ever gave up for Him. May He guide and bless you for Jesus' sake."

To a friend in need of guidance he also wrote in a similar strain :

Light will no doubt be given you. Do not forget, however, in seeking more, the importance of walking according to the light you have. If you feel called to the work, do not be anxious as to the time and way. He will make it plain. . . I desire increasingly to leave all my affairs in the hands of God, who alone can, and who assuredly will, lead us aright if humbly and in faith we seek His aid. . . .

I am sure you will forgive me if I urge on you, as I have on Amelia, the importance of seeking guidance from God for yourself personally, apart from the movements of others. Each one of us has an individual duty and responsibility toward Him The conduct of others cannot make duty, for me, of that which is not so ; nor can the claims of duty be lessened because of the action, right or wrong, of others. We may and should thank God for all the help He gives us through others in the performance of duty. But let us seek to see our own way clearly in the light of His will, and then in trial and perplexity we shall be " stedfast, unmovable," not having trusted to an arm of flesh. The Lord guide and bless you, and give you ever to lean unshaken on His faithfulness.

CHAPTER XXX

ON WHOM THE MANTLE FELL

June–July 1856. Aet. 24.

Six months of intercourse with William Burns had now gone by, and little as either of them expected it they were nearing the close of their helpful, happy fellowship. To them it seemed on the contrary that their work together was only just beginning. The needs around them were so great and the help they were to one another so evident that they could not but look forward to doing something really adequate together by the blessing of God for the important region to which He had called them. But Swatow was only one needy field out of the vast whole of unreached China. For that wider work to be done the Lord was making preparation, as well as for widespread blessing in the region He had specially laid upon their hearts. William Burns for Swatow and other strategic points in the great seaboard provinces, and Hudson Taylor, by and by, for far-reaching inland China :—such was the purpose of Him who sees the end from the beginning. So the days of their pilgrimage together drew to a close, filled as all that went before had been with helpful fellowship in the Lord.

By this time it was the middle of June, and more than ever trying in the little rooms over the incense-shop. It seemed really imperative to get other quarters ; and as this was out of the question in Swatow, they extended the search to neighbouring towns and villages.

" It is much more difficult to itinerate here than it was around Shanghai," Hudson Taylor wrote to his father on June 16. " There the boat one travelled in supplied a home. Here it is not so, excepting in places so near at hand that we should naturally return at night. You must go in most cases on foot, not knowing where or how you will pass the night, and ready to take such accommodation as may offer. It is, of course, an entirely new line of things to me . . . and requires far more faith and self-denial than anything I have hitherto known. But we have the promise that His grace shall be sufficient for us, and we know that in our weakness He will perfect His strength."

All this was of the greatest importance for one who was to be the leader of an evangelistic, pioneering mission. It was needful that he should have a practical, intimate knowledge of many phases of life and work ; and to this end his Swatow experiences were " well and wisely chosen," difficult as they seemed at the time.

On one of these overland journeys, for example, he was brought to the point of having nowhere at all to shelter for the night, a serious position in China. It was in the little town of T'o-p'u, whither he had gone on May 20 to take possession of a cottage they had been enabled to rent. One room below and one above, in the more open surroundings of this country place, promised welcome relief from their overcrowded city quarters. But all unwittingly they were reckoning without their host. For the landlord who had been willing to have them the day before met Mr. Taylor on his arrival saying :

" Go back, go back at once ! My neighbours will not allow me to let you have the house."

A moment's prayer, however, satisfied Mr. Taylor that he must not go back, and dismissing his boat accordingly he went about his Master's business. His servant, who knew the character of the Tie-chiu [1] people, kept asking anxiously :

" What will you do ? Where shall we go when darkness comes on ? We cannot stay out all night." [2]

---

[1] Dialect for Ch'ao-chow, the name of the Prefecture of which Swatow is the commercial centre

[2] On account of danger from evil men, not to mention the malarial climate.

" Never fear," was the quiet answer , " the Lord knows
and He will provide."

So in temple and tea-shop and along the busy streets,
the young missionary gave books to all who could read
them and delivered his message. Rarely had his heart
been so filled with the joy of the Lord in this work, and
the people noticed it.

" Where are you going to sleep," they asked, as the
inwardness of the situation became generally known.

" That I cannot tell you," he frankly replied. " But my
Heavenly Father knows. He is everywhere present, and
never forgets the needs of His people. Nor does He ever
leave them unsupplied."

" Are you not anxious lest you should get into trouble ? "

" No, I am not anxious," he could truly say with a smile.
" My heart is in perfect peace, because the Lord will provide."

" And so it proved," his own letter continued. " I went on distributing books and talking with the people until dark, and then was
invited to sleep over a barber's shop the owner of which was a Ha-ka
man. Some *congee* (rice and water gruel) was prepared, and of this
we made our supper. . . .

" In the evening a great many people came to see me, one man
bringing a present of two very pretty, fragrant flowers. I pointed out
to my visitors that the beauty and sweetness of these flowers was
given them by God ; that birds and insects are all cared for by Him ;
that the many blessings enjoyed even by those who knew Him not,
and sin against Him by worshipping idols, the work of their own hands,
are still given and continued by His grace ; and how much more may
the children of this Heavenly Father look to Him with confidence,
knowing He will supply their every need in life, in death, and in the
world to come ? I was much blessed in soul and greatly helped in
testifying to the love and care of God.

" ' It is curious,' one man remarked, ' how he speaks of God in connection with all things.'

" Poor people ! Truly of them it may be said, ' God is not in all
their thoughts.' "

But the little town of T'o-p'u had the opportunity at
this time of really understanding the message that had
awakened so much interest. For Mr. Burns came over
the next day and stayed almost a fortnight, though his
companion had to return to Swatow.

Later in the month (June) two Chinese Christians joined them, sent by a missionary friend at Hong-kong. They were natives of the Tie-chiu district, and after a brief visit to their homes up-country were to remain with and assist Mr. Burns who was greatly needing such helpers. And the first work with which he entrusted them was the search for a room that could be used for a " street-chapel." As natives of the place he knew they were more likely to be successful than foreigners ; but do what they would, no premises of any kind could be obtained.

Realising afresh through this unsuccessful search the value of the footing they had obtained, Mr. Burns and his companion were more than ever thankful for their little home over the incense-shop, in spite of discomforts that only seemed to multiply with the heat of summer. Some idea of these minor trials may be obtained from a lively passage in a letter from Hudson Taylor to his younger sister, written about this time

SWATOW, *June* 9, 1856.

MY DEAR LOUISA—I must try to answer your note by this mail, or run the risk of leaving it undone. And this I hope to accomplish, if the mosquitoes, flies, cockroaches (two inches long and flying about in all directions), centipedes, lizards, crickets, fleas and all the rest of the tormentors will allow.

While writing these few lines, I have made one successful and two unsuccessful attacks upon as many fleas, so you may imagine how plentiful they are ! Sometimes I stop in the middle of a sentence, catch three or four of these unwelcome visitors, kill a few cockroaches and then go on again. The other night I felt something very strange inside my Chinese garments, and on looking to see what it was, found a centipede two or three inches long ! It bit me severely before I could eject it, and the place swelled up and was very painful ; but I applied carbonate of ammonia with immediate relief. The people of the house made a great stir about it (these bites are very venomous) and soon brought in a hen ! for what purpose I do not know. . . . But I sent the poor creature away, explaining the virtues of my white powder, at which they looked respectfully enough. It was well that I had some. Father's medicine-chest has been about the most valuable thing I brought to China. . .

The rest of the letter is in a more serious strain, for the

spiritual welfare of this dear sister was much upon his heart. She was just leaving school to take up the more leisurely life of home, and as he thought of the opportunities and special dangers this would present, he longed to safeguard her as well as at that distance he was able.

" If you want blessing," he had written in an earlier letter, " ' seek . . . first the Kingdom of God and His righteousness,' and you will be on the high road to all other good. Some people forget this and seek happiness in the world, but it eludes their grasp. . . . They think, plan, contrive, and try this means and that, but get no nearer the mark. While there are others who, seeking nothing for themselves, have joy and peace poured into their hearts. For they put *first* ' the Kingdom of God and His righteousness,' and ' all these things ' are ' added to them ' This I have proved by my own experience, and I can assure you that so it is.

" Pray earnestly, perseveringly, till your prayers are answered, to be truly made a child of God. Then remember you are His . . . but still a child. Your Father knows best where you should be and how. So ask to do His will as the true, the only way to happiness and content. Remember too, when saved you are His servant. All you possess is His. Use it as such. . . . If as His servant you are true to Christ, He as your Master will provide for you and that liberally. It is the Principal of any concern who has the burden of responsibility. So avoid seeking to be head. . . . Be the servant and child in all things. . . . Look for guidance, and commit your way unto the Lord. Thus you will prosper in temporal as in spiritual things, and avoid those grinding cares which wear one down more than actual labour, and sometimes make life itself a burden. And remember to pray for your absent brother, who finds it much easier to tell you what to do than to act it out himself. But he does try to do so, and can tell you that he has never tried altogether in vain, for if he has not come up to the mark he is always blessed in his own soul for trying."

Another paragraph from the same letter is well worth quoting.

There is one thing I would specially warn you against . . . one of the greatest curses I believe of the present day—the practice of novel-reading. If you value your mind and soul, avoid it as you would a dangerous serpent. I cannot tell you what I would give to be able to forget certain novels I have read and to efface their influence from my memory. And I firmly believe, though some would deny it, . . . that no Christian ever did or ever will read them without injury, . . . very serious injury too, if the habit is indulged in. It is like opium-smoking, and begets a craving for more that must be supplied. Better books are neglected, and no one can estimate the mischief that results. Few, I believe, could honestly ask God's blessing upon the reading of a novel, and few would venture to assert that they read them to the glory of God. I dread them for you especially as a temptation to which you are constitutionally disposed . . . for you and I resemble one another very much as to temperament. . . . The only safety lies in avoiding them as one of Satan's most subtle snares.

I often fear that while I may be remembered by you as your brother the missionary in China, you will not feel towards me as to one who has a deep, a constant, and increasing interest in your welfare. . . . May God bless you, my dearly-beloved and often prayed-for sister, and make you all that He Himself would have you be. Good-night, my oil is done. Once more, God bless you.

This was the summer of the disastrous floods, when in the low-lying parts of the Tie-chiu district several cities were inundated and more than two hundred towns and villages. The rice crop, just ready for reaping, was swept away in many places by the tremendous rush of water, that even unearthed coffins and carried them out to sea. Not a few lives were lost, and the distress among all classes was very great. Mr. Burns returned in the middle of June from the neighbouring town of Am-po, where he had been living for ten days. He only came just in time, for the house he had been enabled to rent was flooded breast-high the following day.

He had had an encouraging stay in this busy, important place, a larger town than Swatow though not so crowded. Not only was there a constant stream of visitors coming for books and conversation, but several interested neighbours were regularly attending morning and evening worship. The change back to Swatow was not a little trying, especially as the continued downpour prevented outside work. But it gave a welcome opportunity for prayer and conference over many problems connected with their position.

By the close of the week Mr. Taylor was far from well. The close confinement to their narrow quarters was telling upon him, especially when—with their servants and two native helpers—they were "so thick on the ground" as he expressed it.

" The dark, rainy weather has a depressing effect on one's spirits," he wrote. " I do not feel very well, but trust that in a few days a change of weather will put things right and let me go on with my work again."

Brighter days came and Mr. Burns was able to return to Am-po with his Chinese helpers, but not until it had become evident that he must bid farewell to his English companion for a time. The greatest heat of summer was still before them, and Mr. Taylor was in no condition to meet it under existing circumstances. Providential indications also were not lacking that for the good of the work he ought to pay a visit to Shanghai.

Disappointed as they were about premises for a chapel, their thoughts had naturally turned to other methods of evangelisation. The people of Swatow were far too suspicious of foreigners to let them have a room for nothing but preaching. How could any one be willing to pay the rent of a shop merely to have a place for talking in about religious doctrines ? Clearly there must be something behind such a proceeding. But premises for medical work would be quite another matter. The foreign doctor was always *persona grata*, and if he must tell more or less about his religion—well, his medicines were so good that the preaching could be tolerated.

This being so even in Swatow, Mr. Burns and Mr. Taylor had almost decided to begin hospital work, or at any rate to open a dispensary. They were still praying about it, wondering whether the latter should take the long journey to Shanghai to fetch his instruments and medicines, when the chief Mandarin of the place was taken ill and the native doctors were unable to relieve him. Hearing from a friend that one of the foreigners in native dress was a skilful physician, he sent for Hudson Taylor and put the case into his hands. The treatment proved beneficial, and no sooner was he well himself than he strongly advised his benefactor to commence medical work in Swatow for the assistance of other sufferers. This seemed very like the guidance they were seeking, especially when the Mandarin, in the grateful spirit so characteristic of his people, under-

THE REV. WILLIAM C. BURNS, M.A., OF THE ENGLISH PRESBYTERIAN MISSION.

"In stature he was about middle height, of strong, muscular and well-knit frame, and with a ruddy, pleasant countenance, which is but faintly recalled by the worn and aged features of his Chinese picture, but which doubtless shall reappear in glorified form when He comes again who maketh all things new."—*Picture and quotation from the "Memoir" of Mr. Burns, by his brother.*

To face page 381.

took to help them about premises. Backed by his approval
they were soon enabled to rent the entire house in which
they had hitherto occupied a single room, which gave them
the advantage of beginning in a neighbourhood in which
they were already known and respected.

As though the shadow of a longer parting lay upon his
heart, Hudson Taylor was very reluctant, even then, to
leave his loved and honoured friend. But when just at this
juncture a free passage was offered him all the way to
Shanghai by an English captain, the matter seemed taken
out of his hands. Mr. Burns would not be left alone or
without fellow-workers. One of the native Christians
would assist him in Swatow, and one at Am-po and in the
country districts. It really seemed, at last, as though the
way were opening before them, and all they needed was
the medical outfit waiting in Shanghai to enable them to
enter upon fruitful labours.

And so early in July the parting came ; and full of
thankfulness for the past and hope for greater blessing in
the days to come they committed one another to the care
and keeping that had never failed them hitherto.

" Those happy months were an unspeakable joy and comfort to
me," wrote Hudson Taylor long after, looking back upon the companionship thus ended with William Burns. " His love for the Word was
delightful, and his holy, reverential life and constant communings
with God made fellowship with him satisfying to the deep cravings
of my heart. His accounts of revival work and of persecutions in
Canada, Dublin, and Southern China were most instructive as well as
interesting ; for with true spiritual insight he often pointed out God's
purposes in trial in a way that made all life assume quite a new aspect
and value. His views especially about evangelism as the great work of
the Church, and the order of lay-evangelists as a lost order that Scripture required to be restored, were seed-thoughts which were to prove
fruitful in the subsequent organisation of the China Inland Mission."

For, in the providence of God, they never met again.
All unexpectedly Hudson Taylor found his path diverging
from that of his friend. Dark clouds were gathering over
Southern China, soon to lead to war. On a boat near
Swatow Mr. Burns was taken prisoner and sent under escort,
by river and canal, a journey of thirty-one days to Canton

and the nearest British authorities. Returning to Swatow some months later he was enabled to take advantage of the growing feeling in his favour to establish a permanent work. Known as " The Man of the Book," he was allowed to go in and out freely, the trusted friend of the people, when all other Europeans were confined to their houses and in considerable danger on account of the iniquities of the coolie traffic , and the Swatow Mission of the English Presbyterian Church flourishes to-day as an outcome of those early labours.

Passing on to other fields when initial difficulties were conquered, Mr. Burns was led to Peking at length, and there spent four years in literary and evangelistic work. And then, true to the commanding vision of his life, the veteran missionary turned his face once more to the " regions beyond." North of the Great Wall and stretching far away—an almost unknown world—lay the fair and fruitful plains of Manchuria. A few foreigners were living at the Treaty Port, but as yet no minister or missionary was among their number.[1] Alone, with a single native helper, Mr. Burns set out for Newchwang, his life and teachings so impressing the captain of the junk on which they travelled that he would take no fare from the man whose very presence seemed a blessing.

Then came the closing days, setting the seal of God's own benediction upon this life of singular devotion. Four months of earnest, pioneering work—preaching in English on Sundays to the handful of fellow-countrymen in the Settlement, and in Chinese all through the week in the native quarter in which he lived—and after that an illness, the result as it seemed of chill, brought the quiet, unexpected end.[2]

[1] One missionary journey had been made in Manchuria some time previously, that of Dr. Alexander Williamson, who as Agent of the Scottish Bible Society traversed this important region between the years 1866 and 1868, even reaching a point—San-sin, on the Sungari river—which the Church has not yet overtaken   See *A Century of Missions in China*, p. 206.
[2] The Rev. Wm C Burns passed away on April 4, 1868, just two years after the formation of the China Inland Mission which he had watched with the warmest interest

To the far-away homeland he sent as his last message an appeal to take up the work he was thus laying down ; an appeal nobly responded to by

Alone among the Chinese to the last, planting with his dying hand the standard of the Cross far afield amid the darkness, gathering round it those whose hearts the Lord had opened—a little company, loved, prayed for, taught, and comforted almost to his latest breath, who watching beside him as he passed through the valley learned not only how a Christian should live, but also how he can die— what could be more after the pattern of his whole life, more in keeping with his heart's desire ?

As gazed the prophet on the ascending car,
Swept by its fiery steeds away, afar,
So with the burning tear and flashing eye,
I trace thy glorious pathway to the sky.
Lone like the Tishbite, as the Baptist bold,
Cast in a rare and apostolic mould ,
Earnest, unselfish, consecrated, true,
With nothing but the highest ends in view ;
Choosing to toil in distant fields, unsown,
Contented to be poor and little known,
Faithful to death . Oh, man of God, well done !
Thy fight is ended and thy crown is won.

God shall have all the glory.   Only grace
Made thee to differ.   Let us man abase !
Deep, with emphatic tone, thy dying word,
Thy last was this · " Thine is the kingdom, Lord,
The power and glory ! "   Thus the final flame
Of the burnt offering to Jehovah's Name
Ascended from the altar   Life thus given
To God, must have its secret springs in heaven.

Oh, William Burns, we will not call thee dead !
Though lies thy body in its narrow bed
In far-off China   Though Manchuria keeps
Thy dust, which in the Lord securely sleeps,
Thy spirit lives with Jesus , and where He
Thy Master dwells, 'tis meet that thou shouldst be.
There is no death in His divine embrace ;
There is no life but where they see His face.

the arrival of the first representative of the Irish Presbyterian Mission in the following year, and of the sister Church in Scotland three years later.   The united Irish and Scotch Presbyterian Missions in Manchuria (one Chinese Church) now number no fewer than 16,075 actual communicants, with a missionary staff of sixty-nine Europeans.   Thus blessedly has the confidence of William Burns been justified : " God," he said, " will carry on the good work.   Ah, no, I have no fears for that ! "

And now, Lord, let Thy servant's mantle fall
Upon another   Since Thy solemn call
To preach the Truth in China has been heard,
Grant that a double portion be conferred
Of the same spirit on the gentler head
Of some Elisha—who may raise the dead
And fill the widow's cruse, and heal the spring,
And make the desolate of heart to sing ,
And stand, though feeble, fearless, since he knows
Thy hosts angelic guard him from his foes ,

Whose life an image fairer still may be
Of Christ of Nazareth and Galilee,
Of Thine, oh, spotless Lamb of Calvary !

China, I breathe for thee a brother's prayer,
Unnumbered are thy millions.   Father, hear
The groans we cannot.   Oh, Thine arm make bare,
And reap the harvest of salvation there.
The fulness of the Gentiles, like a sea
Immense, oh God, be gathered unto Thee !
Then Israel save, and with His saintly train,
Send us Immanuel over all to reign !

H. GRATTAN GUINNESS D.D.

PART VI

NING-PO AND SETTLED WORK

1856–1860. AET. 24–28.

We thank Thee, Lord, for pilgrim days
  When desert springs were dry,
And first we knew what depth of need
  Thy love could satisfy

Days when beneath the desert sun,
  Along the toilsome road,
O'er roughest ways we walked with One,
  That One the Son of God.

We thank Thee for that rest in Him
  The weary only know—
The perfect, wondrous sympathy
  We needs must learn below .

The sweet companionship of One
  Who once the desert trod ;
The glorious fellowship with One
  Upon the throne of God ;

We know Him as we could not know
  Through Heaven's golden years ,
We there shall see His glorious Face,
  But Mary saw His tears

The touch that heals the broken heart
  Is never felt above ;
His Angels know His blessedness,
  His wayworn saints His love.

And now in perfect peace we go
  Along the way He trod,
Still learning from all need below
  Depths of the heart of God,

CHAPTER XXXI

MY THOUGHTS ARE NOT YOUR THOUGHTS

July–August 1856.   Aet. 24.

A brief absence was all that Hudson Taylor anticipated
when he parted from Mr. Burns in Swatow.   He was badly
needing change while the hot season lasted, and this journey
to fetch his medicines fitted in very well with the plans they
had in view.   What was his surprise and distress, therefore,
to learn upon reaching Shanghai that the premises of the
London Mission had been visited by fire and that his medical
outfit left there for safety was entirely destroyed.

What could it mean ?   Why had it been permitted ?
Never had he needed these belongings more.   Everything
in Swatow seemed to depend upon the medical work they
were now in a position to undertake—and Mr. Burns was
alone waiting for him.

But what was the use of returning without medicines ?
And where was a new supply to come from, or the means to
obtain them ?   Purchase in Shanghai he could not, on
account of the extravagantly high prices of imported
articles, and six or eight months might be required before
they would reach him from home.   It was a difficult
position, and the young missionary, as he tells us, was
more disposed to say with Jacob, " All these things are
against me," than to recognise with cheerful faith that
" All things work together for good to them that love
God."

" I had not then learned," he records, " to think of God as the One

387

Great Circumstance in whom we live and move and have our being, and of all lesser circumstances as necessarily the kindest, wisest, best, because either ordered or permitted by Him. Hence my disappointment and trial were very great."

The only thing was to write and tell Mr. Burns what had happened, and to put off his return until he could go to Ning-po and see what Dr. Parker could do to help them. If he could spare a small supply of medicines to go on with, they might still be able to begin work as soon as the great heat was over. So in the hope of retrieving his losses, Hudson Taylor set out for the neighbouring city.

And then a whole set of new difficulties began. Three or four days under ordinary circumstances would have taken him to Dr. Parker, but on this occasion he found himself *three weeks after he first started* no nearer his destination than at the beginning. True he had made the trip as much of an evangelistic journey as possible, preaching and distributing literature along the first part of the way. But this was not the reason of his ending up where he began, penniless and destitute, without having reached Ning-po at all or communicated with Dr. Parker.

"It is interesting to notice," he wrote long after, "the various events which united in the providence of God in preventing my return to Swatow and ultimately led to my settling in Ning-po and making that the centre for the development of future labours."

But during this trying summer and the many unsettled months that followed, the young missionary was sorely perplexed to understand the way divine providence was taking in the ordering of his affairs. Life turns at times on a small pivot, and in looking back one is startled to realise the importance of what seemed a very little thing.

How could Hudson Taylor have imagined, for example, that the robbery that left him in such distress upon this journey was to result in the deliverance of the entire Mission he was yet to found, during a period of financial danger? How could he suppose that the upset of all his plans and the severance of a partnership in service more precious than any he had ever known was to prove the crowning blessing of his life on the human side, bringing him into association and at last union with the one of all others most suited both to him and his work ?

But so it is God leads. His hand is on the helm. We *are* being guided, even when we feel it least. The closed door is as much His Providence as the open, and equally for our good and the accomplishment of His own great ends. And one learns at last that it is not what we set ourselves to do that really tells in blessing so much as what He is doing through us, when we least expect it, if only we are in abiding fellowship with Him.

" There was no water beyond Shih-mun-wan," he wrote in relating the latter part of this journey,[1] " so I paid off my boat, hired coolies to carry my things as far as Ch'ang-an, and before sunrise we were on the way. I walked on ahead leaving my servant to follow with the men, who made frequent stoppages to rest, and on reaching the city of Shih-men I waited for them in a tea-shop outside the North Gate. The coolies came on very slowly and seemed weary when they arrived. I soon found that they were opium-smokers, so that although they had only carried between them a load that a strong man would think nothing of taking three times the distance they were really tired.

"After rice, tea and an hour's rest, including, I doubt not, a smoke of the opium-pipe, they were a little refreshed, and I proposed moving on that we might get on to Ch'ang-an before the sun became too powerful. My servant, however, had a friend in the city and proposed that we should spend the day there and go on the following morning. To this of course I objected, wishing to reach Hai-ning (the point of embarkation for Ning-po) that night if possible. . . We therefore set off, entered the North Gate, and had passed through about a third of the city when the coolies stopped to rest saying they would be unable to carry the burden on to Ch'ang-an. Finally they agreed to take it to the South Gate, where they were to be paid in proportion to the distance they had travelled, and my servant undertook to call other coolies and come along with them.

" I walked on before as in the first instance, and the distance being only about four miles soon reached Ch'ang-an and waited their arrival,

---

[1] Up to this point Mr. Taylor had distributed with his usual care as many as 200 copies of the New Testament and 3000 other books and tracts. He had been two weeks upon his way (July 22-August 4) and was able to write : " Never since I have been in China have I had such opportunities for preaching the Gospel."
The account that follows of the rest of the journey is taken from letters to his mother and to the Secretary of the C.E.S., published in part in *The Gleaner* for December 1856.

meanwhile engaging coolies for the rest of the journey to Hai-ning. Having waited a long time I began to wonder at the delay, and at length it became too late to finish the journey to Hai-ning that night. I felt somewhat annoyed, and but that my feet were blistered and the afternoon very hot I should have gone back to meet them and urge them on. At last I concluded that my servant must have gone to his friend, and would not appear until evening. But evening came, and still there was no sign of them.

" Feeling very uneasy, I began diligently to inquire whether they had been seen.

" ' Are you a guest from Shih-mun-wan,' a man at last responded.

" I answered in the affirmative.

" ' Are you going to Hai-ning ? '

" ' That is my destination.'

" ' Then your things have gone on before you. For I was sitting in a tea-shop when a coolie came in, took a cup of tea, and set off for Hai-ning in a great hurry, saying that the bamboo box and bed he carried, just such as you describe yours to have been, were from Shih-mun and he had to take them to Hai-ning to-night, where he was to be paid at the rate of ten cash a pound.'

" From this I concluded that my goods were on before me ; but it was impossible to follow them at once, for I was too tired to walk and it was already dark.

" Under these circumstances all I could do was to seek a lodging for the night, and no easy task I found it. After raising my heart to God to ask His aid, I walked through to the farther end of the town, where I thought the tidings of a foreigner's being in the place might not have spread, and looked out for an inn. I soon came to one and went in, hoping that I might pass unquestioned. . . . Asking the bill of fare, I was told that cold rice—which proved to be more than ' rather burnt '—and snakes fried in lamp-oil were all that could be had. Not wishing any question to be raised as to my nationality, I ordered some and tried to make a meal, but with little success.

" While thus engaged I remarked to the landlord,

" ' I suppose I can arrange to spend the night here ? '

" To which he replied in the affirmative. But bringing out his book, he added :

" ' In these unsettled times we are required by the authorities to keep a record of our lodgers. May I ask your respected family name ? '

" ' My unworthy name is Tai,' I responded.

" ' And your honourable second name ? '

" ' My humble name is Ia-koh ' (James).

" ' What an extraordinary name ! I never heard it before. How do you write it ? '

" I told him, and added, ' It is quite common in the district from which I come.'

" ' And may I ask whence you come and whither you are going ? '

" 'I am journeying from Shanghai to Ning-po, by way of Hang-chow.'

" ' What may be your honourable profession ? '

" ' I heal the sick.'

" ' Oh ! you are a physician,' the landlord remarked, and to my intense relief closed the book. His wife, however, took up the conversation.

" ' You are a physician, are you ? I am glad of that ; for I have a daughter afflicted with leprosy, and if you will cure her you shall have your supper and bed for nothing.'

" I was curious enough to inquire what my supper and bed were to cost if paid for, and to my amusement found they were worth less than three-halfpence of our money.

" Being unable to benefit the girl I declined to prescribe for her, saying that leprosy was a very intractable disease and that I had no medicines with me.

" But the mother brought pen and paper, urging, ' You can at least write a prescription, which will do no harm if it does no good.'

" This I also declined to do, and requested to be shown my bed. I was conducted to a very miserable room on the ground-floor where on some boards raised upon two stools I passed the night, without bed or pillow save my umbrella and shoe and without any mosquito netting. Ten or eleven other lodgers were sleeping in the same room, so I could not take anything off for fear of its being stolen. But I was by no means too warm as midnight came on."

TUESDAY, *August 5.*

Early in the morning I rose, cold, weary and footsore, and I had to wait a long time ere there were any signs of breakfast. After this there was another delay before I could get change for the only dollar I had with me, in consequence of its being chipped in one or two places. More than three hundred cash also were deducted from its price on this account, which was a serious loss in my position.

I then sought throughout the town for tidings of my servant and coolies, as I thought it possible that they might have arrived later or have come on in the morning. The town is large, long and straggling, being nearly two miles from one end to the other, so this occupied some time. I gained no information, however, and footsore and weary set out for Hai-ning in the full heat of the day. The journey (about eight miles) took me a long time, but a half-way village afforded a resting-place and a cup of tea, of which I gladly availed myself. When about to leave again a heavy shower of rain came on, and the delay thus occasioned enabled me to speak a little to the people about the truths of the Gospel.

The afternoon was far spent before I approached the northern suburb of Hai-ning where I commenced inquiries, but nothing could I learn of my servant or belongings. I was told that outside the East Gate I should be more likely to hear of them, as it was there the sea-junks called. I therefore proceeded thither, and sought for them outside the Little East Gate, but in vain. Very weary I sat down in a tea-shop to rest, and while there a number of persons from one of the Mandarin's offices came in and made inquiries as to who I was, where I had come from, etc. On learning the object of my search one of the men in the tea-shop said,

" A bamboo box and a bed, such as you describe, were carried past here about half an hour ago. The bearer seemed to be going toward either the Great East Gate or the South Gate. You had better go to the *hongs* there (business houses) and inquire."

I asked him to accompany me in my search, promising to reward him for his trouble, but he would not. Another man offered to go, however, and we set off, and both inside and outside the two gates made diligent inquiries, but in vain. I then engaged a man to make a thorough search, promising him a liberal reward if he should be successful. In the meantime I had something to eat and addressed a large concourse of people who had assembled.

When my messenger returned, having met with no success, I said to him :

" I am now quite exhausted. Will you help me find quarters for the night, and then I will pay you for your trouble ? "

He was willing to befriend me, and we set off in search of lodgings. At the first place or two the people would not receive me, for though on our going in they were ready to do so, the presence of a man who followed us, and who I found was engaged in one of the Government offices, seemed to alarm them, and I was refused   We now went to a third place, and being no longer followed by the Mandarin's messenger we were promised quarters. Tea was brought and I paid the man who had accompanied me for his trouble.

Soon after he had left some official people came in. They did not stay long, but the result of their visit was that I was told I could not be entertained there that night. A young man present blamed them for their heartless behaviour and said :

" Never mind : come with me, and if we cannot get better lodgings you shall sleep at our house."

I went with him, but we found the people of his house unwilling to receive me. Weary and footsore so that I could scarcely stand, I had again to seek quarters, and at length got a promise of some— but a little crowd collecting about the door they desired me to go to a tea-shop and wait till the people had retired, or they would be unable to accommodate me. There was no help for it, so I went accompanied still by the young man and waited till past midnight. Then we left for the promised resting-place, but my conductor could not find it. He led me about to quite another part of the city, and finally between one and two o'clock he left me to pass the rest of the night as best I could.

I was opposite a temple but it was closed; so I lay down on the stone steps in front of it, and putting my money under my head for a pillow should soon have been asleep, in spite of the cold, had I not perceived a person coming stealthily towards me. As he approached I saw he was one of the beggars so common in China, and had no doubt his intention was to rob me of my money. I did not stir, but watched his movements, and looked to my Father not to leave me in this hour of trial. The man came up, looked at me for some time to assure himself that I was asleep (it was so dark that he could not see my eyes fixed on him), and then began to feel about me gently. I said to him in the quietest tone, but so as to convince him that I was not nor had been sleeping,

" What do you want ? "

He made no answer, but went away

I was thankful to see him go, and when he was out of sight put as much of my cash as would not go into my pocket safely up my sleeve, and made my pillow of a stone projection of the wall. It was not long ere I began to dose, but I was aroused by the all but noiseless footsteps of two persons approaching ; for my nervous system was rendered so sensitive by exhaustion that the slightest sound startled me. Again I sought protection from Him who alone was my stay, and lay still as before, till one of them came up and began to feel under my head for the cash. I spoke again, and they sat down at my feet. I asked them what they were doing. They replied that, like me, they were going to pass the night outside the temple. I then requested them to take the opposite side as there was plenty of room, and leave this side to me. But they would not move from my feet. So I raised myself up and set my back against the wall.

" You had better lie down and sleep," said one of them, " otherwise you will be unable to work to-morrow. Do not be afraid ; we shall not leave you, and will see that no one does you harm."

" Listen to me," I replied. " I do not want your protection. I do not need it. I am not a Chinese, and I do not worship your vain idols. I worship God. He is my Father, and I trust in Him. I know well what you are and what are your intentions, and shall keep my eye on you and not sleep."

Upon this one of them went away, only to return with a third companion. I felt very uneasy but looked to God for help. Once or twice one of them came over to see if I was asleep.

" Do not be mistaken," I said, " I am not sleeping."

Occasionally my head dropped and this was a signal for one of them to rise. But I at once roused myself and made some remark. As the night slowly wore on, I felt very weary, and to keep myself awake as well as to cheer my mind I sang several hymns, repeated aloud some portions of Scripture, and engaged in prayer . . . to the annoyance of my companions, who seemed as if they would have given anything to get me to desist. After that they troubled me no more, and when shortly before dawn of day they left me I got a little sleep.

WEDNESDAY, August 6.

It was still quite early when I was awakened by the young man who had so misled me on the previous evening. He was very rude and insisted on my getting up and paying him for his trouble, even going so far as to try to accomplish by force what he wanted. This roused me, and in an unguarded moment, with very improper feeling, I seized his arm with a grasp he little expected and dared him to lay a finger on me again or to annoy me further. This quite changed his manner. He let me quietly remain till the guns announced the opening of the gates of the city, and then begged me to give him something to buy opium with. Needless to say this was refused. I gave him the price of two candles that he said he had burnt while with me last night, and no more. I afterwards learned he was connected with one of the Mandarin's offices.

As soon as possible I bought some rice gruel and tea for breakfast, and then once more made a personal search for my things. Some hours thus spent proving unavailing I set out on the return journey, and after a long, weary and painful walk reached Ch'ang-an about noon. Here also my inquiries failed to bring any trace of the missing goods ; so I had a meal cooked in a tea-shop, got a thorough wash and bathed my inflamed feet, and after dinner rested and slept until four in the afternoon.

Much refreshed I then set off to return to the city at the South Gate of which I had parted with my servant and coolies two days before. On the way I was led to reflect on the goodness of God, and recollected that I had not made it a matter of prayer that I might be provided with lodgings last night. I felt condemned too that I should have been so anxious for my few things, while the many precious souls around me had caused so little concern. I came as a sinner and pleaded the blood of Jesus, realising that I was accepted in Him—pardoned cleansed, sanctified—and oh the love of Jesus, how great I felt it to be ! I knew something more than I had ever known of what it was to be despised and rejected and have nowhere to lay one's head, and felt more than ever I had before the greatness of the love that induced Him to leave His home in glory and suffer thus for me—nay, to lay down His very life upon the Cross. I thought of Him as " despised and rejected of men, a man of sorrows and acquainted with grief." I thought of Him at Jacob's well, weary, hungry and thirsty, yet finding it His meat and drink to do His Father's will, and contrasted this with my littleness of love. I looked to Him for pardon for the past and for grace and strength to do His will in the future, to tread more closely in His footsteps and to be more than ever wholly His. I prayed for myself, for friends in England and for my brethren in the work. Sweet tears of mingled joy and sorrow flowed freely ; the road was almost forgotten ; and before I was aware I had reached my destination. Outside the South Gate I took a cup of tea, asked about my lost luggage and spoke of the love of Jesus. Then I entered the city, and after many vain inquiries left it by the North Gate.

I felt so much refreshed both in mind and body by the communion I had on my walk to the city that I thought myself able to finish the remaining six miles back to Shih-mun-wan that evening. First I went into another tea-shop to buy some native cakes, and was making a meal of them when who should come in but one of the identical coolies who had carried my things the first stage. From him I learned that after I left them they had taken my luggage to the South Gate. There my servant went away, saying on his return that I had gone on, that he did not intend to start at once, but would spend the day with his friend and then rejoin me. They carried the things to the friend's house and left them there. I got him to go with me to the house, and there learned that my servant had spent the day and night with them and next morning had set off for Hang-chow. This was all I could gather, so unable to do anything but proceed on my return journey to Shanghai with all expedition, I left the city. It was now too late to go on to Shih-mun-wan. I looked to my Father as able to supply all my need, and received another token of His ceaseless love and care —being invited to sleep on a hong-boat, now dry in the bed of the river.

THURSDAY, *August* 7.

The night was again very cold and the mosquitoes troublesome. Still I got a little rest, and at sunrise was up and able to continue my journey. I felt very ill at first and had a sore throat, but reflected on the wonderful goodness of God in enabling me to bear the heat by day and the cold by night for so long. I felt also quite a load taken off my mind. I had committed myself and my affairs to the Lord, and knew that if it was for my good and for His glory my things would be restored. If not, all would be for the best. I hoped that the most trying part of my journey was now drawing to a close, and this helped me, footsore and weary, on the way.

When I got to Shih-mun-wan and had breakfasted, I found I had still eight hundred and ten cash in hand. I knew that the fare by passenger-boat to Ka-shing was one hundred and twenty cash, and thence to Shanghai three hundred and sixty, which would leave me just three hundred and thirty cash (twelve pence and a fraction) for three or four days' provisions. I went at once to the boat-office, but to my dismay found that goods had been delayed owing to the dry state of the river, and that no boat would leave to-day and perhaps none to-morrow. I inquired if there were no letter-boats for Ka-shing, and was told that they had already left. The only remaining resource was to ascertain if any private boats were going in which I could obtain a passage. My search, however, was in vain; and I could get no boat to take me all the way to Shanghai, or my difficulty would have been at an end.

Just at this juncture I saw before me, at a turn in the canal, a letter-boat going in the direction of Ka-shing. This I concluded must be one of the Ka-shing boats that had been detained, and I set off after it as fast as hope and the necessities of the case would carry me. For the time being weariness and sore feet were alike forgotten, and after a chase of about a mile I overtook it.

" Are you going to Ka-shing Fu ? " I called out.

" No," was the only answer.

" Are you going in that direction ? "

" No."

" Will you give me a passage as far as you do go that way ? "

Still " No," and nothing further.

Completely discouraged and exhausted, I sank down on the grass and fainted away.

As consciousness returned some voices reached my ear, and I found they were talking about me.

" He speaks pure Shanghai dialect," said one and from their own speech I knew them to be Shanghai people.

Raising myself I saw that they were on a large hong-boat on the other side of the canal, and after a few words they sent their small boat to fetch me and I went on board the junk. They were very kind and gave me tea, and when I was refreshed and able to partake of it some food also. I then took off my shoes and stockings to ease my feet, and the boatman kindly provided hot water with which to bathe them. When they heard my story and saw the blisters on my feet they evidently pitied me, and hailed every boat that passed to see if it was going my way. Not finding one, after a few hours sleep I went ashore with the captain intending to preach in the temple of the God of War.

Before leaving the junk I told the captain and those on board that I was now unable to help myself ; that I had not strength to walk to Ka-shing Fu, and having been disappointed in getting a passage to-day I should no longer have sufficient means to take me there by letter-boat, an expensive mode of travelling ; that I knew not how God would help me, but that I had no doubt He would do so, and that my business now was to serve Him where I was. I also told them that the help which I knew would come ought to be an evidence to them of the truth of the religion which I and the other missionaries in Shanghai preached.

On our way to the town, engaged in conversation with the captain, we saw a letter-boat coming up. The captain drew my attention to it, but I reminded him that I had no longer money enough to pay for my passage. He hailed it nevertheless, and found that they were going to a place about nine miles from Shanghai, whence one of the boatmen would carry the mails overland to the city.

"This gentleman is a foreigner from Shanghai," he then said, "who has been robbed and has no longer the means of returning. If you will take him with you as far as you go, and then engage a sedan-chair to carry him the rest of the way, he will pay you in Shanghai. You see my boat is now lying aground for want of water and cannot get away. I will stand surety, and if this gentleman does not pay you when you get to Shanghai I will do so on your return."

Those on the letter-boat agreeing to the terms, I bade farewell to my kind friend and was taken on board as a passenger. As I lay down in the bottom of the boat how soft the planks felt, and how thankful I was to be on the way to Shanghai once more !

Long and narrow in build, these letter-boats are very limited as to their inside accommodation, and one has to lie down all the while they are in motion, as a slight movement might upset them. This was no inconvenience to me, however. On the contrary, I was only too glad to be quiet. They are the quickest boats I have seen in China. Each one is worked by two men who relieve one another continuously day and night. They row with their feet and paddle with their hands, or if the wind is quite favourable, row with their feet and with one hand manage a small sail, while steering with the other.

The ninety *li* [1] to Ka-shing Fu were soon passed, and shortly after dark we again left the city—letters having been received and delivered by one of the men, while the other prepared our evening meal.

FRIDAY, *August* 8.

Morning found us at Ka-shan, and while letters were being attended to I went on shore, had my head shaved, and addressed the people

---

[1] Thirty miles, a good day's journey by ordinary houseboat.

who assembled. We then breakfasted and got off. In the afternoon we reached Sung-kiang, and here again I had a good time preaching in an unfrequented quarter.

SATURDAY, *August* 9, 1856.

About 8 A.M. reached Shanghai and the hospitable abode of Mr. Wylie of the London Mission, completing a journey full of mercies though not unmixed with trial. Never since I have been in China have I had such opportunities for preaching the Gospel, and though the termination was far from what I desired it has been greatly blessed to me, and I trust the Word preached and distributed may bear fruit to the glory of God.

CHAPTER XXXII

WHO SHUTTETH AND NO MAN OPENETH

AUGUST–OCTOBER 1856. AET. 24.

AND now the question arose as to what was to be done about the servant who had made off, apparently, with Mr. Taylor's belongings. There was just a possibility that official interference might lie at the root of the matter, and that Yoh-hsi was in detention in one of the Yamens. Before concluding therefore that he had acted dishonestly a messenger was sent to make careful inquiries. But it soon transpired that the case was one of deliberate robbery, Yoh-hsi's own letters bringing the final proof. For the recovery of the property it would not have been difficult to institute legal proceedings, and Mr. Taylor was strongly urged to secure the punishment of the thief; but the more he thought about it the more he shrank from anything of the sort.

Yoh-hsi was one whose salvation he had earnestly sought, and to hand him over to cruel, rapacious underlings who would only be too glad to throw him into prison that he might be squeezed of the last farthing would not have been in keeping, he felt, with the spirit of the Gospel. Finally concluding that his soul was worth more than the forty pounds worth of things he had stolen, Mr. Taylor decided to pursue a very different course.

" So I have sent him a plain, faithful letter," he wrote in the middle of August, " to the effect that we know his guilt, and what its consequences might be to himself; that at first I had considered handing over the matter to the Ya-men, but remembering Christ's command to return good for evil I had not done so, and did not wish to injure a hair of his head.

" I told him that he was the real loser, not I , that I freely forgave him, and besought him more earnestly than ever to flee from the wrath to come. I also added that though it was not likely he would give up such of my possessions as were serviceable to a Chinese, there were among them foreign books and papers that could be of no use to him but were valuable to me, and that those at least he ought to send back.

" If only his conscience might be moved and his soul saved, how infinitely more important that would be than the recovery of all I have lost. Do pray for him."

In course of time, and far away in England, this letter came into hands for which it had never been intended. Mr. George Müller of Bristol, founder of the well-known Orphan Homes, read it with thankfulness to God, finding in the circumstances an exemplification of the teachings of the Lord Himself. His sympathies were drawn out to the young missionary who had acted in what he felt to be a Christ-like spirit, and from that time Hudson Taylor had an interest in his prayers.

But more than this. As soon as the incident became known to him, he sent straight out to China a sum sufficient to cover Mr. Taylor's loss, continuing thereafter to take a practical share in his work, until in a time of special need he was used of God as the principal channel of support to the China Inland Mission. And all this grew out of one little act, as it might seem, of loyalty to the Master at some personal cost. Only there are no little acts when it is a question of faithfulness to God. And it was just his simple adherence, in every detail, to Scriptural principles that gradually inspired confidence in Hudson Taylor and his methods, and won for the Mission the support of spiritually minded people in many lands.

This matter settled, it only remained to set out once more to obtain from Dr. Parker the supplies needed for the medical work at Swatow. This time the journey was accomplished in safety ; and just before setting out Mr. Taylor was encouraged by an unexpected letter that relieved him of what might have been financial embarrassment. For he had declined the generous offer of fellow-missionaries in Shanghai to subscribe towards replacing the most necessary things he had lost. Their own resources as he knew were none too ample, and he felt sure the Lord would provide without drawing upon the little they could spare. The sale of furniture left at the South Gate brought in something, and then—how wonderful it seemed—just as he was starting came this letter that had been eight or ten weeks on the way.

"Please accept the enclosed," it said, "as a token of love from myself and my dear wife." And the enclosed was a cheque for no less than forty pounds from Mr. and Mrs. Berger.

Posted long before Mr. Taylor had left Swatow, it arrived by the very first mail after the robbery: for the promise still holds good, "It shall come to pass that before they call I will answer, and while they are yet speaking I will hear."[1]

"The City of the Peaceful Wave" in which the young missionary now found himself proved even more interesting on this occasion than on his previous visit.[2] Then an attack of illness had obliged him to seek the cooler air of the hills. Now though it was again summer he was able to throw himself heartily into all that was going on, prepared by the experiences of another year in China more fully to appreciate both the missionaries and their work. Never before had he realised the comfort and advantage of labouring among comparatively friendly people, not embittered against the missionary simply on account of his being a foreigner. Although there was of course the usual ignorance and superstition in Ning-po, and at times much anti-foreign feeling, there was also a large element of interest and even inquiry about the Gospel. And then the missionaries themselves—how delightful to be in the midst of so united and efficient a community!

In point of time the two American Missions had the

[1] Isaiah lxv. 24.
[2] Arriving at Ning-po (the "City of the Peaceful Wave" as the Chinese characters imply) on August 22, Mr. Taylor remained for seven weeks with Dr. Parker, taking an active share in his work.

2 D

priority, as well as in strength of numbers ; and an interesting feature in connection both with them and with the Church Missionary Society was that the pioneers were all still on the field, men rich in experience and devotion.

Dr. Macgowan, for example, of the American Baptist Union, was still the leader of their important mission, and with Miss Aldersey divided the honour of having been first to settle permanently in Ning-po. With him were now associated Dr. Lord and the Rev. M. J. Knowlton. Living outside the city wall, these brethren carried on well-organised and extensive operations, extending as far as the island of Chusan, in which they had several converts.

Across the river from this group lived Dr. Parker and his friendly neighbours the American Presbyterians. Splendidly manned from the first, this mission was still represented by its founder, Dr. McCartee, and a group of younger men destined to make their mark in China—including Messrs. Way and Rankin, Dr. W. A. P. Martin,[1] and the late beloved Dr. Nevius.

Within the city itself, enclosed by the five-mile circuit of its ancient wall, lived the pioneers of the Church Missionary Society, and Miss Aldersey with her young companions. From the Taoist Monastery with its surrounding moat, Messrs. Cobbold and Russell had moved as occasion required into school and chapel buildings in various parts of the city, and with their colleague the Rev. F. F. Gough had established themselves in the affections of the people.

So also had Miss Aldersey and her fellow-workers, the only unmarried ladies in that missionary circle. In a large native house in the southern part of the city they were carrying on, it will be remembered, the first girls' school ever established by Protestant missionaries in China.[2]

" It was a model institution," wrote Dr. W. A. P. Martin, with the interest of a contemporary and friend.[3] " For three years at her request I ministered to the Church in her house, and I cherish a

---

[1] The first President of the Peking University, author of *A Cycle of Cathay* and many other works, and now the oldest representative of the missionary body in China.

[2] See Chap XXIV p. 308

[3] Quoted from his well-known book, *A Cycle of Cathay.*

vivid impression of the energy displayed by that excellent woman, notwithstanding a feeble frame and frequent ailments. The impression she made on the Chinese whether Christian or pagan was profound, the latter firmly believing that as England was ruled by a woman so Miss Aldersey had been delegated to be the head of our foreign community. The British Consul, they said, invariably obeyed her commands.

" Several shocks of earthquake having alarmed the people, they imputed the disturbance to Miss Aldersey's magic power, alleging that they had seen her mount the city-wall before dawn of day, and open a bottle in which she kept confined certain strong spirits which proceeded to shake the pillars of the earth.

" No wonder they thought so ! The only wonder is that they did not burn or stone her as a witch. Her strange habits could not but suggest something uncanny. The year round she was accustomed to walk on the city-wall at five o'clock in the morning, and with such undeviating punctuality that in winter she was preceded by a man bearing a lantern. A bottle she carried in her hand did really contain ' strong spirits,' spirits of hartshorn, which she constantly used to relieve headache and as an antidote for ill odours. In summer, unwilling to leave her school for the seaside, she would climb to the ninth storey of a lofty pagoda and sit there through the long hours of the afternoon, sniffing the wind that came from the sea At such times she was always accompanied by some of her pupils, so that her work was not for a moment suspended. So parsimonious was she of time that she even had them read to her while she was taking her meals.

" Many indeed . . . are the households that call Miss Aldersey blessed, and I can truly say that in the long list of devoted women who have laboured in and for China, I know no nobler name than hers."

Scarcely less interesting than Miss Aldersey, if one may venture to say so, were the young sisters Burella and Maria Dyer who so ably filled their place as self-supporting workers in the school. Born under the tropical sun of the Straits Settlements and brought up in a missionary home, theirs had been an inheritance of no ordinary kind. Their father, one of the earliest agents of the London Missionary Society, came of a family in Government service,[1] and was educated at Cambridge for the English Bar. Burning with love to Christ he had left all to go as a missionary to China, " The

---

[1] He was the son of a certain John Dyer, who held a post in the Admiralty about the time of the accession of Queen Victoria.

Gibraltar of Heathenism," almost as unknown in those days as it was inaccessible.   Unable to effect a landing upon its shores, he had devoted himself for sixteen years to work among the Chinese in and near Singapore, and especially to the perfecting of a process by which the Word of God might go where the missionary could not, and the printed page be produced with a facility impossible before.[1] In this task he had been prospered, and though cut off by fatal illness just after the opening of the Treaty Ports— when he with many another was rejoicing in freedom to enter the land for which they had so long prayed and laboured—Samuel Dyer possesses more than a missionary grave upon its shores, the first to mark that great advance.

Acting as Secretary to the General Missionary Conference, the first ever held on Chinese soil, Mr. Dyer spent a week or more at Hong-kong in August 1843.

" From my windows," he wrote to his wife in Singapore,[2] " I look across to the lofty summits of the Chinese hills. . . . The sight is almost overwhelming. In my happiest moments just two thoughts seem to concentrate every longing of my heart.   One is that the name of Jesus may be glorified in China, and the other that you and I and each of our dear children . . . may live only to assist in bringing this to pass. . . . Cease to feel the intensest interest in the spiritual prosperity of China I never can, while this bosom has a heart to feel. Cease to serve the cause of Christ among the Gentiles I never may, while I have head and hands to work. . . . I am as happy as I can be without you, though nothing can compensate for the absence of one who is the joy of my heart. . . . Still, I am about my Father's business. And if I may but do something for the evangelisation of that benighted land, come sorrow, come joy, come grief, come delight, all, *all* shall be welcome for the love I bear to Him Who bled on the mount of Calvary."

And though even then his work was done, and a few weeks later he was laid to rest beside Morrison in the little lonely churchyard at Macao, that spirit still lived on—both

---

[1] To this devoted missionary belongs the honour of introducing a process which greatly simplified the manufacture of movable Chinese type, thus facilitating the way for the rapid production of Christian literature for one-fourth of the human race.

[2] He was singularly happy in his marriage with Miss Maria Tarn, eldest daughter of Joseph Tarn, Esq., one of the early directors of the London Missionary Society.

in the son, whose life was subsequently given to China, and in the daughters who had already been several years with Miss Aldersey. With an exceptionally good knowledge of the Ning-po vernacular these young missionaries were as efficient as they were beloved, and added not a little to the brightness of the foreign community.

Such then was the circle into which Hudson Taylor was introduced for the second time by this visit, and greatly must he have rejoiced to see the value set upon his former colleague by its members. Welcomed in a most generous spirit, Dr. Parker had been successful in building up a practice among the foreign residents, the proceeds of which he devoted entirely to his Medical Mission. Rapidly acquiring the local dialect, in spite of every hindrance to study, he had made the spiritual care of the patients his first work. In this he was assisted by both English and American missionaries, who took in turn to preach in the dispensary (in which nine thousand patients received treatment within the first twelve months) and to visit the temporary hospital.

When as was not infrequently the case these labours resulted in blessing, the converts were free to join any of the Churches, Dr. Parker declining to influence them and making it very clear that his sympathies were with all. At the time of Mr. Taylor's visit he was rejoicing in the conversion of a man whose baptism in connection with the C.M.S. had taken place the week before, and was full of thankfulness also for a forward step in the interests of his projected buildings.

With money contributed in Ning-po he had been enabled to purchase a site on the city-side of the river. And such a site—open, central, commanding, on the brink of the great water-way and close to the Salt Gate with its constant stream of traffic! A better position could hardly have been found for the permanent hospital, and already the energetic doctor was having the ground levelled for building operations.

All this, of course, was deeply interesting to the visitor

from Swatow who was expecting to return to such very different scenes.

"I am now enjoying a season of rest with the friends here," he wrote early in September. "It must be of short duration, however, for long repose begets indolence and weakness, and ill becomes a soldier of the Cross. To me it would be very pleasant to remain on here or at Shanghai, among more civilised and friendly people than we have in Swatow. But my call is to a more arduous post ; and in my dear devoted brother Mr. Burns I have an inestimable companion whom I shall rejoice to meet again.

"I sometimes wonder whether I shall ever be settled, and long for permanent work and a partner to share all my joys and sorrows. I think in His own time I shall be so circumstanced . . . The Lord knows But the only true rest is in following Jesus ' whithersoever He goeth ' ; the only satisfaction is in labouring for and with Him. And while one longs for quiet, even now after a week of it I am eager to be at work again, telling of His surpassing love, His glorious redemption."

And work he did with all his usual energy in spite of summer heat. Careful attention to the peculiarities of local speech soon enabled him to make himself understood even by Ning-po people, and there were so many strangers settled there from other places that he found all the dialects he knew of service.

"The weather is very warm," he continued a little later, "nevertheless I have been twice in the country, once with Mr. Jones to Tse-ki and once with Mr. Quarterman to Chin-hai Hsien. . . . To-day I have been to a small village a mile or two away with Mr. Jones. He took some Portuguese Testaments and found three men able to read them, a Singapore man also who could read English and to whom he gave a Bible ; while I had an attentive audience to whom I told of pardon, peace and heaven through the once-offered sacrifice of Jesus, leaving with them a number of Chinese tracts and Scriptures.

"Oh what an abundant harvest may soon be reaped here ! The fields are white . . . and so extensive round us . . . but the labourers are few ! I do thank God that he has given me such opportunities. . . . I have met with a good many even from Formosa with whom I have been able to speak of Jesus Christ and Him crucified. I sometimes wish I had twenty bodies, that in twenty places at once I might publish the saving Name of Jesus."

The place where the need was greatest, however, had

for him the strongest claim, and before the month was over he was ready to return to Mr. Burns at Swatow. Dr. Parker had fitted him out with medicines, the cost of which had no doubt been covered by Mr. Berger's recent gift, and much benefited by his change of work and surroundings Mr. Taylor was just setting out for Shanghai when a delay arose. Mr. and Mrs. Way of the Presbyterian Mission had to take the journey too. They would have little children with them, and travelling is always so precarious : if Mr. Taylor could wait a day or two, they would hurry their preparations for the sake of joining his party. He was already escorting Mr. Jones and his little son, newly-arrived members of his own Mission, and it would mean a great deal to the Ways to travel in their company.

Regretting the delay but having no reason against it Hudson Taylor waited, and almost a week went by before the final start could be made. And when they did get away the journey proved specially trying. For the winds were against them, which made the actual travelling tedious, and serious illness in the party caused Mr. Taylor much anxiety. His colleague Mr. Jones, to whom he had become sincerely attached during the weeks spent together at Dr. Parker's, developed a painful malady, and as the child was ill too it meant constant nursing.

Early in October they reached their destination, and thankfully exchanged the draughty boat for a missionary home in which they were received as paying guests. And then, having discharged his commissions and handed over the patients to the care of Dr. Lockhart, it only remained for Hudson Taylor to put his things on board the vessel that was taking him to Swatow.

Recent letters from that port made him feel afresh how much he was needed. Though not expecting him back till the great heat was over, Mr. Burns had been sorely missing him, and was now daily awaiting news of his return to take up the work they had planned for the winter. Providentially as it seemed Captain Bowers was again in Shanghai, on the eve of sailing, and cordially welcomed the young missionary as his passenger. So with as little delay as possible Hudson Taylor sent his belongings on board the *Geelong* and prepared to leave Shanghai, it might be permanently.

And then the unexpected happened. A letter from the South coming to one of the members of the London Mission made him go hurriedly in search of Hudson Taylor.

" If he has not started," wrote Mr. Burns, " please inform him at once of this communication."

It was to the effect that all they had looked forward to in Swatow was at an end for the time being, Mr. Burns having been arrested in the interior and sent to Canton. Happily he had escaped summary punishment at the hands of the Chinese, but in all probability it would be long before he could return to the district from which he had been ejected.

.   .   .   .   .   .

It was Thursday morning, October 9. The *Geelong* was sailing in a few hours for Swatow, and all his things were on board. What could be the meaning of these tidings ? Mr. Burns imprisoned and sent to Canton ? The native helpers still in confinement, wearing the terrible *cangue* and in danger of their lives ? The mission-premises empty ? ' The British authorities unwilling that they should return ?

Almost dazed, it all came over him. First one check and then another; medicines destroyed, robbery and all it had entailed, visit to Ning-po, delay in getting away, tedious return journey, and now at the last moment a closed door,—nothing but a closed door and a dear, sick brother waiting to be taken back to the city from which they had come.

Yes, there was no question but to go. But what about Mr. Burns ? Could it be that all they had looked forward to was not of the Lord ?

" Thine ears shall hear a word behind thee saying, This is the way, walk ye in it " . . .

But for the moment the path that had seemed so clear before them was lost in strange uncertainty.

Photograph by G. Whitfield Guinness.

THE QUIET END OF BRIDGE STREET, NEAR THE SUN AND MOON LAKES.

To face page 409

CHAPTER XXXIII

October 1856–May 1857.   Aet. 24–25.

It still stands, that little house on the Wu-Family Bridge Street in which Hudson Taylor made his Ning-po home. To reach this somewhat retired spot one crosses the broad river from the Settlement, and enters the city by the Salt Gate on the east. Thence a walk of rather over a mile through the principal streets leads to the neighbourhood of the Lakes, between the ancient Pagoda and the south-west corner of the city wall. Here a small stone bridge over one of the many canals gives access to a narrow thoroughfare, at the end of which another bridge spans the junction of two large sheets of water, the Sun and Moon Lakes respectively. From the slightly elevated arch of either of these bridges one can look down the little street, and watch the tide of life that eddies in and out of its temple, shops, and homes.

And there on the left, after crossing the canal, stood and still stands the low two-storied building—just an ordinary shop in front and a little yard behind—destined to become the first home and preaching-station of the China Inland Mission. Dr. Parker was using the premises that winter for a boys' school and a dispensary, and was glad to let his former colleague do what he could with the spacious attic above.

"I have a distinct remembrance," said Hudson Taylor many years later, "of tracing my initials on the snow which during the night had collected on my coverlet in the large barnlike upper room, now divided

409

into four or five smaller ones each of which is comfortably ceiled. The tiling of a Chinese house may keep off the rain, if it happens to be sound, but does not afford so good a protection against snow, which will beat up through crannies and crevices and find its way within. But however unfinished may have been its fittings, the little house was well adapted for work among the people, and there I thankfully settled, finding ample scope for service, morning, noon, and night."

The only other foreigners in the southern part of the city were Miss Aldersey with her helpers, and Mr. and Mrs. Jones of his own Mission. The latter had rented an unoccupied house belonging to the American Presbyterians, semi-foreign in style, and were doing their best to acquire the language and adapt themselves to the life of the people.[1]

Upon making their home at *Fu-zin* they had been visited by quite a number of Mandarins and other persons of influence, as well as by hundreds of poorer neighbours. These visits had to be returned as far as possible, and with three little children to take care of as well as the language to study, Mrs. Jones found her hands more than full.

Busy as he was in his own corner, almost a mile away, Hudson Taylor made time to go over frequently to the help of his friends, and the more he saw of them the more he was impressed by their devotion and sweetness of spirit. With his assistance, Mr. Jones was soon able to begin regular meetings, and many were the preaching excursions they made both in and around the city.

Meanwhile Mrs. Jones, too, had found a helper in the younger of the sisters associated with Miss Aldersey at *Siao-kao-tsiang*. When the new family came to settle near them, this bright attractive girl laid herself out to be useful to the busy mother. As often as possible they went visiting together, Miss Dyer's perfect fluency in the language enabling her to make the most of such time as they could give to this work. Young as she was (not yet twenty), and much

[1] Mr. and Mrs. Jones had been seven months in China ; but had not reached Ning-po until June of this year. Detained at Hong-kong by serious illness, and by the death of their eldest child, they had suffered much for the land to which their lives were given. But in it all their faith and love only deepened, and their longing to comfort others with the comfort wherewith they themselves were " comforted of God."

occupied with her school-classes, *Da-yia Ku-niang* [1] could not be satisfied with anything less than soul-winning. With her, missionary work was not teaching the people merely, it was definitely leading them to Christ.

"That was what drew out my interest," said Hudson Taylor long after. "She was spiritually-minded, as her work proved. Even then she was a true missionary."

For it could not but be that the young Englishman living alone on Bridge Street should meet Miss Dyer from time to time at the house of his friends, and it could not but be also that he should be attracted. She was so frank and natural that they were soon on terms of good acquaintance, and then she proved so like-minded in all important ways that, unconsciously almost to himself, she began to fill a place in his heart never filled before.

Vainly he strove against the longing to see more of her, and did his utmost to banish her image from his mind. He was deeply conscious of his call to labour in the interior, and felt that for such work he should be free from claims of wife and home. Besides, all was uncertain before him. In a few weeks or months the way might open for his return to Swatow. Was he not waiting daily upon the Lord for guidance, with the needs of that region still in view? And if it were not to be Southern China, it was his hope and purpose to undertake pioneering work nearer at hand, work that might at any time cost his life. No, it was not for him to cherish thoughts such as would rise unbidden as he looked into the face he loved. And yet he could not but look, strange to say, and long to look again.

And then arguments were not wanting along other lines that would array themselves before him. What *right* had he to think of marriage, without a home, income, or prospect of any that he could ask her to share. Accredited agent of the C.E.S. though he was, it did not at all follow that they were to be depended upon for financial supplies. For months he had not drawn upon his Letter of Credit, knowing the Society to be in debt. Chiefly through the ministry

[1] *Ku-niang* (aunt-mother) is the title in courtesy of an unmarried lady, and the combined monosyllables *Da-yia* form the nearest Ning-po sound-equivalent for the English surname Dyer.

of Mr. Berger, the Lord had supplied his needs. But this might not continue. It could not at any rate be counted on. And what would she say, and those responsible for her, to a life of faith in China, faith even for daily bread ?

Yes, it was perfectly clear · he was in no position to think of marriage, and must subdue the heart-hunger that threatened at times to overwhelm him. And to a certain extent he was helped in turning his thoughts to other matters by events transpiring in the South.

For like a bolt out of the blue had come the sudden tidings that England was involved again in war with China. On the spot and on the spur of the moment we had fanned a tiny spark into a blaze, and the Chinese, all unconscious of results, had dared to disapprove and even resent our high-handed conduct. But this meant war, if war it could be called between combatants so unequal, and within forty-eight hours British guns were thundering at the gates of Canton.[1]

All this had taken place earlier in the autumn, but it was only in the middle of November that the news began to reach the northern ports. When he first heard of it, and saw from the revengeful spirit of the Cantonese in Ning-po how they regarded the attack upon their native city, Hudson Taylor's first thought was for Mr. Burns. What a comfort that he was no longer at Swatow, exposed to the rage of that hot-headed southern people. Now at last a reason was manifest, not only for the removal of his friend, but also for his own detention on the very eve of returning.

" As you are aware," he wrote to his sister on November 16, " I have by various circumstances been detained in Ning-po, and a sufficient cause has at length appeared in the disturbances that have broken out in the South. The latest news we now have is that Canton has been bombarded for two days, a breach being made on the second, and that the British entered the city, the Viceroy refusing to give any

[1] Growing out of the paltry affair of the *Arrow* in October 1856, this war did not come to a final conclusion until four years later (October 1860), when Peking was in the hands of the enemy.

satisfaction. We are anxiously waiting later and fuller accounts. . . .
I know not the merits of the present course of action . . . and therefore forbear writing my thoughts about it. But I would just refer to
the goodness of God in removing dear Mr. Burns *in time*, . . . for
if one may judge of the feelings of the Cantonese in Swatow by what
one sees here at present, it would go hardly with any one at their
mercy."

But following on feelings of thankfulness for the escape
of his friend would come sadder reflections as to the motive
and the meaning of the war. He could not but know that
for fourteen uneasy years [1] England had been pressing
China by every argument that could be devised, to legalise
the importation of opium ; that in spite of the refusal of
the Emperor Tao-kwang to admit at any price " the flowing poison," the smuggling-trade had gone on growing in
defiance of treaty rights ; that one war having failed to
bring the Chinese to our point of view, there had long been
an inclination in certain quarters to bring on a second ;
and that although for the moment the British Admiral had
suspended hostilities, the inevitable outcome of so one-sided
a conflict must be the humiliation of China and the
triumph of our opium-policy.

As to immediate results, they appeared for the moment
to be in the other direction. The Cantonese, in the elation of
their supposed victory over the British fleet, were trying
high-handed measures against the hated foreigner. They
could not know that although Admiral Seymour had withdrawn from Canton, evacuating the dismantled forts along
the river, Sir John Bowring had sent home for reinforcements, and that in spite of the condemning voice of a large
majority in the British Parliament, the war would be
adopted by the nation. They only saw their chance of
retaliation, and very naturally made the most of it. Thus
the British factories were set on fire at Canton, and a price
put on the head of every foreigner. The chief baker at
Hong-kong thought to help on the cause by introducing into
his bread sufficient arsenic to poison the European community. Happily he miscalculated the amount required,

---

[1] Fourteen years since the conclusion, in 1842, of England's first war
with China, justly called " the Opium War." See Chap. VII.

and though four hundred of his victims suffered more or less seriously, in only one case was the result fatal.

All this of course raised a serious question · To what lengths would the revengeful spirit run ? How about others ports and Settlements, and especially Ning-po with its large proportion of Cantonese ? Hitherto they had contented themselves with threatenings merely ; but would it, could it, continue so much longer ?

Up to the end of the year all was quiet, and on Christmas Day Mr. Jones was able to write :

> " The disturbances in the South do not appear to affect the people here in any evil way against us, though there are rumours among them that the Emperor has ordered us all to be expelled. This is probably without foundation, but it makes us realise what it would mean if we were suddenly required to leave. We are just beginning to feel at home amongst the people. Our hearts are drawn out to them in proportion as we know them, and we are longing to enter fully upon our work. Oh, that these threatened hindrances may be averted !

Early in January, however, the hatred of the Cantonese began to take definite form, and a plot was hatched for the destruction of all the foreigners in the city and neighbour-hood. It was well known that in the C.M.S. house (Mr. Russell's), not far from the Salt Gate, a meeting was held every Sunday evening, attended by a large proportion of the European community, Consuls, merchants, and missionaries. They were of course unarmed ; and the plan was to surround the place on a given occasion and make short work of all present. A Mohammedan teacher who had once been employed by one of the missionaries was bought over to lead the assailants, and any foreigners who were not in the habit of attending the service were to be attacked and cut off simultaneously by the other parties.

> " The sanction of the Tao-tai, the chief magistrate of the city," wrote Mr. Taylor, " was easily obtained ; and nothing remained to hinder the execution of the plot, of which we were of course entirely in ignorance. A similar design against the Portuguese community was actually carried out a few months later, between fifty and sixty being massacred in open daylight.

> " It so happened, however, that one of those in the conspiracy was

anxious for the safety of a friend engaged in the service of the missionaries, and went so far as to warn him of coming danger and urge his
leaving the employ of the foreigners. The servant at once made the
matter known to his master, and thus the little community became
aware of their peril. Realising the gravity of the situation, they
determined to meet together at the house of one of their number to
seek protection of the Most High, and to hide under the shadow of
His wings. Nor did they thus meet in vain.

" At the very time we were praying the Lord was working. He led
an inferior Mandarin, the Superintendent of Customs, to call upon
the Tao-tai, and remonstrate with him upon the folly of permitting
such an attempt, which he assured him would arouse foreigners in
other places to come with armed forces, avenge the death of their
countrymen, and raze the city to the ground. The Tao-tai replied
that when they came for that purpose he should deny all knowledge
of or complicity in the plot, and so direct their vengeance against the
Cantonese, who would in their turn be destroyed.

" ' And thus,' he said, ' we shall get rid of both Cantonese [1] and
foreigners by one stroke of policy.'

"The Superintendent of Customs persistently assured him that such
attempts at evasion would be useless ; and finally the Tao-tai withdrew
his permission and sent to the Cantonese prohibiting the attack.

" This took place, as we afterwards discovered, just at the time we
were met together for special prayer and to commit the matter to
the Lord. Thus again were we led to prove that :

Sufficient is His arm alone,
And our defence is sure.

But the Cantonese were not pacified. Prayer had for
the moment prevailed ; but such machinations might
recur at any time, and the foreign community was so
scattered and unprotected that the situation seemed one
of special danger.

" The peril that threatened us," wrote Dr. Parker on the 30th
of January, " was so great, especially last week and this, that the
merchants of the Settlement prepared for flight by keeping at single
anchor the vessel on which their valuables had been stored. They
and some others had their houses guarded by armed men ; and after
much prayer several missionaries, including Mr. Jones and myself,
were led to send our wives and children to Shanghai."

---

[1] "The rapacity and lawlessness of the Cantonese when away from
their native province cause them to be both dreaded and disliked by the
people in general. From their habit of confederating themselves together
in secret clubs or societies, the local government officials are often powerless to act against them."

One reason for this was that the great cold of winter was coming on, and, if flight were left till the last moment, it might mean fatal exposure, especially to delicate children The wildest rumours were everywhere afloat ; and in the event of a general war with China, Shanghai might be the only port held by foreigners. It seemed desirable to secure accommodation there at once. And as it was accessible by regular steamer service, the removal could be accomplished without difficulty, and the return in the spring or summer would be equally simple.

Thus it was that Hudson Taylor, three months after settling in Ning-po, found himself called to move again. No one else seemed so free to escort the party, and his knowledge of the Shanghai dialect made it easy for him to do so. He could be just as useful in Shanghai as in Ning-po, an important consideration when the stay might be a long one.

Personally he would have given a good deal to have remained in Ning-po just then, if only to watch over the safety of the one he loved. For Miss Aldersey would not leave, and her young helpers decided to stay with her. She was just handing over her school, from the superintendence of which she felt it wise to retire, to the American Presbyterian Mission. A connection of the Misses Dyer had come over from Penang, and into her hands the sixty girls with all the school affairs had to be committed. It was no time for unnecessary changes ; and, taking what precautions she could for her own safety and that of her charges, Miss Aldersey stayed to complete her work.

But to leave them then and so was no easy matter to Hudson Taylor. The elder of the sisters had recently become engaged to his friend Mr. Burdon, and seemed in consequence to have a special protector ; but the younger was left all the more lonely, and claimed for that very reason a deeper love and sympathy from his heart. Of course, he dared not show it. He had no reason to think that it would be any comfort to her, and—was he not trying to forget ? So he suffered keenly as he left his little home on Bridge Street, not knowing if he would ever see it or her again.

Photograph

A TEMPLE COURTYARD IN SHANGHAI.

By a Chinese.

To face page 417.

Four and a half months followed, in which the young missionary was engrossed in work in his old surroundings. Living as before in one of the London Mission houses, he might almost have imagined himself back in the old days with Dr. Parker and his family. Only Chinese dress, seven months with William Burns, and the great love that had come to him changed everything for Hudson Taylor. Then, too, he was by this time quite an efficient missionary. Three years in China had given him a good hold of several dialects and considerable experience in work of various kinds. One of the chapels of the London Mission placed at his disposal gave him important opportunities for preaching, besides which he daily addressed large and changing audiences in the Temple of the City God. Returning regularly to these places he and Mr. Jones came to be known and expected, and many were the conversations held with interested inquirers.

"When I first heard you preach," said a young incense-maker, "I found what I was longing for." Illness and desperate troubles had almost driven him to suicide, and he had tried by becoming a devout vegetarian to obtain the consolations of "religion." This involved the recitation of endless prayers to Buddha, and burning incense before many idols.

"It did me no good, however," he continued. "I got no better, until in the temple-garden I heard about Jesus. But He just suits my case ! . . . If you had instructed me to be immersed in fire instead of in water, I should have desired it with all my heart."

During the first three months of their stay in Shanghai (February to April) Mr. Jones and his colleague gave away in connection with such work more than seven hundred New Testaments, besides large numbers of Gospels and tracts. This meant hours and hours of conversation daily, for books were given only to those who could appreciate them, and they were keeping mainly to these two preaching-stations, learning to value increasingly the steady, settled line of things that maintains its influence over the same hearers.

2 E

Meanwhile letters were reaching Hudson Taylor from Swatow, telling of the return of his dear and honoured friend, and the recommencement of work there with many tokens of encouragement. Mr. Burns wrote with all the old affection, anticipating a renewal of their partnership in service. But while rejoicing that Swatow was again occupied, and that Dr. De la Porte had undertaken the medical side of the work, Hudson Taylor had no longer any doubt as to his own relation to it. For him that door was closed. Again and again, while making it a matter of special prayer, hindrances had been put in the way of his return, until he had come to see that it was not of the Lord. That was enough. With him a question once settled in the faith and fear of God there was no reopening it. Throughout life it was one of his outstanding characteristics that he never went back on what had once been made clear to him as Divine guidance.

So the Swatow question was settled, hard though it must have been not to reconsider it in the light of Mr. Burns' letters, and the absence of any personal attraction toward remaining where he was.

For their way was anything but easy at this time. During the whole period of their stay in Shanghai they were surrounded by suffering and distress of the most painful kind. Famine refugees from Nanking had poured into the city until there were thousands of destitute and starving persons added to the ranks of beggary. This meant that one never could go out without seeing heart-rending scenes, which the conditions of life around them made it almost impossible to relieve.

Returning from the city one evening Mr. Jones and his companion were distressed to find the body of a dead beggar lying by the roadside. The weather was bitterly cold, and he had slowly perished for lack of food and shelter. No one seemed to notice, no one seemed to care. It was a sight too common, alas! But the missionaries could bear it no longer.

" We took food with us," wrote Mr. Jones, " and sought out others. Many of these poor creatures . . . have their dwelling literally among the tombs. Graves, here, are often simple arches, low, and from ten to twelve feet long. One end being broken through, they creep inside for shelter, specially at night. . . . We found them in all stages of nakedness, sickness and starvation."

This led to earnest work on their behalf, to the comfort of many.

" In our search," wrote Mr. Taylor, " we came upon the remains of a house bearing witness to the troublous times through which Shanghai had passed. . . . Affording some little shelter from the weather, it had been taken possession of by beggars, and in it we found a large number collected—some well and able to beg, others dying of starvation and disease. From this time we made regular visits to these poor creatures, and helped those who were unable to help themselves. . . . We found, as is always the case, how difficult it is to care for body and soul at the same time. We did, nevertheless, as far as we were able, and I trust the seed sown was not without fruit in the salvation of souls." [1]

Inwardly, too, it was a time of trial. A debt of over a thousand pounds burdened the Society to which they belonged, and burdened still more the consciences of Hudson Taylor and his companions. For some time he had been corresponding with the secretaries on the subject, feeling that, unless a change could be made in the home-management, he would be obliged to withdraw from the service of the Society. This he was most reluctant to do, although the term of years agreed upon in his engagement had expired. He had even suggested that remittances should only be sent when there was money in hand, as he would far rather look to the Lord directly for supplies than draw upon borrowed money. But it seemed as though the Committee could not see anything wrong in their position, and for this reason especially he was much exercised about continuing his connection with them.

Not that he wished then or at any time to be " a free lance," independent of the support and control of others. But as he considered the practical working of things on the

---

[1] One little orphan, *Tien-hsi*, adopted as a result of this work, grew up to be a valued helper at Shao-hing, and one of the first native preachers in connection with the China Inland Mission.

field, it was hard to see in what connection he could labour, seeing he was unordained and without a medical degree.

" I am not sanguine as to any other Society taking me," he wrote to his mother early in the spring : " but, as always, the Lord will provide."

It was in more personal matters, however, that the young missionary was specially cast upon God, through his deep and growing love for the one who he still felt could never be his. He had thought, he had in a sense hoped, that absence would enable him to forget ; that his love for her would be more under control when she was out of sight. And now quite the reverse was the case. Silently but steadily it gained a stronger hold upon his inmost being. He had loved before in a more or less boyish way ; but this was different. A light beyond the brightness of the sun had risen upon him. It flooded all his being. Everything he thought, felt, and did seemed permeated with the sense of that other life—so much a part of his own. He could not separate himself in thought from her ; and when he was most consciously near to God, he felt the communion of her spirit, the longing for her presence most.

In everything she satisfied his mind and heart ; not only embodying his ideal of womanly sweetness, but being herself devoted to the work to which his life was given. As one who having put his hand to the plough dared not look back, he could rest in the assurance that she would help and not hinder him in his special service. And yet the old question remained · How could he marry—with such prospects, such a future ? And, if anything, more serious still—what would she say to it all ?

Of her thoughts and feelings about him, if she had any, he knew nothing. She had always been kind and pleasant, but that she was to every one, with a sweetness of spirit that was unfailing. Apparently she did not wish to marry. Far more eligible men than he had failed to win her ! What chance then could there be for one so poor and insignificant ?

If any one had known, if there had been any one with whom he could have shared the hopes and fears within him,

those first months in Shanghai would have been easier to
bear ; but it was not until the end of March, and through
most unexpected circumstances, that the friends with
whom he was living began to perceive the trouble of his
heart. They had loved him from the first, and had been
drawn very closely to him through their Shanghai experiences, but it was not until Mrs. Jones contracted smallpox among the people she was seeking to relieve, and had
to hand over the care of household and children to their
young fellow-worker, that they fully realised what he was.
Devoted in his care of the little ones, he earned the parents'
deepest gratitude, and in the weeks of convalescence that
followed they were so united in prayer and sympathy that
—how he could not tell—the love he had meant to hide
was a secret no longer from his nearest friends.

And then he was even more surprised at the satisfaction
they expressed. Far from discouraging him, they were full
of thankfulness to God. Never had they seen two people
more suited to each other ! As to the outcome—his duty
was perfectly clear : the rest must be left with Him to
whom both their lives were given.

So the question was committed to writing that had been
burning in his heart for months. Mr. Gough was just
returning to Ning-po, and kindly undertook to place the
letter in the right hands. And then Hudson Taylor could
only wait—a week, ten days, two weeks, how long it seemed !
—until the answer came.

But little was he prepared, in spite of all the prayer there
had been about it, for the tone and purport of this communication. It was her writing surely ; the clear, pretty
hand he knew so well. But could it, could it be her spirit ?
Brief and unsympathetic, the note simply said that what
he desired was wholly impossible, and requested him if he
had any gentlemanly feeling to refrain from ever troubling
the writer again upon the subject.

Could he have known the anguish with which those words
had been penned his own trouble would have been considerably lessened. But the one he loved was far away.
He could not see her, dared not write again after such a

request, and had no clue to the painful situation. Then it was that the tender, unspoken sympathy of his friends, Mr. and Mrs. Jones, became so great a solace. He could hardly have borne it without them, and yet the sight of their mutual happiness reminded him constantly of the blessing he had lost.

Meanwhile, far away in Ning-po, that other heart was even more desolate and perplexed. For the love that had come to Hudson Taylor was no mistaken infatuation : it was the real thing, given of God. Impossible as he would have felt it, it was a love whole-heartedly returned on the part of the one who had always seemed so far above him. Maria Dyer's was a deep and tender nature. Lonely from her childhood, she had grown up longing for a real heart-friend. Her father she could hardly remember, and from the mother whom she devotedly loved she was parted by death at ten years of age, just as she and her brother and sister were leaving Penang to complete their education. After this the doubly-orphaned children had been brought up under the care of an uncle in London, most of their time being spent at school.

Then came the call to China, through Miss Aldersey's need of a helper in her Ning-po school. In offering for this post the sisters were influenced not so much by a desire to take up missionary work as by the knowledge that it was what their parents would have desired. Young as they were they had had some training as teachers (after several years in the Friends' School at Darlington), and, as they were self-supporting and did not wish to be separated, Miss Aldersey invited both to join her instead of only one.

To the younger sister the voyage to China was memorable as the time of her definite entrance into peace with God. Previously she had striven to be a Christian in her own strength, feeling all the while that she lacked the " one thing needful " and seeking vainly to obtain it. Now her thoughts were turned to Christ and His atoning work as the only ground of pardon and acceptance ; the all-sufficient ground to which our prayers and efforts can add nothing at all. Gradually it dawned upon her that she *was* redeemed, pardoned, cleansed from sin, because He had suffered in her stead. God had accepted *Christ* as her substitute and Saviour, and she could do no less. Simply and trustfully as a little child she turned away from everything and every one else, content to take God at His word. "There is therefore now *no condemnation* to them which are in Christ Jesus," and to prove that " The Spirit Himself beareth witness with our spirit that we are " here and now " children of God." [1]

This true conversion with all that flowed from it made her entrance upon missionary work very different from what it would otherwise have been. No longer a philanthropic undertaking to which she devoted herself out of regard for her parents' wishes, it had become the natural and even necessary expression of her great and growing love to Him who was her Saviour, Lord and King. He had changed everything for her, for time and for eternity, and the least she could do was to give herself entirely to His service. So with a peace and joy unknown before she took up her busy and often difficult life in Miss Aldersey's school.

It was a lonely post for a girl in her teens, and especially one of so thoughtful and loving a spirit. Her sister's companionship no doubt was precious, and the missionary circle in Ning-po gave her several attached friends. But her heart had never found its mate in the things that mattered most.

And then he came—the young missionary who impressed her from the first as having the same longings after holiness, usefulness, nearness to God. He was different from everybody else ; not more gifted or attractive, though he was bright and pleasing and full of quiet fun , but there was a something that made her feel at rest and understood. He seemed to live in such a real world and to have such a real, great God. Though she saw little of him it was a comfort to know that he was near, and she was startled to find how much she missed him when after only seven weeks he went away.[2]

---

[1] See Romans viii. 1, 16 ; and indeed the whole chapter.
[2] In the previous October, when he had left Ning-po to return, as he hoped, to Mr. Burns.

Very real was her joy, therefore, as well as surprise, when from Shanghai he had to turn back again. Perhaps it was this that opened her eyes to the feeling with which she was beginning to regard him. At any rate, she soon knew, and with her sweet, true nature did not try to hide it from her own heart and God. There was no one else to whom she cared to speak about him ; for others did not see in him, always, just what she saw. They disliked his wearing Chinese dress, and did not approve his making himself so entirely one with the people. His Chinese dress—how she loved it ! or what it represented, rather, of his spirit. His poverty and generous giving to the poor—how well she understood, how much she sympathised ! Did others think him visionary in his longing to reach the great Beyond of untouched need ? Why, that was just the burden on her heart, the life she too would live, only for a woman it seemed if anything more impossible. So she prayed much about her friend though to him she showed but little. For the love of her life had come to her, and nobody knew but God.

And then he went again, went in the interests of others, and she did not know it cost him anything to leave her. But all the while he was away she prayed to be more like him, more worthy of his love, if that should ever be hers.

Month after month went by, and then, at last—a letter ! Sudden as was the joy, the great and wonderful joy, it was no surprise, only a quiet outshining of what had long shone within. So she was not mistaken after all. They *were* for one another ; " two whom God hath chosen to walk together before Him."

When she could break away from her first glad thanksgivings she went to find her sister, who was most sympathetic. The next thing was to tell Miss Aldersey, then living on the north side of the city with her former ward and fellow-worker, Mrs. Russell. Eagerly the sisters told their tidings, hoping she would approve this engagement as she had Burella's. But great was the indignation with which she heard the story.

" Mr. Taylor ! that young, poor, unconnected Nobody.

How dare he presume to think of such a thing ?   Of course
the proposal must be refused at once, and that finally."

In vain Maria tried to explain how much he was to her.
That only made matters worse.   She must be saved without
delay from such folly.   And her kind friend proceeded,
with the best intentions, to take the matter entirely into
her own hands.   The result was a letter written almost
at Miss Aldersey's dictation, not only closing the whole
affair but requesting most decidedly that it might never be
reopened.

Bewildered and heartbroken, the poor girl had no choice.
She was too young and inexperienced, and far too shy in
such matters, to withstand the decision of Miss Aldersey,
strongly reinforced by the friends with whom she was
staying.   Stung to the quick with grief and shame, she could
only leave it in the hands of her Heavenly Father.   He
knew ; He understood.   And in the long, lonely days that
followed, when even her sister was won over to Miss Aldersey's
position, she took refuge in the certainty that nothing,
nothing was too hard for the Lord.   " If He has to slay my
Isaac," she assured herself again and again, " I know He
can restore."

To Hudson Taylor in his sorrow, sympathising hearts
were open, but for her there was none.   And she did not
know that he would ever cross her path again.   After such
a refusal, if he really cared, he would surely stay away from
Ning-po, especially in view of the recommencement of work
at Swatow which she knew he longed to share.   Nothing
was more probable now than that he would return to his
friend Mr. Burns.   And this, no doubt, he would have done
had he been acting on impulse and not holding stedfastly
to the guidance of God.   As it was, though he knew nothing
of her feelings and had little if any hope of a more favourable
issue, he was winning in the depths of his sorrow just the
blessing it was meant to bring.

" We have need of patience," he wrote to his sister in May, " and
our faithful God brings us into experiences which, improved by His
blessing, may cultivate in us this grace.   Though we seem to be tried
at times almost beyond endurance, we never find Him unable or un-

willing to help and sustain us ; and were our hearts *entirely* submissive to His will, desiring it and it only to be done, how much fewer and lighter would our afflictions seem.

" I have been in much sorrow of late ; but the principal cause I find to be want of willing submission to, and trustful repose in, God, my Strength. Oh, to desire His will to be done with my *whole* heart . . . to seek His glory with a single eye ! Oh, to realise more of the fulness of our precious Jesus, . . . to live more in the light of His countenance; to be satisfied with what He bestows, . . . ever looking to Him, following in His footsteps and awaiting His glorious coming ! Why do we love Him so little ? It is not that He is not lovely. 'Fairer than the children of men !' It is not that He does not love us . . . that was for ever proved on Calvary. Oh, to be sick of love for Jesus, to be daily, hourly longing, hungering, thirsting for His presence ! . . . May you find your love to Him ever increasing, and His likeness in you be apparent to all. . . . Continue to pray for me . . . that God will supply all my need, Jesus be all my delight, His service all my desire, rest with Him all my hope."

It is perhaps not surprising that one book in the Bible, that had never meant much to him before, should have opened up at this time in undreamed-of beauty. His deep understanding of the Song of Solomon seems to have begun in these days, when the love that welled up so irresistibly within him could only be given to God. Never had he understood before what the Lord can be to His people, and what He longs to find in His people toward Himself. It was a wonderful discovery, and one that only grew with all the glad fruition that lay beyond this pain. To those who knew Hudson Taylor best in later years, nothing was more characteristic than his love for the Song of Solomon and the way in which it expressed his personal relationship to the Lord.[1] Here is the beginning of it all, culled from letters to his mother and sister in that sad spring of 1857.

My dear Amelia, it is very late, but I cannot retire without penning a few lines to you. All below is transitory ; we know not what a day or an hour may bring forth. . . . One thing only changes not—the love of God. Our precious Jesus is the same and ever will be, and soon He will come and take us to Himself.

---

[1] Mr. Hudson Taylor's Bible Readings on the Song of Solomon are published under the title *Union and Communion*

What will it be to see Him with unclouded vision, and be ravished with His transcendent loveliness ? . . . And not only shall we be with Him ; we shall be *His*. " My Beloved is mine and I am His " is true for us even now. But then He will share with us not only His power and glory, but the very beauty of His character and person. When we see Him " we shall be like Him , for we shall see Him as He is." Precious Jesus, oh, to be more like Thee now ! to manifest Thy grace as Thou didst the Father's

Have you thought much about the Song of Solomon ? It is a rich garden to delight in, and so is the forty-fifth Psalm. To think that even the sweetest, dearest of earthly ties but faintly shadows forth the love of Jesus to His redeemed . . . to me . . . is it not wonderful ? . . . Oh, how can we love our precious Jesus enough, how do enough for Him ! . . . Soon will He call us to a wedding-feast, the marriage supper of the Lamb. Not as guests, but as *the bride* shall we take our place with joy, arrayed in the spotless robe of His righteousness. The time is short. May we live as those who wait for their Lord, and be ready with joy to meet Him.

And again, in connection with the happiness of her engagement to Mr. Broomhall ·

These feelings are implanted by God Himself, and all the circumstances connected with them are ordained or permitted by Him for our highest spiritual good as well as temporal happiness . In nearly every book in the Bible they are used by the Holy Spirit to illustrate the relationship between God and His people, and very specially do they belong to those who have been " espoused . . as a chaste virgin to Christ." With the love with which you love your husband (in fact or in anticipation) you are to love the Lord Jesus, nay, *more* Are you lonely when he leaves you ? So you should be while Jesus is absent. Do you long for the time when you can always be together ? So you should for the return of Jesus to take you to Himself. Is service for your loved one freedom? "No," you will say, "that is far too cold a word. Freedom ! It is joy, delight, the desire of my heart." So should you serve Jesus. Would you do what you could to remove the obstacles and hasten the day of your union ? Then look for and hasten the day of *His* return. . . . See Jesus in everything, then in everything you will find blessing. Keep looking to Jesus. Do nothing but for Him, but as in Him and by His strength and direction. Christ all and in all ! And oh ! may He abundantly and personally manifest Himself to you."

God's plans ever go forward, though to us they may appear at times to retrograde. That is due to our imperfect point of view. May we ever grow in grace, and be made vessels such as our Master can use.

. . . We *have* our portion—the " chiefest among ten thousand," and the " altogether lovely."

> All that my soul has tried
> Left but an aching void ,
> *Jesus has satisfied*
> *Jesus is mine.*

May we daily see more of Him, daily see more *in* Him. . . .

I have been much tried of late. Seeking to do all to the glory of God, I do nothing that is not mixed with self and sin. Oh, how fit is our Jesus for us ! perfect righteousness for ruined sinners, a glorious robe for the tattered and filthy, gold, fine gold for the poor, sight for the blind—all, all we need or could desire. Precious Jesus ! may we love Thee more, and more manifest our love by deadness to the world. Come, Lord Jesus, come quickly !

CHAPTER XXXIV

THE GOD THAT IS ENOUGH

MAY–SEPTEMBER 1857. AET. 25.

WINTER was over, summer was drawing on, and with the
first hot days came a change in the conditions that had
detained Hudson Taylor and his colleagues in Shanghai.
For one thing the famine refugees began to disappear.
Spring harvests drew them back to country villages all
over the plain, and for the few who could not leave a local
missionary undertook to care.

Then, a lull in the war with England made aggressive
work in Ning-po and the neighbourhood more possible ; and
though the house Mr. and Mrs. Jones had previously occupied
was no longer available, other and even better premises were.
The retirement of Mr. Cobbold for health reasons had left
one of the C.M.S. buildings vacant, and this Mr. Jones
was able to rent for a moderate sum. Dr. Parker also was
glad to hand over the entire premises on Bridge Street
part of which Hudson Taylor had formerly occupied. Thus
without any effort on their part they were provided with a
dwelling-house and a street-chapel in the busiest parts of
the city.

With growing experience Hudson Taylor was increasingly
drawn, it should be said, to the more settled forms of
missionary work. The war with England made it out of
the question to attempt to live at any distance from the
Treaty Ports. Itinerations were still possible, but speaking
generally the interior was more inaccessible than ever.
Believing, however, that the time was near for a change in

this respect, Mr. Taylor and his colleague realised the importance of labouring in some one, settled spot, until a native church could be raised up that should afford them, by the blessing of God, pastors and evangelists for the wider opportunity of coming days.

With this hope in view, therefore, they turned their faces to Ning-po again, but not before they had taken a step of great importance in its bearing on the future.

For it was in the month of May, three years and three months after his arrival in China, that Hudson Taylor felt the time had come to resign his connection with the Chinese Evangelisation Society. Not all the difficulties under which he had laboured would have led him to this step. He loved the Secretaries and many members of the Committee known to him personally, and valued their sympathy and prayers. But the Society, as we have seen, took a very different position from his own in the matter of debt, a position in which he felt he could no longer participate.

"Personally," he wrote in recalling the circumstances, " I had always avoided debt, and kept within my salary, though at times only by very careful economy. Now there was no difficulty in doing this, for my income was larger, and the country being in a more peaceful state, things were not so dear. But the Society itself was in debt. The quarterly bills which I and others were instructed to draw were often met with borrowed money, and a correspondence commenced which terminated in the following year by my resigning from conscientious motives.

"To me it seemed that the teaching of God's Word was unmistakably clear : ' Owe no man anything.' To borrow money implied, to my mind, a contradiction of Scripture—a confession that God had withheld some good thing, and a determination to get for ourselves what He had not given. Could that which was wrong for one Christian to do be right for an association of Christians ? Or could any amount of precedents make a wrong course justifiable ? If the Word taught me anything, it taught me to have no connection with debt. I could not think that God was poor, that He was short of resources, or unwilling to supply any want of whatever work was really His. It seemed to me that if there were lack of funds to carry on work, then to that degree, in that special development, or at that time, it could not be the work of God. To satisfy my conscience I was therefore compelled to resign my connection with the Society. . . .

"It was a great satisfaction to me that my friend and colleague, Mr. Jones, . . . was led to take the same step, and we were both profoundly thankful that the separation took place without the least breach of friendly feeling on either side. Indeed, we had the joy of knowing that the step we took commended itself to several members of the Committee, although the Society as a whole could not come to our position. Depending on God alone for supplies, we were enabled to continue a measure of connection with our former supporters, sending home journals, etc , for publication as before, so long as the Society continued to exist.

"The step we had taken was not a little trying to faith. I was not at all sure what God would have me do, or whether He would so meet my need as to enable me to continue working as before. . . . I was willing to give up all my time to the service of evangelisation among the heathen if, by any means, He would supply the smallest amount on which I could live ; and if He were not pleased to do this, I was prepared to undertake whatever work might be necessary to support myself, giving all the time that could be spared from such a calling to more distinctly missionary efforts.

"But God blessed and prospered me, and how glad and thankful I felt when the separation was really effected ! I could look right up into my Father's face with a satisfied heart, ready by His grace to do the next thing as He might teach me, and feeling very sure of His loving care.

"And how blessedly He did lead me I can never, never tell. It was like a continuation of some of my earlier experiences at home. My faith was not untried ; it often, often failed, and I was so sorry and ashamed of the failure to trust such a Father. But oh ! I was learning to know Him. I would not even then have missed the trial He became so near, so real, so intimate. The occasional difficulty about funds never came from an insufficient supply for personal needs, but in consequence of ministering to the wants of scores of the hungry and dying around us. And trials far more searching in other ways quite eclipsed these difficulties, and being deeper brought forth in consequence richer fruits. How glad one is now not only to know, with dear Miss Havergal, that

> They who trust Him wholly
> Find Him wholly true,

but also that when we fail to trust fully He still remains unchangingly faithful. He *is* wholly true whether we trust or not. " If we believe not, He abideth faithful ; He cannot deny Himself." But oh, how we dishonour our Lord whenever we fail to trust Him, and what peace, blessing and triumph we lose in thus sinning against the Faithful One ! May we never again presume in anything to doubt Him."

What the more searching trials were that brought forth
richer blessing it is not difficult at this point to divine.
Twice daily in his walks to and from Bridge Street, Hudson
Taylor had to pass very near Miss Aldersey's School. Carried
on now by Mrs. Bausum and her young relatives it was
still the home of the being dearest to him on earth. He
had seen her again since returning to Ning-po in June, but
a barrier had been raised between them that was hard to
pass. Kind and gentle as she still was, he could not forget
that she had charged him never again to trouble her upon
a certain subject ; and Miss Aldersey had so spoken her
mind to the friends with whom he lived that the position
was doubly trying.

For soon after their return from Shanghai Mrs. Jones had
invited Miss Dyer to go out visiting with her as before.
There was no one else to whom she could look for help,
and the need was very pressing. Besides it was the best,
the only way in which the young people could see more of
each other. To the girl herself she said nothing, nor did
Maria allude to the matter of which their hearts were full.
But Miss Aldersey knew no such reticence, and seeking
Mrs. Jones after the Ladies' Prayer Meeting, in another
part of the city, poured out the vials of her wrath. She
had good reason, she felt, to be indignant. Miss Dyer
belonged to a different social circle from that of Mr. Taylor,
and had a small but reliable income of her own. She was
educated, gifted, attractive, and had no lack of suitors far
more eligible in Miss Aldersey's eyes. It was unpardonable
that this person should presume upon her youth and
inexperience, and still more so that he should return to
Ning-po after its having been made plain that he was not
wanted.

In the course of such a conversation many things come
out, and before it ended Mrs. Jones could see pretty clearly
how the land lay. Miss Aldersey's object was to obtain
from her a promise that she would do nothing to forward
Mr. Taylor's suit, and that the latter would never see or
speak to Miss Dyer in their house. While not committing
herself as far as this, Mrs. Jones felt it desirable to state

that she would refrain from throwing the young people together, and that Mr. Taylor would not take advantage of Miss Dyer's visits to attempt to see her alone. At the same time she earnestly put before Miss Aldersey the other side of the matter, trying to make her feel how serious a thing it is to tamper with such affections. But the older lady would hear no good of Hudson Taylor, and deeply pained by her criticisms Mrs. Jones came away.

After this, of course, Hudson Taylor felt himself bound by Mrs. Jones' promise. He could not write to Miss Dyer or seek an interview in the house of his friends ; and yet as the days went by he found it impossible to let matters drift indefinitely. Having learned that Miss Aldersey was not related to the Dyers and was not even their guardian, he determined to call on the sisters both together and ask whether he might write to their uncle in London for permission to cultivate a closer acquaintance. More than this he dared not venture at present, nor was it necessary after his Shanghai letter.

Taking a sedan-chair, therefore, as the etiquette of Chinese dress demanded, Hudson Taylor went over to the school, only to meet the young ladies going out. So without waiting for the ceremony of sending in his card, he requested the privilege of a few minutes' conversation.

" Come in," responded the elder sister, " and we will ask Mrs. Bausum."

But when Mrs. Bausum appeared he found that both girls had gone over to see Miss Aldersey. Burella divining the purpose of his visit had insisted upon her sister's leaving the house at once, and for the sake of avoiding an open rupture Maria had consented.

It was hard just then not to look at second causes. But though everything and every one seemed against him Hudson Taylor was enabled to leave it all with God, confident that He understood best how to manage such matters. If an interview were necessary He could and would bring it about, and cause it, moreover, to accomplish the desired results. Personally there seemed nothing he could do. But the Lord has ways of working beyond our ken ; and

2 F

in spite of everything he could not help a growing impression that his love was returned and that, in the way he hoped, faith would be rewarded.

Meanwhile the trial through which he was passing was not allowed to interfere with daily duties. Situated on a crowded thoroughfare the house at *Kuen-kiao-teo* was within a stone's throw of the main street of the city. " By day and far into the night the clink and ring of smiths' and tinkers' hammers close by and the busy hum from neighbouring tea-shops could be heard." The air was close and oppressive, a population of half a million being gathered within and around the city wall. But from a summer-house on the roof a refreshing view could be obtained of the surrounding hills, and many an early hour the young missionary must have spent there alone with God. For he had learned that only in such communion could freshness of spirit be maintained both for work and burden-bearing.

Street-chapel preaching is far from easy, and both at *Kuen-kiao-teo* and in the little house across the city Hudson Taylor was carrying on daily services as well as medical work. Nothing but the attraction of the Lord's own love and presence in the speaker's heart could hold the changing audiences or turn argumentative conversations into blessing. But the young missionary kept on, always patient and pleasant, always ready with some helpful word or kindly act, until the neighbours could not but be impressed by such a message delivered in such a spirit

" Next door to our premises on Bridge Street," wrote Mr. Jones, " there is an opium den. The men who keep it are southerners and . . . at first looked upon us with little favour. But one and another dropped in to our services, Brother Taylor sometimes addressing them in their own dialect, until they became quite friendly. One of them who was suffering much from his eyes was cured by careful treatment, and now they often shew us little attentions of one sort or another. People also who frequent their house are constant in attendance at our meetings, and one at any rate has a good understanding of the Gospel."

Thus the Friend of publicans and sinners was able to

come very near even to these poor, unhappy opium-smokers, through a life made attractive by much fellowship with Him.

The evening meeting at *Kuen-kiao-teo* was perhaps the most important of the day's proceedings. People were more willing to come out after the sun went down, and the big bell soon filled the hall with an audience willing to listen for an hour or two. All this, of course, meant hard work for the young missionary on whom most of the speaking devolved. It was his fourth hot season, and one's powers of resistance seem to lessen with each succeeding summer. But not the intense heat nor yet the work kept up with unremitting vigour were the chief strain upon Hudson Taylor. The trial of suspense meant more, far more, involving as it did the dearest hopes of his heart.

But in this also he was wonderfully sustained. The matter had been left entirely in the hands of God, and though Hudson Taylor had no means of communicating with the one he loved it was not difficult for the Lord to bring them together. He who can use ravens, if need be, or angels to do His bidding was answering His children's prayers, and on this occasion He seems to have employed a waterspout !

It was a sultry afternoon in July, shortly after Hudson Taylor's unsuccessful visit to the school, when in regular rotation the Ladies' Prayer Meeting came to be held at *Kuen-kiao-teo*. The usual number gathered, representing all the Societies, but as the sequel proved it was easier to come to the meeting that day than to get away. For with scarcely any warning a waterspout, sweeping up the tidal river, broke over Ning-po in a perfect deluge, followed by torrents of rain. Mr. Jones and Mr. Taylor were over at Bridge Street as usual, and on account of the flooded streets were late in reaching home. Most of the ladies had left before they returned, but a servant from the school was there who said that Mrs. Bausum and Miss Maria Dyer were still waiting for sedan-chairs.

" Go into my study," said Mr. Jones, to his companion, " and I will see if an interview can be arranged."

It was not long before he returned saying that the ladies were alone with Mrs Jones and that they would be glad of a little conversation.

Hardly knowing what he did Hudson Taylor went upstairs, and found himself in the presence of the one being he supremely loved. True others were there too, but he hardly saw them, hardly saw anything but her face, as he told much more than he would have ever thought possible— in public. He had only meant to ask if he might write to her guardian for permission. . . . But now it all came out ; he could not help it ! And she ?—— Well, there was no one present but friends who loved them and understood, and it might be so long before they could meet again ! Yes, she consented, and did much more than that. With her true woman's heart she relieved all his fears, as far as they could be relieved by knowing that he was just as dear to her as she to him. And if the others heard—were there not angels too ? And presently Hudson Taylor relieved the situation by saying :

" Let us take it all to the Lord in prayer."

.   .   .   .   .   .

So the letter was written about the middle of July upon which so much depended, and they had to look forward to four long months of prayer and patience before the answer could be received. Under the circumstances they did not feel free to see one another or even communicate in writing, for they had as far as possible to mitigate Miss Aldersey's displeasure. Maria of course informed her that Mr. Taylor had written to her uncle asking permission for a definite engagement. That matters should have come to such a pass in spite of all her precautions seemed incredible to the older lady. But they should proceed no farther She would at once communicate with Mr. Tarn herself, and he of course would see the impropriety of the request. So with the keenest desire for her young friend's happiness she set to work to bring the distant relatives to her own point of view.

This of course made it very hard for the lovers, especially as Miss Aldersey observed no reticence on the subject.

Impressions she had gained about Hudson Taylor, happily as unfounded as they were unfavourable, were soon made known to the rest of the community. Her object was to alienate the affections of Miss Dyer from one whom she considered unworthy of her, and she did not hesitate to encourage the attentions of other suitors with the same end in view. The Chinese dress worn by Hudson Taylor was one strong point against him, and seemingly awakened not aversion only, but contempt. His position also as an independent worker, upon the uncertain basis of " faith," was severely criticised ; and he was represented as " called by no one, connected with no one, and recognised by no one as a minister of the Gospel." Had this been all it would have been bad enough, but other insinuations followed. He was " fanatical, undependable, diseased in body and mind," and in a word " totally worthless ! " And the two most concerned could not tell how far all this would influence Mr. Tarn in London, to whom Miss Aldersey had written in a similar strain.

As month after month went by and these strange misrepresentations came to be believed in certain sections of the community, Hudson Taylor had to learn in a new way what it was to take refuge in God. It was a fiery furnace seven times heated ; for he knew how his loved one must be suffering, and he could not explain anything or reassure her even of his devotion. And what was to be the outcome ? What if her guardian in London were influenced by Miss Aldersey's statements ? What if he refused his consent to the marriage ? If there was one thing of which Hudson Taylor had no doubt it was that the blessing of God rested upon obedience to parents or those in parental authority. Nothing would have induced him to act contrary to a command from his own parents, nor could he encourage the one he loved to disregard her guardian's wishes. Years after, when experience had confirmed these convictions, he wrote upon this important subject :

I have never known disobedience to the definite command of a parent, even if that parent were mistaken, that was not followed by retribution. Conquer through the Lord.[1] He can open any door. The responsibility is with the parent in such a case, and it is a great one. When son or daughter can say in all sincerity, " I am waiting for you, Lord, to open the door," the matter is in His hands, and He will take it up.

But at this time it was theory more than experience ; his conviction of what must be rather than his knowledge of what was ; and the test was all the more severe.

No wonder he needed to be very still in those days before the Lord. Never before had he had to walk so carefully, or so felt his helplessness apart from sustaining grace.

" It is not sufficient," he wrote to his sister early in August, " to have the every road pointed out merely, to be prevented from straying to the right hand or to the left, though this is no little blessing. . . . We need Him to direct our *steps* . . . step after step. Nay more, we need to pass through this wilderness *leaning*, always leaning on our Beloved. May we in reality do this, and *all* will be well."

Meanwhile in another part of the city another lonely, suffering heart was learning the same lessons. Deeply she too felt the sacredness of parental authority, and that the divine blessing could not rest upon a step taken in defiance of its control. She would have waited if need be for years had her guardian disapproved the marriage, and as the slow months went by times of desolation could not but come over her in view of all he was likely to hear.

She was visiting Mr. and Mrs. Gough of the C.M.S. on one such occasion, who entertained a warm regard for Hudson Taylor. He may have been spoken of with appreciation : at any rate the longing for him that was always there filled and overflowed her heart. It was a summer evening, and going to her room alone the poor child knelt long in silent grief. But her Bible was at hand, and as she turned its pages the precious words shone out : " Trust in Him at all times ; ye people, pour out your hearts before Him : God is a refuge for us." And that just met her need.

" I marked it at the time," she wrote to her loved one

[1] Mr Taylor was then dealing specially with the question of a call to missionary work, the consent of one or both parents being withheld.

seven years later, "and the light-coloured ink still remains to remind me of that night."

"My soul, wait thou only upon God ; for my expectation is from Him."   He only, He alone ; always *El-Shaddai*— "The God that is Enough."

CHAPTER XXXV

SEPTEMBER AND OCTOBER 1857. AET. 25.

IT was about this time that a pair of scrolls made their appearance in the sitting-room at *Kuen-kiao-teo* that were as new as they were perplexing to the little company of Christians and inquirers gathered there on Sunday mornings for worship. Beautifully written in Chinese each character in itself was intelligible, but what could be the meaning of the strange combination, *I-pien-i-seh-er ; Je-ho-hua I-la* ?

The young missionary who had been ill and confined to his room for a month could have explained. For it was there in quiet communion with God those inspired words had come to him in such fullness of meaning as to make them for ever memorable. *Ebenezer* and *Jehovah Jireh*: " Hitherto hath the Lord helped us," and for all coming need " The Lord will provide " ;—how he rejoiced as strength came back again to unfold to his Chinese friends their precious message, leading them on to a deeper knowledge of the infinite God they too were learning to trust.

That little inner circle, small though it was in numbers, was the joy and rejoicing of Hudson Taylor's heart, and the illness that laid him aside during the whole of September was made the most of for prayer on their behalf. Taken out of the busy round of preaching and medical work he was able to give more time to individual inquirers, amongst whom Mr. Nyi, a business man in the city, was perhaps the most encouraging.

Passing the open door of the mission-house one evening soon after Mr. Jones and his colleague had settled there, he observed that something was going on A big bell was ringing, and a number of people were passing in as if for a meeting. Hearing that it was a " Jesus Hall," or place where foreign teachers discoursed upon religious matters, he too turned in ; for, as a devout Buddhist, there was nothing about which he felt more concern than the pains and penalties due to sin, and the transmigration of the soul on its long journey he knew not whither.

A young foreigner in Chinese dress was preaching from his Sacred Classics, and this was the passage he read .

As Moses lifted up the serpent in the wilderness, even so must the Son of Man be lifted up . that whosoever believeth in Him should not perish, but have eternal life.

For God so loved the world, that He gave His only begotten Son, that whosoever believeth in Him should not perish, but have everlasting life. For God sent not His Son into the world to condemn the world ; but that the world through Him might be saved.

It is scarcely possible to imagine much less describe the effect upon such a man of such a message, heard for the first time. To say that Nyi was interested scarcely begins to express all that went on in his mind. For he was a seeker after truth, one of the leaders of a reformed sect of Buddhists devoted to religious observances. The story of the brazen serpent in the wilderness illustrating the divine remedy for sin and all its deadly consequences ; the facts of the life, death, and resurrection of the Lord Jesus ; and the bearing of all this upon his own need, brought home to him the power of the Holy Spirit—well, it is the miracle of the ages, and thank God we see it still ! " I, if I be lifted up . . . will draw all men unto Me."

Nyi came into the hall that evening one of the vast—the incredibly vast multitude—who " through fear of death are all their lifetime subject to bondage " ; and as he sat there listening, hope dawned in his heart, old things for ever passed away and he was conscious of the sunrise that makes all things new.

But the meeting was drawing to a close ; the " foreign

teacher " had ceased speaking. Looking round upon the audience with the instinct of one accustomed to lead in such matters, Nyi rose in his place and said with simple directness ·

I have long sought the Truth, as did my father before me, but without finding it. I have travelled far and near, but have never searched it out. In Confucianism, Buddhism, Taoism, I have found no rest; but I do find rest in what we have heard to-night. Henceforward I am a believer in Jesus.

The effect of this declaration was profound, for Nyi was well known and respected. But no one present was more moved than the young missionary to whom he specially addressed himself. Many interviews followed, and Hudson Taylor experienced the joy no words can express as he saw the Lord working with him and claiming this soul for His own.

Shortly after his conversion, a meeting was held of the society over which Mr. Nyi had formerly presided, and though he had resigned from its membership he obtained permission to be present and to explain the reasons for his change of faith. Mr. Taylor, who had the pleasure of accompanying him, was deeply impressed by the clearness and power with which he set forth the Gospel. One of his former co-religionists was led to Christ through his instrumentality, and with Nyi himself became of great value to the *Kuen-kiao-teo* church. Nyi, as a dealer in cotton, frequently had time at his disposal which he now devoted to helping his missionary friends. With Mr. Jones he went out almost daily, taking no payment for his services, and everywhere winning an entrance for the message he was so keen to bring.

He it was who, talking with Mr. Taylor, unexpectedly raised a question the pain of which was not easily forgotten.

" How long have you had the Glad Tidings in England?" he asked all unsuspectingly.

The young missionary was ashamed to tell him, and vaguely replied that it was several hundreds of years.

" What," exclaimed Nyi in astonishment, " several

hundreds of years ! Is it possible that you have known about Jesus so long, and only now have come to tell us ? "

"My father sought the truth for more than twenty years," he continued sadly, "and died without finding it. *Oh, why did you not come sooner ?* "

.   .   .   .   .   .

Hardly had Hudson Taylor recovered from his illness and resumed his former activities when a call came to very different service—as difficult as it was unexpected.

Over on the compound of the Presbyterian Mission his friend Mr. Quaterman was taken seriously ill. A devoted pioneer evangelist, he had remained unmarried during the ten years of his life in China, finding a congenial home with his sister Mrs. Way. His brother-in-law, one of the Presbyterian missionaries, was absent on a journey, and with several children to care for Mrs. Way discovered that her brother was suffering from smallpox. Sadly Dr. Parker pronounced it that dread disease in its most malignant form. The patient had of course to be isolated, and to her great distress Mrs. Way could not undertake the nursing.

No one else seemed in a position to do so, and the sufferer would have been left to the care of native servants had not Hudson Taylor heard of it. But to him the circumstances were a clear call to go to the help of his friends. He was unmarried and knew that could he have consulted the one he loved she would not have held him back. As it was he had to leave it to others to tell her, and almost at a moment's notice hastened across the river to take up his sorrowful task.

Night and day he tended the dying man, with no thought of self, doing duty as doctor and nurse in one, that others might be spared the risk of infection.

"He has been taken home to be with Jesus," he wrote a week later, "and great was my privilege in being permitted to minister to the Lord in his person, and to see the power of sustaining grace "

But he did not say how cast upon God he had been all through those terrible nights and days, nor how he felt the strain now that it was over. For the moment, indeed, more pressing considerations occupied him, and he was reminded in a practical way of the scrolls at *Kuen-kiao-teo* with their precious message.

For hardly had he performed the last offices for his friend before he found himself in an unforeseen dilemma. In his attendance night and day upon the patient he had been obliged to change his clothing frequently, and now all the garments used in the sick room had to be discarded for fear of spreading the infection. A Chinese tailor could soon have provided others, but as it happened the young missionary could not afford a fresh supply. It was not that he had been suffering from shortness of funds. On the contrary, ever since leaving the C.E.S he had received from other sources more than he personally required. But he was sharing all that came to him with Mr. Jones and his family, and had had the pleasure of helping others also in different parts of China. During his recent illness he had written to his mother (September 20) of a gift of thirty-seven pounds that had just reached him, and of the thankfulness with which he had forwarded it to a brother-missionary in need

"Do not be uneasy about . . . money," he continued. "The Lord directs. I do not get it to lay by in store, but to use for Him."

And there were always ways in which it could be used to more advantage, it would seem, than on himself.

Thus his supply of clothing had run short, and now that the infected garments had to be destroyed there were none to fall back upon, and he would have been in serious difficulty but for the resource of prayer.

And just then, strange as it may seem, a long-lost box arrived containing among other belongings all the clothing he had left in Swatow fifteen months previously. For the promise still holds good, " Before they call I will answer, and while they are yet speaking I will hear."

A little incident ? Yes, but one that added meaning to the motto of the Mission that was yet to grow out of the growth of his soul

Hitherto hath the Lord helped us.
The Lord will provide.

CHAPTER XXXVI

JOY COMETH IN THE MORNING

OCTOBER AND NOVEMBER 1857. AET. 25.

IT is hardly to be wondered at that his attendance upon
Mr. Quaterman should have proved too much for Hudson
Taylor at this time. But for recent vaccination the illness
that followed might have been much more serious, for it
was undoubtedly smallpox, and the fever ran high. As it
was, it was chiefly memorable for the mercy that averted
worse developments, and for an experience toward the
close that brought him untold comfort.

It was early on October 20, before day-dawn indeed,
when some noise in the street awoke him with a sudden
start. He could not sleep again, and though outwardly
quiet was distressed by palpitation due to his exhausted
condition. And then, with the fatal ease of disordered
nerves, one thing led to another until he was overwhelmed
with painful apprehensions.

All the suspense and anguish of the long months of
his love for the one who might never be his seemed to
come back like a flood, gathering itself up in a great fear
of what was yet to come. They had suffered so much;
their love for one another was so intense, and the opposition it
awakened so persistent that it seemed more than he could
bear. In a few weeks now the letter would come that must
decide their future. Unreasoning anxiety laid hold upon him,
and though he tried to quiet his distress of mind by handing
it all over to the Lord, the very effort added to his sufferings.

But " underneath," all the while, were " the Everlasting

Arms." One Whose comprehension is infinite was watching over His suffering child ; and in the way of all others most sure to help, relief was given.

" All at once," he wrote to his sister later in the day, " I became conscious of dear Maria's presence. She came in silently as a breath of air, and I felt such a tranquillity steal over me—I knew she must be there. I felt spell-bound for a short time, but at length without opening my eyes I put out my hand, and she took it in such a warm, soft grasp that I could not refrain from a look of gratitude. She motioned me not to speak, and put her other hand on my forehead, and I felt the headache which had been distracting and the fever retire under its touch and sink as through the pillow. She whispered to me not to be uneasy . . . that she was mine and I was hers, and that I must keep quiet and try to sleep. And so I did, awaking some hours later well of the fever though very weak.

" A sweet dream, I would call it; only I was as wide awake as I am now, and saw and felt her touch as plainly as I do now pencil and paper. All my fear in the fever had been that our love would come to nothing, so you may guess how it soothed me."

It was with pleasure Hudson Taylor found on recovering from this illness that his friend Mr. Burdon of Shanghai was again in Ning-po, this time to arrange for his wedding. He had been engaged to the elder Miss Dyer for almost a year, and now on November 16, they were to be married. Without in the least grudging them their happiness, he could not but feel the contrast with his own circumstances very keenly, especially in view of Miss Aldersey's growing dislike. For as time went on she seems, if anything, to have increased her opposition to the younger's sister's engagement. Not content with having written fully to Mr. Tarn in London, she continued to bring accusations of a serious nature against Hudson Taylor. It came to such a pass at length that Maria herself almost wondered that her confidence did not waver in the one of whom she knew so little. But their love was too deep, too God-given. She suffered none the less, however, especially during these weeks of illness, his own and Mr. Quaterman's, when she could neither come to him nor do anything to show her sympathy. Yet she had come, although she knew it not.

It was rarely the young people could meet even in public

at this time, for the school in which the Misses Dyer were
teaching had been moved across the river to the compound
of the Presbyterian Mission. Living with Mrs. Bausum in
the brown, gable-roofed house adjoining the school-building
they were near neighbours of the Ways, whose love and
admiration for Hudson Taylor must have been a comfort
to the younger sister. He would be frequently spoken of
with gratitude as one who had risked his life in ministering
to their brother,[1] and Maria's fingers may have lingered on
the keys of the harmonium that had belonged to Mr.
Quaterman and was now to be given to her friend.

Not that Hudson Taylor felt free to accept the gift.
Much as he would have valued it, he dared not lay himself
open to further misrepresentations.

"I could not have taken it," he wrote to his mother, "without
its having been considered by some as a sort of payment, and that
of course I guard against. For I would not have anyone imagine
that I desire payment in this life for service to the Lord's people."

For this same reason—that he might avoid causes of
offence—he refrained from visiting Mr. and Mrs. Way on
the Presbyterian compound, and waited as patiently as
he might without communication of any kind with the
one who was in all his thoughts until the letter should
arrive on which so much depended.

Meanwhile with returning strength he was more than
ever busy in the city. The work both in the home he

[1] In August 1905, nearly fifty years later, a sister of Mrs. Way's wrote
as follows —

"Letters from Mrs R. Way of Ning-po would have given delightful
reminiscences of Mr. Hudson Taylor, but these letters, so much prized,
were unavoidably lost . . Mr. Way was absent from the city when the
sickness of Mr. Quaterman, proving to be smallpox, rendered the situation
of Mrs. Way and her children very alarming. The doctor had him isolated,
and I suppose he would have been left to the care of the Chinese, had not
our Heavenly Father interposed and moved the heart of His faithful
servant, Mr. Hudson Taylor, to take upon himself to be nurse, brother,
and comforter in one Actuated by the very spirit of Christ, he cut himself
off from every one, and devoted himself to the care of my suffering brother.

"The sad details—his sore sickness and death—brought sorrow to our
hearts; but how this was tempered by the knowledge that loving hands
and devoted care had done all that could be done for our brother ! "

"For this dear servant of the Lord, Mr Hudson Taylor," added another
member of the family (Miss G. S. Way, of Savannah, Georgia), " we have
always felt the deepest gratitude , and we ever rejoiced in the great things
he was enabled to accomplish in winning China for Christ."

shared with Mr. and Mrs. Jones and in their preaching-station was full of encouragement, and they had added to it " free breakfasts " for the very poor that were a special source of satisfaction to Hudson Taylor. The Lord was supplying his needs more bountifully than ever before, and in the spirit of the words " freely ye have received, freely give," he rejoiced to pour out all that he was and had in the service of others.

Feeding sixty to eighty people every day was a considerable tax on their resources however, and once and again they had actually come to the last penny before fresh supplies were received. This very naturally was misunderstood in some quarters, as may be seen from Dr. Martin's interesting recollections.[1] But both Hudson Taylor and his colleague were walking prayerfully before God in the matter, and He honoured their faith while allowing it also to be tested.

" Many think I am very poor," wrote the young missionary in the middle of November. " This certainly is true enough in one sense, but thank God it is ' As poor, yet making many rich ; as having nothing, yet possessing all things.' . . . I would not if I could be otherwise than as I am—entirely dependent myself upon the Lord, and used as a channel of help to others "

An instance was before him at the moment of the care and faithfulness of God that he could not but share with his home-circle. For only a few days before they had found themselves in " sore straits " at *Kuen-kiao-ieo* through their work of love and mercy. Seventy hungry people, the poorest of the poor, had had their breakfast that morning,

---

[1] " I conclude," writes Dr W. A P Martin recalling early Ning-po days, " with two names more eminent than any of the preceding, the names of Robert Hart and Hudson Taylor. From a budding interpreter the former has blossomed into the famous statesman known as the ' Great I.G ' (Inspector-General of the Chinese Customs Service). His career to which there is no parallel in East or West will be further noticed in connection with Peking. The latter, who rules as many men and with a sway not less absolute, is the Loyola of Protestant Missions When I first met him he was a mystic absorbed in religious dreams, waiting to have his work revealed ; not idle, but aimless. When he had money he spent it on charity to needy Chinese, and then was reduced to sore straits himself. When the vocation found him it made him a new man, with iron will and untiring energy. He erred [?] in leading his followers to make war on ancestral worship, instead of seeking to reform it ; still in founding the China Inland Mission he has made an epoch in the history of missionary enterprise " (from *A Cycle of Cathay*).

and had listened for an hour or more to the story of Redeeming Love. Nyi, who had just been baptized, and others of the native Christians were very helpful on these occasions, and no doubt found their own faith strengthened by the experiences they witnessed.

"Well, on that Saturday morning," continued Hudson Taylor, " we paid all expenses and provided for the morrow, after which we had not a single dollar left. . . . How the Lord would care for us on Monday we knew not, but over our mantelpiece hung two scrolls in Chinese character—*Ebenezer* and *Jehovah Jireh*—and He kept us from doubting for a moment."

And then, that very day, letters that had travelled half across the world reached Ning-po when no mail was expected. Posted in England two months previously, they had been brought in safety over land and sea, and so prospered on their journey that the prayer " Give us this day our daily bread " was answered before the sun went down.

"That very day," concluded Hudson Taylor, " the mail came in a week before it was due, and Mr. Jones received a bill for two hundred and fourteen dollars. So once again we thanked God and took courage.

" The bill was taken to a merchant, and though there is usually a delay of several days before we can get the money, this time he said : ' Send down on Monday and I will have it ready.' We sent, and though he had not been able to buy all the dollars he let us have seventy on account. So all was well.

" Oh it is sweet to live thus in direct dependence upon the Lord who never fails us !

" On Monday the poor had their breakfast as usual, for we had not told them not to come, being assured that it was the Lord's work and that He would provide. We could not help our eyes filling with tears of thankfulness as we saw not only our own needs supplied, but the widow and orphan, the blind, lame and destitute together provided for by the bounty of Him who feeds the sparrows. . . .

" ' Oh taste and see that the Lord is good : blessed is the man that trusteth in Him. Oh fear the Lord, ye His saints : for there is no want to them that fear Him. The young lions do lack and suffer hunger : but they that seek the Lord shall not want any good thing '— and if not good, why want it ? "

Very soon after this Hudson Taylor found that the Lord had been working for him in other ways also. For it was

2 G

toward the end of November the long-looked-for letters came—and were favourable ! After careful inquiry in London, Mr. Tarn had satisfied himself that Hudson Taylor was a young missionary of unusual promise. The Secretaries of the Chinese Evangelisation Society had nothing but good to say of him, and from other sources also he had the highest references. Taking therefore any disquieting rumours he may have heard for no more than they were worth, he cordially consented to his niece's engagement, requesting only that the marriage should be delayed until she came of age. And that would be in little more than two months' time !

Oh China, China ! How the said young missionary longed, after that, to see what some one else would say, and how distractingly difficult it was to arrange an interview ! To cross the river forthwith and present himself at Mrs. Bausum's would have outraged all proprieties. Anywhere on the compound where she lived, indeed, they could not have met under the circumstances ; and his own home was still more out of the question. But news of this sort flies fast, and in some way Mrs. Knowlton of the American Baptist Mission heard of the situation. She was in favour of the engagement, and lived in a quiet place outside the city-wall and close to the river. She would send a note to the school. Miss Dyer could come to see her at any time ; and if somebody else were there—well, such things will happen, even in China !

So it was in Mrs. Knowlton's drawing-room he waited while the messenger went slowly, slowly across the river and seemed as if he never would return. Let us hope that the windows overlooked the ferry, and that Hudson Taylor had not to keep up the form of conversation. At last, at last ! The slender figure, quick step, bright young voice in the passage—then the door opened, and for the first time they were together alone.

Fifty years later the joy of that moment had not left him : " We sat side by side on the sofa," he said, " her hand clasped in mine. It never cooled—my love for her. It has not cooled now."

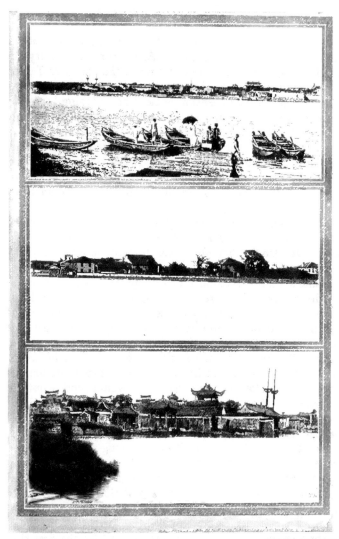

Photographs by   G. Whitfield Guinness.

1. THE FERRY BETWEEN THE FOREIGN SETTLEMENT AND NING-PO.
Showing the Salt Gate and City Wall near Dr. Parker's Hospital.

2. PART OF THE PRESBYTERIAN COMPOUND OPPOSITE THE HOSPITAL.
Showing the Girls' School and House among the trees, from which Mrs. Hudson Taylor was married.

3. A VIEW FROM BRIDGE STREET NEAR THE JUNCTION OF THE SUN AND MOON LAKES.

To face page 450.

CHAPTER XXXVII

●

PERFECT IN ONE

AFTER this they were openly engaged, and could meet from time to time in the company of friends : and how those happy winter days made up for all that had gone before !

"I never felt in better health or spirits in my life," wrote Hudson Taylor. "To God who alone doeth wondrous things, who raiseth up those that are bowed down and has caused every effort to injure me to work only for good . . . to Him be praise and glory."

The engagement was not to be a long one, for on January 16 Miss Dyer would be twenty-one years of age and free to follow the dictates of her heart. So the closing weeks of the year were full of joyous anticipation.

It is good to know that in a life so serious as regards its outward surroundings there were still times when they could be young and gay. One refreshing glimpse into this side of things is afforded by an intimate friend of those days, now the widow of the devoted and beloved Dr. Nevius.

"To those who only knew Mr. Taylor in later life," wrote Mrs. Nevius, "it may be a surprise to learn that when he ' fell in love ' it was a headlong plunge, and by no means a slight or evanescent passion. And his fiancée with her strong, emotional nature was in this respect not unlike him. My husband was rather a special friend of both, and he sometimes indulged his propensities for good-natured teasing at their expense. I was in America, sent home on account of ill-health, when the following little ' passage at arms,' or rather *hands*, took place.

"One evening the young people were seated round a table playing a

451

game that required their hands to be hidden beneath it. To his surprise Mr. Nevius received an unexpected squeeze. Guessing at once that it was a case of mistaken identity, and enjoying the situation, he returned the pressure with interest. In a moment ' Maria ' his next neighbour discovered her mistake, but when she would have withdrawn her hand it was held fast by its captor's strong fingers. Not until flushed cheeks and almost tearful eyes warned him that the joke had gone far enough did he release her. Those were days when to laugh was easy, and not such very funny things were sufficient to evoke much merriment.

" Perhaps still another person whose name is known round the world was sitting at that table, for Mr. (now Sir Robert) Hart was a frequent visitor in our home. And it is quite possible that the now venerable and even then learned Dr. W. A. P. Martin was also a guest that evening. How little we imagined in those days the remarkable careers in store for some of those bright, merry young people ! But cares and responsibilities were to come upon them soon enough ; and what could have been better, in the midst of more serious preparation, than just such times as these ? They were hard students even then, every one of them, and probably erred on the side of overwork."

A very different experience and one that might well have given the young girl pause, had her character been other than it was, occurred on the eve of their marriage a few weeks later.

" It was the 6th of January," said Mr. Taylor, recalling the circumstances in conversation with the writers, " and the bride-elect was coming to tea at *Kuen-kiao-teo* in company with Mrs. Bausum. This had been arranged some time previously, when we were under no anxiety as to supplies. But when the time drew near we found ourselves in serious difficulty. Expenses had been heavy on account of our work among the poor, and mail after mail had come in bringing nothing from home. At last on the morning of the day in question one solitary cash—the twentieth part of a penny—was all that we had left between us. But though tried we looked to the Lord once again to manifest His gracious care.

" Enough remained in the house to supply a modest breakfast; after which, having neither food for the rest of the day nor money to obtain any, we could only betake ourselves to Him who is a *real* Father, and cannot forget His children's needs. And you may be sure that what was to me the most painful element in the situation— our unpreparedness for the guests who were coming that evening— was specially remembered before Him.

" After prayer and deliberation Mr. Jones agreed with me that we ought to try to dispose of some saleable article in order to supply our immediate needs. But on looking round we saw nothing that could well be spared, except perhaps a clock, and little that the Chinese would purchase for ready money. Credit to any extent we might have had, but that would not have been in accordance with our principle in the matter of debt. So the clock was taken to a neighbouring merchant, who proved a willing purchaser.

" 'But of course you must leave it for a week,' he said, 'that we may see how it goes. No one would think of paying money down for an untried clock ! '

" This was so reasonable from the Chinese point of view that there was no gainsaying it, and we saw there was no help for us in that direction.

" One other article remained, an American stove that could have been sold for old iron, but we much regretted parting with it. Still, it seemed necessary, so we set out for the foundry which was at some distance. On the way, however, our path was unexpectedly closed. The bridge of boats, by which we had intended crossing the river, had been carried away in the night, and all that remained was a ferry, the fare for which was two cash each. As we only possessed one cash between us our course was clearly to return and await God's own interposition on our behalf.

" Upon reaching home again we found that Mrs. Jones and the children had gone to dine with a friend. The invitation, accepted some days previously, had included Mr. Jones, but under the circumstances he would not hear of leaving me. So we set to work and carefully searched the cupboards, and though there was nothing to eat we found a small packet of cocoa which with a little hot water somewhat revived us.

" Our Chinese cook then came and begged his master to make use of the small sum left of his wages. But to this Mr. Jones could not agree, as he explained to the man, adding that although we could not go into debt, even for necessary food, our Heavenly Father knew all about it, and would soon supply His children's needs.

" But though he spoke with confidence, our faith was not a little tried as we went into his study and gave ourselves to waiting upon God. We cried indeed unto the Lord in our trouble, and He heard—and delivered us out of all our distresses.

" For while we were still on our knees, the cook came to the door. ' Oh Teacher, Teacher,' he exclaimed, ' here are letters ! ' Once again a mail had arrived from home several days before it was expected, bringing, as we found to our thankfulness, a generous gift from Mr. Berger. ' Whoso is wise and will observe these things, even they shall understand the loving-kindness of the Lord.' Who that ever trusted in Him was put to shame ? "

Over a happy tea-table that evening the whole story came out, for their hearts were so filled with joy and praise that they could not keep it to themselves. The wedding had been arranged for January 20, just two weeks later, but in the light of what had taken place Hudson Taylor felt that he must put before his loved one the more serious aspects of the step she was taking. Very fully he told her, when they were left alone, just what the trial had been.

" I cannot hold you to your promise," he continued, " if you would rather draw back. You see how difficult our life may be at times "——

" Have you forgotten ? " the sweet voice interposed. " I was left an orphan in a far-off land. God has been my Father all these years ; and do you think I shall be afraid to trust Him now ? "

" My heart did sing for joy," he said as he told the story. And well it might ! For the price of such a woman is " far above rubies."

So the preparations for the wedding went on,—outwardly with the kind help of many friends, and inwardly with the blessing of God. Some of the lessons he was learning at this time may be gathered from the last letters Hudson Taylor penned before the happy event.

I can scarcely realise, dear Mother, what has happened ; that after all the agony and suspense we have suffered we are not only at liberty to meet and be much with each other, but that within a few days, *D.V.*, we are to be married ! God *has* been good to us. He has indeed answered our prayer and taken our part against the mighty. Oh may we walk more closely with Him and serve Him more faithfully. I wish you knew my Precious One. She is such a treasure ! She is all that I desire.

Yet the first place in his heart was truly given to Him " whose love exceeds all human affection," as he wrote in another letter, " and who can fill the soul with gladness to which all other joy is unworthy to be compared."

Now I know what it is to have my name written on His heart . . .

and *why* He never ceases to intercede for me . . . His love is so great that He *cannot*. It is overwhelming, is it not ? Such depths of love, and for me !

.　　.　　　.　　　.　　　.　　　.

The Wedding Day was perfect, setting a crown on all that had gone before.[1]

In brilliant sunshine Hudson Taylor crossed the river and made his way to the old temple, near the Presbyterian compound, that did duty as a Consulate. The Rev. F. F. Gough was there already in his office as Chaplain, with friends from all the different Missions, officers from the British gunboat and a few other foreigners. Mr. Robert Hart represented the absent Consul ; and Mr. Way the father of the bride.

Very sweet and fair she looked in more than Hudson Taylor's eyes that day, in her simple grey silk gown and wedding veil. He was wearing ordinary Chinese dress, and to some the contrast between them must have seemed remarkable. But to those who could see below the surface the noteworthy thing about this wedding was the way in which bride and bridegroom were already " perfect in one."

The reception afterwards in the hospitable home of Mr. and Mrs. Way, the speeches and all the kind congratulations passed like a dream ; but it began to seem more real when early sunset found them alone together among the Western Hills. And the days that followed were better far than any dream.

From the guest-room of the Nioh-wang monastery Hudson Taylor wrote a week later :

Jan. 28. We are so happy ! The Lord Himself has turned our sorrow into joy, giving us " the garment of praise for the spirit of heaviness." . . .

Jan. 29. He has answered all our prayers ; overruled the opposition of those who would have separated us ; justified the confidence He enabled us to place in Him, and made us very, very happy indeed.

And from Ning-po, when six weeks had gone by ·

Oh, to be married to the one you *do* love, and love most tenderly

---

[1] January 20, 1858.

and devotedly . . . that is bliss beyond the power of words to express or imagination conceive ! There is no disappointment *there*. And every day as it shows more of the mind of your Beloved—when you have such a treasure as mine—makes you only more proud, more happy, more humbly thankful to the Giver of all good for this best of earthly gifts.

CHAPTER XXXVIII

1858–1859. Aet. 26.

A NEW home, especially if it is to receive a bride, is just as interesting in China as elsewhere; and Hudson Taylor found himself quite popular on Bridge Street when in the early spring he remodelled the barn-like attic in which he had formerly dwelt alone. Not only was he married, a change that in itself entitled him to consideration, but he had married the well-known *Da-yia Ku-niang* who for five years had lived and worked in that part of the city. In addition to being a bride she was the trusted friend of many a woman and girl throughout the neighbourhood, so that visitors were numerous when the young couple came into residence, as they did toward the end of April.

This was three months after their marriage, and in the interval they had broken ground in a country district eight or ten miles from the city. From the quiet of the Nioh-wang monastery they had moved to a busy little town (*Moh-tz-in*) on the shores of the Eastern Lake. Surrounded by a large fishing population they had spent a happy month living and preaching Christ among those who had never heard. Love and joy, it seemed, were a wonderful talisman with which to open hearts, and it was a real sorrow when illness obliged them to abandon the native cottage in which they had been living and return to more suitable quarters in the city.

Long weeks of nursing followed, for the fever was nothing less than typhoid, which attacked them one after the other. It was evident that it would not do to return to *Moh-tz-in*

457

for the summer ; so while continuing to visit it as an outstation Mr. Taylor decided, as we have seen, to occupy the
premises on Bridge Street, where it would not be necessary
to sleep on the ground floor.

So it was there over the chapel, between the narrow
street in front and the canal behind, in the little rooms that
were to form the cradle of the China Inland Mission and
are now its oldest home, that the young missionaries began
their settled work. Downstairs everything remained as
before, but a few small chambers were fashioned above,
with inexpensive partitions. Chinese furniture was easily
to be had, and housekeeping was a simple matter to one so
familiar with the language and ways of the people.

Then it was that Hudson Taylor discovered fresh meaning
in the inspired word, " Whoso findeth a wife findeth a good
thing, and obtaineth favour of the Lord." Missionary
life was no longer a one-sided, bachelor affair, but rounded
out and complete in all its relations. He began to feel in
touch with the people in a new way, and was able to understand and serve them better at every point. And the
gentle presence that made the sunshine of his home was
loved and welcomed by the neighbours all about them.
Quite freely she went in and out of their courtyards, seeking
pupils for her little school, chatting with the children,
delighting the women with her understanding of their
everyday affairs, and cheering the old people with ready
sympathy. There was something about her bright face
and pleasant ways that made them want to know the secret
of the peace she possessed, and many came to the meetings
in the Mission-house to hear more from her lips of the Saviour
who made her life so different from their own. Thus a
light began to shine from the new home on Bridge Street
that brightened many a heart in that great heathen city,
and both husband and wife discovered how much marriage
may help the missionary in his work when it is not only
" in the Lord," but " of Him, through Him, and to Him."

They were not without their anxieties, however, in
common with all others in Ning-po this summer, for it was

THE HOME TO WHICH MR. TAYLOR BROUGHT HIS BRIDE, ON BRIDGE STREET, NOW THE OLDEST STATION OF THE CHINA INLAND MISSION.

a time of painful excitement both in and around the city. The Tai-ping Rebellion, still at the height of its power, was moving rapidly toward the rich province of Cheh-kiang, upon the conquest of which its leaders had determined ; and the inhabitants of Hang-chow, Shao-hing, Ning-po and other important places saw themselves powerless to avert a calamity that defied imagination.

Little or no assistance could be expected from Peking. Worsted in the unequal conflict with England, the broken-hearted Emperor had witnessed the collapse of all his hopes as to protecting his country from foreign opium, and the capital was about to surrender before the might of European arms. With such affairs on hand what help could be given to a distant province over which were hovering the harpies of civil war ? And as to self-defence, the experience of eight terrible years had taught the people only too well that success lay with the Rebels and there was no safety but in flight. And for flight the panic-stricken inhabitants of Ning-po were already preparing.

" Great alarm has been felt in this city," wrote Mr. Taylor early in June, " on account of the approach of the Rebels. . . . Many wealthy men have moved their families and effects into the country, and pawn-brokers have been fortifying their places of business. You will be aware that the latter are a wealthy class in China, something like bankers at home, and are therefore the most likely to be attacked in the event of serious disturbance. Passing along the street, making purchases in shops and even when one is preaching, people stop one to ask if the Rebels are coming ; and though the excitement is less than it was, this still continues." [1]

Even the capture of the forts at Tien-tsin, guarding the approach to the capital, aroused but little interest. It was too far off to make much difference ! But here close at hand were the dreaded " long-haired Rebels." And Heaven itself seemed indifferent to the calamities of the people !

For, to add to their distress, the spring and autumn crops

[1] It was a needless alarm for the time being, for not until three and a half years later (December 1861) did the Rebels succeed in possessing themselves of Ning-po. But the tragedy when it came justified only too fully all the terrible apprehensions, reducing the population of the city and its immediate surroundings to barely a twentieth part of its former number.

were largely ruined through an unusual rainfall all over
this part of China. Day after day, week after week, the
clouds poured out their torrents. Rich and poor were alike
filled with consternation, and large sums of money were
lavished at the shrine of many an idol.

"The Mandarins, great and small, have been to the principal
temples to pray for fair weather," Mr. Taylor continued, "but of
course in vain. When will this poor people cease to lean on them,
and turn to the only living and true God ? Never, I suppose, until
He comes whose right it is to reign, and to whom shall ' the gathering
of the nations be.' "

All this, of course, seriously affected missionary work
at Bridge Street as well as in other parts of the city. Sometimes the preaching-hall was almost empty, and hardly a
passer-by was to be seen on the streets. This was when the
rain was specially heavy. Again at other times Mr. Taylor
had all he could do to keep the crowds in order, and the
preaching was constantly interrupted by questions as to the
troubles that engrossed the thoughts of the people.

There were not wanting difficulties also in the work
itself that called for faith and patience, chief of which
was the lack of native helpers. Mrs. Taylor, happily, had
succeeded in obtaining one or two servants, although they
were wont to disappear on the least provocation, or even
without any. But Christian fellow-workers they had none.
Preaching, teaching, prescribing and dispensing medicines,
as well as entertaining visitors by the hour, Mr. Taylor
had to manage single-handed, in addition to business
affairs, correspondence, and evangelistic excursions with
Mr. Jones.

It would have been possible, of course, to employ a heathen
teacher in the school to which Mrs. Taylor gave six or seven
hours daily ; and they might also have taken on some of
the inquirers with a view to training them for positions of
usefulness. But either of these courses would have been
a hindrance, they considered, rather than a help. To pay
young converts, however sincere, for making known the
Gospel must inevitably weaken their influence if not their
Christian character. Later on the time might come when

the call of God to such service would be evident to all ; but in their spiritual infancy, at any rate, they should be left to grow naturally in the circumstances in which God had placed them, strengthened by the very trials with which they found themselves surrounded.

Meanwhile special faith and devotion were needed to enable the missionaries to do so much themselves. And in their insufficiency, God worked, bringing them in contact with hearts ready to receive the Gospel, and giving them as their children in the faith men and women who should become *soul-winners* and in the fullest sense their " joy and crown of rejoicing."

One of the first of these after their marriage was the basket-maker, Fang Neng - kuei. Introduced at Bridge Street by his friend Mr. Nyi, there was a something about the Christians that greatly attracted him. Long had he been seeking peace of heart, but neither in the ceremonies of Buddhism nor the philosophy of Confucius had he found any help. He had even attended for a time the services of the Roman Catholics, but not until he joined the little circle at Bridge Street did he begin to understand the rest of faith. Then nothing would satisfy him but to be there every night as soon as his work permitted, following eagerly all that was said and done.

It was about this time that Mr. Taylor, finding his audiences diminishing, bethought him of a plan to arouse fresh interest. He had at hand a set of coloured pictures illustrating the Gospel stories, and put up a notice to the effect that these would be on view at the evening services, when they would also be fully explained. The result was all he had hoped, for the Chinese dearly love pictures and stories.

One night the subject was the Prodigal Son, and the young missionary preached with more than ordinary freedom. With the crowded room before him and eager faces peering in from the street, one can well imagine how he would speak on the experiences of the wanderer and all the father's love. The thought of God as such a Father was strangely new to most of his hearers, and when at the close Mr. Taylor invited any who wished to hear more to stay behind for conversation almost the whole audience remained. Among the most interested were Neng-kuei and two friends whom he had brought to the meeting. Others drifted out by degrees, but these three stayed on, and seemed much in earnest when they said they wished to become followers of Jesus.

Mr. Taylor had recently started a night-school in which inquirers might learn to read the New Testament by means of Roman letters. This exactly suited Neng-kuei and his friends, and for some time they were regular in their attendance. Then it began to be rumoured abroad that the basket-makers were becoming Christians, and they had a good deal of persecution to put up with. This of course tested the reality of their faith, and to the sorrow of the missionaries first one and then another ceased to come. Would Neng-kuei too drift away ? But in his case the work proved deep and real. Persecution only brought him out more boldly as a " good soldier of Jesus Christ," and ridicule taught him to defend his new-found faith in such a way that he became a most effective preacher of the Gospel.

But Neng-kuei's earnestness in making known the truth as it is in Jesus was due to something deeper than external opposition. He was a man called of God to a special service, and placed by divine providence in a special school. In spite of more than one fall like Peter's, whom he closely resembled in character, Neng-kuei was to be widely used in winning souls to Christ. Wherever he went in later years, he was enabled to raise up little churches that continued to thrive and grow under the care of others. Neng-kuei was not one who could long minister to them himself ; but he realised this, and was always ready to pass on to new fields when his special work was done. And the zeal and devotion that characterised him must be attributed, under God, to the influences by which his Christian life was formed and nurtured.

Few though they were in number, Hudson Taylor gave

himself to the young converts at this time, as if the
evangelisation of China depended upon their future efforts.
In addition to all his other work he devoted several hours
daily to their instruction. Mr. Jones was the recognised
Pastor of the church, and the Sunday services were held in
his house;[1] but the older Christians, several of whom were
already baptized, were just as eager to attend the Bridge
Street classes as were the most recent inquirers.

First came the public meeting every evening, when the
little hall would be filled with more or less regular attendants;
and when that was over, and outsiders had for the most
part withdrawn, three periods were given to regular and
carefully considered study.

To begin with, a lesson was taken from the Old Testament,
the young missionary delighting to dwell upon the spiritual
meaning of its matchless stories; then a chapter was read
from some important book, frequently the *Pilgrim's Progress*;
and finally a passage from the New Testament was talked
over, the version used being the Romanised colloquial.

Nor was this all. Sunday with its special meetings,
morning, afternoon and evening, was made the very most of
for the inner circle. It cost the Christians a great deal to
leave their regular employments, sacrificing the practical
possibilities of one day in seven. It was perhaps the
hardest thing their Christian faith required of them. Yet
the command was plain, " Remember the Sabbath day to
keep it holy "; and Mr. Taylor and his fellow-missionaries
were convinced that no strong, self-propagating church
could be built on any other basis. So they constantly
enjoined upon the native Christians, by teaching and
example, the requirements of Scripture in this connection.

And as due compensation, if it may be so expressed, they
felt it incumbent upon them to make the sacrifice worth
while, as far as in their power lay, by filling the hours thus
given to God with profitable occupation. In addition,
therefore, to the regular meetings, they had two periods of
teaching after the fashion of the American Sunday School,

---

[1] The *Kuen-kiao-teo* house had been given up soon after Mr Taylor's
marriage, and Mr. and Mrs. Jones were now living in a purely Chinese
residence, about a mile from Bridge Street.

when old and young—Christians, inquirers, patients, school-children and servants—were divided into classes and taught in a helpful, personal way. This made Sunday a heavy day for the missionaries, of whom there were only four, but if it cost some toil and weariness they were the better able to appreciate the sacrifices made by the converts.

Some had to walk long distances and go without food for the greater part of the day, and others had to face perse-cution and financial loss. Neng-kuei, for example, found that it cost him a full third of his weekly wages to attend the meetings on Sunday. He was a skilled workman, and his master was quite willing that he should get through all there was to be done in six days—provided he went without pay on the seventh. If it gave him satisfaction to waste four days in every month he was at liberty to do so, only he must of course provide his food on those occasions and draw wages only for the time in which work was done. It was a clever arrangement as far as the master was con-cerned, but one that told heavily on the poor basket-maker. Two pence a day and his food had been little enough before, but now out of only twelve pence a week (instead of fourteen) he had to spend two or three on provisions for Sunday—which meant a total lessening of his hard-earned income by a third. But he was willing, quite willing for this, if only he could have the Lord's Day for worship ; and there could be no doubt that he was richly repaid in the strength and blessing it brought him all through the week.

Another element of great importance in the training of these young converts was the emphasis placed on reading for themselves the Word of God. This it was that brought out the exceeding value for the uneducated among them of the Romanised version of the Ning-po New Testament. For the local dialect differed greatly from the written language, and hence the more literary versions were unin-telligible to the majority. But there was no one who could not understand the Romanised version. It was a very fair translation, direct from the original language, into the vernacular in everyday use, and as such had a special charm for the women, who could soon read it easily and found that what they read was understood by others.[1]

Mrs. Taylor was fully one with her husband as regards the importance of teaching every inquirer to read, including women and children, and gave a good deal of time to preparing and even printing on her own printing-press suitable literature in the Romanised colloquial. She found that by the use of this system a child of ordinary intelligence could read the New Testament in a month. Older people with less time at their disposal might take longer ; but even for busy women it was no difficult task ; and experience proved that those who accomplished it rarely if ever failed to become Christians.

Mrs. Tsiu, the Teacher's mother, was a case in point. When her son was first employed at *Kuen-kiao-teo* she was angered and distressed by his interest in the Gospel. Reading the Scriptures daily with Mrs. Jones and other foreigners, he had a good opportunity for studying the practical effects as well as the teachings of Christianity, and before the missionaries had any idea that a deep work was going on in his heart, the young Confucianist had become a humble follower of Jesus.

" May I purchase a New Testament ? " he inquired one day. " I want the easy kind, printed in Roman letters."

" But you can read Wen-li," replied his pupil. " Would you not rather have it in the scholarly character ? "

" It is not for myself," said the young man earnestly, " but for my mother. And will you not pray that she may learn to read it, and obtaining heavenly influences may have her heart changed and her sins forgiven ? "

Full of thankfulness over the conversion of the son, the missionaries joined him in earnest prayer for his mother, sharing also his conviction that if only she would learn to read the Gospels she too would love and believe in Jesus.

And so it proved. For though Mrs. Tsiu refused for a

---

[1] Mr. Taylor spent the larger part of his first furlough (in association with the Rev. F. F. Gough) in carefully revising this Romanised New Testament, and supplying it with marginal references : a work which Archdeacon Moule of Ning-po stated many years later to have been of " the greatest value to Christians throughout the province."

long time to have anything to do with the religion of the
foreigners, her desire to be able to read at last won the day.
She was flattered by her son's assurance that she would
soon master the new system and be as fluent a reader as
those who had long studied character, and that moreover
everybody would understand the meaning of what she read.
With his help she made rapid progress, and meanwhile the
message of the book was doing its work in her heart.

Taking her stand boldly as a Christian, Mrs. Tsiu was a
great cheer to the little company of believers all through
those summer months For she was full of joy and courage.
She opened her house for a weekly prayer-meeting which
became a centre of blessing in the neighbourhood, and was
never so happy as when reading and explaining to her
neighbours the precious Book and its story.[1]

This was of course a great encouragement to the
missionaries, and quickened their zeal for the instruction of
all over whom they had any influence. The burden on
their hearts increasingly was that of raising up, as workers
together with God, a band of native evangelists for the as
yet unreached interior of China. To go themselves seemed
for the time being out of the question, and yet the country
was accessible as never before. The Treaty of Tien-tsin
signed during the summer had opened the way at last to all
the inland provinces.[2] Foreigners had now the right to
travel freely, under the protection of passports, and it only
remained to make use of the facilities for which they had
prayed so long.

Tidings brought by Lord Elgin of his recent journey with

[1] Those were red-letter days indeed when Neng-kuei the basket-maker
and the Teacher's mother were baptized and received into the little Church.
This took place on August 15 and 29, Sundays when the Chapel of the
American Baptist Mission was available. Mrs. Tsiu was the first Chinese
woman Mr. Taylor had ever baptized, and his address on the reproach of
Christ as greater riches than the treasures of Egypt came from a full heart.

[2] This Treaty, signed on June 26, 1858, was of the utmost importance
in our relations with China. It contained excellent provisions, such as the
right of maintaining an Ambassador at Peking, freedom for foreigners to
travel in the interior of China, and toleration for Christianity, so that
" persons teaching it or professing it should alike be entitled to the protection of the Chinese authorities." But alas, under the Tariff Supple-
ment, it also contained a clause legalising the importation of opium, against
which the Chinese had striven so long!

a view to testing the new order of things were deeply stirring. No hindrance had been put in his way as he steamed slowly up the Yangtze, six hundred miles to the newly-opened Port of Hankow, the commercial metropolis of central China. Nothing was to prevent foreigners from settling there now— ministers of the Gospel as well as Government officials and merchants—and many were the missionaries who longed to enter that open door.

" You will have heard before this all about the new Treaty," wrote Mr. Taylor in November. " We may be losing some of our Ning-po missionaries . . . who will go inland. And oh, will not the Church at home awaken and send us out many more to publish the Glad Tidings ?

" Many of us long to go—oh how we long to go ! But there are duties and ties that bind us that none but the Lord can unloose. May He give ' gifts ' to many of the native Christians, qualifying them . . . for the care of churches already formed, . . . and thus set us free for pioneering work."

Nothing else, nothing less would have kept Hudson Taylor and his young wife from proceeding at once to the interior. But the claims of that little band of believers could not be set aside. They were their own children in the faith, and though not a large family as yet were just at the stage when they most needed watchful care. It was to *their* love, *their* prayers, these souls had been committed, and to leave them now, even for the good of others, would have been to disregard that highest of all trusts, parental responsibility. And they were right in this conviction, as the blessing of God abundantly proved.

For these Christians, Nyi, Neng-kuei and the rest, were men whom the Lord could use. Poor and unlearned like most of the first disciples, they too were to become " fishers of men." No less than six or seven, indeed, of the converts gathered about Mr. and Mrs. Taylor this winter were to come to their help in later years as fellow-workers in the China Inland Mission.[1] But for them the planting of that

[1] The labours of Mrs. Tsiu and her devoted son, of Nyi the cotton-merchant, Neng-kuei the basket-maker, Wang the farmer and Wang the painter (see next chapter), not to speak of Loh Ah-tsih and others, can never be forgotten. It would be difficult to overestimate the services of

little seed amid so many difficulties would have been almost impossible and much of its promise might never have come to fruition.

Already in the winter of 1858-1859 there were signs that rejoiced the missionaries in the midst of much to try both faith and love. But, even so, they little realised the importance of the influence they were exercising, directly and indirectly. What they were themselves, in the deepest things, this to a large extent their children in the faith became ; and there is no better, surer way of passing on spiritual blessing.

" Imitators of us and of the Lord."

" Those thing which ye have both learned, and received, and seen, and heard in me, do : and the God of peace shall be with you."

Thus it was the Lord trained His own disciples in the three wonderful years ; and thus it must be still to-day.

---

that little band in connection with the earliest stations of the Mission—services extending over ten, twenty, forty and even fifty years, and ending in unclouded testimony to the glory of God.

CHAPTER XXXIX

1858–1859.   Aet. 26.

Among all the characteristics caught by the converts from their missionaries at this time, none was more important in its results than love for souls—that sure evidence of a heart in fellowship with the Lord Himself. When this is not found in the missionary is it ever developed in his native helpers ? And can anything make up for its absence in either the one or the other ? Learning, eloquence, natural gifts, all, all go up in the balances as lighter than nothing, if not permeated with this supreme endowment.

" Though I speak with the tongues of men and of angels, and have not love, I am become as sounding brass, or as a tinkling cymbal. And though I have the gift of prophecy, and understand all mysteries and all knowledge, and though I have all faith so that I could remove mountains, and have not love, I am nothing."

But in the little home on Bridge Street, in spite of all that may have been deficient on less important lines, there was no lack of love—love for God and love for man—the essential qualification for leading men to God. Nyi was a soul-winner, Neng-kuei was a soul-winner, and, to go no farther, Mrs. Tsiu and her son were soul-winners in the good, old-fashioned meaning of the term. They believed in heaven and they believed in hell, and longed to bring those around them to the Saviour whose blood alone cleanses " from all sin."

No sooner had Mrs. Tsiu learned to read, as we have

seen, than she longed to share with her neighbours the
blessings of the Gospel. Taking her precious Testament
wrapped in a coloured handkerchief, many were the hours
she spent in going from courtyard to courtyard, reading
to women at their sewing, and telling the old, old story to
all who would listen. She was a welcome visitor, and
made the most of her opportunities for being useful. But
there was one old woman who seemed beyond her reach.
Very deaf and almost blind, she could think of nothing but
her troubles, and had long ago given up hope of better
things. Yet there was love and rest for her in Jesus ; and
with earnest prayer the Teacher's mother set about winning
this poor, dark soul to Him. But what a difficult task
it was, when every word had to be shouted into her ear,
and she could not catch the love-light in the speaker's
eyes !

This only made it the more wonderful, when the darkened
mind at length was penetrated with some gleam of light
from above. She consented then to go to the Mission-
house, and was conscious in its very atmosphere of a peace
she had never known.

" Why does my heart feel so much *wider*," is the oft-
repeated question, " when I come inside these doors ? "

"Mrs. Tsiu taught her syllable by syllable," wrote Mr. Taylor,
" to repeat verses of hymns and passages of Scripture, . . . and the
Holy Spirit made the Word effectual to her conversion.   Much
prayer and many persevering efforts were rewarded as new light, new
love, sprang up within her.   Now she had found something to think
of, now she had a Friend to converse with, now she had comfort both
for time and for eternity.   A happier Christian than that old woman
I have seldom if ever met.   She loved the house of God, she loved the
people of God.   In fair weather or in wet, in hot weather or in cold,
she was to be found leaning on the shoulder of her grandchild, and
wending her way to the meetings, some of which were more than a
mile from her home.   She could see nothing and hear nothing, but
she met with God and He blessed her ; she met with His people, and
their hearty salutations did her good.

" After a time she was taken ill, and all believed that she was about
to die.   She was very happy, especially in the thought that she would
be neither blind nor deaf in heaven.   One day, however, some
neighbours, to whom she had been talking about the Lord, jeeringly

replied that she should pray to Him, since He was such a wonderful Saviour, to raise her up to health again. Left alone, she pondered the matter until convinced that her recovery in answer to prayer would be to the glory of God ; and upon Mrs. Tsiu and another friend coming in she told them about it, and requested them to kneel down and pray that she might be raised up

"This they willingly did, asking God for the honour of His own great Name to make her well ; and the old woman added her Amen to the prayer she knew had been offered though she heard it not. Within a few days she was in her usual health, and to my astonishment took her accustomed place in one of the meetings. And not until a year later did she finish her course with joy."

Meanwhile Mrs. Tsiu and her son were rejoicing over another soul they had been permitted to win for Jesus. He was an old man and had seen many sorrows, for his sons had turned out badly and through evil ways had ruined the family fortunes. Dying early, they had left their parents to the sorrow and disgrace of a childless, poverty-stricken old age. Scarcely can there be in China a sadder lot, and old Dzing as he peddled his wares thought bitterly of the days when he had been well-to-do and respected. Now he must travel the streets with a pack on his back, depending for a livelihood upon the odds and ends he could sell for women's embroidery and children's caps and shoes. Only at night when every door was shut could he turn homeward to the miserable room where little comfort awaited him.

Persuaded by Mrs. Tsiu and her son to accompany them to Bridge Street, a new interest had found its way into his once dreary existence. So this was the meaning of the change he had noticed in the very faces of his friends ! They had something worth living for ; something that could turn sorrow into joy and brighten even the shadows of the tomb. It was a great discovery.

Many an evening was now spent in the inquirers' classes, the old intelligence waking up in response to their helpful influences. It restored his self-respect to be addressed as "Teacher Dzing" on account of his knowledge of the classics, and appealed to from time to time for the name or meaning of a character. But a deeper work was going on within him, under the touch of a Hand that brought deeper healing.

"As a poor, helpless sinner," Mr. Taylor wrote, "he cast himself upon God's forgiving mercy, and found peace in believing."

His love for the Bible was great, and he spent every available moment over its pages. Perhaps it was this that made his Christian life so restful. Wherever he went he carried a blessing with him, and many a woman on a back street first heard the message of redeeming love from his lips.

Neng-kuei, too, from the very first was a soul-winner. Not unlike Peter in his fervent, devoted spirit, he also was used to bring the message of salvation to seeking souls whose prayers were known to God alone. One such was daily traversing the streets of Ning-po at this time, in search of a religion of which he knew nothing save that it would bring him peace ; and but for a great trial coming into Neng-kuei's life, he might have been long without finding it.

It was the busy season for basket-makers, and Neng-kuei's master insisted that he must work on Sunday. It was no use reminding him of his agreement, or suggesting that he should call in additional help. No, this idea of resting one day in seven was all very well for foreigners, but, now there was work to be done, Neng-kuei must be broken of it.

"Come to-morrow, or not at all," was his ultimatum. And the Christian basket-maker knew himself dismissed.

Nor was this the worst of it. For on Monday morning, when he set about seeking other employment, every door was closed. No one wanted workmen, busy season though it was, and Neng-kuei tramped the city in vain.

"The devil is having hard at me," thought he at last; "but I must and will resist him. If he will not let me have other employment, I will give my time to plucking souls from his kingdom."

And this he did by spending the rest of the day in distributing tracts, and talking in the streets and tea-shops with all who were inclined to listen.

Far away from Ning-po, in the beautiful valley of the Feng-hwa river, lay the farming district from which Neng-kuei himself had come. There he had learned his trade and married the young wife from whom he had been parted in little more than a year. Her death had been terrible—a death in the dark, like so many thousands, alas, in China every year! Poor Neng-kuei could speak no word of comfort as she was passing from him in anguish and fear. And still there was no voice to tell among all those hills and valleys of Jesus and His redeeming love.

The basket-maker drifted to Ning-po a little later, and there found, as we have seen, the Light of Life; but who was to care for Wang the farmer, in the little village of O-zi, when he became concerned about eternal things?

Not far from Neng-kuei's former home he lay ill and apparently dying, alone in the empty house. The family were all out in the fields, having supplied his needs as well as they could; and there was no one to whom he could turn for help in the great distress of his soul. For Wang regarded death with terror, as introducing the dreaded day on which he must "reckon up accounts." Somehow, somewhere, he must meet the gods his sins had angered; and the balance to his credit was pitifully small. Whether his heart went out in a longing cry for mercy we cannot tell. At any rate his need was great, and he was dimly conscious of it.

And then a strange thing happened. In the silence of the empty house he heard himself called. The voice though unknown was so real that he got up and made his way to the door, but on opening it could see no one. Painfully he crept back to bed, only to hear the same voice a little later calling more urgently. Again he rose, and, supporting himself by the walls and furniture, managed to reach the door. But again no one was in sight. Greatly alarmed, he buried his face beneath the coverlet. This was none other than the approach of death!—the dreaded summons of the King of Hell, at whose bar he must shortly appear.

And now the voice spoke a third time, and told him not

to be afraid. He was going, it said, to recover. An infusion of a certain herb would cure his sickness, and as soon as he was able he was to go into Ning-po, where he would hear of a new religion that would bring him peace of heart.

All this was so reassuring that Wang determined to do exactly as he was instructed. He persuaded his wife to prepare the medicine, and to the surprise of all began forthwith to recover. Going to Ning-po, however, was another matter. The city was thirty miles away, and Wang had nothing to live on while seeking the new religion. His farm-produce he could not carry with him, and besides it was all needed at home. The only plan would be to work for his living ; and finally the farmer set out to support himself by cutting grass along the wayside and selling it to people who had cattle.

Thus he had managed to earn a scanty subsistence in Ning-po for some time, without finding anything that met the longings of his heart. Under the city-wall and amid the many grave-mounds he gathered a supply of grass day by day, which he sold in the city, but no one paid much attention to his questions about religious matters. Still, Wang was sure that what the voice had told him would come true.

At length one day in a tea-shop—what was that he heard ? A simple working-man like himself was leaning across one of the tables, talking with those nearest him. Something about " the Jesus-doctrine " he said, and about sins being forgiven. Greatly interested Wang drew nearer, and listened for the first time—try to imagine it—to the glad tidings of salvation.

Neng-kuei's heart was full that day, and he spoke long and earnestly. Some went out and some came in, but the O-zi farmer never lost a word. When Neng-kuei had finished he introduced himself, and asked many questions. Seeing his interest Neng-kuei said :

" You must draw water yourself from the fountain. There is a book God has given us in which everything is made plain. You shall have a copy and study the matter fully."

" Alas," replied the farmer, " I do not know how to read, and I am now too old to learn ! "

" Far from it ! " exclaimed his new-found friend. " For with the Glad Tidings an easy method of reading has been brought to us. I did not know a single character when I became a Christian, but now I can read the New Testament quite easily. If you like I will be your teacher. Let us begin at once ! "

Wang needed no second invitation. It did not take long to move his few belongings to the house in which the basket-maker lodged, and before the sun went down he had mastered the first six letters of the alphabet, besides acquiring a much fuller knowledge of spiritual things. And how happy they were over the lesson ! It is doubtful whether anywhere in the city there were more thankful hearts, for had not the farmer found the treasure he had been seeking, and Neng-kuei a new jewel to lay at his Master's feet ?

No doubt they prayed together that evening over Neng-kuei's difficulty in obtaining employment, for which a sufficient reason was found the following day. His former master, angered by his adherence to Christian principles, had sent round to all the basket-makers of the city asking that if this particular workman applied to them on Monday morning they would turn him away. As members of the same Guild they had thought it best to comply. But the promise was for Monday, not for subsequent days ; and the first employer to whom he went on Tuesday was glad enough to engage the clever workman. So Neng-kuei's troubles, too, were happily ended ; and his new master living not far from Bridge Street, he was able to run in during the breakfast-hour and tell his missionary friends all that had happened.

Introduced in this way to the farmer from O-zi, Mr. Taylor hardly knew at first what to make of his story. But as time went on the sincerity of the man became apparent to all. He remained in Ning-po for some months, still supporting himself as a grass-cutter, and when he returned to O-zi it was to set apart the best room in his house as a little chapel, in which for fifty years he lovingly and faithfully made known the Gospel.

But this was not the only time Neng-kuei was enabled, through fidelity to Christian principle, to win a soul destined to become specially useful in winning others. Another man named Wang was living in Ning-po at the time who was yet to be numbered among the Bridge Street Christians, and to exceed them all in the fruitfulness of his labours. But as yet he knew nothing of the Master he was to love and serve.

A busy workman, employed from morning till night in painting and decorating houses, how was he to come under the influence of the Gospel? He had no time to listen to preaching, though he seems to have been religiously inclined, and was no frequenter of tea-shops, his own home being at hand with the attractions of wife and infant child. So the Lord, who had chosen him for His service, sent across his pathway one whom He could trust to be faithful in little things, and who "in season and out of season" would deliver His message.

It was a beautiful house young Wang was in that day, decorating one of the guest-halls. Presently a stir began— servants came hurrying from the inner apartments, a man with a load of baskets was ushered in, and several ladies, richly dressed, came out to give their orders. Of all this the painter on his scaffolding took little notice, but when the ladies began to speak in tones of some annoyance he pricked up his ears to listen.

"What! Not make baskets for holding incense? Refuse an order for anything to be used in the service of the gods?"

"Do not be angry, ladies," replied the simple basket-maker. "I am sorry not to comply with your wishes, but I cannot make or sell anything for the worship of idols."

"And pray, why not?" was the astonished question.

"I am a believer in the Lord Jesus," Neng-kuei answered respectfully; "a worshipper of the true and living God." And he went on to put before these ladies, who might never hear again, the way of pardon and peace through a dying, risen Saviour.

" What was that you were saying ? "

The ladies had grown tired of listening, and had tottered away on their tiny feet, but Neng-kuei's attention was arrested, as he was about to leave, by a man in working clothes, who went on earnestly :

" You did not see me. I am painting up there," indicating his ladder. " What was it you were saying ? I heard, but tell me again."

That conversation, too, we are left to imagine. We only know that Wang Lae-djün took the first step that day in a lifetime of devoted service to the Master.

CHAPTER XL

WHAT HATH GOD WROUGHT

FEBRUARY–AUGUST 1859. AET. 26-27.

IT was February 9, and in a darkened room Hudson Taylor knelt beside the bed-side of his dying wife. Only a few weeks had elapsed since the New Year dawned upon their perfect happiness, and now—was she to be taken from him, and his life shadowed with irreparable loss ? Internal inflammation, the result apparently of chill, had brought her so low that life seemed ebbing fast away, and every remedy the physicians could suggest had proved unavailing.

Elsewhere in the city the united prayer-meeting was going on, and the knowledge that others were praying with him upheld the lonely watcher as nothing else could have done. Noting with anguish the hollow temples, sunken eyes, and pinched features, all indicating the near approach of death, Hudson Taylor was indeed "shipwrecked upon God." Faith was the only spar he had to cling to ; faith in the Will that even then was perfect wisdom, perfect love.

Kneeling there in the silence—how was it that new hope began to possess his heart ? A remedy ! They had not tried it. He must consult Dr. Parker as quickly as possible. But would she, could she hold out until he came back again ?

"It was nearly two miles to Dr. Parker's," he wrote, "and every moment appeared long. On my way thither, while wrestling mightily with God in prayer, the precious words were brought with power to my soul, ' Call upon Me in the day of trouble · I will deliver thee, and thou shalt glorify Me.' I was enabled at once to plead them in faith, and the result was deep, deep unspeakable peace and joy.

"All consciousness of distance was gone. Dr. Parker approved the use of the means suggested ; but upon arriving at home I saw at a glance that the desired change had taken place in the absence of this or any other remedy. The drawn aspect of the countenance had given place to the calmness of tranquil slumber, and not one unfavourable symptom remained to retard recovery."

The Great Physician had been there. His Presence had rebuked the approach of death. His touch had once again brought healing.

This experience of what the Lord could and would do for His people in answer to believing prayer was one of the most wonderful Hudson Taylor ever had, and strengthened him for many an emergency including those of the summer near at hand. Never could he forget those days and hours in which it seemed as though the Lord were saying : "Son of man, I take from thee the desire of thine eyes at a stroke." But it was not on his home the sore affliction fell.

Very refreshing, after this dangerous illness, was a visit to the new hospital outside the city. For Dr. Parker's building operations were finished, including chapel, dispensary, and dwelling-house, and he had accommodation for European as well as Chinese patients and guests, Everything was new, fresh, and attractive, and the house itself, standing back a little from the river, was crowned with a watch-tower commanding a view of unusual interest.

"The situation of Dr. Parker's new hospital," wrote Dr. W. A. P. Martin about this time, "is the best that could have been selected in the vicinity of this port. Separated on the one hand from the impure atmosphere of the city by the city-wall, and removed on the other from the noisome exhalations of the paddy-fields by the breadth of the river, it enjoys the best air that blows over the plain of Ning-po. Close to one of the city gates, near a much-frequented ferry, and overlooking, too, a river which is the main thoroughfare from the sea-coast to many large cities in the interior, its handsome and commodious buildings daily attract the notice of thousands of passers-by.

"The number of in-patients is already so large as nearly to fill the neat little chapel which the doctor has erected as a dispensary for the soul. They form the nucleus of a very interesting congregation, to which I have preached several times ; and the probability of their obtaining permanent good is the greater as they remain many weeks together, receiving daily instruction in divine truth."

It was delightful to see how much had been accomplished by the courage and perseverance with which the Doctor had worked at his long-cherished plan, raising within three years, without help from his Society, this well-equipped medical mission.

" May the Lord who has aided me thus far," he wrote, " now use all for the advancement of His cause and the glory of His Name."

Four years had now elapsed since the beginning of 1855, when Dr. Parker and his young colleague had been writing home about their " plans of usefulness." How differently everything had turned out from their expectations ! And yet, with these commodious buildings round them representing so important a work, Dr. Parker must have felt thankful that he had not remained in Shanghai ; and Hudson Taylor, as he thought of the Christians in the city, and the loved one given and spared to him in answer to prayer, could not but overflow with gratitude and praise. It was all they had hoped or dreamed, only better—" our plans of usefulness," but with added elements of blessing they could never have devised, much less brought to pass.

" Commit thy way unto the Lord ; trust also in Him. . . . Delight thyself also in the Lord, and He shall give thee the desires of thine heart."

" Yesterday (February 28) was a glad day for us," wrote Mr. Taylor while still at Dr. Parker's, " for our servant who has been with us almost ever since our marriage was received into the Church by baptism, as well as a woman who works for Mrs. Jones. We have now eight native Christians in communion with us, of whom the second (Mr. Tsiu) was baptized a year ago yesterday. Truly we may say with thankfulness, ' what hath God wrought ! ' " [1]

" I am very busy," he continued after their return to the city. " So many patients, meetings, and other matters need attention that

---

[1] Seven baptisms within a year was cause indeed for thanksgiving, representing as it did fully as much of prayer, labour and progress as would ten times that number in the same localities to-day. One Mission then in Ning-po, after fifteen years of faithful labour, had a Church Roll of only twenty members ; though another, not quite so long in the field, had considerably more.

I am puzzled which to take up first. . . . Our work here is becoming more important day by day, as God is adding to our numbers. . . . May His great work go on, and the multitudes of China yet see a glorious day when in every part of this populous empire . . . the saved of the Lord shall be many."

Thus spring-time came again, and in April a little holiday was taken, that proved most beneficial in view of the difficult summer before them. Travelling in houseboats with Dr. Parker and his family, Mr. and Mrs. Taylor spent a week among the Western Hills, covered at this season with azaleas, hawthorn, dwarf lilac, wistaria and violets.

"The quiet retirement," wrote one whose name has long been associated with Ning-po, "the blue heavens above and the green hills around, the sound of rippling brook or singing bird, the flash of summer lightning, the echoing storm, the cry of roaming deer at night, the indescribable beauty of the carpet of flowers in spring-time are pleasant and refreshing sights and sounds indeed after the toil, dust, and oppressiveness of a great city." [1]

Leaving their boats the little party explored some of the side streams, tracing one almost to its source by means of light rafts of bamboo.

"The scenery was very beautiful," Mr. Taylor wrote to his mother. "Waterfalls abound, one of which leaps seven hundred feet in a sheer descent, and another that we saw about six hundred. . . . The views above, below, and around were wonderful . . . something to be remembered for a lifetime."

Great was the contrast on their return to Ning-po with the heat and manifold distresses of that summer. Following upon the floods of the previous year came an unusually hot season, and at the same time a wave of anti-foreign feeling swept over the city, due to daring outrages perpetrated in connection with the coolie-traffic, which was "rapidly assuming all the features of the African slave-trade." Hitherto its ravages had been confined to the Southern provinces, but now men and lads were disappearing from this region also, carried off on foreign ships to the plantations

[1] The Ven. Arthur E. Moule, B.D , Archdeacon in Mid-China and C.M S. Missionary at Ning-po. Quoted from *The Story of the Cheh-kiang Mission*, p 76.

of Cuba and South America, most of them never to return. And these outrages were the more alarming because of their connection in the minds of the people with the renewal of hostilities between China and the Allied Powers.[1]

" You will not be surprised to hear," wrote Mr. Taylor in the middle of August, " that while God is granting us blessing, Satan is manifesting his malice. Owing to the kidnapping villainies of those engaged in the coolie traffic—forcibly seizing villagers, and carrying them off in sacks to their vessels—public excitement has reached a very high pitch. Rumours have been circulated that these persons are being seized at the instance of the ' defeated British,' who wish to reinforce their numbers and again attack Tien-tsin. Violent incendiary papers have been posted up, and our lives and property have been in imminent danger. The excitement is decreasing a little now, and we hope the worst is over, as the people know that measures are being taken by the foreign authorities to search to the bottom of this disgraceful affair."

But before this letter was written and a measure of tranquillity restored, the missionary household in Bridge Street had passed through some anxious hours. As many Europeans as possible had left the city, taking shelter in the Settlement or on foreign vessels, but Mr. and Mrs. Taylor would not leave the native Christians, whose danger was little less than their own.

Those were days in which the young husband could not but long for quiet and the blessed sense of security that would have meant so much to the one dearer to him than life. Protect her he could not from the knowledge of surrounding danger, but taking such precautions as were possible he stayed his heart on God. It was not much that could be done to facilitate escape, should it be necessary. A boat lay in readiness at the back door, and a rope was

---

[1] For the Treaty of Tien-tsin, signed in June of the previous summer, was to have been ratified at Peking a year later. Upon the arrival of the fleet of nineteen vessels representing the Allies (England, France, Russia and America) they were attacked in the mouth of the Pei-ho river and driven back with considerable loss ; and the capture of Peking itself was necessary before the Chinese Government realised that they must carry out their terms of surrender   The Treaty was finally ratified in October 1860   In August of the following year the heart-broken Emperor (Hien-feng) died.   The ratification of these Treaties had swept away the barriers he had so long striven to maintain against the importation of opium, which, from this time, alas ! spread with fatal rapidity throughout the length and breadth of the land.

Photograph   By a Chinese.

THE BEDROOM WINDOW, MARKED WITH A ✗, WHICH WOULD HAVE AFFORDED
MR. AND MRS. TAYLOR THEIR ONLY WAY OF ESCAPE, IN THE EVENT OF
A NIGHT ATTACK ON THE BRIDGE STREET PREMISES.

To face page 483.

strongly fastened in their bedroom window by means of which it might be possible to reach the canal under cover of darkness. But full well he knew the complications that might arise, and it would have been a time of agonising suspense but for the peace of God.

For it was then, and under those circumstances, the hopes of many a long month were fulfilled, and the little daughter came to them for whom they could find no sweeter, truer name than Grace.

" My dear Parents," wrote the father a week later, " though this is the Lord's Day I find myself able to pen a few lines, which will no doubt surprise you as much as it does myself. The reason is that I am at home taking care of my wife and baby-girl—your first grand-child ! Oh, my dear Parents, God has been so good to me, to us all ! better far than my fears. ' O magnify the Lord with me, and let us exalt His Name together ! ' "

The thermometer was at 104° F. in the coolest part of the house when on July 31 this little one was born, and once only in the week that followed did it drop as low as 88°—at midnight, during a thunderstorm. So that this period was not without its trials. But the worst had been averted, although for a few hours it came very near.

Surging crowds about the mission-house had almost broken into a riot a few days previously, while cries of " Beat the foreigner," " Kill the foreign devils," rent the air. In some wonderful way, however, a restraint was on the people, and no attempt was made to batter in the doors, easy as it would have been.

And, if anything, more wonderful still was the peace in which the mother's heart was kept, both before and after. " Notwithstanding, the Lord stood with me and strengthened me," was indeed true in her experience. Nothing retarded her recovery, and so conscious was she of the inflow of divine grace for every need that she would not have been without the trials that revealed to her new depths of the heart of God.

The dangers did not pass away for some time, and

combined with the intense heat might well have proved
overwhelming.

" We feel that we are living only from night to day and day to
night," wrote Mr. Jones, who also remained in the city. " The people
are thirsting for revenge. . . . They mix up together missionaries,
traders, and the government, the war, and the coolie traffic, . . . and
say that the kidnapped Chinese are put in the front of the fight against
their own Emperor. . . . They have placarded the streets calling for
our blood; one of the foremost in all this being a man who supplies
the Mandarins with buckets to contain the heads of the decapitated,
a fearfully large trade here.

" We are now, as I write, in the midst of all this, our wives and our
little ones in the same danger. But we are resting on Him who
restrains our enemies with ' Thus far, but no further ' ; and who to
us is saying, ' I will never leave thee.' He has made His Word very
precious to our hearts, . . . and even in these trying times we have
been encouraged by some inquiring the way of salvation."

For the work of God went on, and was more deep and
real for the testing through which the converts had to pass.
Wang the grass-cutter, for example, who was accepted for
Church-membership in August, was frequently upbraided
on the streets for casting in his lot with the Christians.
His simple faith, however, was proof against all attacks.
When told that foreigners were at war with his country,
and were carrying off people to make them fight against
their own Emperor, he would say :

" There must be a mistake somewhere. Satan surely
has blinded your eyes. These missionaries do not fight
at all. They heal the sick, relieve suffering, and show us
the way of eternal happiness. Nothing but good can come
of joining them."

And from this position he was not to be moved.

That he really knew the Lord was very evident to those
who watched his life at this time.

" I think much of heaven and Jesus," he said to Mr.
Taylor one day, " the weather is so hot."

" Indeed," replied his friend, waiting to hear more.

" You see," he continued, " I have to cut grass out in
the burning sun, and sometimes I hardly know how to keep

on. And then I think of Jesus—Jesus and heaven—and my mind becomes peaceful and my body so much rested that I can do twice as much as before. Oh, it is wonderful the difference it makes when you just think of Jesus!"

And so the missionaries found it too.

CHAPTER XLI

A WEALTHY PLACE

SPARED thus in the mercy of God the loss of his own loved one, Hudson Taylor felt the more deeply for Dr. Parker when the angel of death visited his home. With scarcely any warning, on August 26, Mrs. Parker was stricken with dangerous illness, and passed away at midnight leaving four little ones motherless. The young missionaries at Bridge Street did what they could to come to the help of their friend, and others were ready with practical sympathy, but the shock proved too much for the bereaved husband. One of the children was seriously ill, and amid the difficulties of his changed position the doctor began to realise how much his own health was impaired by five years spent in China. He had neither heart nor strength for added burdens and decided before long to take his family home to the care of relatives in Scotland.

But what about the medical mission, outcome of so much prayer and labour ?   The hospital was full of patients, and the dispensary crowded day by day with a constant stream of people, all of whom needed help.   No other doctor was free to take his place, and yet to stop the work seemed out of the question with the winter coming on.   How would it be, in default of better arrangements, to ask his former colleague, Hudson Taylor, to continue the dispensary at any rate ?   He was quite competent for this, and with the hospital closed would not have much financial responsibility.

The suggestion, it need hardly be said, came as a great

surprise to Mr. and Mrs. Taylor, and sent them to their knees in earnest prayer. All they wanted was to know the Lord's will in the matter, and as they waited upon Him for guidance it was clearly given, but in a direction they little anticipated.

Yes, the dispensary must be kept open ; and more than that, the hospital must not be closed. The Lord had given them helpers just suited for such an emergency—a band of native Christians who would rally round them and make the most of the opportunities which the hospital especially afforded. And as to funds, or lack of funds—for Dr. Parker had very little to leave—the work was not theirs but the Lord's. To close it on account of the small balance in hand would practically mean that prayer had lost its power, and if so they might as well retire from the field. No, for the good of the native Christians, the strengthening of their own faith and the comfort and blessing of many, *they must go forward*, and above all for the glory of God.

" After waiting upon the Lord for guidance," wrote Hudson Taylor, " I felt constrained to undertake not only the dispensary but the hospital as well, relying solely on the faithfulness of a prayer-hearing God to furnish means for its support.

" At times there were no fewer than fifty in-patients, besides a large number who daily attended the dispensary. Thirty beds were ordinarily allotted to free patients and their attendants, and about as many more to opium-smokers who paid for their board while being cured of the habit. As all the wants of the sick in the wards were supplied gratuitously, as well as the medical appliances needed for the out-patient department, the daily expenses were considerable. A number of native attendants also were required, involving their support.

"The funds for the maintenance of all this had hitherto been supplied by the proceeds of the doctor's foreign practice, and with his departure this source of income ceased. But had not God said that whatever we ask in the name of the Lord Jesus shall be done ? And are we not told to seek first the kingdom of God—not means to advance it—and that " all these things " shall be added to us ? Such promises were surely sufficient."

Strong therefore in the Lord and in the inward assurance of His call to this enlarged service, Mr. and Mrs. Taylor prepared to move over to Dr. Parker's. The care of the

Bridge Street Christians remained in the hands of their beloved colleague Mr. Jones, who from the first had been Pastor of the little Church, and cordial indeed was the prayer and sympathy with which all its members endorsed the action of their missionaries.

To Mrs. Taylor, as she thought over it all, it must have seemed very wonderful, this sudden change that brought her husband into a position of usefulness he was so well qualified to fill. They had sought nothing for themselves, but in going about their work had quietly lived down misunderstandings, leaving their reputation in the hands of God. And now He had led them out into " a wealthy place," putting them in charge of a work second to none in Ning-po in its importance, and the common meeting-ground of all the other missions.

Looking across the river to the Presbyterian Compound, Mrs. Taylor could not but recall a conversation of the previous summer, to which she alludes in the following letter.

NING-PO, *September* 30, 1859.

MY DEAR MOTHER—Hudson has again been prevented from writing to you, which makes the fourth fortnightly mail since he was able to send off a letter. I hope you will not . . . I know you will not . . . begin to think that his dear little daughter is winning his heart away from his beloved parents. If he could steal some hours from the night he would do so, as he often has before, but his occupations leave him none to steal. He comes upstairs usually between ten and eleven o'clock, tired out with the long day's work, and after resting a little down he goes again to see some of his patients or make up medicine for others.

You will no doubt be surprised at my speaking of patients in this way, but perhaps still more so when I mention that Dr. Parker is leaving his hospital in dear Hudson's care. A few months ago I was walking with a friend (Mrs. M'Cartee) in one of the gardens of the Presbyterian Mission, when she said .

" Do you know what I prophesy ? That in a few years Dr. Parker will be taking his family home, and that you and Mr. Taylor will come to live in his large house and carry on the work."

I reminded her that Hudson was not a qualified medical man, and said I did not think we should ever live outside of the city.

Little could we have imagined that in a few short months Dr.

大英內地會公所

Photograph by   *G. Whitfield Guinness.*

ENTRANCE TO DR. PARKER'S PREMISES.

One of the hospital buildings just showing on the left, and the doctor's house on the right. Through the farther doorway may be seen the river and part of the foreign settlement.

To face page 489.

Parker would be on his way home with his motherless children, and that we should be in his house and Hudson taking charge of his work.

She herself, far though she was from supposing it, was one of the most important elements in his success at this time. For God works through human means, and but for his wife and Chinese helpers this winter could never have been what it was in Hudson Taylor's experience and in the annals of the Ning-po hospital. Thoroughly competent to undertake the direction of their enlarged establishment, Mrs. Taylor relieved him of account-keeping, correspondence and all household cares, managing the servants and to a certain extent the staff so admirably that his strength was conserved for the medical and spiritual part of the work. She even found time to do a good deal in the wards herself, especially among the women patients, and spent many an hour caring both for body and soul in the dispensary.

"Her influence over the patients," wrote her husband, "was great and most beneficial. They saw and felt that there must be something deserving of attention in the religion that led an English lady to labours so peculiar and naturally repulsive. Over her domestics, too, she exerted an influence only to be won by genuine sympathy and continuous efforts for their good. She looked upon them not so much as persons paid for serving her, but as persons brought under her care that she might seek to lead them to Christ. She encouraged and helped them to learn to read and had some of them taught to write, and not a few who for longer or shorter periods were connected with her in this way came to know and love the Master she so faithfully served. . . .

"She was accustomed to take real comfort from a heart-felt belief in the overruling providence of God in small as well as great matters. If His Word said ' The very hairs of your head are all numbered,' she did not, could not doubt it. She was accustomed, too, to seek His counsel in all things, and would not write a note, pay a call, or make a purchase without raising her heart to God."

In the same way he too drew upon divine resources. Outwardly he was carrying on a great work ; inwardly he was conscious of a great cry to Him without whom it could not be sustained for a moment. Had he been depending upon man for help, he would have waited until the need could be made known before assuming such heavy responsibilities. But it had come about so suddenly that no one at any distance was aware of the position or could be more prepared than he himself.

" Eight days before entering upon the care of the Ning-po hospital," wrote Mr. Taylor, " I had not the remotest idea of ever doing so ; still less could friends at home have foreseen the need."

But the Lord had anticipated it, and already His provision was on the way, as events were happily to prove.

The first step taken by the young missionary upon assuming independent charge of the hospital was to call together the assistants and explain the real state of affairs. Dr. Parker, as he told them, had left funds in hand for the expenses of the current month, but little more. After this provision was used up they must look to the Lord directly for supplies ; and it would not be possible to guarantee stated salaries, because whatever happened he would not go into debt. Under these circumstances, any who wished to do so were at liberty to seek other employment, though he would be glad of their continued service if they were prepared to trust the simple promises of God.

This condition of things, as Mr. Taylor had expected, led all who were not decided Christians to withdraw and opened the way for other workers. It was a change Dr. Parker had long desired to make, only he had not known how to obtain helpers of a different sort. But Mr. Taylor did ; and with a greatly lightened heart he turned to the little circle that at this critical juncture did not fail him. For to the Bridge Street Christians it seemed quite as natural to trust the Lord for temporal as for spiritual blessings. Did not the greater include the less ? And was He not, as their " Teachers " so often reminded them, a *real* Father, who never could forget His children's needs ? So to the hospital they came ; glad not only to strengthen the hands of their missionary friends, but to prove afresh both to themselves and all concerned the loving-kindness of God.

Some worked in one way and some in another ; some giving freely what time they could spare, and others giving their whole time without promise of wages, though receiving their support. And all took the hospital and its concerns upon their hearts in prayer.

No wonder a new atmosphere began to permeate dispensary and wards ! Account for it the patients could not —at any rate at first—but they enjoyed none the less the happy, homelike feeling, and the zest with which everything was carried on. The days were full of a new interest. For these attendants—Wang the grass-cutter and Wang the painter, Nyi, Neng-kuei and others—seemed to possess the secret of perpetual happiness, and had so much to impart ! Not only were they kind and considerate in the work of the wards, but all their spare time was given to telling of One who had transformed life for them, and who they said was ready to receive all who came to Him for rest. Then there were books, pictures and singing. Everything indeed seemed set to song ! And the daily meetings in the Chapel only made one long for more.

There are few secrets in China, and the financial basis upon which the hospital was now run was not one of them. Soon the patients knew all about it, and were watching eagerly for the outcome. This too was something to think and talk about ; and as the money left by Dr. Parker was used up and Hudson Taylor's own supplies ran low, many were the conjectures as to what would happen next. Needless to say that alone and with his little band of helpers Hudson Taylor was much in prayer at this time. It was perhaps a more open and in that sense crucial test than any that had come to him, and he realised that the faith of not a few was at stake as well as the continuance of the hospital work. But day after day went by without bringing the expected answer.

At length one morning Kuei-hua the cook [1] appeared with serious news for his master. The very last bag of rice had been opened, and was disappearing rapidly.

" Then," replied Hudson Taylor, " the Lord's time for helping us must be close at hand."

[1] This was the same valued servant who had been with Mr Taylor in Shanghai, Tsung-ming and elsewhere ; and who was now a bright Christian.

And so it proved. For before that bag of rice was finished a letter reached the young missionary that was among the most remarkable he ever received.

It was from Mr. Berger, and contained a cheque for fifty pounds, like others that had come before. Only in this case the letter went on to say that a heavy burden had come upon the writer, the burden of wealth to use for God. Mr. Berger's father had recently passed away, leaving him a considerable increase of fortune. The son did not wish to enlarge his personal expenditure. He had had enough before, and was now praying to be guided as to the Lord's purpose to what had taken place. Could his friends in China help him? The bill enclosed was for immediate needs, and would they write fully, after praying over the matter, if there were ways in which they could profitably use more?

Fifty pounds! There it lay on the table; and his far-off friend, knowing nothing about that last bag of rice or the many needs of the hospital, actually asked if he might send them more. No wonder Hudson Taylor was overwhelmed with thankfulness and awe. Suppose he had held back from taking charge of the hospital on account of lack of means, or lack of faith rather? Lack of faith—with such promises and such a God!

There was no Salvation Army in those days, but the praise-meeting held in the chapel fairly anticipated it in its songs and shouts of joy. But unlike some Army meetings it had to be a short one, for were there not the patients in the wards? And how they listened—these men and women who had known nothing all their lives but blank, empty heathenism!

"Where is the idol that can do anything like that?" was the question upon many lips and hearts. "Have they ever delivered us in our troubles, or answered prayer after this sort?"

MR. WILLIAM T. BERGER OF EAST GRINSTEAD AND OF CANNES.

The first Home Director of the China Inland Mission, and throughout life its valued and most generous friend.

To face page 492.

CHAPTER XLII

JANUARY–JULY 1860; AND ONWARDS.

NOTHING is more contagious than spiritual joy, when it is the real thing, and of this there was abundance in the Ning-po hospital that winter. For answers to prayer were many, in connection with other than financial needs. There were critical cases of illness in which life was given back when every hope seemed gone; there were operations successfully performed under unfavourable conditions, and patients restored from long and hopeless suffering. And best of all there were dead souls brought to life in Christ Jesus, and slaves of sin set free, so that within nine months sixteen patients had already been baptized and more than thirty others were enrolled as candidates for admission to one or other of the Ning-po Churches.

This did not come all at once, it need hardly be said but only as the result of unremitting prayer and labour. One man from the hospital was desiring baptism by the end of October. In November there were four new candidates for Church-membership. More than six hundred out-patients were treated before the end of the year, and sixty in-patients had been for longer or shorter periods under the influence of the Gospel. A new glow of spiritual life and love pervaded everything. All felt it, and Mr. Taylor was able to write:

Truly the Lord is with us, and is blessing us abundantly.[1]

---

[1] This was on February 13, 1860, when to his parents he wrote: "You will rejoice to hear that on the 5th inst. we received five men into our

And in the midst of it all came the home-going of the first of that little group to be called into the presence of the Lord—the first death, one may almost put it, in connection with the China Inland Mission, or at any rate with its forerunner. And when one thinks how many thousands shine and shall yet shine in eternal glory through the labours of that widened circle, a quite peculiar interest invests this first passing-over.

It was dear old Dzing to whom the summons came, and the closing days of the year were bright with his beautiful end.

" He was upwards of sixty years of age," wrote Mr. Taylor, " and it was only during the last twelve months of his life that he found the Saviour."

But it was a good year, and going about with his pedlar's pack he was a messenger of glad tidings to many who but for him would never have heard.

In the chilly days of December he fell ill with bronchitis, and Mr. Taylor had him brought to the hospital. There in a warm, dry room, very different from his own quarters, he was encompassed with kindness. His gratitude was touching, and as the end drew near, the spirit in which he met it made a profound impression on those about him.

His difficulty in breathing was great at times, and it was hard not to be impatient.

" If only the Lord would take me ! " he exclaimed again and again.

" He will," replied his missionary friend, " just as soon as you are ready. He loves you better far than we do, and will not let you suffer a moment longer than He sees needful. He wants you to trust Him, and be willing to wait His time. Will you show your love for Him by being patient, even in this ? "

It was a difficult lesson, but he was given grace to learn

---

little Church, to whom I had the privilege of administering the Lord's Supper yesterday. . . . We have now therefore eleven men and six women in fellowship with us, though one, I regret to say (dear Neng-kuei), is suspended for the present May God grant him speedy restoration. To-morrow we are to have a Church-meeting, D.V., to consider the cases of other candidates, twelve in all, I believe "

it, and, wonderful to say, never again showed any sign of impatience.

"To-morrow is the Lord's Day," he said on New Year's Eve, " but I shall not be able to join in worship."

When reminded that the Lord was just as near him on his bed of sickness, and that he could praise Him there in a way specially to His glory, he seemed comforted and said :

"Yes, it is so. He promised never to leave me, and He never has ; and soon will take me to Himself."

During the day—New Year's Day—he was failing fast, but enjoyed passages of Scripture read to him at his own request, including the twenty-third Psalm. Hymns also gave him pleasure, especially a translation of

> Who are these in white array,
> Brighter than the noonday sun ?

"I shall soon shine too," whispered the dying saint, " but all the praise will belong to Jesus."

After the evening service he received with much affection some of the Christians who came to see him, and pleaded earnestly with his wife to turn to the Lord. Then losing consciousness a little he seemed to be seeking something.

"What do you want, Elder Brother ? " inquired one of those beside him. Opening his eyes with a smile he slowly but distinctly said, " Jehovah *my* Shepherd," and soon after fell asleep in Jesus.

.   .   .   .

But it all told, this blessed work, upon those whose hearts were in it. "Nothing without the cross " is true above all in spiritual things, and for Hudson Taylor the price that had to be paid was that of health, almost of life itself. Six years in China, six such years, had left their mark ; and now, under the strain of day and night work in the hospital, entailing much exposure to wintry weather, strength was failing fast.

But in a sense his work was completed—or the preparation, rather, for which he had been sent to China. " Whosoever will be great among you shall be your minister ;

and whosoever of you will be chiefest, shall be servant of all." " He that is faithful in that which is least is faithful also in much." " Faithful over a few things, I will make thee ruler over many."

Not that any thought of large developments was in Hudson Taylor's mind as he faced the probability that he must return to England before long. He was conscious only of two things—great and growing opportunities on the one hand, and rapidly failing health on the other; so that while longing to multiply himself into a hundred missionaries he was increasingly unequal to the work of one.

It is deeply interesting to notice, at this juncture, the means the Lord was using to bring about purposes of His own in connection with this little Ning-po Mission of which those most interested in it never dreamed. Poor, uninfluential and without what would ordinarily be regarded as training or talent for leadership, how unlikely that Hudson Taylor should ever become the founder and director of a world-wide organisation embracing missionaries from all evangelical denominations and every Protestant land. Yet this was indeed to be the case, for He who is the great, the only Worker still delights to use what has been well called " God's five-rank army of weakness."

Not many wise after the flesh, not many mighty, not many noble, have part therein : [1] but God hath chosen the foolish things of the world to confound (or put to shame) the wise ; and God hath chosen the weak things of the world to confound the things which are mighty ; and base things of the world, and things which are despised, hath God chosen, yea, and things which are not, to bring to nought things that are : that no flesh should glory in His presence. . . . According as it is written, He that glorieth, let him glory in the Lord.

A beginning was to be made even now along the lines of that future development, and how were Hudson Taylor and his colleague to be launched upon it but by a constraining sense of the greatness of the need and their own insufficiency to meet it. Fellow-workers they *must* have to enter doors of opportunity that never before had seemed so open. And all unconscious of what lay beyond the

[1] 1 Cor. i 26 ; R V. margin ; and vers. 27-31 from A.V.

step to which he felt himself led, Hudson Taylor wrote home early in the New Year : [1]

> Do you know any earnest, devoted young men desirous of serving God in China, who not wishing for more than their actual support would be willing to come out and labour here ? Oh for four or five such helpers ! They would probably begin to preach in Chinese in six months' time ; and in answer to prayer the necessary means would be found for their support.

Had he gone on living quietly at Bridge Street it might have been long before the young missionary would have been driven to such a step. There he and Mr. Jones were able to overtake the work, and with the help of the native brethren might have carried it on for years. But removed suddenly from that position and entrusted with larger, more fruitful labours, the result was very different. Here was something too great for him ; and as the Lord wrought with them, confirming His own Word " with signs following," the outlook and possibilities were over-whelming.

If souls had not been saved in the hospital and the Christians had not developed in usefulness and promise, the situation would still have been other than it was. But with a growing family manifesting no little gift for spiritual ministry, Hudson Taylor was impressed as never before by the need of watchfulness in utilising the resources of the native church. This it was that brought him to the point of appealing for fellow-missionaries. The converts must have supervision ; as yet they could not stand alone. The fall through pride and even dishonesty of the basket-maker, their most devoted worker, had burned this upon his heart. Prayer and loving personal influence alone could restore him and safeguard others ; and all needed, as he had learned from experience, the most painstaking instruction in spiritual things.

And beside all this, the care of the hospital was proving too much for his strength. With sixteen members in fellowship and a dozen or more awaiting baptism ; with

---

[1] In a letter to his parents in Barnsley, dated January 16, 1860.

work opening up in the villages round about, and native
Christians fitted to undertake it if only they could have
supervision ; with no difficulty as to funds, for the Lord
was abundantly supplying their need, both he and Mr.
Jones were so run down that it was with difficulty they
could get through present duties. Had any of these elements
been lacking the effect produced might have been less
definite, but taken all together one conclusion only was
possible. Help they must have, the help of fellow-
missionaries willing for their own simple line of things.
So the appeal went home that was to result in the coming
out, to begin with, of just the workers prayed for, two of
whom are still labouring in China as the senior members
of the Inland Mission.[1] But there was no thought in
Hudson Taylor's mind that he would have to be their
leader, indeed there was no immediate thought at all, save
that he must seek in one way or another to meet the claims
of the ever-growing work.

" I have this morning sent out forms and tables," he wrote in
February, " to a house in a neighbouring village that we have been
enabled to rent for a school, and we have engaged Mrs. Tsiu and her
son, the Teacher, to commence work both among boys and girls. . . .
Their home will I trust be an influence for good in the neighbourhood
and a centre from which we may preach the Gospel."

And then, thinking of all that might be done if his
suggestions about five new missionaries were carried out,
he continued :

I do hope father will take up the idea. . . . The people are perishing,
and God is so blessing the work. But we are wearing down and must
have help. . . . Pity poor China ! You have given your son, give
your influence too.

But month after month went by bringing no response
from home. There was sympathy of course in his desires,

[1] First of the five was the Rev. J. J. Meadows, who, after half a century
of devoted labours in China, is still working within a hundred miles of Ning-
po. And fifth of that little group was the Rev. J. W. Stevenson, now and
for more than twenty years the Deputy Director on the field of the China
Inland Mission

but no encouragement to expect that helpers would be forthcoming.

Hoping much from a brief holiday, Mr. Taylor closed the dispensary as spring came on, and went with his wife and child to the neighbouring hills.   They were away ten days, and he seemed greatly benefited ; but the heavy work of the hospital soon bore him down on their return.   Then it was he first wrote to his parents about the precarious state of his health, and that he had reason to suppose his lungs were affected with tubercular trouble.[1]

" It is a comfort under these circumstances," he concluded, " to have no doubt it was God who guided us into the position we now hold ; and the supply of funds for the work as well as the blessing that has rested upon it confirms one in this conviction.   Here at any rate is my present post of duty, and I trust that by His Grace who has led me hitherto I shall not leave it before, nor remain in it longer than it is His will. . . ,

" Dearly as I should love to see you all . . . may I never, never be permitted to turn back from the Gospel plough, or to lay down my works save as He directs who has called me to so honourable, if in some respects so trying a post."

Yet at the very time this letter was written, tokens for good were not wanting to cheer them on their way.   It was a time of wonderful blessing in the home-lands, and the rising tide of revival was sweeping many into the kingdom of God.   Prayer and sympathy, in consequence, were steadily on the increase for missionary work.

" A kind friend has been raised up," wrote Mr. Pearse in a communication received at the end of March, " who sends a hundred pounds each to Brother Jones and yourself. . . . You will be glad to hear that the revival has reached London and hundreds are being converted."

And only two weeks later a letter was received in Mrs. Berger's handwriting containing a bill for fifty pounds.

" My husband is very anxious," she said amongst other encouraging things, " that the hospital should be sustained.   It appears to be such

---

[1] A letter written on March 25.

a means of blessing. And as other openings occur he hopes you will be able to follow them up.

"Surely this is a day calling for no ordinary activity. People are beginning to wake up. You doubtless see *The Revival* and other papers. Stirring meetings have been held all over London and in many parts of England, arising out of the week set apart for prayer at the invitation of Christians in India (the second week in January), to plead for the mighty working of the Holy Spirit in the Church and in the world.

"Such a week this earth never before witnessed. Oh that glorious results may follow ! I feel so cold and lifeless, and long to be in the heart of these mighty workings. But such is not my privilege. One has to learn to deal with the Lord alone, and not to limit His power to seasons or even places. Ask and have, is His way of it. Believe, and the blessing is ours."

Into the prepared soil at home a little seed was to fall that would take root and grow all the more surely because the time was so opportune. Hudson Taylor's life, past, present and to come, was needed in the providence of God to foster that little seed. He must be taken home, and that before long. So the trial of failing health continued until it was evident that a voyage to England was the only hope of saving his life.

"What I desire to know is how I may best serve China," he had written early in May. "If I am too ill to labour here and by returning home might re-establish health, if only for a time, or if I might rouse others to take up the work I can no longer continue, I think I ought to try."

But now in June his letters took another tone.

"I trust, if it is the will of God," he wrote to his parents, "that . . . I may be spared to labour for China. If not, all is well. I am very happy in Jesus. Never before have I felt Him to be so *precious* a Saviour, Lover, Friend. Sometimes I think I may not live to see you ; sometimes I hope to be spared to labour long and more earnestly than ever for China. All, all is known to Him who needs to know all . . . and He will do all things well.

"Do not think me selfish. I do sorrow for the grief my removal would be to you and to my dear, so dear wife. I would fain live for your sakes. But Jesus is so lovely, so precious ! All must sink in comparison with Him."

Still there seemed a probability that the voyage might prolong his life, if nothing more, and closing the hospital with great reluctance the Hudson Taylors set out for Shanghai toward the end of June. And they did not go alone. Means having been abundantly supplied by recent gifts, Mr. Taylor felt gratified in accepting the services of the young painter Wang Lae-djün, who saw that his beloved missionaries were unfit to travel alone. Immense as was the distance between China and England in those days, Lae-djün was willing to leave his wife and child in his father's home and go to the ends of the earth with those to whom he owed so much. And they—well they never could have managed the journey without him. His presence also was a precious link with the past they were leaving behind, and encouraged the hope that fellow-workers might be given them in England to whom he could be useful as a teacher of the language.

Many arrangements had to be made in Shanghai, and they were thankful for the two weeks that elapsed before they could sail for home. It was providential that they were able to secure passages at all, for the *Jubilee*, bound for London, was the only vessel by which they could have travelled for a long time to come.

"The Captain has his wife with him," wrote Mr. Taylor, "and seems to be a gentlemanly though unconverted man. He looks irritable, and I fear may make it hard for us at times. But we look to God as our stay. . . . The season is against us. We shall have to beat down the China Sea, and may expect typhoons. But winds and waves obey Him still, and
. . . The worst that can come
But shortens the journey and hastens us Home."

One great mercy remained to fill their cup to overflowing. A much-loved sister in the home-circle had not yet given herself to the Lord, and during all the years of their separation Hudson Taylor had daily cried to God on her behalf. Many were the letters he had written pleading with her to decide the question of her soul's salvation, but as far as he was aware she was still putting it off. And then, the very day before they sailed, a mail came in bringing glad tidings. His prayers were answered! They were united at last, an unbroken family in the Lord.

Unable to write to her before nightfall, the brother roused himself at three o'clock next morning, and in spite of great weakness traced a few lines in pencil, the last he was to write from China for several years.

" In view of my ill-health," they read, " and the possibility of my removal, a burden has been on my mind, now thank God removed. Cleave to the Lord, my doubly-dear sister, with full purpose of heart, and you will indeed find your joy to be full."

.   .   .   .   .   .

Daybreak that summer morning — and as the brown waters of the Yangtze were left behind them, how the travellers' hearts would go up to God ! With what thankfulness they looked back over long years of " goodness and mercy " in China ; with what confidence they looked forward to " goodness and mercy " still through all the untried way.

> He cannot have taught us to trust in His Name,
> And thus far have brought us, to put us to shame :
> Each sweet Ebenezer we have in review,
> Confirms His good pleasure to help us right through.

The voyage, though not prolonged beyond four months, was an unusually trying one, on account of illness and the awful temper of the captain, and the little party had no comfort but in one another. Often they prayed together in Chinese, and talked over Ning-po days the way in which the Lord had led them. Often too they thought of the future, and dwelt on the time when with restored health and fellow-workers given in answer to prayer they might be returning to China by the blessing of God. But never on quiet nights in the prow, never under the shining stars, never in moments of most earnest prayer or appropriating faith did they imagine what really was to be.

What dream or desire could reach to it ? China open, open from end to end ; an " Inland Mission," working in its most distant provinces ; a thousand stations and out-

stations manned by hundreds of missionaries—what! more
than *nine hundred*, when they were praying for five? Yes,
and the converts! How could they picture the thirty
members of the Church so dear to them multiplied to more
than thirty thousand, and the little company of native
workers increased to more than two thousand—pastors,
teachers, evangelists, Bible-women, all following in the
steps of Nyi and Tsiu and Wang Lae-djün? And as to
money, what flight of imagination could have suggested a
million and a half sterling given in answer to prayer within
the next fifty years? A million five hundred thousand
pounds, not dollars, put into their hands for the spread of
the Gospel in China, and that without a collection or a
single appeal for financial help. Impossible indeed would
it have seemed, even with all their knowledge of Him
with whom they had to do ·

" A God that worketh for him that waiteth for Him."

No, they only prayed and trusted, the future veiled from
their eyes. All that Hudson Taylor saw was the great need
and the unutterable privilege of giving oneself, one's all, to
meet it, in fellowship with Christ. Going home, invalided
though he was, few if any expecting to see him return, one
longing only filled his heart, one prayer—with his remaining
strength to do something more for China, whether by life
or by death.

" Oh there is such a boundless sphere of usefulness," he had written
in one of his last letters, " but the labourers are few, weak, worn and
weary. Oh that the Church at home were awake to its duties, its
privileges! How many would then come and labour here. . . .

" I have not given up hope of seeing you and your dear husband
join us. [Written to his sister Amelia, recently married to Mr.
Broomhall.] I believe you will yet come. I believe you will be sent
by God. And a happy work you will find it. We have only the
Lord to look to for means, for health, for encouragement—and we
need no other. He gives us all, and He best knows what we need.

" Dear Brother and Sister, do come! . . . 'Come over and help
us.' . . . Had I a thousand pounds China should have it. Had I
a thousand lives China should claim every one. No, not China, but
Christ! Can we do too much for Him? Can we do enough for
such a Saviour?

> Were the whole realm of nature mine,
> That were an offering far too small ;
> Love so amazing, so divine,
> Shall have my life, my soul, my all."

And as they followed faithfully, living out the spirit of their prayers, the reality of their consecration, God in His infinite faithfulness did the rest.

To be continued, *D.V.*, in

HUDSON TAYLOR AND THE CHINA INLAND MISSION:

The Growth of a Work of God.

How good is the God we adore,
  Our faithful, unchangeable Friend;
Whose love is as great as His power,
  And knows neither measure nor end.

'Tis Jesus, the First and the Last,
  Whose Spirit shall guide us safe home;
We'll praise Him for all that is past,
  And trust Him for all that's to come.

J. HART.

INDEX

THE END

Printed by R. & R. Clark, Limited, Edinburgh.

THE CHINA INLAND MISSION.

LONDON, PHILADELPHIA, TORONTO, MELBOURNE, & SHANGHAI

Founder: The late Rev. J. HUDSON TAYLOR, M.R.C.S.
General Director. D. E HOSTE.
Director for North America. HENRY W. FROST.

Philadelphia, Penna. . . 1329 Walnut Street.
Toronto, Ont. . . . 507 Church Street.

OBJECT

The China Inland Mission was formed under a deep sense of China's pressing need, and with an earnest desire, constrained by the love of Christ and the hope of His coming, to obey His command to preach the Gospel to every creature

CHARACTER.

It is evangelical, interdenominational, and international. It is supported entirely by the free-will offerings of God's people, no personal solicitations and collections being authorised.

PROGRESS.

On January 1, 1911, there were in connection with the Mission, 968 missionaries and associates (including wives), 18 ordained Chinese pastors, 551 assistant Chinese preachers, 304 Chinese school teachers, 263 Colporteurs, 200 Biblewomen, and 702 unpaid Chinese helpers. There are 615 organised churches, 271 schools, 46 dispensaries, 59 opium refuges, and 8 hospitals. There are now 25,155 communicants; 36,469 converts have been baptized since the commencement of the work.

HOME EXTENSION.

The Mission originated in England, in 1865. In 1888 it was extended to North America, and in 1890 to Australia and New Zealand. Also there are connected with it several Associate Missions, in the United States, Norway, Sweden, Finland, and Germany.

NORTH AMERICA.

There are two centres in North America, as above, one in Philadelphia and one in Toronto At these centres there are Mission Offices and Homes, at these places funds are received, applications from candidates are dealt with, and outgoing and returning missionaries are cared for. Correspondence may be addressed to the Secretary, at either Office

MAP OF CHINA.

All Protestant Mission Stations in China up to June, 1866 (when the C.I.M. *Lammermuir* Party sailed) are underlined in black.
All other places are the Stations of the China Inland Mission only, which (with the exception of Ningpo and Fenghwa) have been opened since June, 1

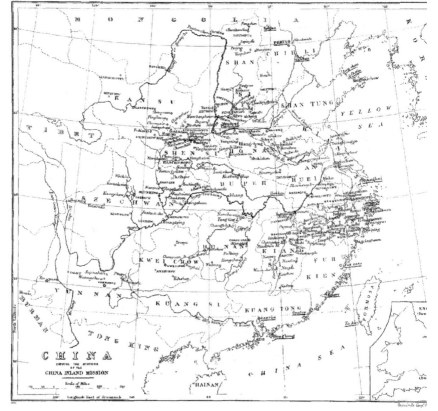

CPSIA information can be obtained
at www.ICGtesting.com
Printed in the USA
BVHW040003230120
570202BV00003B/41